CASUISTRY AND MODERN ETHICS

Casuistry and Modern Ethics

A POETICS

OF

PRACTICAL

REASONING

Richard B. Miller

THE UNIVERSITY OF
CHICAGO PRESS
CHICAGO
AND LONDON

RICHARD B. MILLER is professor and director of graduate studies in the Department of Religious Studies at Indiana University. He is the author of *Interpretations of Conflict: Ethics, Pacifism, and the Just-War Tradition* (1991), published by the University of Chicago Press.

The University of Chicago Press, Chicago 60637
The University of Chicago Press, Ltd., London
© 1996 by The University of Chicago
All rights reserved. Published 1996
Printed in the United States of America
05 04 03 02 01 00 99 98 97 96   1 2 3 4 5

ISBN: 0-226-52636-4 (cloth)
      0-226-52637-2 (paper)

Library of Congress Cataloging-in-Publication Data

Miller, Richard Brian, 1953–
    Casuistry and modern ethics : a poetics of practical
reasoning / Richard B. Miller.
        p.   cm.
    Includes bibliographical references and index.
    ISBN 0-226-52636-4 (cloth : alk. paper).—
    ISBN 0-226-52637-2 (pbk. : alk. paper)
    1. Casuistry.   2. Ethical problems.   3. Ethics,
Modern—20th century.   I. Title.
BJ1441.M55   1996
170—dc20   96-17324
                                                CIP

TO THE MEMORY OF MY FATHER,

Henry Louis Miller

1912–1993

CONTENTS

ACKNOWLEDGMENTS

This book has grown out of conversations with friends, colleagues, and students who are bound together by an interest in practical reasoning. I wrote it out of a desire to join interests in religion and ethics with developments in public philosophy and cultural inquiry. The heterogeneity of sources that such a work involves is reflected in the debts I wish to acknowledge. Barry Kroll followed this project with great interest from its inception, and I could not have envisioned many of its parts had it not been for his ongoing input. Salena Fuller Krug, Judy Granbois, Jim Hart, and David H. Smith provided insightful readings of the entire manuscript, teaching me in their own ways about the virtue of interpretive perspicuity. David Boeyink, Charles E. Curran, Lois Daly, William French, James M. Gustafson, John Kelsay, Oz Kenshur, David Klemm, Julia Lamm, Terence Martin, Jr., William Meyer, Doug Ottati, Francis Schüssler Fiorenza, William Schweiker, Mark Kline Taylor, and Charles Wilson all provided intellectual acuity and goodwill along the way. Scott Ellis, Mark Graham, Lisa Sideris, and Lucinda Peach served in helpful ways as research assistants. A Summer Faculty Fellowship in 1995 and a generous grant-in-aid from Indiana University ensured that this book would come to fruition.

My interests in casuistry were deepened in a graduate seminar I taught during the fall of 1992, and I wish to thank my students for their imaginative probing into the subject during that term. Todd Sullivan, who died tragically in December 1993, was an especially energetic and provocative participant.

My thoughts on casuistry and war gained greater clarity from conversations with Chris Brown, Jean Bethke Elshtain, John Finnis, Ted Koontz, David Mapel, Jeff McMahan, Terry Nardin, Peter Steinfels, and Michael Walzer at a conference titled "The Ethics of War and Peace" in Jerusalem in January 1993, sponsored by the Ethikon Institute. I wish to thank Philip Valera and Terry Nardin for their generous invitation to participate in the conference. Earlier versions of my chapter on the Gulf War were presented at the University of Notre

Acknowledgments

Dame, the University of Pittsburgh, Georgetown University, and Saint Mary's College (Indiana). I am grateful to George Lopez, Alex Orbach, Jack Haught, and Terence Martin, Jr., for their kind hospitality during my visits, and to J. Bryan Hehir for his insights and criticisms during my visit to Georgetown.

My work toward chapters 3 and 4 was enriched by graduate seminars I taught in the fall semesters of 1990 and 1993, and I wish to thank professors Dan Conkle and Kevin Brown of the Indiana University Law School for their attendance and incisive participation. Chapter 3 was greatly improved as a result of conversations I had at a luncheon gathering of moral philosophers at Indiana University and at an annual meeting of the Theology and Ethics Colloquy at the American Academy of Religion. Chapter 4 served as the basis for a departmental colloquium in the fall of 1992, and I wish to thank my colleagues and doctoral students in the Department of Religious Studies for their comments and criticisms.

I presented an abbreviated version of chapter 5 at the 1992 annual meeting of the Society of Christian Ethics, where I received helpful comments toward producing a final draft. Milton Fisk, Oz Kenshur, and Fred Beiser also made imaginative recommendations toward improving this chapter at a spring 1991 meeting of the Ad Hoc Committee on Political and Social Thought here in Bloomington. Mary Jo Weaver pointed me toward important materials representing the views of the Catholic right.

Chapter 6 is reprinted here in revised form, with permission, from the *Journal of Medicine and Philosophy* 14 (December 1989): 617–40. It grew out of research supported by the National Institutes of Health and the Poynter Center at Indiana University in the summer of 1988. I benefited greatly from conversations with Judy Granbois, Robin Levin Penslar, David H. Smith, and Carol Weil on the ethical and legal issues surrounding this case.

An earlier version of chapter 7 appeared in *Soundings* 69 (Fall 1986): 326–46, and appears here in its revised form with permission. The staff at the Kinsey Institute library at Indiana University provided invaluable assistance in tracking down materials for the chapter.

I presented chapter 8 during a visit to Saint Mary's College (Indiana) in the fall of 1993, and I am grateful to the faculty in the Department of Religious Studies for their critical responses.

I wish to thank the staff at SIS on South Walnut Street, whose sojourn to the East End enabled me to rediscover my back pages in March 1994. Also, Kim and Ash Nichols, Charles L. Garrettson III, and Claire and James N. McKean have nurtured me with friendship and conversation over several decades. As always, my deepest debts are to Barbara Klinger for her levity, affection, and good cheer, and to Matthew Miller for (among other things) his weekly hikes—re-plete with wild boars, butterfly witches, saber-toothed dragons, pirate penguins, tree sharks, flaming arrows, and forest ghosts.

R. B. M.
Bloomington
September 1995

PART ONE

Preliminary Inquiry

Casuistry, Politics, and Moral Complexity

A Poetics of Practical Reasoning

This is a book about practical reasoning and the use of cases in moral inquiry, developing an approach commonly known as *casuistry*. My goal is to cast ethical analysis in a case-based method, not unlike legal inquiry as it is generally understood. Like jurists, casuists are interpretive and practical: They seek to reflect about the merits of our conduct in one situation or another, help us perceive the morally salient features of human experience, and render judgments that are fair. Cases require us to develop our powers of perception and to produce judgments as guides for action. Such is the task of practical reasoning, which, I hope to show, is itself a nonformalized skill. In any event, throughout these pages I will illustrate some of the more obvious features of a case-based method, keeping in mind its main rivals on the landscape of moral inquiry today, applied ethics and narrative ethics.

Readers familiar with the history of ethics know that a case-based approach has a long and impressive pedigree. Indeed, in Western philosophy and religion, literature devoted to resolving practical problems of ordinary life, or "cases of conscience" (*casus conscientiae*), comprises a tradition in its own right. In the hands of biblical writers, Cicero, Augustine, medieval rabbis, Muslim jurists, Jesuits, and English Protestants, casuistry has traditionally sought to solve real-life problems in moral experience. May a merchant increase his prices during times of famine? Is one obligated to reveal information that would jeopardize innocent persons? Does one tell a lie by telling the truth to a disbelieving colleague, hoping to deceive her? To what extent may someone inflict harm in defense of his honor? May we steal in circumstances of duress? To what degree am I liable when a third party steals property that a friend has entrusted to me? Addressing these kinds of questions, casuists have produced a wealth of ethically sensitive literature to advise—and perhaps liberate—the consciences of the morally anguished.

Yet when most people hear the word *casuistry* today they imagine something vaguely medieval, suggesting a kind of scholastic sophistry in the service of moral mediocrity. Casuistry has no place in religion or ethics, many would say, because it is a form of chicanery. However venerable it may have been in its formative years, by the sixteenth and seventeenth centuries casuistry degenerated into a form of reasoning characterized by moral permissiveness and disingenuous argument. During this time moral theologians often advised "liberty over law," hoping to prevent penitents from being overly scrupulous. But the spirit of liberty was seen by many as moral laxity, leading Blaise Pascal to produce his hilarious lampoon of casuistry in *The Provincial Letters.*[1] Summarizing the suspicions that haunted casuistry, the seventeenth-century theologian Jeremy Taylor remarked: "By these doctrines a man is taught how to be an honest thief, . . . and by these we may not only deceive our brother, but the law; and not the laws only, but God also."[2] The charges of laxism, chicanery, and sophistry stuck, and casuistry acquired the tarnished image that still lingers in the popular imagination.[3]

Its reputation notwithstanding, casuistry is receiving new attention in religious ethics and philosophy, owing largely to uncertainties in modern life and the inability of conventional ethical approaches to deal with them adequately. This new attention, I hope to show, is richly deserved. Casuists' claim to distinction lies not in their sophistry, but in their efforts to provide resources for making practical judgments about real-life issues, and to do so by heeding the richness and complexity of everyday life. Casuistry seeks to deliver us from those occasions when rules are unclear, when conflicting rules pull us in opposite directions, or when we must ascertain degrees of moral culpability. Such occasions are often a function of our diverse—and competing—duties, loyalties, and roles. Casuistry thus teaches that we are not sufficiently equipped when we have merely determined the rules of morality; nor is it enough simply to appeal to the strengths of moral character. Rather, our rules and our character must be put to practical use in our day-to-day lives, and casuists seek to show in concrete terms how we are to put morality into action.

4

What, more precisely, is casuistry? Generally speaking, casuistry is a problem-solving endeavor, seeking to interpret and resolve practical issues of the day. The overall goal is to settle "cases of conscience," instances in which we are unsure about how to judge or carry out an action. With clear parallels to legal (especially common law) reasoning, casuistry is a genre of moral inquiry focusing on concrete moral problems, their proper interpretation, and their reasonable resolution.

Two of casuistry's more important devices are paradigms and presumptions. *Paradigms* are exemplary moral frameworks that enable us to classify a case taxonomically. They furnish a gestalt, a way to see a case's morally relevant details. Paradigms articulate clear models from which we can reason analogically, enabling us to move from familiar results of ethical reasoning to new or strange cases. They include *presumptions*, which enshrine moral rules and maxims, those prima facie obligations that bear upon a case. Expressing in a condensed or elliptical way certain attitudes about how to live a good life, presumptions hold generally and for the most part, but not absolutely. We presume, as a commonplace, that they ought to orient our response to a situation. Such presumptions or moral orientations may give way when they conflict with rival duties in a situation of genuine moral perplexity, or when their applicability is extended beyond their normally circumscribed situations.[4] Casuistry also draws upon expert moral opinions, and attends carefully to the circumstances that surround the case in question.

In its traditional guise, casuistry involves five components. First, casuists attempt to classify the event in question, drawing upon paradigms and taxonomies. Frequently this process involves analogical reasoning, drawing together similarities and differences between well-established paradigms and novel cases as an initial step toward "getting a handle" on such cases. Second, casuists identify which presumptions are relevant to the event, and how those presumptions add to our perception of the morally salient features of the case. Third, casuists comment on the case's circumstances and how these might affect our overall judgment of the event in question. Fourth, casuists often reflect upon the opinions of prior authorities as these might bear upon our moral assessment of the case. Fifth, bringing together the materials from the first four components, casuists render a verdict. Sometimes this is done with a view as to how that verdict, and the process of reasoning that led to it, might function as a precedent for similar cases in the future.[5]

A careful look at recent events suggests that we all engage in casuistry, if only inchoately. Did the Gulf War defend moral principle or American imperialism, oil interests, and loyal clients? Is liberalism's protection of pluralism to be celebrated or viewed as corrosive of

5

communal ties? How are we to view gender roles and sexual practices in a society undergoing massive changes in traditional attitudes toward men and women? Does transplanting fetal tissue produce therapeutic benefits or redeem abortions and generate incentives for women to have them? Is violent pornography an act of free speech or an act of violence against women?

This book will show how casuistry provides tools for addressing these and other practical problems. The main goal is to deepen our understanding of casuistry's contributions to moral deliberation and to enrich our use of casuistry by joining it to important developments in the philosophy of science, rhetorical studies, the history of religions, and ethical method. Seen in this way, casuistry provides not a method of medieval logic-chopping, but *a poetics of practical reasoning*, furnishing rich resources for addressing some of the most pressing issues in public life today.

That casuistry implies the exercise of practical reasoning is, I hope, obvious. If nothing else, casuists are known for providing reasonable opinions about how individuals should act. The idea that casuistry implies a *poetics* is less than clear, however. Given its obvious associations with case analysis and legal reasoning, casuistry would seem to inhabit an intellectual world quite foreign to imaginative reflection. Yet quite the contrary is true. Practical reasoning requires us to be perceptive in our analysis of circumstances; without the ability to discern carefully, our moral deliberations become sterile and repetitive, insensitive to the demands of the moment. Indeed, recent discussions of ethical reasoning show that practical deliberation without the skills of perception and interpretation lacks the full excellence of virtue.[6] Moral reasoning demands that we first perceive the ethically salient features of a case, that we make sense of our problems and circumstances. In this process no simple rules or formulas exist. Instead, casuistry requires that we provide "strong readings" of our experiences, drawing upon a wide range of diagnostic tools to help us in the difficult task of moral discernment. Seen in this way, a casuistical poetics bids us to be producers of meaning, meaning to develop our capacities of discrimination, insight, and social criticism. As a form of practical reasoning, casuistry includes an "illative sense," where *illative* is understood according to its Latin root (*illatum*): to carry in. We can speak of a creative, poetic dimension to casuistry, then, insofar as practical deliberation invites us to "carry in" wisdom, insight, and interpretive perspicuity in order to settle new cases.[7]

Albert Jonsen and Stephen Toulmin have taken an important first step toward reopening the case for casuistry's merits. In *The Abuse of Casuistry: A History of Moral Reasoning*, they provide a history and repristination of casuistical inquiry.[8] Perhaps for the sake of simplicity they select one foil against which to argue, namely, rigid, ahistorical modes of moral analysis. Their goal is to slay the dragon of the "tyranny of principles," a form of dogmatic, apodictical ethics premised on a geometrical model of rationality. Following Aristotle, Jonsen and Toulmin argue on behalf of a more flexible, practical attitude toward ethics, in which discretion and judgment replace the attempt to invent fixed, timeless rules.[9]

But casuistry has even more to offer than Jonsen and Toulmin suggest. When viewed expansively, casuistry is an interdisciplinary genre, borrowing insights from the philosophy of science, legal reasoning, literary theory, comparative religion, and hermeneutics. Casuistry's use of paradigms, precedents, and latent meanings bears strong likenesses to scientific, legal, historical, and interpretive inquiry. Casuistry is not a strange form of argumentation, to be cordoned off from other attempts to argue and solve problems. Rather, it is a genre of practical reasoning—the task of forming judgments—that we practice in a variety of everyday settings and, ideally, with an interdisciplinary set of diagnostic tools.

In order to develop this point, I will situate casuistry within a wider horizon of intellectual inquiry, going beyond (but not forgetting) the problems posed by the tyranny of principles. Very generally, I hope to strengthen our appreciation of casuistry by using its tools to address a variety of debates in our public and intellectual life—debates about war, politics, sexuality, medicine, women in society, and the study of religion. One aim is to illumine what is at stake in those debates and to suggest an ethical resolution to some pressing issues of the day. Yet I also hope to expand our understanding of practical reasoning by showing how casuistry itself can be enriched by tapping into recent currents in the humanities. Thus another, equally important, aim is to show how taxonomies, precedents, and tools of hermeneutics open up further terrain to explore in casuistry and—along the way—produce more dragons to slay.

This study will thus employ the terms, questions, and concerns of casuistry with a twofold agenda. On the one hand, I address cases of conscience, issues that have presented themselves in public discourse and moral debate. When we turn, for example, to the Gulf War or the question of whether to transplant human fetal tissue, I proceed with somewhat traditional casuistical strategies in view, drawing in part on insights about casuistry's terms and procedures, described in chapter 1. On the other hand, I hope to deepen our appreciation and use of casuistry by calling attention to how its tools shed light on some practical and philosophical issues, as in my discussions of liberalism in chapters 3 and 4. I also hope to show how casuistry can be enriched by ideological and cultural criticism, as we shall see in my discussions of Catholic sexual ethics and depictions of women in popular culture. These two agendas are by no means separate; in many ways they overlap. But in either case—in its more traditional guise or as an interdisciplinary genre—casuistry calls for a poetics of practical reasoning, various aspects of which I hope to illustrate throughout these pages.

Vision and Deliberation

As a book about moral cases and practical reasoning, this work raises questions that hark back to traditional Greek philosophy and ethics. Indeed, in less than a generation Greek philosophers marked off two main paths along which Western philosophical and religious ethics would travel for over two millennia. The first, provided by Plato, holds up the ideal of moral knowledge as an epiphany, a flash of insight in which the soul is illumined by the Form of the Good. This first path envisions moral knowledge as a kind of wisdom that enables the knower to distinguish between the Real and the Deceptive. Equipped with such knowledge, philosophers have a power of vision that enables them to distinguish between reliable and unreliable appearances; they are no longer dependent on social conventions or the opinions of the masses.

The experience of such an epiphany produces, among other things, freedom from internal discord. Our inner voices and impulses are domesticated by wisdom, which directs our powers to their appropriate channels. Ambition and appetite are thus constrained, ruled by sovereign reason. However difficult it may be for groups to harmonize their interests, the self can be governed as the republic within.

By Plato's account, the task of solving cases evidences a breakdown in order, a loss of harmony and balance, a weakness of character. Cases presuppose competing images of the good life or rival recommendations about the proper course of action. Those who are divided or perplexed by cases, then, are somehow deficient, for the very presence of confusion reveals a prior absence of internal order and moral insight. Cases threaten to tear the self apart, pulling us in different directions with their ambiguous or conflicting claims. Casuistry, in short, is symptomatic of a lack of character. The freedom provided by *nous,* in contrast, delivers the wise individual from the task of settling conflicts, of resolving differences. In Platonic thought, the revelation of the Good liberates the philosopher from the tasks that we associate with casuistry.

This view of moral wisdom was roundly rejected by Aristotle, for whom ethical reasoning required individuals to immerse themselves in the contingent, the changing, the "particular." By his account, the task of practical deliberation marks the exercise, not the deficiency, of moral excellence. Plato's mistake, Aristotle alleged, was to equate moral knowledge with scientific knowledge (*epistēmē*), hoping to deliver ethics from the perils of relativism and flux. In making this equation Plato abstracted moral excellence from its proper forum, namely, the realm of mundane life—with all of its contingency. The particularity and novelty of everyday experience militate against the idea that morality can be regulated by a timeless vision, modeled on an ideal of mathematical fixity and certainty. Aristotle thus distinguishes between theoretical and practical sciences.[10] Ethics, as a practical science, should aspire to reasonableness rather than exactness.[11]

For those who follow Aristotle, ethics must build into itself the skill of discerning judgment, which defies tidy formulas and crisp shibboleths. For Aristotle, the virtuous person is not the individual who is removed from the realm of chance and finitude. Instead, the person of virtue must negotiate that realm by discerning the "ultimate particular fact" from an array of competing loyalties, duties, and emotions. This exercise requires the excellence of practical deliberation, "which is rightness with regard to the expedient—rightness in respect . . . of the end, the manner, and the time."[12] Such is one task of *phronēsis*, or practical wisdom.

When carried out with care, casuistry stands somewhere between the alternatives provided by Plato and Aristotle, although it is considerably closer to the latter's than to the former's. Like Aristotle, I hold to the idea that moral reasoning requires us to scrutinize the details of our experience and to proceed with a sympathetic eye to moral complexity. Each chapter of this book is devoted to such a task, premised on the notion that casuistry is an honorable and important discipline, and that the experience of complexity is an inevitable feature of a morally rich life. But as Plato suggests, ethical inquiry succeeds not simply by deliberating and producing a solution to a problem. Rather, it succeeds by furnishing a flash of insight, a new way of seeing.[13] Casuistry is successful not merely because it offers a solution to a case; it must also strengthen our vision, our insight into the meaning and value of moral particulars. Casuists rely on optical skills. At their best, they produce small epiphanies, new ways of seeing the intricate texture of the moral life. Casuistry does not enable us to redescribe ourselves with a new vocabulary, as Plato might have it. But we may be able to redescribe the terms of our topical commitments, those more quotidian dimensions of our experience.

By the conclusion of this book I hope it will be clear how casuistry can join a concern for seeing with a concern for producing judgments. In this respect casuistry constitutes an alternative to narrative ethics and applied ethics. Casuists echo narrativists' concern for vision, yet they also embrace applied ethicists' desire to produce judgments or arguable opinions. Owing to the importance of vision and deliberation in casuistry, I hope to show, casuists can seek the best of both worlds. I will return to these ideas at the end of this book, perhaps after they have been forgotten. For the moment we should direct our attention to two immediate complaints about casuistry.

Topical Inquiry and the "Habits of Democracy"

For many persons casuistry poses two obvious problems. The first concerns casuistry's lack of ambition, its intellectual narrowness. It would seem that a genre devoted to everyday affairs is an underachiever, at least when compared with the challenging rigors of philosophical or historical inquiry. Casuists appear to shy away from Big Questions and thus lack the kind of high seriousness that we often associate with intellectuals. Concerns about war, or sex, or politics, or medicine are the proper subject for professional pundits, talk-show hosts, writers for opinion magazines, and syndicated columnists—those "retail commentators" of popular culture. Given the time needed to confront issues on our philosophical and historical agenda, it seems unwise to write about such mundane, transient problems as those associated with cases of conscience. It would appear more appropriate, contemporary intellectuals might say, to address those comprehensive issues without which specific ethical matters would be unintelligible. It is better, in other words, to write about the intractability of will-to-power, the evils of the nation-state, our narcissistic culture, the failure of foundationalism, or a philosophy of "dwelling." Having clarified lofty, sweeping themes in philosophy or theology, we can then leave topical questions—like when to go to war, or whether to transplant human fetal tissue—to answer themselves.

This first reservation about casuistry should not suggest, however, that casuists can find allies among other, more practically minded intellectuals today. Quite the contrary: In the language of the pragmatic intellectual, casuistry seems insufficiently "political," unreflective about how social and political structures shape human thought and agency. Herein lies the second worry: Casuistry is insufficiently aware of the effects of history and society on our habits. Its focus on the puzzled conscience seems to reflect naïveté about the ways in which social and institutional forces construct the individual's identity. Casuists thus seem politically "innocent." They lack ideological suspicion about cultural forces and their effect on our self-interpretations.

Without accepting all of the implications (and conceits) of these two sets of concerns, this book has been written with both of them in mind. To the first set I have suggested that casuistry occupies an important place in ethical theory, with roots in Aristotle's account of practical judgment and deliberation. In the concluding chapter I will show that casuistry is an important genre of moral discourse, providing a suggestive alternative to dominant approaches on the map of ethics today. For those uninterested in methodological debates in ethics, I will illustrate how casuistry can be joined to other developments in the humanities, especially in the philosophy of science and rhetorical studies. For persons who worry about Big Questions and high seriousness, casuistry is hardly unambitious or lacking in contentious theoretical claims.

For that matter, casuistry is scarcely innocent and apolitical. As we shall see in chapters 3 and 4, the tools of casuistry provide important resources for understanding the current debate between liberals and communitarians in political philosophy. But even apart from issues in contemporary political theory, the excellences required by casuistical practice are vital for what John Dewey called the "habits of democracy." Democratic politics is, if anything, an invitation to deliberate collectively over matters of shared importance, requiring citizens to attend carefully to details. Collective deliberation is notoriously inefficient, requiring time to gather information and to organize forums for debating facts, interests, and practical needs. Political conversations force us to clarify our terms, to accumulate relevant data, and to consider the possible effects of our judgments. We must weigh public matters prudently, reflecting on their implications for ourselves, our children, and our neighbors. We must also be able to articulate our judgments to others, hoping to secure agreement. We must be able, in short, to make a case for our views.

When seen in this way, the habits of democracy should welcome the practice of casuistry and the skills that it nurtures as a contribution to public philosophy. Civic discourse in a democratic regime must be able to sustain vibrant public argument, providing an alternative to vacuous sound bites, academic fashions, and anemic ideologies. Owing to the importance of the "particulars" in moral life, the value of deliberation, and the arguability of ethical matters, casuistry asks us to develop the habits of persuasion and painstaking reflection. It leaves policy to those who make the best case for their practical judgments, given available knowledge and a commitment to social responsibility.[14]

11

Proceeding Incrementally

In addition to suspicions about casuistry's ambitions and political innocence, there are methodological doubts about the merits of using cases in moral reasoning. These concerns have emerged in connection with casuistry's use of historical conventions and paradigms. Here I want to call attention to such questions, which I will address in more detail in subsequent chapters. Those chapters comprise neither a story of casuistry nor an abstract account of its merits and deficiencies. Rather, as I have suggested, I will proceed topically, focusing on several practical issues in our public life and calling attention to casuistry's strengths and foibles along the way. I make no claim to providing a comprehensive treatise of casuistry's history or methodology. I suggest instead that we proceed inductively, deriving insights into casuistry from the cumulative effects of casuistical practice. Proceeding incrementally thus requires that we postpone a discussion of methodology to the conclusion of this book. At that juncture we will be in a position to cull the chief methodological assumptions of casuistry from preceding chapters, paying special attention to its poetic features.

Perhaps the most obvious question that emerges for casuistry concerns the *problem of application:* How do casuists apply presumptions and paradigms to historical events? In particular, how is casuistry different from applied ethics? The method of applied ethics, as John Arras observes, begins "from 'on high' with the working out of a moral theory and culminate[s] in the deductivistic application of norms to particular factual situations."[15] Casuistry, in contrast, is more dialectical, moving from presumptions and paradigms to cases and back again.

To illustrate this dialectical method, in chapter 2 I focus on the case of the Gulf War, drawing on just-war criteria to assess Operation Desert Storm. In this instance, a genuinely dialectical casuistry must take into account several morally relevant facts that complicate traditional notions of just cause and competent authority, as well as the idea that Western leaders can take the moral high road when opposing a tyrant whose despotic power they once assisted. Beyond rendering a judgment about the Gulf War, one goal of the chapter will be to show that ethical criteria should not be applied to experience in a "top down" fashion, that history and ethics ought to inform each other in casuistry.

Another problem for casuistry concerns its alleged tendency toward laxity and moral mediocrity. If the history of casuistry tells us anything, critics argue, it is that casuists were renowned for developing ways to justify reprehensible behavior. This is the reason that Pascal ridiculed casuistry. Thus we face a second general question in casuistry: the *question of moral expectations*, pitting *realists* against *idealists*. How demanding should a moral theory be?

Typically, realists seek to craft a morality that can commend itself without asking too much from us, premised on the belief that a morality will not gain many adherents if it requires us to become saints or martyrs in the process. Idealists, in contrast, argue that a morality that makes nonutopian demands encourages moral mediocrity. Echoing a perfectionist sensibility, idealists often point to the higher standards of a religious ethic, which they perceive to be compromised by casuistry's realism.

These terms provide a new way of entering the recent debate between liberals and communitarians, which is the topic of chapter 3. Although casuistry is not typically associated with political philosophy, I want to show that recent debates between liberals and communitarians can be seen afresh through a prism provided by casuistical terms and tools. Indeed, casuistry can inform our critical imagination when we sort through ambitious political theories and the expectations they wish to impose on citizens of modern society. Echoing a realist, nonutopian refrain, liberals such as John Rawls and Ronald Dworkin seek to craft a political theory suited to fit the circumstances of cultural pluralism in the modern nation-state. Communitarians gesture in an idealist direction: They complain that liberalism's protection of freedom and diversity disregards the more intimate ties that bind, or ought to bind, people together. Solidarity, communitarians insist, requires greater sacrifices than does a liberal polity.

Against the communitarians, I try to show that solidarity within liberalism is possible. Following John Stuart Mill, my argument is that liberals should view cultural pluralism as a source of experimentalism, self-correction, aesthetic enrichment, and human flourishing. Among other things, pluralism can provide a good (or set of goods) that we share in common. I also argue that pluralism is a feature of modern society that religious adherents can (and ought to) embrace. With this defense of liberalism in place, then, we can see that a nonutopian political theory is neither deficient owing to its realism nor inimical to religious commitment.

This appeal to the merits of pluralism invites liberals to excavate and interpret latent values of a democratic culture. Such a move provides a segue into chapter 4, where I examine, in the works of Michael Walzer, how casuistry has taken a hermeneutical turn. Seeking to assess moral experience within real-life situations, Walzer uses case histories to illustrate the main lines of his social philosophy. He thus attempts to map our social life by drawing on our customs, habits, and cultural meanings, using tools drawn from anthropology and ethnography.

Here I will address the *problem of interpretation* in hermeneutical casuistry. Essentially my argument is that, for Walzer's map to be compelling, we must be able to locate ourselves on it. That Walzer extends his analysis in a Jewish direction complicates matters for him, especially when he asks us to remain faithful to our shared meanings and to maintain clear boundaries between the distinct spheres—education, leisure, religion, and politics—of our public life. These aspects of Walzer's work invite a reading of his social philosophy as covenantal and levitical, deeply informed by religious themes. I conclude by arguing that Walzer's appeal to shared meanings and the duty to keep our spheres distinct generate considerable tensions in his casuistry, especially when we consider the cases on which he relies. For, as we shall see, it is by no means obvious that our shared meanings make for covenantal unity, or that the levitical mandate to keep our spheres distinct is as possible (or as desirable) as Walzer suggests.

The role of shared history and moral custom in casuistry naturally raises the *question of ideology:* To what extent does casuistry enshrine long-standing biases, special interests, and social attitudes about, for example, gender? Is casuistry incurably conservative, unable to provide resources for social and cultural criticism? If so, how might we expose the ideologies of casuistry?

By drawing on stable paradigms and conventions of moral reasoning, casuistry may provide concreteness at the expense of a critical edge. Such conventionalism, as Arras observes, may lead us merely to refine our prejudices.[16] Accordingly, the task of exposing the problem of conservatism in casuistry requires a subtle set of critical tools. In a study of *Humanae vitae,* Pope Paul VI's famous encyclical banning artificial contraception, I carry out an ideological analysis of casuistry by focusing on the encyclical's covert attitudes toward gender. I show that *Humanae vitae* glosses "nature" and "culture" with the language of gender, creating an allegory in which *nature* refers to femaleness and regularity and *culture* refers to maleness and freedom. This analysis is meant to show the importance of a hermeneutics of suspicion in casuistry, arguing that until Paul VI's ideology is unveiled, interpretations of *Humanae vitae* will continue to overlook its enduring appeal in patriarchal circles.

The role of history in shaping cases and moral reasoning also raises questions about the experience of *novelty* for casuistry: How do we move from customs and conventional ideas to uncharted terrain in moral experience? In chapter 6 I focus on the novel case of transplanting fetal tissue. Arguing in favor of fetal tissue transplantation, I draw on moral arguments that allow us to override strong presumptions against using the dead in medical practice. To provide structure to that argument, I revisit the just-war tradition, this time supplemented by the provisions of the Uniform Anatomical Gift Act. This chapter is meant to underscore the importance of interpretation and analogical reasoning in casuistry, and to illustrate how we might use verisimilitude when confronting novelty in moral experience.

Matters connected to history and a hermeneutics of suspicion also suggest the *question of radical evil:* Is it not true that casuistry's use of nuanced, careful reasoning lacks the suspicion necessary to uncover malicious motives and institutional, conspiratorial evils? In chapter 7 I address this question in relation to the case of violent pornography, viewed as media of vicious cruelty. My main point is that prior assessments of violent pornography are confounded by the fact that radical nihilism lurks beneath the surface of the violent pornographic text, ridiculing and subverting the conventions on which ethical inquiry rests. Previous casuistry in this area has failed, due to the fact that this nihilistic undercurrent has remained hidden from view. Effective casuistry, I argue, cannot take for granted that its diagnostic tools are obviously or immediately helpful. Rather, casuists must be wary of efforts to subvert the categories and assumptions on which they rely.

In chapter 8 I address the problem of *extrinsicism* and rigidity in practical reasoning. *Extrinsicism* refers to adopting an alien ("extrinsic") principle in ethics, requiring us to assess our actions in light of principles that have been imposed from without. Practical reasoning becomes extrinsicist when we ignore the particularities and subtleties of the moral life, attempting instead to force a set of foreign codes or expectations to fit our experience.[17]

I address this danger by examining what might seem to be an unlikely case for such an analysis, the academic study of religion. This extrinsicism is evidenced, I argue, by those who insist on an approach to the study of religion that excludes theology. I focus on those who insist on studying religion "scientifically," explaining religious phenomena according to their genetic causes and invoking canons of scientific objectivity. My main charge is that such an approach is antiliberal, seeking to impose a criterion for the study of religion that would in effect censor much of what actually occurs within the academy of religion. The impact of such approaches, if they were put into actual practice, would be to eliminate the rich, experimental, and pluralistic study of religion that we presently enjoy.

In chapter 9 I conclude by developing two features of casuistry as I have presented it here: its poetic and rhetorical dimensions. The fact that casuistry demands attention to the kaleidoscopic details of a case means that we must develop skills of interpretive perspicuity, the power to discern the salience of moral particulars and to apprehend their meaningful configurations in human affairs. Understood in poetic terms, casuistry has an aesthetic dimension, focusing our attention on the nuances and subtexts of moral experience. The idea that casuistry has rhetorical aspects means that we approach practical deliberation as local, topical, and persuasive, seeking to provide sound judgments about substantive issues of the day rather than airtight demonstrations about what abstract, theoretical principles entail for human action. A rhetorical approach to practical reasoning invites us to draw upon presumptions and paradigms that have stood the test of time, and to develop them in light of practical concerns. I then sharpen these features of casuistry by contrasting them with two influential approaches in ethics today, applied ethics and narrative ethics.

Before we consider these specific questions and what they suggest for casuistry, it is important to describe the occasions of casuistical inquiry in some general terms. In many respects it resembles what Thomas Kuhn calls "normal science": Both casuistry and normal science are problem-solving practices, providing a particular community of researchers with a foundation for further inquiry.[18] In chapter 1, therefore, I draw parallels between casuistry and Kuhn's account of scientific problem-solving, focusing especially on their respective uses of paradigms and analogical reasoning. In considering casuistry's causes and philosophical dimensions we will see, among other things, what kind of portrait of the moral life casuists traditionally paint, and what kinds of expectations they generally impose on the rest of us.

CHAPTER ONE

The Occasions of Casuistry

Interpretation as Specification

Casuistry's basic premise is that virtue is incomplete without the skill of practical deliberation—that appeals to character, integrity, or purity of heart alone are insufficient for ethical theory and the moral life. The conscience needs counsel about the concrete details of acting well and practicing the requirements of virtue. Thus, one of casuistry's basic tasks is to make judgments and guide our decisions when we are ethically puzzled. Casuistry addresses itself to a reflective clientele, those who regularly interrogate the moral dimensions of their everyday lives. The casuist's overriding raison d'être is founded on the idea that even the well-intentioned conscience needs practical wisdom about managing day-to-day affairs. Given our diverse loyalties (and the pressures they generate), our particular circumstances, and our complex moral heritages, it is not always obvious what virtue requires.

Primarily a problem-solving endeavor, casuistry seeks to furnish answers to tangible, practical questions. It arises naturally—almost inevitably—in religious traditions that esteem the role of law, practical reasoning, and moral action. But here I am suggesting that the kinds of problems that emerge for practical deliberation are by no means simple or monolithic. For those whose

conscience hath a thousand several tongues,
And every tongue brings in a several tale,[1]

the conscience may be puzzled for a variety of reasons. Thus we must explore the occasions of casuistry, instances that require us to develop and

17

refine the skill of practical deliberation. This exploration may help us to understand more precisely the purposes to which casuists direct their intellectual energies, the kinds of expectations they typically impose on us, and how they envision the moral life.[2]

One occasion derives from the experience of ambiguity, especially when the *range of application* of a principle is unclear. Casuists ask how a general, commonly acknowledged rule is to be interpreted and applied within a particular set of circumstances. We engage in casuistry, in other words, in order to clarify the practical applicability of an otherwise vague piece of legislation. As Kenneth Kirk observes, casuistry is prompted by doubt about how to interpret and apply moral principles. In "doubtful cases," Kirk writes, "we hesitate between obeying and ignoring a principle which has indeed some support in authority, but no final support in conscience."[3] Where hesitation is compounded by the suspicion that custom or authority prefers one course to another, we find ourselves in a moment of interpretive and moral uncertainty.

The occasions of doubt provide the general contours for one of casuistry's more famous concerns, namely, the tensions between liberty and law. As Aristotle observes, owing to the law's generality it cannot cover all imaginable cases, and any application of law in doubtful situations must be carried out with *epikeia,* or a prudent sense of equity.[4] When a law is doubtful we may be free of its strictures, but laws are not to be dismissed lightly lest we become disorderly or morally lax.

To clarify how we are to balance the authority of law with equity and common sense, casuists developed three schools of thought to determine when obedience to law was "probable," that is, arguably stronger than the permissions of freedom. *Probabilism* is the doctrine that, in cases of doubt, a probable opinion in favor of liberty may be followed even if the contrary opinion is stronger. It relies on the idea that a doubtful law does not apply and remains uncertain even when more probable opinions weigh in its favor. Arguments can be *intrinsically probable,* based on excellent arguments, or *extrinsically probable,* drawing on the authoritative opinions of moral experts. *Probabiliorism,* seeking to correct the permissiveness implied by probabilism, is the doctrine requiring one to act on the assumption that the moral principle in question obliges when arguments in its favor are more probable than arguments in favor of liberty. Arguments for liberty must be clearly weightier, in other words, to override the law. *Equiprobabilism,* developed by Alphonsus Ligouri in the eighteenth century, is the idea that cases of doubt turn on matters of "possession." If the doubt concerns the existence of a particular duty, and if the argument in favor of liberty is at least equally probable, then our liberty is confirmed, since it is already "in possession." If doubt concerns not the existence but the cessation of a duty, and if liberty is no more than equally probable, the duty—which is already "in possession"—still obtains.[5]

During and after the period of "high casuistry" (1556–1656), moral theology often drew upon the doctrines of probabilism, probabiliorism, and equiprobabilism—so much so that casuistry is still often equated with one or another form of probable reasoning. But it would be a mistake to make this identification with casuistry *tout court*, because it confuses one of the more general occasions of casuistry—doubt—with the strategies that some moral theologians used to cope with it.

It is more accurate to say that casuistry is hermeneutical rather than probabilistic, because it is frequently occasioned by interpretive uncertainties and the need to decipher the practical meaning of an obligation. Casuistry thus represents an attempt to overcome ethical, social, or interpretive alienation, to clarify why and when we are to adopt a certain moral code. Yet unlike many hermeneutical philosophers, casuists are scarcely worried—if at all—about exploring the deeper assumptions of their own inquiries. Instead, they devote their energies to refining the actual practice of interpretation and application. Casuistry is more of an interpretive practice than a self-reflexive theory.[6] Casuists are hermeneutical in the sense that they adhere to the notion that "by discussing cases new light is thrown upon the principle,"[7] in the process of which our obligations can be put into action. As a result, one of casuistry's main goals is to provide *specification*. Hoping to eliminate confusion about how to interpret moral rules, casuists move from the general to the specific, seeking to show more precisely how a moral rule ought to regulate our lives.[8] In the process, they help us apprehend the concrete, substantive meaning of the general principle in question.

Consider, for example, the relation between the Decalogue and the Covenant Code in the Hebrew Bible and, in particular, the ethics of killing (Exodus 20: 1–17; 20: 22–23, 33). The Fifth (or Sixth) Commandment prohibits killing, but it is by no means clear how far this prohibition should extend. Does the law forbid all forms of killing, even in self-defense? Are all forms of killing *equally* wrong? What of accidental deaths and injuries? The redactor of Exodus sought to answer these kinds of questions by attaching the Covenant Code to the account of Moses' revelation at Mount Sinai. And in this code it is quite clear that numerous casuistical practices operate, many of which attempt to specify the range of application of the commandment.

We are told, for example, that "whoever strikes a man so that he dies shall be put to death" (Ex 21: 12). But this blanket condemnation of killing is not as simple as it might seem. Killing in defense of one's property is not absolutely forbidden: If, during the night, "a thief is found breaking in, and is struck so that he dies, there shall be no bloodguilt for him" (Ex 22: 2). We also learn that an accidental death is not punishable as a capital offense; only "if a man willfully attacks another to kill him treacherously, you shall take him from my altar, that he may die" (Ex 21: 14). For that matter, not all forms of killing are equally wrong, regardless of intention: If a pregnant woman is struck and her fetus dies, then the offender must provide financial restitution. Only if the woman dies should "life for life" be the compensation for her injury. Slaves, too, complicate matters: If a man strikes his slave and the slave immediately dies, the owner shall be punished. But if the slave survives a day or two, no penalty should be exacted (Ex 21: 20).

One result of these efforts at specification is to suggest a range of *permissible* actions, often cast in terms of *exceptions to the moral law*. This dimension of casuistry has often been associated with laxity, or finding easy excuses for avoiding the rigors of moral life. But as the Covenant Code illustrates, such an assessment of casuistry would be simplistic. It is more accurate to say that casuists seek to clarify an uncontroversial distinction of morality, namely, between those acts that I *ought* to do and those acts that I *may* do. The task of specification can thus open the door to a class of *indifferent* acts, acts whose moral content is negligible.

Aquinas's account of the morality of theft provides an instructive case in point. In the *Summa Theologiae,* he attempts to specify the range of application of the Sixth (or Seventh) Commandment, "Thou shalt not steal." Among other reasons, theft is wrong because it is "contrary to justice, which is a matter of giving each person his due."[9] But the general prohibition against stealing does not hold always and everywhere. One instance is when an individual is extremely impoverished, and has no alternative but to take another's property. About such circumstances, Aquinas writes, "everything is in common. Therefore a person who takes somebody else's property which necessity has made common again so far as he is concerned does not commit theft."[10] The category of "theft," in other words, includes circumstances of moderate provision. Within those circumstances, it is possible to justify the institution of private property. But such a justification is relative to conditions that are not pertinent to those who suffer from extreme deprivation.

Aquinas's attention to circumstances is not an attempt to *justify* theft for persons who lack basic provisions. Rather, he is arguing that absent some background conditions, the protections that normally surround property do not obtain. He seeks not to justify theft but to *reclassify* the act in question. So he concludes: "If one is to speak quite strictly, it is improper to say that using somebody else's property taken out of extreme necessity is theft. For such necessity renders what a person takes to support his life his own."[11] Indeed, to take property that necessity has rendered "common" is to acquire one's just due.

Aquinas's discussion of theft (and its redescription) illustrates another dimension of casuistry, namely, the importance of classifications, definitions, or taxonomies for moral analysis. Casuists often begin by providing a clear, brief definition of an action—e.g., lying, theft, abortion, obliteration bombing in war—before assessing the merits of a particular case or policy. Owing to the importance of taxonomic description for casuists, several parallels between casuistry and the role of paradigms in scientific research naturally suggest themselves. As Kuhn observes, paradigms in science provide examples in which investigative procedures are relatively clear and well tested. They provide the route to what he calls "normal science," shaping a gestalt, a way of seeing, for scientific practitioners.[12] Similarly, casuistry is paradigm-based research in the sense that it begins with accepted examples of ethical analysis, standard approaches that become familiar to practitioners in the course of their professional initiation. Such paradigms, as Kuhn writes, provide "models from which spring particular coherent traditions of . . . research." Without paradigms or taxonomies in casuistry, our interpretations would be random and ad hoc, not unlike those moments when science lacks a paradigm for inquiry and problem-solving. Kuhn continues, "In the absence of a paradigm or some candidate for a paradigm, . . . early fact-gathering is a far more nearly random activity than the one that subsequent scientific development makes familiar."[13]

When used as a means to approach the unfamiliar, taxonomies in casuistry require us to reason analogically. We solve our puzzles by modeling them on previous puzzle solutions, keeping an eye to relevant similarities and differences between the familiar and the new. In this way, paradigms resemble models or matrices when learning a language. "Type cases" enable us to infer how to conjugate a verb in a foreign language: We begin from a standard conjugation and then puzzle out the tenses of similar verbs. As Kuhn observes about analogies in science, research about the unfamiliar can be conducted "by resemblance and by modeling to one or another part of the scientific corpus which the community already recognizes as among its established achievements."[14] Similarly, in ethics we can seek a solution by first seeing how a novel case resembles a problem that ethicists have already encountered and for which they have developed a clear taxonomy.[15] In this way, Jonsen and Toulmin write, practical arguments "depend for their power on how closely the *present* circumstances resemble those of the earlier *precedent* cases for which this particular type of argument was originally devised."[16]

One clear example of analogy in casuistry appears in the work of Henry Davis, S. J. Writing in 1938, Davis sought to develop some specific guidelines about the morality of surgery for women suffering from ectopic pregnancies. He confronted the quandary: Does the removal of the fallopian tube and the inevitable loss of fetal life constitute an abortion? Or can we justify the surgery because the death of the fetus is unintended? On the one hand, removing a fallopian tube carrying fetal life resembles a craniotomy, in which the emerging child's head is crushed in order to save the life of the woman. Such an act would be prohibited by the rule that evil cannot be willed to produce a good. If used as the taxonomy of ectopic pregnancies it would produce *a fortiori* a prohibition. Yet ectopic surgery also resembles the removal of a cancerous uterus from a pregnant woman. In this second case, the loss of fetal life is foreseen, but not intended, and is justified as a proportionate measure. Davis set out to address the case of ectopic surgery by first seeking to ascertain which case provides the best way to classify—by analogy—the surgical removal of a fallopian tube in which an embryo is lodged. Drawing on the advice of medical professionals experienced with the case, he concluded that the latter analogy was more appropriate.[17]

Davis's discussion of ectopic pregnancies and Aquinas's treatment of theft point to a vital dimension of casuistry: its attention to the circumstances that surround an agent or an act. For, as we attempt to specify the meaning and implications of a law, we must also consider the particular context in which it might be pertinent. Yet attention to circumstances in casuistry does not produce the kind of ethical relativism associated with situation ethics. Situation ethics bids us to determine the "loving thing" within a situation as an alternative to invoking prescriptive rules.[18] Typically such determinations involve calculating what will produce the greatest good for the greatest number of people, regardless of the principles that are relevant to a case. Casuists, in contrast, set out to ensure the fitting application of a rule to a case as a vital feature of practical deliberation.

Circumstances impinge upon moral reasoning in five ways, two of which I have obliquely suggested. First, circumstances can aggravate or attenuate the seriousness of a moral action. For example, Aristotle's argument that committing an injustice to a friend is worse than committing an injustice to a stranger is premised on the idea that debts accruing to familiar relations aggravate a wrongdoing.[19] Alternatively, factors over which I have little control can mitigate the seriousness of my moral failure. If I commit a moral misdeed when fatigue has prevented me from attending to my duties, then I am less culpable than if I had acted deliberately and with full intent, all else being equal.

Second, as Aquinas's discussion of theft indicates, attention to circumstances can produce an alternative paradigm for classifying an action. Here circumstances have less to do with determining degrees of blame or merit than with determining the correct taxonomy of the deed in question. Aquinas's discussion of theft and necessity is an attempt to show how some acts fall outside the parameters of a paradigm case and thus require another taxonomy, a rectification of names. For Aquinas, taking property under conditions of necessity is not to be classified under the rubric of *theft*. Within the context of duress, an act that would otherwise count as an injustice must be redescribed. In this way circumstances—phenomena that literally "stand around" one's decision—can have a direct bearing on how we are to interpret someone's behavior.

Circumstances can affect our assessments of behavior in a third way if we consider how cultural forces can influence our habits, perceptions, or institutional practices. Knowing how history can shape our prejudices is part of a genuinely self-reflexive casuistry, requiring casuists to be conscious of the ways in which culture and history affect our views of others, especially the less fortunate in society. Awareness of the effects of history on our ways of seeing, in other words, is a crucial component of casuistical deliberation. When discussing proxy consent for experimenting on children, for example, Richard McCormick argues for special protections for institutionalized children, given the temptation to regard them as "lesser human beings." Since "medical history shows our vulnerability to this type of judgment," McCormick argues, special cautions should be imposed when seeking consent from institutionalized noncompetents.[20] Similarly, Daniel Maguire develops a sustained defense of preferential affirmative action, insisting that interpretations of social justice must include an honest account of the history of race relations in the United States. Without attention to the effects of history on our perceptions of others, appeals to justice will lack sufficient attention to the problems of racial discrimination.[21] In both cases the point is to remind us that practical deliberation can easily be affected by bias or prejudice, that casuistry can be tainted by partiality and privilege.

Fourth, casuistry attends to circumstances insofar as casuists assess the effects of a decision or policy on the future mores of a culture. Such concerns are typically captured by the image of a slippery slope. When debating some difficult cases in which abortion might be necessary, for example, the Jewish ethicist David Novak counsels caution.

His main point is that liberalizing abortion policy in order to deal with rare cases poses the danger of cheapening the value of vulnerable human life as a whole. Novak writes:

> The fundamental question is whether the life of a fetus may be destroyed at will. If this is permitted for utilitarian reasons (overpopulation, convenience, etc.), then the right to life of the severely retarded, the hopelessly psychotic, the senile, could be questioned next. Are not the senile, the retarded, and the psychotic more "trouble" than an unwanted fetus? Reverence for life is at a low ebb, and the clamor for open abortion is just one symptom of the moral climate of our times. Jews especially, who have been the most tragic victims of the contempt for life, should be the last people in the world to support legislation that would give *carte blanche* and moral sanction to abortion.[22]

Novak's argument concerns not only the way history affects our perceptions of one group, such as institutionalized noncompetents or victims of racial prejudice. It also concerns the *widening* effects of a policy on *analogous* members of society: the marginal, the vulnerable, the powerless. Casuistry attentive to circumstances sometimes asks us to imagine how a policy might resemble ripples that spread from a rock thrown into a pond. Such ripples literally "stand around" the initial splash, as a consequence. Or, to return to the original image, attention to the circumstances of casuistry in this fourth sense must include some consideration of the *many* downward directions in which a slippery slope can take us. We are asked, then, to consider not only the circumstances that surround a decision now, but also the problems that are likely to emerge in the future. With such anticipated dangers in view, casuists frequently advise us to take the safer course, to act with caution.

Fifth, circumstances bear upon casuistry in the sense that custom, or repeated actions, can produce codes for moral behavior.[23] As Aquinas argues, custom can gain the force of law, "for when a thing is done again and again it seems to proceed from a deliberate judgment of reason."[24] Customs constitute the unarticulated backdrop, the embodied understanding of a group, enshrined in their everyday practices.[25] The habits of a people, in other words, contribute to the formation of their laws and mores. As Aristotle remarks about practical affairs, the wisdom of moral sages emerges inductively, "for experience has given them an eye [with which] they see aright."[26] In ethics no less than in common law, the moral understanding of a culture grows out of reflections on shared practical experience.[27] In casuistry this means that moral directives can "bubble up" from our everyday practices, producing general conclusions about the moral life from the accumulation of particular facts and individual cases. Seen in this way, circumstances can provide an orienting vision, a set of anticipatory judgments, based on action and wisdom that have stood the test of time.

The fact that circumstances bear on casuistry in these five ways suggests that casuistry must include "thick descriptions" of moral action. For this reason (in addition to those I mentioned in the last chapter), casuistry is poetic, requiring us to attend to the nuances, details, resonances, and implications of human behavior. In the attempt to specify the meaning of a moral principle, no simple, crisp answer to a problem will do. Instead, casuists expect (or ought to expect) no less than a careful, discerning interpretation of the relevant particulars of a case. Circumstances include the "who, what, when, where, and why" of an action. Casuists' attention to such contextual factors means that their efforts to overcome ambiguity are likely to be long and arduous.

Generative Conflicts

Ambiguity in moral experience provides one occasion of casuistry, requiring casuists to *specify* a rule's range of application, *distinguish* between permitted and prohibited actions, develop *paradigms and taxonomies,* reason by *analogy,* and attend in various ways to the *circumstances* surrounding an action. In this way the practical meaning of an obligation can become clear—or at least less unclear—for the reflective conscience.

A second, quite different, occasion results from the experience of moral conflict. In this case we are concerned not with interpretive ambiguity, but with the need to settle a conflict between rules that are quite clearly understood. The casuist's task, then, is not to specify a duty, but to order or rank competing obligations.[28]

Casuists typically handle such problems by drawing on an account of presumptions in moral disputes.[29] Presumptions enshrine commonplace attitudes and maxims, a set of general obligations that bear upon a case. They hold generally and for the most part, but may give way to rival considerations in a situation of moral perplexity.

Arguments in casuistry thus throw the advantage of presumption on one side, or the burden of proof on the other, when addressing a case. In this way casuistry thus has clear parallels with legal argumentation. As Nicholas Rescher observes, in legal disputes "a presumption indicates that in the absence of specific counterindications we are to accept how things 'as a rule' are taken as standing, and it places the burden of proof upon the adversary's side."[30] Adopting a presumption is to impute to facts or attitudes a prima facie significance, and thus to throw upon the party against whom it works the challenge of bringing forward arguments to meet it.[31] In legal trials, for example, American jurists presume that an accused is innocent until proven guilty, that a child of less than seven years of age cannot commit a crime, and that a person lost for seven or more years is dead.[32] Such presumptions are potentially or probably true, pending further inquiry, evidence, and argumentation. Like precedents in common law, presumptions "fix the point of departure" from which the labor of casuists (or jurists) begins.[33] They lend structure to an argument, but do not foreclose its development.

This means that presumptions are defeasible, not absolute and invariable. They have a probative status, and may be overridden when weightier rival considerations are brought to bear. In casuistry, presumptions express in a condensed or elliptical way certain attitudes about how to live a good life. As such, they articulate general, uncontroversial beliefs or shared assumptions; these hold generally and for the most part, furnishing substantive starting points for knowledge and understanding. As a candidate for truth, a presumption enjoys the benefit of the doubt. It is a plausible pretender to the truth, and to accept a presumption is to engage in "a conditional epistemic inclination towards it."[34] But such acceptance is provisional and *pro tem*, until other relevant issues that "remain to be seen" are brought to light.

Conflicts in casuistry take three specific forms: between *rival moral principles or goods;* between *principles and pragmatic or utilitarian concerns* (e.g., between justice and expedience); and between *relative evils,* requiring us to choose the less undesirable alternative. In each instance casuists must ascertain which presumptions ought to shape our initial response to the case, and then determine whether rival considerations trump the presumption, producing an alternative verdict or course of action.

Consider, first, the clash of principles or goods. Here the conscience is bound by two clear and specific imperatives, one of which requires us to sacrifice the other.[35] The duty to uphold a promise to meet a friend, for example, may have to be sacrificed on behalf of the duty to care for an ill spouse. A physician's duty to protect the confidentiality of an AIDS patient may clash with the duty to protect public health. A lawyer's duty to defend a client who threatens to perjure herself on the witness stand may conflict with the duty to uphold justice.[36] Parental duties notoriously conflict with professional or other commitments. Not infrequently in modern society, tensions between the goods of family life, recreation, friendships, and professional responsibilities are all too acute. Such conflicts typically require us to choose between competing obligations. The experience of complexity is familiar to citizens who carry out different roles and partake in the pluralism of associations in liberal society. Casuistry arises from the need to develop an ordering of charity—a hierarchy of duties and loyalties to settle dilemmas that arise on a daily basis.[37]

A less obvious—but no less difficult—series of conflicts arises when principles clash with practical concerns, like those between duty and utility. Sometimes this conflict is cast in terms of the tensions between morality and necessity, where the latter often qualifies the former.

Casuists address this second source of conflict in one of several ways. First, one can argue on behalf of heeding the demands of utility if it clashes with a *moral permission*. Here Paul's first letter to the Corinthians provides a classic example. One of the questions put to Paul by the church in Corinth concerned eating meat sacrificed to pagan idols. Members of the local church wondered, Is it proper to eat meat sacrificed to other deities? What about those who object to eating such meat? To these questions Paul replies that for Christians all things are lawful. His basic claim, developed more fully in his letters to the Roman and Galatian churches, is that Christians are now free from the Jewish law, that practices like circumcision are no longer necessary as a condition for membership. It is life as a new creature, life in the Spirit, that serves as the basis for membership in the community. As a result, eating meat sacrificed to idols is a matter of moral indifference.

Yet Paul refuses to overlook the problem of scandal and weaker consciences. That is, even if all things are lawful, not all things are useful. Not all actions are conducive to the upbuilding of the community. So in the presence of those with weaker consciences—Christians who scruple about eating meat sacrificed to pagan gods—it is fitting to find an alternative. Concessions to harmony may be necessary, even at the expense of the Christian's freedom.

Paul thus argues for a form of moral condescension, where I must restrict my action in order not to pique my neighbor's conscience, even when I know that my neighbor is overly scrupulous. But insofar as my concessions to utility—social harmony—compromise my freedom (only), self-restraint is called for. To extend Paul's logic, consider the case of swearing. We may be untroubled by those who swear casually or for rhetorical punctuation, believing that swearing is relatively harmless. But we probably do not swear in the company of our elders—when that distant aunt is visiting—lest we upset the social applecart. Even if swearing is lawful, it is not always useful.

Paul's case is one of the easier ways of resolving tensions between morality and expediency, because the moral principle involved is a permission instead of a commandment or a prohibition. The dilemma of 1 Corinthians, then, is between liberty and socially harmful acts. But for the most part the tension between morality and necessity involves obligations or prohibitions (not permissions), creating conflicts that are more difficult to resolve.

One approach to this latter kind of tension is to argue it away, claiming that what appears to conflict with duty is illusory. So, for example, Cicero argues about the tension between the honorable and the beneficial in *On Duties*. For Cicero there is only an apparent, but no real, tension between honorable acts—or acts from duty—and acts done for the sake of benefit or utility. One of the chief tasks of *On Duties* is to provide a "rule of procedure" to help us adhere to the demands of duty and resist the temptation to follow what seems useful.[38] To this end Cicero provides countless cases that are meant to illustrate the unity of the honorable and the beneficial. His casuistry, then, is occasioned less by the need to resolve moral conflicts than by the desire to dissolve them away.

In Cicero's mind the harmony of duty and utility derives from two basic facts. First, one's reputation would be blemished from acting unjustly, thus creating more disutilities in the long run. As Cicero remarks, a person who seeks his own advantage at the expense of others is "a twister, mysterious, cunning, tricky, ill-intentioned, crafty, roguish, and sly." Thus he asks, "Surely it is not beneficial to subject oneself to all these allegations of viciousness and many others?"[39] Second, and perhaps more important, unjust acts injure the larger community of humanity. Drawing on the Stoic account of the law of nature, Cicero adheres to the notion that individuals are parts of a larger whole—the whole of humanity—and to injure another is to do indirect, but real, damage to oneself. "Suppose," he writes, "that each limb were disposed to think that it would be able to grow strong by taking over to itself its neighbor's strength; necessarily the whole body would weaken and die." In the same way, then, "if each one of us were to snatch for himself the advantages other men have and take what he could for his own profit, then necessarily fellowship and community among men would be overthrown."[40] Without community the individual is removed from the conditions of a genuinely human life. Those who believe that dishonest acts can be beneficial are therefore deluded about the real meaning of their good.

The natural law premises on which Cicero relies are by no means self-evident today, especially when they are meant to articulate a vocabulary of universal human community. But when we rank the value of particular communities above that of a universal community, the tensions between morality and expedience return, as we can see in Michael Walzer's well-known contribution to just-war theory. According to Walzer, the ethics of war must keep in mind two concerns:

human rights and utility. We enter war in order to restore rights that have been violated, but we may do so only if we respect the rights of those who are not contributing to the opponent's war effort. In the normal course of war, the rights of noncombatants may not be sacrificed for the sake of utility—that is, as a means of prosecuting the war more efficiently.[41] And, while Walzer is generally averse to speaking about universal community, he nonetheless holds to the idea that rights are universal in that we ascribe them to humans regardless of their particular memberships.[42]

But unusual circumstances may exist in war—what Walzer calls the "supreme emergency"—when necessity may justifiably trump the protections that surround human rights. Walzer defines such an emergency by two criteria: "The first has to do with the imminence of the danger and the second with its nature."[43] When a community confronting a wholly nefarious opponent finds its back against the wall, anything goes. A supreme emergency allows one to override strict prohibitions—like the duty not to harm innocent persons intentionally—in the desperate situation in which a community's survival is at risk. Necessity overrides moral obligation, in other words, in those circumstances in which "our history will be nullified and our future condemned unless I accept the burdens of criminality here and now."[44] In the supreme emergency, evil may be done to achieve the good of protecting the future of a particular collective life. Thus for Walzer, casuistry in war can be occasioned by the need to determine when duty and utility clash, and when it is appropriate to sacrifice the former on behalf of the latter.

Augustine's famous discussion of truthtelling in *On Lying* provides an alternative attempt to manage the tensions between duty and utility, paving a middle path between Cicero and Walzer. Augustine argues that the duty to tell the truth is indefeasible *and* that considerations of utility enable us to conclude that not all lies are equally wrong. One might serve lesser goods—temporal goods—by lying. Accordingly, some lies are worse than others, depending on whether they satisfy some other need. Lying in order to convert another to believe in Christianity is more serious than lying to protect an innocent party from unjust arrest, which is worse than lying to protect oneself from sexual violation. The first lie is worse than the second because lying for the sake of spreading piety is a corruption of Truth itself. Such a lie is a self-contradictory act, a violation of "chastity of mind," from which no temporal good can be achieved.[45] And, while the second lie at least serves some temporal good, it is worse than the third because hindering public authority is more heinous than failing to protect a private individual's body. In contrast to Walzer, Augustine

29

does not allow utility to trump duty, while conceding that considerations of utility nonetheless complicate the final evaluation of the seriousness of a sin.

Augustine's way of handling duty and utility is, in effect, an attempt to join the "one and the many" in moral experience. The "one" is the mandate to tell the truth in all circumstances, a mandate that is constrained by Augustine's belief in theodicy. Central to the task of *On Lying* is to show that the biblical commandment to tell the truth is not unfair, that God does not demand more from us than we can be expected to achieve.[46] *Deus impossibilia non iubet.* So Augustine concludes his treatise, citing 1 Cor 10: 13: "God is faithful, Who will not suffer you to be tempted above that ye are able to bear, but will with the temptation make also a way to escape, that ye may be able to bear it."[47] God would not ask us to abide by a duty that is contrary to our own good as humans; indeed, an inhuman ethic would seem unjust, and would cast doubt on the fairness of God's design.

We must be assured, then, that we will flourish, not suffer, if we adhere to moral principle and resist temptations to lie. This means, among other things, that Augustine's theological ethic links theodicy and moral motivation. Augustine seeks to join the right and the good, saying that it *is* in our interest to be honest, that we *will* flourish by always telling the truth. A cosmos that is on the side of justice assures us that virtue is its own reward, that honesty is the best policy.

In this way theological reasons shape Augustine's attempt to handle the conflicts between duty and utility. Against Walzer's position, Augustine's belief in theodicy makes it inconceivable that revelation or the natural law would allow some kind of evil so that good may come. The conviction that the cosmos is on the side of justice means that the right will always be joined to the good, although the realization of the good might lie in the future. If, by contrast, those who are righteous will suffer for their righteousness, the system seems unfair and reflects badly on the morality of the Designer. Similarly, if I must do evil so that good may come, it would seem that injustice has an advantage over justice.

Yet this absolute prohibition of lying is not uncomplicated, for it admits of several gradations. The "one" to which I have referred pertains to the absolute mandate not to lie; the "many" pertains to the several degrees of wrongdoing that may occur by violating the biblical commandment in the service of other, temporal goods. For this reason Augustine provides an instructive contrast with Cicero. In *On Duties* Cicero refuses to allow us to break the unity of the honorable and the beneficial. Augustine generally agrees with this line of thought, given his belief that honesty is the best policy. But he nonetheless qualifies it, arguing that considerations of utility and disutility are not illusory, but have "relative" reality.

Once again, theological considerations are important. Augustine's belief that creation constitutes a realm of relative goods prevents him from dismissing the tension between duty and utility as illusory. Hence, the temporal benefits wrought by a lie make it more or less grievous, depending on the temporal goods that are served or evils that are avoided. Indeed, if temporal suffering had no exigency, then Augustine would be forced to divorce the order of redemption from the order of creation, and would find himself embracing a version of Manichaeanism. Manichaeans considered the created order to be ontologically indifferent, if not evil. But Augustine sought to affirm the relative goodness of the temporal, created order, which led him to weigh the reality of temporal goods (like procreation) and temporal evils (like bodily pain or sexual violation) in his casuistry. Thus for Augustine all lies are unlawful, but not equally unuseful. Lies on behalf of utility have a certain "weight," depending on the nature of the temporal goods that they might serve.

Casuistry is thus occasioned by conflicts between rival duties or between duty and utility, providing a host of questions for casuists to examine. Yet no discussion of moral conflict and casuistry would be complete if we overlooked those instances in which we are met with nothing but undesirable alternatives, forcing us to choose the lesser of two evils. As Aristotle observes about the requirements of virtue, at times we must make the best of our circumstances, "as a good general makes the best military use of the army at his command and a good shoemaker makes the best shoes out of the hides that are given him."[48] Not infrequently circumstances present us with options that resist our higher ideals and wishes. About these problems Aristotle remarks: "Since to hit the mean is hard in the extreme, we must as a second best . . . take the least of the evils."[49] Perhaps here more than elsewhere the moral life is especially difficult—even tragic—requiring us to decide between two unattractive possibilities.

Many of those who defend a prochoice position in debates about abortion, for example, adopt a version of Aristotle's line of argument. Whatever may be the problems surrounding the decriminalization of abortion, the reasoning goes, we would be worse off in a society that banned abortion. Criminalizing abortion would not eliminate abortions, but would only force many women to induce their own abortions, greatly increasing risks to themselves. It would also create the conditions for an expensive medical black market, to which only affluent women would have access. The effect of banning abortion would thus be to endanger poor women and make safe abortions a matter of financial privilege. Given our options, a policy that permits elective abortion is tragic but acceptable, in that it settles for the least undesirable of the imaginable alternatives.

Action and Liability

The experiences of ambiguity and conflict help us understand two of the more general occasions of casuistical inquiry, along with two of its more important tools (the paradigm and the presumption). But as the examples from Aquinas and the Covenant Code suggest, casuists also seek to determine conditions in which individuals are to be held morally accountable for their behavior. Casuistry thus seeks to assign blame and merit, hoping to clarify when the moral law applies. And, as Augustine's discussion of lying indicates, casuists attempt to ascertain the *degree* to which the moral law applies, assuming that some actions are more praiseworthy or blameworthy than others. Many casuists may believe in the "equality of sin," owing to Christian notions of original or inherited sin. But they also believe in the "inequality of guilt," or degrees of culpability, the determination of which requires casuists to provide a fine-grained description of action.[50]

To this end casuists have developed an elaborate set of distinctions to clarify whether or to what degree moral responsibility is to be imputed to an individual. (Casuistical distinctions are also meant to guide practical judgments in the future, assuming that casuistry can be prospective as well as retrospective.) Equipped with the vocabulary of blame and praise, casuists (or the individuals they advise) articulate a poetics for conscientious action and practical deliberation.

In the casuist's attempt to determine degrees of liability, general paradigms and presumptions are not always sufficient. Left to themselves, they might lend the false impression that practical reasoning is uncomplicated, that assigning praise or blame need only rely on conventional descriptions or cultural slogans. One reason casuistry involves a poetics is that it bids us to enter into a fine-grained analysis of human conduct, requiring us to supplement paradigms and presumptions. Consider the following, which are among the most prominent terms in casuistry for measuring moral accountability:

(1) *Formal and material acts.* A formal act is one in which an agent is deliberately and willfully engaged. In such instances the agent is culpable for her behavior. A material action differs in that it leaves open judgments of moral responsibility. Actions that materially violate a moral law may have been coerced, accidental, or the result of necessities over which the agent had little control. Accordingly, an act may be materially wrong from the point of view of an outside

observer, but whether the agent is responsible for *moral* wrongdoing requires further examination. Catholic medical professionals are forbidden to cooperate formally in elective abortions, but nurses who can find employment only in hospital clinics that require them to assist in performing abortions may be excused insofar as their actions remain material but not formal. Traditional Catholic casuistry holds that the importance of gainful employment provides the nurse with a proportionate reason for cooperating in the practice of abortion.[51] So long as the nurse does not consent to the morality of the practice, the rule forbidding assistance with direct abortion can be set aside.

(2) *Intended versus foreseen but unintended effects of an act.* This distinction, central to the principle of double effect, reflects the effort to provide a disciplined acceptance of tragedy in moral experience. It presupposes that there are some acts whose principal aim is to produce good, but which may also produce some untoward outcomes as a foreseeable by-product.[52] Such consequences are unfortunate, a source of regret or reluctant acceptance. A doctor who injects a painkiller into a dying patient should intend to ease her suffering; yet we also know that such treatment may hasten the patient's death as an unintended but predictable result. Typically, casuists argue that such unintended effects are acceptable when they do not outweigh the overall good that is deliberately sought by the doctor. Adverse effects exemplify the fact that well-intended actions are not always free of complications or regrettable results.

One formulation of the distinction can be found in Aquinas's attempt to revise the views he inherited from Augustine on the ethics of homicide. Augustine argues that private citizens are prohibited from using lethal force in self-defense. Only those commissioned with protecting the commonweal are authorized to kill. In effect, Augustine endorses an ethic of nonresistance for private individuals; in the civic realm their only recourse for protection is to summon public officials. Private citizens who kill in self-defense simultaneously act as vigilantes and depart from the Sermon on the Mount, thereby violating both the natural law and commands of the Bible. But into this paradigm Aquinas introduces the distinction between intended and foreseen outcomes of an act, the effect of which weakens the force of the Augustinian paradigm and opens the door for the use of force by private individuals in self-defense. By Aquinas's account, private citizens who intend to defend themselves conform to the natural law, which includes the inclination toward self-preservation. Injury to an attacker is foreseeable, to be sure. But so long as such injury remains *praeter intentionem,* beside the intention, the use of force by private individuals in self-defense is warranted. While retaining an important dimension of the Augustinian paradigm—especially its attention

33

to charitable motives and controlled passions in violence—Aquinas's distinction nonetheless modifies the inherited taxonomy and produces an alternative paradigm for the future of moral theology.

(3) *Negative versus positive duties.* The former designate prohibitions ("thou shalt not"), while the latter designate requirements to carry out moral obligations ("thou must"). In general, Western legal, philosophical, and religious traditions have found it easier to specify acts that we should not do than those we are obligated to carry out.

This does not mean, however, that positive duties are insignificant. It means only that negative duties generally take precedence over positive duties. Thus, positive duties that override negative duties—e.g., harming third parties in order to protect innocent people from injury—must overcome a special burden of proof.[53]

(4) *Sins of commission versus sins of omission.* The former category refers to wrongdoing that is deliberately willed; the latter category refers to wrongdoing that results from moral delinquency, or the failure to act when duty calls. Sins of commission typically draw our immediate attention in casuistry, but sins of omission are hardly to be overlooked. Telling a lie is a sin of commission, while mental reservation—uttering a partial truth, while keeping the full truth reserved in the mind—is a sin of omission against the virtue of truthfulness.[54]

Casuists typically view sins of omission as more difficult to specify, given the general priority of negative to positive duties. This priority makes it easier to indicate what we should not do than to specify positive obligations. Thus, absent a robust account of positive duties, it is often difficult to hold individuals accountable for delinquency in exercising (positive) moral responsibility when, for example, others are in need.

(5) *Sins that are committed versus sins that are permitted.* Like the other distinctions, this one concerns matters of moral culpability. But while the others seek to define conditions in which one agent is blameworthy or praiseworthy, this distinction suggests that it is better to allow *others* to sin rather than to commit a sin ourselves. In *On Lying,* for example, Augustine argues that it is wrong to lie as a means of protecting a third party from being harmed by someone else. Deliberately to provide false information about an innocent neighbor so that he will not be captured by an unjust authority is, by Augustine's account, sinful.[55] To commit a wrong in order to prevent others from wrongdoing is, in effect, a commitment to utilitarian ethics. Such an act is a violation of the Pauline principle, which prohibits doing evil so that good may come.

(6) *Ordinary versus extraordinary means.* This distinction provides an important set of terms in medical ethics about doctors' duties to

treat or withhold treatment from their patients. When is a doctor obligated to treat a patient, and when is treatment optional?[56]

Ordinary means refer to those treatments that promise a definite hope of proportionate benefit to a patient. On balance the benefits to the patient must outweigh the burdens of cost, pain, travel, or anxiety. Ordinary means are thus required as part of the medical professional's duty to care for the well-being of the patient. *Extraordinary means,* in contrast, are treatments that promise no proportionate benefit. Whether treatment is ordinary or extraordinary is relative to the patient's condition; what may be ordinary for one patient may be proportionately burdensome, and therefore not obligatory, for another.

In concrete terms, this distinction is meant to justify withholding or withdrawing extraordinary forms of treatment, even if the medical professional foresees that the patient will die as a result. In such instances, death is "permitted" but not "committed" by those in charge of the patient's care. Withholding or withdrawing extraordinary means, then, does not fall under the prohibitions that might surround active euthanasia.

The distinction between ordinary and extraordinary means is not the same as that between natural and artificial means. Depending on the patient's condition, natural means may be extraordinary—depending on whether the treatment augurs more burden than benefit. In such circumstances, natural treatments may be omitted.[57]

(7) *Venial and mortal sins.* These terms specify degrees of wrongdoing in Catholic casuistry. Various factors—circumstances, lack of full evil intention, or a conflict of duties—may attenuate the gravity of an evil deed. As I have indicated, one of the principal tasks of casuistry is to determine not whether but how much an individual has fallen away from the moral law. In *On the Good of Marriage,* for example, Augustine argues that fornication and adultery are both immoral, but that the latter is more sinful since it includes a breach of marital trust.[58]

Drawing on 1 John 5: 17 ("All wrongdoing is sin, but there is sin which is not mortal"), subsequent Catholic moral theology refined the distinction between mortal and venial sins.[59] The former refers to a sin committed with a clear knowledge of guilt and with full consent of the will, and which concerns "grave matter." The latter disposes the soul to death, but unlike mortal sin does not deprive the individual of sanctifying grace. To be sure, this distinction was roundly rejected by the Protestant Reformers, who saw sin as an expression of idolatry or disloyalty, not vice or discrete wrongdoing.[60] And in contemporary Roman Catholic ethics the tendency has been to reinterpret mortal sin not so much as a discrete deed, but as a fundamental orientation away from God's self-communication.[61] Yet the general spirit of this distinction is scarcely an artifact of traditional Roman Catholic moral theology; it persists today in a variety of attempts to establish a hierarchy of evil. Christian pacifists who place a premium on selfless love, for example, might find wars of humanitarian intervention less sinful than wars of self-defense.[62]

(8) *Commands and counsels of perfection.* Distinguishing between perfect duties and imperfect duties, Ambrose attempted to interpret the Gospel account of the young man whom Jesus exhorted to "keep the commandments," and then added, "If you wish to be perfect, go sell all and follow me" (Mt 19: 16–22).[63] The distinction produced, in the Catholic tradition, two sets of categories: *commands,* which pertain to precepts that are imperative for all Christians, and *counsels of perfection,* which are discretionary. Also called "evangelical counsels," the counsels of perfection pertain to the vows of poverty, chastity, and obedience.[64] They specify behavior that is expeditious to attaining charity and form the basis of the religious life for laity and clergy in Catholicism.

The hierarchy of duties implied by this distinction provides a vocabulary of moral expectations: Commands can be realistically expected of individuals, whereas counsels, being more demanding, require special gifts and echo an idealist sensibility. But this is not to say that the religious life is superior to a life based on commands, especially when counsels are obeyed and commands are disregarded.[65] Consider again Augustine's treatise on marriage. Augustine held that a drunken virgin is less admirable than a chaste spouse, given the fact that the latter obeys a command while the former obeys a counsel but disobeys a command.[66]

The language of commands and counsels has given rise to the distinction between obligatory acts and acts of supererogation. The latter are understood to be morally praiseworthy acts that extend above and beyond the call of duty. Acts of supererogation are heroic deeds, surpassing our ordinary obligations, and are usually performed by certain individuals who are graced with the disposition to do them.[67]

(9) *Permitting an action versus consenting to an action.* This distinction pertains to the general topic of complicity. In particular, it designates two ways in which an individual might relate to a foreseeable outcome produced by someone else. To permit an action is not necessarily to approve or wish it. If, for example, preventing an evil deed is reasonably beyond my capacities, then I am free from complicity; my inaction is neither a sin of commission nor a sin of omission. But if I consent to the action, then I am formally implicated in the wrongdoing because I have joined my will to the morality of those

carrying out the evil deed. Civilians who endorse an unjust war carried out by their leaders are formally complicit, and thereby morally implicated, in their government's wrongdoing. Similarly, as Augustine argued, an individual who refuses to bear false witness rather than suffer bodily violation is sinless insofar as he permits the evildoer's action. But if the victim consents to the violation, then he sins against chastity.[68]

(10) *Proximate and remote occasions of sin.* An *occasion of sin* refers to circumstances in which the temptation to wrongdoing occurs. The occasion is not chosen in order to commit a sin; rather, it is chosen for some other reason and creates the temptation to sin owing to external pressures or circumstances.[69] At times we need to weigh the moral risks of the company we keep. When a Wall Street broker is invited by his colleagues to share information necessary for insider trading, the temptation to divulge his secrets puts him in an occasion of sin. An occasion is "proximate" depending on the likelihood that sin is probable, the gravity of the sin in question, and the extent to which the agent has power to avoid the circumstances. Fewer constraints on moral freedom, the lack of probability, or the lack of gravity can render the occasion "remote" rather than proximate.[70]

Casuistry and Particularity

I have remarked that the experiences of ambiguity, conflict, and liability generate numerous questions for casuistical deliberation. These experiences energize the doubts and anxieties to which casuistry regularly devotes its skills and toward the resolution of which it has developed an elaborate set of diagnostic tools. The occasions of casuistry suggest that even the well-intentioned conscience needs guidance in the realm of everyday, practical affairs. For casuists, having strong character or firm integrity is morally insufficient. Indeed, cases of conscience arise not from a weak character, but from a thoughtful one. Thus it is important to attend to the particulars of moral life: the meaning of our responsibilities, the complexity of our loyalties, and the external factors that provide the possibilities and limits for moral accountability.

I have also remarked that particulars are relevant to casuistry insofar as customs and habits can assume the force of law, especially when casuists wish to specify the meaning of a paradigm or presumption. Experience provides not only the problems to which casuists attend, but also the stuff of casuistical insight. A genuinely practical and historical casuistry, in other words, draws from the dynamics of experience itself. We have also seen that the work of casuists is occasioned by the experience of conflict—for example, when one duty competes with another. But how history contributes to the formation of our paradigms and presumptions or the resolution of our conflicts is by no means simple. The Gulf War is one instance in which a conflict of duties produced an occasion for casuistical deliberation, to which historical developments made no small contribution. But few if any discussions of the Gulf War attended to its complexity with genuine casuistical sophistication. Instead, the temptation was to apply moral principles deductively, in a "top-down" fashion, as if history itself had no "new light" to throw on our principles. In order to understand more precisely how the particulars of experience might contribute to our moral taxonomies and our understanding of conflicting duties, let us turn now to the case of the war against Iraq.

PART TWO

Casuistry and Society

CHAPTER TWO

Justice, Complicity, and the War against Iraq

Aggression, Annexation, Intervention

When 100,000 Iraqi troops crossed the border into Kuwait in August 1990, they were not expecting—nor did they meet—significant military resistance from local forces. The fiercest fighting occurred at the royal palace in Kuwait City, where the emir's brother died resisting the invasion. The emir himself quickly fled to Saudi Arabia, and Kuwaiti forces soon found themselves overwhelmed by the Iraqis. Emboldened by his victory, Saddam Hussein warned that he would make "a graveyard" for anyone who tried to oppose him. Soon the Iraqis set up a provisional nine-man government, which disbanded within a week when Hussein declared the annexation of Kuwait. By the end of August Hussein announced that Kuwait was Iraq's nineteenth province, to which he appointed his cousin, Ali Hassan al-Majid, as governor. Meanwhile Iraqi forces moved toward the emirate's border with Saudi Arabia, another crucial player in the international oil market. Having spent billions of dollars to procure arms over the previous fifteen years, Hussein was in great need of money, and the wealth of his neighbors proved to be irresistible. Neither Kuwait nor Saudi Arabia was ready to forgive the $35 billion debt that Baghdad accrued during the Iran-Iraq war, and oil prices had plummeted to a historic low.[1]

Hussein argued that Kuwait had initiated a war on Iraq by pumping more crude oil than was allotted under quotas set by the Organization of Petroleum Exporting Countries (OPEC), thereby driving down international oil prices. This excess pumping, Baghdad claimed, cost Iraq $14 billion in lost oil revenues, and Hussein wanted $27 billion in return from Kuwait alone. Moreover, Iraq had tried without success to lease from Kuwait two islands that control the approaches to Iraq's sole functioning port on the gulf, Umm Qasr. Baghdad had also staked a claim to the oil-rich northeastern strip of Kuwait as part of an ongoing territorial dispute. Citing these reasons, Hussein sought to justify his aggression as, in effect, an act of collective self-defense.

But the Iraqis had designs on more than Kuwait's vast petroleum wealth. Immediately after the invasion, the international press and Amnesty International alleged that occupying forces were engaged in widespread destruction and looting of Kuwaiti property, torturing and executing civilians, raping numerous Kuwaiti women before executing them, and deporting thousands of local citizens. Kuwait appealed to the world for assistance, and soon leaders in Middle Eastern and Western countries were faced with the alternatives of *nonintervention, economic coercion* (through sanctions), or *military intervention.*

The United States responded by imposing an embargo on most U.S. trade with Iraq and freezing $80 million in Kuwaiti and Iraqi assets; subsequent embargoes followed from the European Community, the Soviet Union, and Japan. Four days after the invasion the United Nations Security Council passed Resolution 661, calling for economic sanctions against Iraq and freezing all of its assets until its forces withdrew from Kuwaiti territory. Soon the Security Council passed Resolution 665, authorizing member states to use their vessels to inspect all ships in the Persian Gulf to ensure enforcement of the U.N. embargo. Over the next three months the council met several times to reiterate and develop its resolutions, culminating in November 1990, when it authorized member states to use all necessary means after January 15, 1991—including military force—to uphold the U.N. resolutions should Iraqi forces remain in Kuwait. In the face of these ultimata, Hussein nonetheless held his ground.

A coalition of Western and Middle Eastern forces, led largely by the United States, began the first phase of war—an air war—on January 16. Not long thereafter the Allies were flying 2,000 to 3,000 sorties daily over Iraqi targets. By mid-February the infrastructure of Baghdad was virtually destroyed. The city was without water and electricity, sewage overflowed into the streets, and the danger of widespread disease increased precipitously. For those who had failed to gather provisions, food was scarce.

Air raids sent Iraqis into bomb shelters and Israelis into sealed rooms, as Baghdad responded by sending the first of what would be eighty-one SCUD missiles into Israel, hoping to divide the Allied coalition and its Arab membership by drawing Israel into the fray. In addition, Iraqi troops embarked on a campaign of ecological terrorism in Kuwait's oil fields, creating an oil spill in the Persian Gulf that was reported to be one hundred miles long and ten to twenty miles wide.

On February 23 Operation Desert Storm began a ground war, first by invading from the south and then swinging east to envelop Iraqi forces. To the surprise of the Allies, forces on the ground met little resistance: Tens of thousands of Iraqi soldiers, many of them young boys, surrendered almost immediately. Hoping to complete their campaign of ecological terrorism, retreating Iraqi soldiers set hundreds of Kuwaiti oil wells ablaze, producing thick clouds of smoke and stench that soon stretched from Turkey to Iran. Iraqi soldiers fleeing along the road north to Basra were pummeled by Allied fighter-bombers, leaving a "wall of death" thirty-five miles long and four columns wide.[2] Exactly one hundred hours after the ground war began, a cease-fire was declared, ending the seven-month-long occupation.[3]

Theory and Tradition

Here I wish to assess the events surrounding Iraq's invasion of Kuwait and the Allied response, keeping in mind the ways in which casuists differ from applied ethicists when thinking about moral cases. But first it is important to observe that, however controversial this war may have been, it did not involve anyone in the herculean effort of inventing *ex nihilo* a moral language for assessing the merits of Operation Desert Storm. Rather, parties to all sides of the debate drew from moral vocabularies that have developed over centuries in Western thought and culture: pacifism and the just-war tradition. Pacifists oppose all wars and sometimes all forms of killing to protect themselves or others, while nonpacifists often invoke just-war criteria. These criteria presuppose that a war may be, but is not necessarily, justified. In the United States, assessments of the war against Iraq pitted pacifists against nonpacifists, and some nonpacifists against other nonpacifists.

Recently it has become a commonplace to say that pacifists and just-war theorists need each other when war becomes a topic of social criticism.[4] Just-war theorists need the pacifist voice to remind them of basic values that are central to Western culture, values like the virtue of compassion for those who suffer, the intolerance of cruelty and wanton injury, and the obligation not to harm other persons. Just-war theorists need pacifists, in short, to help them identify the tradeoffs that shape justifications of war. And, although pacifists reject the

institution of war as a whole, they can nonetheless use just-war criteria, assuming that some wars are more pernicious than others. At the
very least, pacifists can refer to just-war criteria to identify incongru-
ities between political discourse and events in war, especially when
that discourse invokes just-war categories. In this way pacifists can
use just-war criteria to accuse political leaders of moral inconsistency
or hypocrisy.[5]

Pacifists can also use just-war criteria to expose discrepancies
between the principles of limited war and the actual practices in a
specific war, hoping to keep international conflict from assuming the
magnitude of total war. Using just-war criteria in this way enables
pacifists to obey the general mandate to make the world less violent.[6]
For these reasons, pacifists have a vital stake not only in using just-
war criteria, but also in ensuring that the just-war tradition is not
co-opted by those who may wish to cloak political interests in moral
dress. When co-optation occurs, just-war criteria can conceal the
practices of total war, which are premised on values contrary to those
of just-war theorists and pacifists alike.[7]

The just-war tradition comprises a detailed body of criteria or
conditions for judging the events in war, originating fifteen centuries
ago in the writings of Augustine and subsequently developing in
canon law, medieval theology, and early international law.[8] Its values,
terms, and distinctions have found their way into the Hague and Ge-
neva conventions, which are meant to establish rules of war. Indeed,
despite the frequent accusation that just-war criteria are ineffective or
obsolete in public discourse,[9] recent events testify to the remarkable
tenacity and pertinence of these ideas for evaluating the war against
Iraq.

Yet using just-war criteria cannot guarantee a consensus about the
morality of any particular war. Considerations of justice provide a
vocabulary for interpreting the moral dimensions of international
conflict, and in this way just-war criteria focus our attention on salient moral features of war. But interpretations and judgments may
differ, depending on how much weight we place on each criterion and
on specific events in war.

Among those who have drawn on just-war criteria to assess the
Gulf War, judgments vary significantly. For some just-war theorists
the Allied cause was dubious, dangerous, imperfect, unwise[10] if not
wholly immoral,[11] while for others the war was unequivocally justified.[12] What is notable about these verdicts is not only that they differ,
but also that they result from mechanistic applications of just-war
criteria. As I aim to show in this chapter, such an approach is misguided since it obscures the extent to which the Gulf War raises questions that cannot be easily subsumed under the terms provided by

the just-war tradition. In order to ascertain the justice of the war against Iraq, we must therefore uncover the problems that would otherwise be obscured by deductive applications of just-war criteria.

I want to argue that the war against Iraq was justified but regrettable, that it satisfied several, but not all, just-war criteria. Equally important, the Allied cause raises significant methodological questions about how to consider the justice of war, especially given the collective nature of the Allied commitment, the procedures according to which this commitment was authorized, and the complicity of Western forces in Hussein's rise to power. I should say at the outset that I see no clear or obvious answers to all of the problems I will pose below; such issues in all likelihood will find pragmatic solutions as citizens and policymakers cobble together answers given the materials and options available to them. But to those committed to just-war criteria, a pragmatic route scarcely reduces the relevance of such problems. Quite the contrary: As studies of the development of just-war tenets have shown, this tradition has been shaped by changing practices in society, practices that have developed in response to historical contingency, technological novelty, and unique circumstances in the relations between communities or nation-states.[13] The development of the just-war tradition *as a tradition*, then, will owe no small debt to the judgments that were made in the war against Iraq, or to decisions that must be made in the war's aftermath. For future casuists who view history as a resource for ethics, it will be necessary to heed the judgments and policies that emerge in the wake of the Allied cause.

This means that we have two questions to consider here, relevant to pacifists and nonpacifists alike: How can just-war criteria serve as a framework for assessing Operation Desert Storm? What features of this war might contribute to future casuistry about the justice of war?

Harm and Moral Discourse

To understand how the just-war tradition can shape an interpretation of war, we must first examine its basic moral logic. Without some understanding of this logic, its specific conditions are hardly intelligible, and perhaps arbitrary. To begin, consider the following imaginary case, developed by Jeffrey Stout:

> Suppose that yesterday, in New York City, in the presence of witnesses, a middle-aged black man took a knife and stuck it into the belly of an elderly white woman. Blood oozed out. The woman, unable even to cry out, lay there passively. Before long, she had lost vast quantities of blood, and the doctors could not save her. She never spoke again to her loved ones, never again enjoyed a stroll in Central Park. And make

45

no mistake about it, she died because of what that man did to her, deliberately and with premeditation. He knew very well that this might be the outcome, and he did it anyway. No doubt, he will soon be spending her money. On what he will spend it, we do not know. The witnesses did nothing to stop him. They neither called the police nor testified against him. One of them, in fact, handed over the knife.

What can be said about such a case? It may help to know that the scene was Mount Sinai Hospital. The black man was a surgeon, the woman his patient. It was a nurse who handed over the knife—a scalpel—in the hope that the operation might save or prolong this poor woman's life. The other witnesses, all of them hospital personnel, agreed that the surgery, though risky, was the woman's due. As for the money, it was nothing more than the fee she agreed to pay for services rendered, whatever the outcome.[14]

If not pressed too far, this analogy sheds light on two dimensions of just-war criteria (neither of which is intended by Stout).

First, this example suggests that we must begin our thinking about harm or injury with a moral presumption *against* the practice. Without further description, acts of suffering are typically associated with wrongful injury. At the very least, we feel compassion for those who suffer and alarm about their pain. Indeed, our compassion is such that we might hastily impute malicious intentions to agents of harm, judging them as aggressors or muggers. In any event, this presumption against harm designates a moral bias against the act. It means that all else being equal, it is wrong to injure another person, that there is a prima facie duty not to harm.

A presumptive or prima facie duty is weighty, but not absolute. Such a presumption resembles the way Americans typically think about whether to increase tax revenues: Raising taxes is not necessarily unjust, but there is a strong presumption, an anticipatory judgment, against doing so. Americans are generally suspicious of increased taxes given a recent history of inefficiency, mismanagement, and corruption by governmental officials responsible for allocating public revenues. Those who propose an increase in taxes, then, must provide clear and convincing evidence that there is no other way to finance public programs that are vital to the common good.

Understood in more technical ethical terms, a presumptive or prima facie duty is *generally* binding, unless it clashes with another duty.[15] When such a clash occurs, the prima facie duty may have to give way, given the judgment that competing obligations are more pressing. Seen in this way, presumptions place the burden of proof on anyone who wishes to override them when they conflict with other moral obligations. Prima facie duties point us in the general direction of what is morally correct, but what is *finally* imperative may differ, depending on a fuller account of the situation in question.

For the case of surgery, the presumption against injury means that if nonsurgical methods provide a reasonable hope for success, then they should be tried first. But if such methods are unavailable, then the presumption against harm may be overridden. The general idea is that for the care of the patient, for the sake of her health, it is justifiable to carry out acts of physical injury—but only after the doctor (on whom rests the burden of proof) acquires the patient's consent. In a medical context, the duty to care "trumps" the duty not to injure. We are thus faced with a situation of moral conflict, where health and harm coexist.

Just-war theorists argue that war constitutes an analogous situation of moral conflict. Here, too, the idea is that when someone needs protection against aggression, the duty not to harm may conflict with other duties, like the duty to defend or protect. The duty not to harm may be overridden by the obligation to protect oneself or third parties from aggression.[16]

At the same time, however, to override a presumptive duty is not to abandon it. Such duties continue to exert their force in the subsequent course of action. That is, a prima facie duty leaves "residual effects" or "moral traces"; after overriding such a duty, our behavior must still be affected by it. Our conduct should approximate as closely as possible the values enshrined in the overridden duty. For practical purposes, this means that those who use force to defend or protect must carry out their duties with the least amount of necessary harm.

This first point about the medical analogy is meant to show how pacifists and just-war theorists share some common ground. For both of them there is a prejudice—and I mean this, following Hans-Georg Gadamer, as an anticipatory judgment—against harming others. Prejudices, Gadamer argues, are productive rather than debilitating, providing substantive starting points for knowledge and understanding.[17] Prejudices serve an important rhetorical function in moral discourse: They articulate general, uncontroversial beliefs or shared assumptions. In this way presumptions allow us to "foreground" important ideas when we form arguments or seek public agreement.[18]

In the ethics of war we begin our interpretations of conflict from anticipatory judgments against injury; these judgments shape the way we start to discern the agonizing moral questions that arise when others are forced to suffer. As I suggested in the previous chapter, presumptions distill in technical ethical language the general, customary prejudices that shape our elementary moral perceptions. For the pacifist the prejudice against injury produces, in the final analysis, an absolute duty not to go to war: This duty may not be compromised or sacrificed. For the just-war theorist, the presumption against harm is not necessarily the last word about the ethics of war. Indeed, in the cases of war and surgery a moral conflict arises between the *duty not to harm* and the *duty to protect* victims of harm.[19]

The second point to be drawn from the medical analogy is that in surgery the problem of harm is not the only moral consideration. Rather, the vital point is that the *harms are foreseen, but unintended*. We intuitively distinguish surgery from mugging, even though in many cases a person can suffer more from surgery than from a mugging on the street. The *moral* difference lies not in the extent of injury, but in the orientation of intention. Unlike the surgeon, the mugger cannot say that harms to the victim are *praeter intentionem*, beside the intention. For the surgeon, such harms are foreseen and regrettable, but not necessarily unjust.

How does this situation resemble war? In surgery the general idea is that the operation should be aimed toward a moral good, the health and well-being of the patient. Those items that are "attacked" include agents of harm, like tumors or unhealthy organs. Other harms may foreseeably and regrettably occur, such as physical pain and financial cost, but such harms must not be part of the surgeon's overall goal. If they are, we accuse the surgeon of a moral wrong. Moreover, if foreseen but unintended burdens outweigh the prospective benefits of surgery, the operation is considered extraordinary means and is not morally required, owing to judgments about proportionality.[20]

Similarly, the goals in war must be ordered toward self-defense, defending sovereign boundaries, or protecting the innocent. Such goals are analogous to the health of the patient insofar as they are aimed toward fulfilling objective goods, i.e., self-preservation or the protection of others. Further, the victims of attack must be agents of harm, like troops, weapons, and related industries. Other harms, such as the death of civilians, may foreseeably occur, but they must not be planned or intended. Moreover, to continue the analogy, if foreseen but unintended suffering outweighs the prospective benefits, the war would be considered a disproportionate risk.

In its simplest form, then, the logic of just-war criteria begins with a presumption against harm, which places a strong burden of proof on those who argue on behalf of using coercion or lethal force to settle disputes. Such justifications must show why it is necessary to override the presumption against harm, specifying other duties that must be met. Even then, however, such presumptions leave moral traces, which require us to provide clear reasons for resorting to war, and to inflict the least amount of necessary harm in the course of war. Moreover, we must examine carefully the intentions of a war, and we must examine the costs that would accompany wars whose intentions seem praiseworthy. If those costs appear to be excessive, the goal of the war may not be enough to override the prima facie prohibition against harming others.[21]

The War against Iraq

The medical analogy is meant to point to considerations relevant to the justification of injury: cause (illness), authority (surgeon, with the consent of the patient), intention (restoration of health), last resort, hope for success, proportionality, and limited means. The just-war tradition includes a clear set of criteria for refining our understanding of such means; it is premised on the notion that not all is fair in war, even for those whose cause is just. Given this concern for both justification and limitation, just-war criteria have developed on two pillars, respectively, the *jus ad bellum* and the *jus in bello.*

The *jus ad bellum* is designed to answer the "when" or "whether" question: When, if ever, is resort to war ethically justified? The components within this pillar consist of several criteria, defined below.

The *jus in bello* is designed to answer the "how" or "methods" question: What methods are morally acceptable once recourse to war has been justified? Here the idea is that the justification for entering war does *not* extend to all possible methods of war itself: The ends do not justify the means. Accordingly, even those engaged in a just cause may not intentionally kill or terrorize noncombatants as a means of prosecuting a war more efficiently.

Given the structure and the details of this tradition, what can be said about the morality of the Allied cause? *Ad bellum* criteria involve the following considerations:

1. *Just cause:* War is justifiable only in occasions of unwarranted aggression—as a defense against threats to national self-determination and basic human rights. War is not justifiable as an exercise of revenge or domination.

Just cause, then, allows for two kinds of wars: wars of *self-defense* and wars of *intervention* on behalf of other victims of aggression. The first is premised on the notion that nations have the right of self-preservation, which may be defended by force. This first justification, obviously, has little direct bearing on the Allied cause. Rather, Operation Desert Storm was an intervention, justification for which is premised on the idea that it is permissible for third parties to use force to protect others from aggression.[22]

The category of third-party intervention must include several considerations that are not germane to the case of self-defense.[23] These additional considerations make intervention more difficult, although not impossible, to justify. For one, the oppressed nation must lack the

49

means necessary for its own defense when its sovereignty is violated. Also, it must summon the support of external aid; otherwise the intervening forces are themselves guilty of invading a sovereign nation. Moreover, its cause is surely helped if it can show that human rights are being systematically violated by the aggressor, that victims are unable to carry out self-rule and self-determination.[24]

All of these considerations about intervention are relevant to the Allied cause, and each was satisfied as a condition for entering the war against Iraq. Yet several questions are pertinent, for psychological and perhaps moral reasons, about the calculus of intervention: Does the cause of intervention require as strong a commitment as does the cause of self-defense? Does the fact that *other* parties are being defended allow for a different kind of commitment than a commitment to one's own preservation? If a war of third-party intervention proceeds with less success than anticipated, is it permissible to cease or lessen one's commitment, given that one's own vital interests are not at stake?

These questions derive from other *ad bellum* considerations, namely, proportionality and reasonable hope for success. Generally, each of these conditions requires us to reach a judgment about risks to ourselves in the recourse to force. Such conditions enable us to ask, Do we measure risks to ourselves differently in the case of intervention than we do in the case of self-defense? If so, and if such dangers begin to materialize in a war of intervention, may one's commitment to the cause decrease?

I recognize that for the case of the Gulf War these questions about commitment are only hypothetical. They are meant to suggest that, in general, judgments about just cause in the case of intervention should be informed by prospective judgments deriving from other relevant *ad bellum* criteria. On this matter it is instructive to recall the U.S. Catholic bishops' suggestion that just-war criteria should be holistically weighed in judgments about the justice of modern war. According to the bishops, *in bello* criteria ought to be integrated *prospectively* among *ad bellum* judgments when considering recourse to war.[25] Their general point is that the military and political dangers involved in war must be anticipated in moral deliberations about whether to enter war. The case of third-party intervention would seem to require a similar holism when measuring the justice of war, a form of deliberation in which cause, proportionality, and reasonable hope for success are factored together.[26] Such a composite approach would assist in making judgments about the degree of legitimate risk-taking in contexts that differ from the case of self-defense.

2. *Right intention:* This condition requires us to evaluate the pur-

poses in pursuit of which war is being waged. Having a just cause, in other words, is not enough: We must be *intending peace* as the goal of war. As G. E. M. Anscombe once argued, it is not enough to say that we are fighting *against* an unjust cause; we must also be fighting *for* a just one.[27] Force may not be used to acquire control over the adversary, although this criterion does permit relevant parties to establish stronger conditions of peace than those that preceded war. At the very least, it requires us to consider how peace is to be reestablished in the aftermath of war.

In the case of the Gulf War, considerations of intention suggest the following questions: What did the Allies seek to accomplish in the war? Did they seek only the expulsion of Iraq from Kuwait and the restoration of the Kuwaiti government? Or were their purposes more expansive? Should such purposes have included disarming Iraq, removing Saddam Hussein from power, or occupying Iraq? Should the Allies have pressed the Kuwaitis to generate democratic reforms once their government was restored? Initially, policymakers moved toward the first, more modest, reply: a "military peace." But right intention also requires us to consider the kind of peace that is to be established in the aftermath of war: a "political peace."

In response to these questions, critics of the war alleged that Western interests were too complicit in Hussein's rise to power to render credible an appeal to right intention. (I will outline the extent of such complicity below.) And, to make matters more complex, the issue of complicity and its relevance for assessing war have received scant attention in ethical commentary. If anything, reference to complicity typically casts doubt on the intentions of those involved in a third-party intervention.

Consider the writings of H. Richard Niebuhr about an analogous event, the Japanese invasion and occupation of Manchuria. In the early 1930s, as in the early 1990s, citizens of the United States considered the morality of third-party intervention to repel aggression and subsequent annexation of an area whose boundaries had been subject to historical dispute. Niebuhr argued on behalf of national repentance instead of intervention, asking each individual to reflect "upon the fact that his inability to do anything constructive in the crisis is the inability of one whose own faults are so apparent and so similar to those of the offender that any action on his part is not only likely to be misinterpreted but is also likely—in the nature of the case—to be really less than disinterested." In such a situation, he added, "righteous indignation is not wholly righteous." It was Niebuhr's hope that, in place of military actions, self-analysis would produce a new way of interpreting the meaning of events. Then it might be possible

51

to see the Chinese as "being crucified . . . by our sins and those of the whole world."[28] In such a context, appeals to moral language to justify military action seem hypocritical.

Present studies indicate that Western interests were profoundly complicit in Hussein's aggression at military and diplomatic levels. Kenneth Timmerman's chilling account of the international arms market reveals a widespread and elaborate set of arrangements between Iraq and numerous Western companies and governments between 1975 and 1990.[29] During this period Hussein invested billions of dollars in his pursuit of nuclear and chemical technology, surface-to-surface missiles with the capacity of hitting Tehran and Tel Aviv, and engineering capabilities that would enable the Baghdad government to build its own weapons. By 1976 Iraq was one of the top five arms-importing nations in the world, and by 1984 Hussein was spending $14 billion annually—half of his gross domestic product—on arms procurement and manufacture.[30] Among Timmerman's more startling revelations:

• Between 1975 and 1990 Hussein spent over $20 billion on French arms, trying to free Baghdad from its dependence on Soviet weapons without having to fall into the lap of U.S. arms producers. The advantage of French weapons was that they came with no political strings attached. Among the purchases from France, Iraq acquired Mirage fighter planes, various missiles, a navy yard, gas liquefaction complexes, radar, a bacteriological laboratory, and a nuclear reactor capable of making bomb-grade uranium.[31] It was France, more than any other nation, that opened the door to the widespread arms trade with Iraq during the 1970s and 1980s.

• In 1981 the West German firm Thyssen Rheinstahl Technology signed a contract for DM 21.4 million to build a laboratory outfitted with special equipment capable of producing highly toxic materials. These included phosphorus pentachloride, a starting chemical for nerve gas. Although spokespersons for Thyssen Rheinstahl denied knowledge of Iraqi intentions in producing nerve gas, from the day when ground was broken for the laboratory the site was heavily guarded by Iraqi soldiers, and Soviet-built SA–2 missile batteries were installed to protect the site against an air attack.[32]

• The West German company Karl Kolb built six chemical weapons lines in Samarra during the 1980s. These plants made everything from mustard gas to the nerve gas compounds Sarin and Tabun. Poisons were funneled to an underground packing plant, where they were put into artillery shells, rockets, and other munitions. By the end of 1984 the Samarra plant was capable of producing sixty tons of mustard gas per month. In March and August of 1988, Hussein used chemical weapons produced at Samarra against two Kurdish villages. They were dropped from Soviet-made fighter planes and German-made helicopters.[33]

• MBB, a multimillion-dollar West German company, provided the bulk of technology for a project designed in Argentina for producing a missile capable of carrying a nuclear warhead. MBB had a significant share of the Pentagon's most advanced weapons projects, and the record suggests "that much of the expertise MBB gleaned from its Pentagon contracts ended up in the hands of Saddam Hussein."[34]

• Belgian, French, and British firms built a variety of strategic underground shelters, hardened air bases, and underground highways to the tune of $2.5 billion between 1982 and 1987.[35]

• British sales in machine tools jumped from £2.9 million in 1987 to more than £31.5 million in 1988. British firms explicitly acknowledged that their tools were programmed to produce mortar shells ranging from 60 to 120 mm.[36] Moreover, the British government approved sales of nuclear materials and chemical weapons precursors such as thiodiglycol in 1988 and 1989, despite the fact that Hussein had used chemical weapons against the Kurds and that he was suspected of possessing a nuclear weapons program.[37]

• In 1990 Portuguese officials admitted selling 252 tons of uranium yellowcake to Iraq on the black market from 1980 to 1983.[38]

• Chile sold Iraq $467 million worth of cluster bombs, fuses for which were purchased by the Chilean entrepreneur Carlos Cardoen from a Pentagon contractor in Lancaster, Pennsylvania—despite a U.N. arms embargo prohibiting sales to Chile.[39]

• In 1976 Hussein agreed to purchase 150 armored cars, 150 scout trucks, and 2,000 military trucks from Petrobras, a Brazilian conglomerate. A ten-year nuclear cooperation agreement with Brazil, sealed in 1979, committed Brazil to supplying Iraq with large quantities of natural and low-enriched uranium, reactor technology, and training.[40] Perhaps most important, Brazilian engineers worked side by side with Iraqis to convert Soviet SCUD-Bs to ballistic missiles with enough range to hit Tel Aviv and Tehran.[41]

• The Soviets, squeezed out of the Iraqi arms market by the French and West Germans, sought to restructure their relations with Baghdad in 1983 by replacing all ground equipment and providing $4.5 billion in new weaponry. Moreover, they rushed a delivery of MiG–21 and MiG–23 fighter planes, helicopter gunships, 350 SCUD-B missiles, and 200 PT–76 light amphibious tanks, accompanied by a $2 billion long-term loan to ease the financing. Three years later they sold 60 MiG–29s for $600 million, and $3 billion worth of assault helicopters, rocket launchers, artillery, and tanks.[42]

• From 1985 on, the U.S. Commerce Department referred many critical Iraqi license requests to other agencies for review. Iraq obtained twenty-one separate licenses for computer equipment during this time, and $94 million worth of high-tech computer equipment was sold directly to Iraqi weapons plants with the approval of the Commerce Department. A subcommittee of the House Committee on Governmental Operations has now reported that these computers helped Iraq develop long-range ballistic missiles and advance its nuclear program. Indeed, from 1985 to 1990 U.S. companies, with the approval of the Commerce Department, sold $500 million worth of sensitive technology to Iraq.[43]

• At the diplomatic level, U.S. officials sought to placate rather than deter Hussein as he increased his thinly veiled threats to the United States and Kuwait, starting in February 1990. Remarking on July 24, 1990, about Hussein's bellicose language, Margaret D. Tutweiler, the State Department spokeswoman, stated: "We do not have any defense treaties with Kuwait," adding that the United States was committed to "the individual and collective self-defense of our friends in the Gulf with whom we have deep and long-standing ties."[44] These remarks could not be heard by Hussein as describing the ties between the United States and Kuwait, whose relations since the Second World War had been sketchy at best. Equally important, a week before the invasion April C. Glaspie came to the Iraqi Foreign Ministry to convey Tutweiler's remarks and, after Hussein complained once again about his relations with Kuwait, assured him that "we have no opinion on the Arab-Arab conflicts, like your border disagreement with Kuwait."[45] Glaspie subsequently sought to vindicate her actions and her conversation with Hussein, arguing that her comments included the claim that "we would defend our vital interests, we would support our friends in the Gulf, and we would defend their sovereignty and integrity." Yet given the history of U.S.-Kuwaiti relations, there was little to suggest that the United States considered Kuwait a friend worth defending.[46] Summarizing the account of the events preceding Iraq's invasion, Theodore Draper remarks: "If Saddam had been trying to gauge what the United States was likely to do in the event of a full-fledged invasion, he had reason to feel reasonably safe. He had been escalating his demands publicly for months without getting any indication that the United States was seriously upset or even realized how serious the situation was."[47]

One way for policymakers to deflect some of these concerns about complicity is to adhere to a narrow notion of right intention, interpreting *intention* merely to refer to the military goal of thwarting aggression. And such an interpretation is not without moral advantages: By describing the Allies' goals in terms of removing Iraq from

Kuwait, policymakers appeared to adopt a moderate set of purposes, in keeping with the politics and ethics of limited war. Yet such actions are premised on a thin account of right intention, focusing on the goal of victory instead of political peace, and masking the extent to which Western forces were implicated in Hussein's ability to carry out aggression.

A robust notion of right intention, in contrast, requires more of the Allied forces than the removal of Iraq from Kuwait. It also requires that the Allies consider their own implication in Saddam Hussein's rise to power, especially in the area of arms proliferation. Efforts to reestablish peace in the Middle East must include further study of how Western leaders aided and abetted Hussein's efforts to destabilize the region, and how they failed to deter Hussein after he provided signals about his aggressive intentions. A robust criterion of right intention, in short, requires a more expansive set of analyses and directives, emphasizing the requirements for establishing genuinely peaceful conditions in the region and examining the habits and practices that eroded peaceful relations. On this score, ceasing arms proliferation and the marketing of weapons technology by the West to Iraq should be of paramount importance in postwar settlements. They should be combined with a more coherent and disciplined set of diplomatic policies than have characterized Western leaders' ad hoc relations with Arab nations during the past three decades.

A thick rendition of right intention, in other words, calls attention to the political as well as the military dimensions of war, especially the political decisions made in the aftermath of war. Seen in this way, a robust understanding of right intention requires us to ask, What political arrangements will emerge in the wake of war, and to what extent can such arrangements mark an improvement for justice and peace?

However much Operation Desert Storm may have been a military success, it was a massive political failure. Indeed, politically speaking the war against Iraq was remarkably conservative. The Kuwaiti regime that was subsequently restored to power showed little promise of democratic or economic reform. Saddam Hussein retained his power and strengthened his hand against rebel Shiite and Kurdish factions. Sanctions aimed at coercing Hussein to submit to U.N. inspections and to sell oil to pay for reparations only augmented structural violence against civilians, and showed little sign of a reasonable hope of success.[48] As a form of indiscriminate harm, sanctions should never have been implemented once the war ceased. Regional peace, understood as the *status quo ante bellum,* was restored insofar as Iraq was removed from Kuwait, and it was strengthened to the extent that

Iraq was militarily defanged. But peace understood in terms of just and harmonious relations, the equitable sharing of power, escaped the reach of Allied leaders.

3. *Legitimate authority:* This criterion precludes resort to war by private individuals, allowing only those who are responsible for the public order to declare war and organize a defense.

On this point citizens in the United States engaged in an important constitutional debate in December 1990: Who has the authority to declare war and marshal a defense, the Congress or the president? The U.S. Constitution grants Congress the right to declare war, but the War Powers Resolution empowers the president to carry out certain initiatives, within a sixty-day grace period, absent such a declaration. After sending more than 400,000 troops to the Gulf Region by mid-November, President Bush turned to the United Nations to seek authorization to use force by January 15, 1991, to which the Security Council agreed. Having secured military commitment and international consent, the president turned to Congress for authorization to use American forces.

While this solution apparently smoothed over tensions between the legislative and executive branches, it nonetheless generated several difficult issues. The first is a problem that may forever accompany public discourse about war—at least in democracies—concerning the relationship between governmental action and the collective will: Is the president bound to calibrate his commitment to war with the sentiments of the populace? If the nation is divided, should the military commitment be qualified and limited? Does stronger public support empower the president to use more expansive methods? How do we gauge public support, and how often do we do so? In a democracy, legitimate authority is a highly complex matter, given that such authority is representative. Americans have yet to clarify the complex relation between the citizenry, their many representatives, and the president when it comes to the authorization of war and the *relationship* of that authorization to the subsequent commitment to war. Here is the dilemma: If the decision and subsequent commitment to use force reflect a tentative, divided nation, then we may send our troops to fight, in the (clumsy) words of President Bush, "with one arm tied behind their back." Yet if forces and troops are committed quickly and without reservation, public policy may not reflect the collective will. Hence the problem: Representation and military resolve are not always compatible.

The second issue concerns the relationship between the United States' authorization to use force and that of the U.N. Security Council. The president sought to move the question of authority up one echelon to the United Nations. He then acquired authorization laterally, from Congress, to carry out actions authorized by the Security Council. Policymakers suggested that reference to the Security Council Resolution marks one aspect of a new world order, the first page in a new chapter of international relations. To be sure, viewing authorization in this way creates an even more complex array of players in the game of authorization than does my first set of questions. Whether this pattern will serve as a model for future international action will be for the next decade to determine.

Should international authorization become paradigmatic, a further set of questions emerges: In an *allied* cause, how shall the risks of war be fairly shared? Having a plurality of players acting against a common foe sharpens the question of distributive justice in war, that is, the equitable allocation of the burdens of war in a collective effort.

Such questions open up a special range of issues about justice in war. Typically, *ad bellum* and *in bello* criteria enable us to weigh the justification for entering war and the justice of using lethal practices in war. In other words, just-war criteria distill rules about justifiable suffering. Such criteria seek to ensure that war does not become a form of domination or oppression for the nonparticipants, that the burdens of war are fairly distributed to the relevant opponents. To that end, just-war criteria seek to make evident the distinction between killing and murder so that those who abide by just-war tenets will keep the killing in war from becoming murderous. In short, just-war criteria shape judgments about what may and may not be done to an adversary. But international authorization for collective action adds another set of problems about the justice of war. Now, such judgments will have to contend with questions of fairness *internal* to the collection of players pursuing a just cause. Citizens in a nation that is acting in a just cause may be driven to object to their nation's role if they conclude that the risks of war have been unfairly allocated in an allied endeavor.[49]

Yet it is also true that concerns about distributive justice should not be applied as if wars emerge in a historical vacuum. Given what I have said about Western and Soviet implication in Hussein's rise to power and subsequent aggression, it would seem only fair that the coalition be composed primarily of Western and Soviet forces. Those who contributed to the problem ought at the very least to shoulder a commensurate burden in seeking a solution. It seems morally incongruous—putting it mildly—to expect Hondurans to risk their lives on behalf of a tragedy in which Americans, Brazilians, the French, the West Germans, and the Soviets are primarily complicit.

The third issue concerns the fact that the president's turn to Congress came after large numbers of military personnel were mobilized and tremendous political and diplomatic efforts were made to secure international consent to use military force against Iraq. Such maneuvering put immense pressure on Congress to authorize the use of force. Given this fact, it was remarkable that the congressional debate was so vigorous and that the vote in the Senate, 52 to 47, was so close. Clearly the burden of proof was placed on those who voted against authorization. The structure of just-war criteria, as I outlined it above, suggests that this burden was wrongly placed. While it may seem necessary to mobilize forces and to secure international assent for political reasons—"to prepare the country for war"—such efforts as a prelude to official debate pose the danger of turning congressional authorization to use force into a *fait accompli*.

Finally, there is the question, Does the Allies' implication in Hussein's rise to power and subsequent aggression disqualify them from taking a moral stand against Iraq? To state the issue more precisely, it would seem hypocritical, critics might argue, for the United States to enter the war, given the fact that U.S. leaders turned a blind eye toward Hussein or aided in his ascendancy. There appears to be a huge moral incongruity about the fact that those who aided and abetted a dictator then turned around self-righteously to reproach him, as if his ascendancy developed in a political and historical vacuum. At the very least, evidence of complicity raises the specter of scandal, endangering the public trust. When it comes to assessing the morality of public authorities, in short, Niebuhr's worries about the dangers of self-righteousness and hypocrisy once again seem apropos.

To these questions it should be said that such complicity, even if potentially scandalous, does not automatically nullify the claims of a legitimate authority to wage war. That is, complicity in the problems of the Middle East is not sufficient to render such authority illegitimate. Nor is it the case that a history of prior political or military mistakes disqualifies a legitimate authority from committing itself to moral aims, as many critics of the U.S. administration alleged. The United States' implication in the moral blunders of Vietnam, Grenada, or the Iran-Contra affair, for example, does not render the U.S. government illegitimate as an authority for going to war, at least according to just-war criteria.

Here it is important to understand properly the meaning of *legitimate*. The condition of legitimate authority is meant to prevent non-public officials from setting out to wage war; it is a prohibition of paramilitary groups from embarking on vigilantism. In short, legitimate authority is tested by considerations of political legitimacy, understood in terms of how a government rules its citizenry. It is *not* a condition that imposes on a government the burden of maintaining morally pure relations with other nations as a condition for embarking on a just cause. As a criterion of the just-war tradition, legitimate authority must be interpreted in terms of the relationship between an administration, the military, and the citizens. It does not require nations to have an unblemished record in foreign affairs, "clean" rather than "dirty" hands.

These ideas bear directly upon how we ought to understand some background features surrounding the criterion of just cause. Having a just cause means that one is justified (only) in one's recourse to force, not that one is righteous as a player on the field of international affairs. Satisfying the criterion of just cause is a specific verdict, confined by fairly narrow circumstances: Does the occasion of aggression warrant recourse to lethal force in this instance? Understanding the criterion of just cause in this way helps to clarify that even those with less than perfect moral or political records can be justified in resisting aggression. In effect, just-war criteria suggest something about moral expectations, allowing us to justify self-defense or intervention by those who are less than morally pure.

These ideas can easily be overlooked, especially by those who allege that the West's implication in Hussein's rise to power should have disqualified the Allies from acting on behalf of Kuwait. But just-war criteria provide grounds for talking about *justified* actions only; invoking them does not imply that countries acting in defense of a just cause are incarnations of political virtue. As I have presented it, the criterion of legitimate authority suggests that it would be too heavy a burden to insist that nations must satisfy conditions of righteousness as a prerequisite for defending a just cause. Contrary to Niebuhr's suggestions in the 1930s, genuinely *righteous* indignation, or pure disinterestedness, is not a condition for entering war.

4. *Last resort:* This criterion holds that all peaceable means of settling disputes within reasonable reach of the public authorities must be exhausted before resort to war is justifiable. If successful defense of a just cause is reasonably possible according to nonviolent methods, then there is a duty to use them.

In my judgment, arguments about whether last resort was satisfied fail to produce a definitive verdict either for or against Operation Desert Storm. This is not to say that considerations of last resort are unimportant or uninstructive, however. Indeed, judgments about last resort were foremost in the minds of many who questioned the justice of this war. Were sanctions given enough time?[50] Were all reasonable diplomatic avenues tried? When the Allies attacked in January 1991, did they act prematurely?

On this point the U.S. Catholic bishops spoke in November 1990, urging policymakers to continue the course of "peaceful pressure" in the form of economic sanctions as an alternative to war.[51] They argued against intervention in light of a strong presumption against force and sought to underscore the importance of last resort. Not long before war broke out, various religious leaders appealed to this condition to criticize preparations for the Allied intervention.[52]

Those who cite the criterion of last resort are open to the charge that policy requires decisive action within a limited time frame, and that this condition imposes a barrier to leadership. As Michael Walzer remarks, "We can never reach lastness, or we can never know that we have reached it. There is always something else to do: another diplomatic note, another U.N. resolution, another meeting."[53] Walzer reminds us that last resort is very difficult to satisfy. According to what evidence, and by what standards, can one determine that peaceful efforts have been "exhausted"?

This question suggests that we must have clarity and certainty when satisfying the condition of last resort, which is doubtless a great deal to ask. It seems more plausible to admit that this condition resists any clean, crisp, clear application. Instead we must make judgments based on perceptions and intuitions about when it is prudent to cease diplomatic actions and shift to military methods. Walzer's dissatisfaction with the bishops' appeal to last resort is premised on an overly demanding view of how it should be applied.

Yet even a more flexible interpretation of last resort does not necessarily support the bishops' plea to give sanctions more time to work. There is little evidence to suggest that Hussein would have cared much about the effects of sanctions on his people. Sanctions take time—in this case perhaps a year—before pressure is fully exerted. No less than war, sanctions should be subject to the *ad bellum* criterion of reasonable hope of success. Those who decided to move to military intervention might well argue, then, that their disagreement with the U.S. Catholic bishops turns on a difference of moral judgment about sanctions, a judgment shaped by the spirit if not the letter of other just-war criteria.

Moreover, during the time that sanctions were imposed, individuals in Kuwait were being deported, tortured, or executed. From the point of view of those persons living under such threats, the condition of last resort was surely met. Or, to put it more precisely, to expect Kuwaitis to continue to suffer while sanctions were given time to take effect would seem to ask a lot. Surely we would not expect Kuwaitis themselves to galvanize an international embargo against Iraq, especially an embargo that might require a year to become effective, as an alternative to the use of force. And if we would not expect Kuwaitis to wait as an alternative to their own military defense against occupation and ongoing aggression, why should we expect their proxies to do so? Are those who have the capacity to assist, but who expect Kuwaitis to suffer while sanctions take effect, not committing a sin of omission?

An additional problem surrounding sanctions is that they are by no means morally unambiguous or materially harmless. For those concerned about structural violence, sanctions impose tremendous hardships on the social and economic infrastructure of a society. To consider sanctions a "peaceful" method is to indulge in semantic sophistry, the kind of reasoning that often gives casuists a bad name. Sanctions are a form of "compellence," which, as Thomas Schelling remarks, seeks to induce "withdrawal, or . . . acquiescence, or . . . collaboration by an action that threatens to hurt."[54] Those who insist on "sanctions first" in fact commit themselves to compellence in the form of economic coercion as an alternative to, or as a prelude to, military intervention. True, sanctions did not include food and medicine and were not aimed at the civilian population of Iraq. But in the Iraqi context it would be naive to think that food and medical supplies would find their way into civilian hands. Sanctions are effective because they hurt, and it seems excessively sanguine to think that somehow the civilian population of Iraq would or could be removed from such harms.

If sanctions are to have moral credibility, then, we must first recognize that they can be implicated in acts of omission and are harmful to civilian populations. Those committed to "sanctions first" may have to reconsider how a strategy of compellence is morally required by the criterion of last resort. To that end, two additional considerations are relevant, even if finally inconclusive.

First, it might be argued that sanctions are appropriate in the Allied cause given the fact that *our* soldiers would otherwise be put at risk in defense of Kuwaiti life.[55] There is a moral difference, I suggested above, between Kuwaiti self-defense and the risks that others may be expected to assume in a third-party intervention. If American, Canadian, French, British, or Soviet troops are going to risk their lives, it would seem appropriate to test methods of compellence first. It may be much to ask Kuwaitis to suffer ongoing aggression, but their lives are not the only lives at risk. To call for prompt intervention is also to expect a lot of the Allied forces when alternatives are available.

Second, there is the danger of escalation of war in the political and military tinderbox of the Middle East. Considerations of proportionality require that alternatives to war be tried first. As before, weighing *ad bellum* criteria holistically suggests caution about recourse to war. Indeed, the presumption against war would suggest that compellence ought to precede recourse to war. Otherwise the Allies may have acted to worsen a situation about which they have already made serious prior mistakes. *"Sanctions first," then, would follow not from the notion of last resort, ahistorically applied.* It would rather devolve from the need not to aggravate a problem in which Western and Soviet policies were already complicit.

Let us suppose, at least for the sake of argument, that the criterion of last resort was not met in Operation Desert Storm. A difficult question remains: Does such a verdict lead to the conclusion that individuals fighting in the Allied forces were committing an evil? Does violating the condition of last resort nullify the justice of the Allied cause? Once the Allies were "in there," did their hasty entrance require them to withdraw immediately?

These questions might be sharpened with another medical analogy, one that distinguishes between *withholding* medical care and *withdrawing* such protection. In the medical world the distinction is premised on the general belief that it is sometimes easier to argue for nonintervention than it is to justify withdrawing treatment in cases of extraordinary means. Even those who reject the distinction acknowledge that it has psychological appeal to medical professionals.[56] As Jeff McMahan remarks, withdrawing aid in progress is more like killing than nonintervention, "perhaps because withdrawing aid may involve action, or because releasing a threat that has been blocked is more like initiating a threat than simply failing to block a threat is."[57] In medicine no less than in war, once you have intervened something has changed. The doctor now has a different relationship with the patient than she did before treatment began. A commitment to the patient develops. The doctor has crossed the threshold separating diagnosis from ongoing medical treatment. Expectations are raised for the patient and the family. In religious language, a covenant has been sealed. And all of these changes are relevant despite the fact that the doctor may have intervened prematurely.

Such actions alter the situation, requiring us to ask, Is it *now* still better for the doctor to deny treatment? Perhaps the patient is being cared for in ways that were unforeseen before intervention occurred. The point of the analogy is to call attention to the fact that intervention can change the patient's situation or can produce new, morally relevant facts that figure in the decision about whether to withdraw treatment. Even if the doctor crosses the threshold from diagnosis to active intervention before she should, the error of her decision does not lead automatically to the judgment that treatment should cease.

In several cities in the United States, antiwar protesters expressed their views on street signs, making them read STOP WAR and DO NOT ENTER WAR. But this medical analogy is meant to suggest that arguments for not entering war and for stopping war are not necessarily identical. Once the Allies acted, they committed themselves to protect. They did more than save face by remaining in Kuwait, especially given the fact that other moral criteria were being satisfied by the intervention.

5. *Relative justice:* Harking back to Vitoria's notion of ostensible simultaneous justice, this criterion is rooted in the idea that impartiality is impossible in war, that one's perspective in judging the morality of events will be skewed by one's motives and interests.[58] Relative justice, in short, is premised on epistemic fallibilism. But its implications can be extended beyond the recognition of human finitude to include some methodological claims about how to consider the moral complexity of war.

As it is typically interpreted, relative justice is understood to mean that no state may act as if it possesses absolute justice, that neither side may claim a monopoly of justice in defense of its cause. Rather, the justice is relative, especially given the problems of measuring justice objectively in the drama and passion of war.

In many respects this condition is less of a rule-term governing our conduct than a character-term, designed to discipline our attitudes and affections, our noncognitive responses to war. The idea is to chasten civic virtue by prohibiting sanctimonious attitudes or self-righteous political language, all-too-familiar rhetoric in war. The category of relative justice is meant to humanize war by reminding us that the other side should not be demonized during the course of war as a way of motivating soldiers and citizens. Popular support for war must come from other sources, other arguments, other cultural symbols. Demonizing the enemy makes it easier to develop a holy-war attitude, the idea that "God is on our side." But relative justice is meant to underwrite the notion that neither side should be viewed as wholly righteous—or, for that matter, wholly unrighteous.[59]

In the context of the United States, relative justice should work to deflate appeals to American exceptionalism, the idea that Americans transcend the moral canons according to which other cultures should be evaluated.[60] Seen in this way, relative justice ought to function, in part at least, as a counterideological criterion, reminding us that the language of saints and sinners is inappropriate when describing the parties involved in war. Relative justice ought to keep us sober and honest when assessing the war's justice, calling attention to the limits of human judgments and our moral visions.

Consider, by way of contrast, the following description of the war by George Weigel:

> A brutal dictator, armed to the teeth with offensive military capabilities and busily developing weapons of mass destruction (including those nuclear weapons that so exercised religious leaders during the

1980s) invades, occupies, and dismantles a neighboring country. The invaded country is an Arab country, with a substantial number of Palestinian workers. The leading Arab financial power (Saudi Arabia) and the leading Arab military power (Egypt) support the United States in its resistance to Iraqi aggression. The president locates U.S. policy in terms of supporting a "new world order" in which the rule of law replaces the law of the jungle. The United Nations, in an unprecedented collective security action, moves against the aggressor. The Soviet Union joins with the United States in garnering the votes on the Security Council. A program of economic sanctions is undertaken. Israel stays on the sidelines. The world decides, through the Security Council, that enough time has expired: Saddam has been in Kuwait for five-and-a-half months, on any day of which he could have brought the Gulf crisis to a non-military resolution by the simple expedient of withdrawing his army of occupation. The Security Council and the Congress authorize the use of U.S. armed forces. Our Arab allies join us in the campaign.[61]

A less complicated description of events could hardly be imagined. Notice what is missing: Weigel (a) makes no mention of how Hussein became "armed to the teeth"; (b) omits reference to the fact that U.S. officials discussed with Hussein his imminent invasion of Kuwait, yet sought no deterrent measures before the invasion; (c) provides no indication of how the defense of sovereign boundaries constitutes a genuinely "new" world order; (d) fails to specify how the "world decides" through the Security Council; and (e) overlooks how the preparations for war in the fall of 1990 established a strong presumption in favor of war and against nonintervention for those congressional leaders who were finally required to settle the matter of U.S. intervention.[62]

These observations were raised by more than a few critics of the war. But for Weigel, those who criticized the war not only made a serious error of judgment, they also expressed a "deep-set alienation that constitutes the temporal and ideological link between much of the American religious leadership and 'Vietnam.'" That alienation included the anxiety not that American military efforts would fail, but that they would succeed. Church leaders "instinctively understood," Weigel asserts, that success in the Iraq war "would be the end of 'Vietnam,' the prism through which their politics had been focused for a generation and the paradigm by which they had persistently read (which is to say, misread) the international politics of the 1970s and 1980s." In mainline Protestant and Roman Catholic churches, criticism of the war was a testimony to the triumph of "functional pacifism," rooted in the "profound alienation from the American experiment and in a deep conviction that American power cannot serve good ends in the world."[63]

This account only exaggerates the moral stakes in the public debate about the Gulf War, obscuring the conditions for sober public discourse and revealing the exceptionalist refrain deep in the heart of Weigel's analysis. To be sure, more than a few critics of the war found occasion to vent their alienation from the American experiment. But many of those who criticized the war—like the U.S. Catholic bishops—expressed genuine counterideological anxieties. Their anxieties drew from quite legitimate suspicions about the exceptionalist temptation, that is, the inclination of Americans to view their suffering as part of a cosmic struggle between the powers of light and darkness, devoid of moral ambiguity or dirty hands. Such suspicions are by no means reducible to anti-Americanism or intellectual alienation. Rather, they are an expression of connected criticism, alert to public pronouncements about war, its likely co-optation of just-war criteria, and its tendency to depict political or military struggles in terms of moral simplicity. For the connected critic, to justify the war as an effort against an intractable evil—as President Bush did when drawing parallels between Hussein and Hitler—can only be viewed as incurably naive, if not ideologically distorted.

For obvious political reasons, appeals to relative justice had little currency among policymakers. U.S. leaders took a different route, expressing the conviction that the Allies possessed a monopoly on justice. Iraq was guilty of crossing sovereign boundaries in violation of international law, occupation and declared annexation, and ongoing, villainous aggression against innocent people, about which there was little or no ambiguity. Moreover, relative justice is difficult to accept for motivational reasons, especially in a democracy in which public support is important to the authorization to enter war. After all, who can be enthusiastic about a war that is described in terms of moral complexity?

Yet when viewed from a different angle, the ideas I have developed throughout this chapter suggest that reference to relative justice *in some sense* is virtually inevitable when it comes to measuring the justice of war. Those who conclude that the Allied cause was *arguably* justified are committed to the fact that this cause includes a mixture of justice and injustice. Consider again those who would accept the idea that last resort was not satisfied, but who say that the Allies were nonetheless obliged to continue fighting if other moral criteria were met. Such persons embrace—if only implicitly—a version of relative justice. Relative justice distills the sense of war's moral ambiguity, the fact that judgments must balance competing and conflicting verdicts when assessing the overall justice of war. This means that the overall verdict about war will in all likelihood include a mixed argument, one that relies on a composite of considerations, not all of which may harmonize. Accordingly, public discourse about war is likely to be vexed by moral complexity and ambiguity. The application of rules or conditions requires practical reason—what Aristotle knew as *phronēsis*—for which there is no clear and simple formula. Those who say that a justified war can satisfy some but not all just-war criteria in fact embrace relative justice.[64]

Seen in this way, just-war criteria require an interpretation of conflict midway between the views of Weigel and those of the early Niebuhr. Social critics who adopt the account of legitimate authority and relative justice that I have developed above must view Weigel as expecting too little by way of admission of guilt and Niebuhr as expecting too much by way of moral purity during the Manchurian crisis. Interpreting a war as I have here provides an alternative to the claims of the children of light and the children of darkness. The former, to paraphrase Reinhold Niebuhr, want to prove our guiltlessness in order to be able to act, while the latter refuse to act because we cannot achieve guiltlessness.[65] In contrast, those who embrace the relativity of a just war find it permissible to tolerate political imperfection and fallibilism in Western and Soviet leadership, perhaps even complicity in the woes of the Middle East. For them the moral issue is *not* whether Western and Soviet leaders are ethically qualified to pass judgment on Hussein's actions before entering the war, or during the war. Rather, as I have suggested, the central moral issue requires us *to clarify their appropriate moral responsibilities, given the facts of prior complicity.*

6. *Proportionality:* Within *ad bellum* criteria, proportionality requires one to determine whether the prospective suffering, the costs incurred in war, are balanced by the overall values that are being defended. Is the war, in moral terms, worth risking?

Proportionality has an arcane and mathematical ring to it, seemingly dissonant to careful ethical analysis. How do we measure body counts against values like sovereignty and international law? But reference to proportionality was a recurrent dimension among those who expressed anxieties about what might happen. Questions were numerous before the war: Can the coalition endure a protracted ground war in defense of Kuwaiti sovereignty? What will happen if other parties are drawn into battle? What if war expands into a regional conflagration? Will the Allied action lead to terrorism against Americans and their allies? Will segments of the Arab world harbor resentment against Westerners for generations to come? These questions provide the content for proportionate judgments: Are these risks so grave as to render the Allied cause imprudent? Is it possible to take sufficient precautions against escalation, resentment, and/or future terrorism? Furthermore, judgments about proportionality must be made as any war proceeds. If risks begin to exceed the values defended, then the balance may shift for those who consider a just cause to be only arguably justified. As the U.S. Catholic bishops contended in 1968, when judgments about proportionality in war change for the worse, one's commitment to war may need to change as well.[66]

Those who look back upon the war and judge it proportionate or disproportionate have the advantage of hindsight, which is not how *ad bellum* judgments of proportionality are meant to apply. Rather, such judgments are meant to shape decisions about whether to enter or to continue in war. And on this score information suggests that, despite the dangers of military conflict in the Middle East, the decision to act was reasonable and proportionate. The Allied forces entered only after considerable planning and collective organization. They committed their air forces first, thereby preparing the way for a less dangerous ground assault and reducing risks to ground forces. Allied air forces abstained from entering Iran, despite the danger that Iraqi pilots flying to Iran might be securing an advantage against attack. Iraqi forces were deceived into thinking that the Allies would attack from the sea, leaving their western flank vulnerable and enabling coalition forces to strike and then envelop the Iraqi army with unexpected efficiency.[67] Israel displayed remarkable restraint, despite Iraq's numerous attempts to draw Israeli forces into battle. Each of these decisions considerably reduced risks to Allied forces and prevented the war from unduly escalating.[68]

7. *Reasonable hope for success:* A corollary of proportionality, this criterion excludes reckless or futile fighting in defense of a cause. Although it may at times permit a defense of very noble values against tremendous odds, its general purpose is to prevent irrational uses of force.

On this point citizens worry about the prospective length of war. How long was it reasonable to think that the war would continue, and would the Allies be able to bring this war to a satisfactory conclusion? Again, information like that pertinent to proportionality suggests that the decision to commit Allied forces was shaped by a reasonable calculation of the odds of success.

Yet several questions arise about how to view this condition in relation to other criteria. For example, how one approaches the condition of reasonable hope for success depends on how "right intention" is defined in principle and, more important, in practice. Intentions to disarm Iraq require different expectations about what counts as "success" than do intentions to remove Iraq from the sovereign boundaries of Kuwait. Moreover, as I indicated above, reasonable hope for success seems more important in cases of intervention than in cases of self-defense. Third-party interventions invite us to consider how long the Allies should be willing to sustain losses to help others in need.

In bello criteria, establishing the moral limits to the use of force, are two, and are applied according to the rule of double effect:

1. *Discrimination:* This criterion prohibits the intentional attacking of civilians, the shorthand for which is the phrase "noncombatant immunity." It has two key distinctions.

The first distinction draws a line between combatants and noncombatants. *Combatant* denotes anyone who is materially cooperating with the war effort, such as soldiers and those working for war-related industries (e.g., bomb factories).[69] *Noncombatant* denotes anyone who is not contributing materially to the war, including children, the disabled, the sick, farmers, teachers, and health-care professionals, to name a few.

The second distinction draws a line between intentional (i.e., purposeful) and foreseen, but unintentional, effects of an act.

According to the logic of these distinctions, *intentional* attacks against noncombatants are tantamount to murder. Such attacks are inflicted on people against whom defense is unnecessary. Such persons are "innocent" in the sense that they are not engaged in carrying out acts of lethal force, even if they support the war effort "in their hearts." Nor are they in any active way contributing to the war—for example, by working in bomb factories or related industries. The foreseen, unintentional loss of innocent life passes the test of discrimination, but it is subject to moral scrutiny required by the second *in bello* criterion, proportionality.

2. *Proportionality:* As an *in bello* criterion, proportionality requires us to balance the foreseen, unintended losses against the values that are defended in a particular act of war. Here we must think about the morality of specific tactics: Does the good that is being pursued or defended outweigh the regrettable, unintended losses that may reasonably be expected? Tactics are immoral when the foreseen, unintended loss of life outweighs the defended values, even if those tactics are discriminate.[70]

In bello criteria take on special relevance for military forces that rely on air power. Were bombs and missiles targeted in a manner that respected civilian life? The effectiveness of *in bello* criteria seemed evident in military leaders' and public officials' efforts to show that the rules of engagement were designed to avoid civilian casualties. According to *in bello* considerations it is not the case that the loss of innocent life is immoral, only that intentional killing of innocent people, excessive collateral damage, or culpable negligence in military strategy is immoral. Doubtless the loss of innocent life is tragic, requiring a response of remorse or regret. But whether it is a barbarous act of injustice is a difficult judgment to render, and often turns on considerations of proportionality.[71]

Of greater concern are problems that haunted Iraqi citizens in the wake of widespread collateral damage. As I noted earlier, within a month of the war Baghdad was without water and electricity. Food was scarce for those who failed to stockpile it earlier, and the sewage system overflowed, creating the danger of widespread disease. Reports indicate that citizens were cutting down trees for fuel, and that the city's infrastructure as a whole was virtually destroyed.[72] The 300,000-barrel-a-day oil refinery in Bejii in northern Iraq, far from the war's chief theater of operations, was not bombed until the final days of the air war.[73] Such data raise suspicions about whether late bombing missions over Iraq can satisfy the condition of proportionality, and perhaps discrimination. Such suspicions find further warrant in the U. N. report that described the landscape of Iraq after the war as "post-apocalyptic" and warned that it threatened to reduce "a rather highly urbanized and mechanized society to a pre-industrial age."[74] After the war ended, a Harvard public health team reported that the lack of electricity, fuel, and transportation links in Iraq led to acute malnutrition and epidemic levels of cholera and typhoid, and that at least 170,000 children under five years of age would die in 1992 from the delayed effects of the Allied bombing.[75]

These facts raise moral concerns about the extent to which Iraq's infrastructure was damaged, and the toll of such damage on civilians. How are we to evaluate the massive loss of civilian life owing to disease and famine in the wake of war? Are water supplies and electrical sources, vital for civilian life, proper targets? Even if the loss of civilian life is construed as an indirect effect of military targeting, is it not true that such effects are so clearly foreseeable as to be morally questionable? How are we to assess the damage to the material conditions for livelihood?

Although prohibitions against the wanton destruction of an enemy's infrastructure have rarely been explicit in the just-war tradition, at least two sources in religious ethics could be invoked to strengthen our moral sense that such destruction is profoundly wrong. The first, from Deuteronomy 20: 19, states:

> When you besiege a city for a long time, making war against it in order to take it, you shall not destroy its trees by wielding an axe against them; for you may eat of them but you shall not cut them down. Are the trees in the field men that they should be besieged by you? Only

the trees which you know are not trees for food you may destroy and cut down that you may build siegeworks against the city that makes war with you, until it fails.

Philo extends these prohibitions to include vandalizing a besieged city, and Josephus argues that despoiling enemy countryside comes under the proscription of profligate destruction.[76] The general point is that there are *conditions* of livelihood that deserve protection, that civilian life—and its immunity from direct attack—should not be viewed in isolation from the wider "externalities" of human existence. To distinguish sharply between physical life and the external necessities of human livelihood is to ignore the extent to which we depend on our political and economic infrastructures for our well-being. The principle of noncombatant immunity, understood with these conditions of human survival and flourishing in mind, would suggest that much of the Allied bombing of Iraq was wrong. Indeed, Paul Ramsey once argued that nuclear war would become disproportionate well before it became indiscriminate. The Gulf War raises the case that nonnuclear wars may become indiscriminate well before civilians are directly targeted.

Consider, second, the ethics of Aquinas on homicide and war. For Aquinas, killing in self-defense must be aimed at the goal of self-preservation; harm to the attacker is permissible only *praeter intentionem*. It would be immoral purposefully to cripple the attacker as part of the act of individual self-defense. By the same token, public authorities who are responsible for the defense of the body politic are allowed to harm the enemy's corporate body only as a secondary effect of self-protection. Generalizing from Aquinas's view of justified homicide, one could infer that intentionally crippling the infrastructure of an enemy nation would be an excessive use of force, one that failed to discriminate between legitimate objects of attack and those that form the backbone of everyday life. Harm to the conditions of an enemy's corporate life must remain beside the public authority's intention, an accident of acts on behalf of collective self-defense.[77]

Moreover, if late bombing missions were aimed at the psychological goal of demoralizing the city's populace, the Allies are open to the charge of violating the spirit if not the letter of noncombatant immunity. During the last days of the war, numerous bombing missions were carried out over Baghdad and over Iraq's northern provinces. Targets in those regions posed little if any actual threat to the Allies; the decisive battles were being waged in Kuwait City, southern Iraq, and along the Iraq-Kuwait border, and no supply lines between northern and southern sectors of Iraq were identified by military officials who were asked about the bombing. About these missions, moral questions would take the following form: Assuming that these Allied bombing missions in the late stages of war satisfied the principle of discrimination (strictly speaking), what do we make of certain foreseeable, unintended effects of such acts, like civilian death and demoralization? Is such demoralization ethically acceptable, given the kinds of immunities that ought to surround civilians in time of war?

Two analogies might help us address this issue of demoralization. The first was developed in response to concerns about the morality of the strategic nighttime bombing of German cities during World War II. These bombing missions inspired little commentary in religious and philosophical ethics, with the notable exception of the Jesuit ethicist, John C. Ford, whose essay on the subject has become a minor classic.[78] Although Ford did not address the issue of terror bombing, his comments about the rule of double effect pertain to the problem of bombing military targets of doubtful military utility as a possible means of terrorizing the "enemy people." Ford asked,

> When is it possible, psychologically and honestly, for one to avoid the direct willing of an evil effect immediately consequent upon one's action; or to put it another way, when can an action, estimated morally, be considered really twofold in its immediate efficiency? Secondly, when is the evil effect to be considered only incidental to the main result, and not a means made use of implicitly or explicitly to produce it?[79]

Ford's questions raise doubts about whether we may define an "intention" simply in terms of deliberate volition when intentions are tightly linked to foreseeable outcomes, some of which may hasten the end of a war. Drawing the line too sharply between what is intended and what is merely foreseen is often counterintuitive, allowing us (falsely) to exonerate ourselves from the harmful effects of our actions. When the results of our actions are causally connected, or when such connections follow each other closely in time, it seems disingenuous to draw a sharp division between willed purposes and "merely foreseen" effects. Indeed, to draw such a sharp distinction seems casuistical in the pejorative sense of the term.

A second analogy, with more permissive implications, might be drawn from Ramsey's attempt to join a justification of nuclear deterrence with a "fight-the-war" policy that is shaped by just-war criteria. Ramsey sought to derive deterrent "cash value" from the anticipated but unintended effects of discriminate nuclear targeting. According to Ramsey, discriminate nuclear targeting poses the danger of widespread collateral damage. Such damage, foreseeable to an opponent, is sufficiently menacing to deter aggression.[80] Given the case presented by the Allied cause, someone like Ramsey might argue that widespread collateral damage is inevitable in war—even in discriminate targeting—and that the foreseeably demoralizing effects of such acts are proportionate to the goals of terminating the war. So long as the targeting is discriminate, one might argue, the Allies' methods were an acceptable way to bring coercion to bear on Iraq, coercion necessary to hasten the war's conclusion.[81]

The problem with this argument is that it leaves unanswered the question of whether the bombing and its collateral damage were (a) necessary as a military objective and (b) proportionate within the constraints of *in bello* considerations. If the damage was either unnecessary (from a purely military point of view) or disproportionate as a method in war, then to argue that such methods are proportionate to the goals of demoralization allows the ends to justify the means. The only way to justify these bombings would be to show that they were indeed discriminate, proportionate, and *necessary* to the Allies' military purposes, and that the Allies acted conscientiously to limit the collateral damage as much as possible. But the events of the last few days of the war generate real questions about whether the bombing was necessary for military aims or whether it was gratuitous, designed to instill fear or foment dissent against Hussein. If the bombing had these wider political goals, they were carried out against those who ought to be immune from intentional or foreseeably disproportionate harms of war. The fact that citizens are not to be directly attacked or terrorized derives from the conviction that they are immune from being instrumentalized in the Allies' efforts to prevail.

One possible justification for attacking Iraq's infrastructure is that the bombing would intensify the economic and psychological impact of international sanctions. Insofar as sanctions were designed to coerce Hussein to withdraw from Kuwait, augmenting their effects would seem to be an efficient use of force. As one planning officer remarked, "Well, what were we trying to do with [United Nations–approved economic] sanctions—help the Iraqi people? No. What we were doing with the attacks on infrastructure was to accelerate the effect of the sanctions."[82] But this rationale only begs the question of the morality of sanctions. If "targeting" civilians directly through blockades and sanctions is morally problematic, then augmenting that pressure with military force is no less so.

It must also be added that judgments deriving from *in bello* considerations are necessarily constrained by the government's control of the press during the war.[83] Indeed, perhaps the most nettlesome issue for those engaged in casuistry during a war concerns the extent to which moral judgments will be constrained by fragmentary and highly controlled information. Estimates about the toll of death and destruction in Iraq have come from various sources and have ranged widely. As a result, verdicts about the overall morality of means are, at best, speculative. In the wake of the war against Iraq, appeals to just-war criteria in future wars stand in tremendous danger of being hostage to official press releases and sanitized information.

Inductive Casuistry

Given the qualifiers and distinctions above, just-war considerations support the following judgment: There was arguably a justification for the Allied intervention to remove Iraqi forces from Kuwait—or at least for not withdrawing once intervention occurred—given the fact that the conditions of cause, authority, proportionality, and reasonable hope for success were satisfied, and that at least a thin account of intention appears to have been part of the Allies' plans. (Last resort remains too arguable a condition in this case, in my judgment, to count for or against Operation Desert Storm.) But problems surrounding the *in bello* criteria of discrimination and proportionality count against the cause, leaving us with a war of qualified justice and considerable—indeed, torturous—regret.

It must be added, however, that this war is not merely a test for familiar just-war considerations. It raises questions pertaining to

(1) how just-war criteria are to be applied holistically (in light of each other) in the case of war;

(2) how wars are authorized in a representative democracy;

(3) the relationship of democratic authorization to international authorization, prior military initiatives by the president, and the subsequent commitment to act;

(4) how burdens might be fairly allocated in a collective effort;

(5) how such allocations ought to be affected by a nation's prior complicity in arms proliferation or political support;

(6) how commitments to self-defense differ from commitments in third-party intervention;

(7) how such differences might affect the application of last resort;

(8) the ethics of economic sanctions, and the extent to which economic sanctions may be required by the criterion of last resort;

(9) how relative justice points to the arguable, mixed judgments about the justice of one's commitments;

(10) whether a robust rendition of "right intention" can be exercised in the aftermath of war; and

(11) whether information, obviously vital for moral analysis, will be freely available.

These issues are anomalies in the just-war tradition, falling outside the normal scope of its application. This means that it is likely that such issues will be settled in practice before they find a solution in theory. But casuistry cannot, or ought not, set up obstacles to the energetics of practice, blocking the contribution that history can make to ethics. Rather than repress the historical features of Operation Desert Storm, it is salutary to uncover how history can assist us when considering the justice of this war and, for that matter, future wars. If practice is to inform theory, we must avoid the temptation to proceed deductively in casuistical reflection. As I indicated in the previous chapter, custom contributes to the development of our moral knowledge, and custom begins with actual practices and human experience. True, the developments that occurred during and immediately after the Gulf War are too recent to constitute a custom in the ordinary sense of the term. But as Kirk suggests, casuistry relies not only on "custom come into its own," but also on "custom in the making."[84] Casuistry that fails to attend to such developments risks becoming rigid and ahistorical.

Sublimating the drive of historical experience into an application of the just-war tradition enables us to see a broad range of ethical dimensions of the Gulf War; it might also expand the range of relevant considerations necessary for judging the morality of future international conflict. By examining the anomalous features of this war, casuistry of a more inductive sort might deliver us from an ahistorical application of just-war tenets, requiring us to operate self-consciously, and pragmatically, by joining history and ethics. Then, and only then, will we be able to craft resources for determining the full justice and injustice of future wars that resemble the war against Iraq.

CHAPTER THREE

The Case against the Case against Liberalism

Liberalism and Solidarity

In the last chapter I indicated that a nation may make a lesser commitment to a war of third-party intervention than to a war of self-defense. Casuistry must calibrate what we can expect of nations acting on behalf of a just cause, given the different circumstances in which they may find themselves. We may expect stronger commitments to self-defense than to third-party interventions, owing to an order of charity in which duties to the self are more pressing than duties to others. The result of such casuistry is to render tangible the distinction between wars that are morally imperative and wars that are (only) permitted.[1]

A more nettlesome question in Western politics is whether liberal democracies can inspire civic loyalty and commitment *at all*, not merely when it comes to war. By *liberalism* I mean the theory, developed by philosophers such as John Rawls, Bruce Ackerman, and Ronald Dworkin, that assigns priority to liberty over social welfare; accordingly, any improvements in social welfare cannot sacrifice individual freedom.[2] Defenses of liberty, moreover, provide a strong basis for ethical and cultural pluralism: Our pursuit of diverse and potentially conflicting interests, liberals argue, may be restricted only for the sake of others' liberty, but not for majoritarian reasons.

Thus understood, liberalism seems to make few if any appeals to goods that people might share in common, goods that would inspire allegiance, solidarity, and civic loyalty. It should come as no surprise, then, that debates about the morality of war seem sociologically counterintuitive in a liberal culture. In many respects war provides a litmus test for liberal solidarity: Given that liberals require us to take a neutral attitude toward comprehensive visions of the good, liberalism appears hostile to entreaties that would motivate citizens to risk their lives in war. In a liberal regime, it would seem that appeals to a just cause for war—whatever the circumstances—would fall on deaf ears. Liberalism, prizing individualism and freedom, and solidarity, prizing collective identity and allegiance, seem to pull in opposite directions. If just-war tenets presuppose an inchoate sociology of civic loyalty and public spirit, can they gain a hearing in liberal regimes?

Owing to these kinds of questions, the tenets of liberalism are increasingly under fire, arousing a new round of intellectual debate in political philosophy and religious ethics. Attention to the importance of solidarity has developed under the aegis of communitarianism, receiving its most sustained expression by Stanley Hauerwas, Mary Ann Glendon, Alasdair MacIntyre, Michael Sandel, and Charles Taylor. Despite some genuine diversity, communitarian thought is held together by several common threads:

1. Liberalism's emphasis on individual freedom presupposes an atomistic view of the self and moral identity, failing to recognize our lives as embedded in and shaped by local commitments, social relations, and shared projects. Liberals construct contract theory by imagining a generic self, detached from time, social roles, and personal relations. Viewing moral identity as partially constituted by its attachments and personal ties, in contrast, communitarians typically argue on behalf of an intersubjective self. The effect is to blur the boundaries between what is "me" and what is "mine." The idea of a liberal self asks that we conceive of "me" apart from those commitments or relationships that are "mine."

2. Liberalism's notion of detached selves provides the breeding ground for alienation, political apathy, and social fragmentation. Liberals are thus naive about the sociological and psychological costs of maintaining a liberal ethos. Moreover, insofar as "intolerance flourishes most where forms of life are dislocated, roots unsettled, traditions undone,"[3] the sociological costs of liberalism undermine the commitment to tolerance that is central to liberal philosophy.

3. Liberalism elevates justice to the highest virtue, conceiving justice as a principle to regulate our various pursuits of happiness. Liberals thus fail to see that justice is a remedial virtue, required only when communal ties have broken down.

4. In the absence of communal ties and local custom, liberalism requires a strong state apparatus to protect human liberty and the

rights that accrue to individuals in a society in which justice is the highest virtue.

5. Liberalism is part of the wider Enlightenment project, which seeks an impersonal, ahistorical, detached perspective from which to view human commitments and endeavors. Such an epistemology fails to take account of the ways in which our points of view are implicated in the traditions, thought-forms, and languages of a culture. Instead, we must recognize that our moral visions are shaped by communities and their constitutive narratives or final vocabularies. Liberalism's quest for detachment, owing to its Cartesian roots, is blind to the epistemological insights wrought by historicism and hermeneutical philosophy.

6. Liberalism parades itself as the heir to the Age of Reason and the aspirations for liberty and equality in seventeenth- and eighteenth-century Europe. But this legacy is only a part of the recent past; liberalism represses another voice of Europe's heritage, namely, Romanticism. Linked to Romantic forebears, communitarianism is not alien to the sources and movements that have helped to shape the present age.[4]

Given these complaints, a strong presumption against liberalism seems to exist. In particular, it seems appropriate to ask, Is liberal solidarity possible?

Casuistry Revisited

The fact that virtually none of the authors I have mentioned is known for work in casuistry might obscure the fact that, in many respects, the debate between liberals and communitarians is but a variation of an old casuistical issue that pits realists against idealists. In this context, *realism* and *idealism* denote rival attitudes about how demanding a moral theory ought to be. Realists and idealists differ, in short, over what I have called the issue of *moral expectations.* Realists seek to craft a morality that can commend itself without demanding too much from us, or to show that obedience to their principles would in fact produce better long-term consequences than obedience to rival moralities. As a nonutopian doctrine, realism accepts the view that a theory will not gain many adherents if it requires us to become saints or martyrs. And if a theory cannot gain a sufficient number of followers, then it can hardly avoid the charge of perfectionism or sectarianism—a doctrine for the few, the elect, the strong, the countercultural, or the otherworldly. Idealists, in contrast, argue that a morality that makes moderate demands is open to the charge of encouraging moral minimalism or mediocrity.[5] As Pascal asked in *The*

Provincial Letters, if moral thought cannot push us to new levels of performance, then by what account should it claim our admiration?

In the present context, liberals such as Rawls echo a realist, non-utopian refrain by seeking to craft a contract theory of justice suited to the constraints of mutual disinterestedness, moderate scarcity, religious diversity, and cultural pluralism. Such an account is designed to fit the circumstances of the nation-state as it has developed since the Reformation. Seen in this way, Rawls remarks, liberalism is to be contrasted with the more exacting requirements of utilitarianism, which demands "the sacrifice of the agent's private interest when this is necessary for the greater happiness of all."[6] Utilitarianism produces an unstable political arrangement, "unless sympathy and benevolence can be widely and intensely cultivated."[7] For reasons I will elucidate below, Rawls develops a contract theory in which substantial sacrifices and benevolence "are not demanded as a matter of justice by the basic structure of society."[8]

Communitarians in turn echo an idealist refrain when they argue that Rawls's account of justice is inattentive to the more intimate ties that bind, or ought to bind, persons together. Such ties constitute the identity of persons and would impose greater sacrifices on individuals than would liberal theory. Communitarians such as Sandel argue that an ethic drawing upon *philia* or "circumstances of benevolence" demands more than adjudicating conflicting claims or protecting individual rights. In order to be friends we must be more than fair with each other; we may even need to tolerate some measure of injustice. In this vein Sandel asks, "Does it go without saying that a rent in the fabric of implicit understandings and commitments is fully morally repaired so long as everyone 'does what he ought' in the aftermath?"[9] If we expect more from our friends than simple fairness and respect for rights, should we not also expect more from a genuinely robust ethical theory?

Liberals have sought to deflect such idealist queries by employing a standard casuistical weapon: the distinction. For liberals the decisive distinction is between *moral theory* and *political morality.* Moral theory is concerned with fundamental assumptions about agency and the moral life of individuals, or metaphysical concerns. Political morality, in contrast, devotes itself to narrower tasks, namely, justifying political action and political institutions, setting the terms for the proper limits of the power of the state.[10] Accordingly, Rawls remarks, the primary subject of justice "is the basic structure of society, . . . the way in which the major social institutions distribute fundamental rights and duties and determine the division of advantages from social cooperation."[11] Liberals, viewing liberalism as *only* a political morality, argue that communitarians are imposing an inappropriate set of expectations by raising questions of identity, constitutive goods, and intersubjectivity. Liberal conceptions of justice are moral conceptions in that they place ethical limits on the role of the state, but they are not intended as a "comprehensive moral doctrine," which includes metaphysical conceptions about selfhood or human well-being.[12]

Distinguishing between political morality and comprehensive moral doctrines allows liberals to restrict the range of application of communitarian ethics. Liberals thus seek to weaken the force of anti-liberal philosophy by confining matters of identity and community to a separate sphere of inquiry, one that cannot annex the main interests of contract theory. The distinction works to insulate liberalism from more controversial problems of metaphysics and comprehensive definitions of the good. Typically, liberals then try to show how communitarian doctrine is deficient as a political program, arguing that communitarians are notably reticent about the political implications of their antiliberalism.[13]

Communitarians typically respond by invoking another distinction, one that allows them to re-annex contract doctrine under a broader set of questions than those provided by liberal philosophy. So Charles Taylor claims that liberals falsely charge communitarians with a deficient political program because liberals have failed to distinguish questions of political advocacy from those of ontology. Communitarians like Sandel, Taylor asserts, are raising ontological questions, which are more general than but not irrelevant to the political ideas advocated by liberal theory. Posing ontological questions is meant neither to settle metaphysical questions nor to advocate a specific political program. Rather, Taylor remarks, such questions "structure the field of possibilities in a more perspicuous way."[14] Communitarian criticisms of liberalism, then, are not attempts to advocate a society that would be structured like a family; their chief goal is to show that liberals like Rawls hold together an egalitarian difference principle, which involves treating the endowment of each part as a common asset, with a notion of social contractors who are mutually indifferent. By posing ontological questions, communitarians thus want to show how liberals seek the best of both worlds, namely, a theory that presupposes both encumbered and unencumbered selves.[15]

In this crossfire between liberals and communitarians, it is easy to lose sight of the issue over which the lines of argument initially developed. The wealth of discussion, like much casuistical commentary, all too easily departs from the fundamental sources and questions from which communitarian critiques emerged. Casuistry can become baroque today no less than in the seventeenth century, and no less among political philosophers than among more traditional casuists. Is there a basic issue beneath the rococo?

It is tempting to answer this question by viewing debates between liberals and antiliberals as an instance of foundationalists arguing against nonfoundationalists about the wisdom of seeking a vantage point that is detached from experience or historical tradition.[16] Seen in this way, the differences between liberals and communitarians reduce to methodological concerns about the place of history and context in political theory. But as I shall point out, the charge of foundationalism has scarcely bothered liberals such as Rawls; indeed, Rawls has readily owned up to the importance of Western history and politics for his liberal theory. A more nettlesome problem—one with which Rawls has wrestled on numerous occasions, however obliquely—concerns the issues of moral motivation and civic loyalty in liberalism. *These related issues are practical, not abstract and methodological.* They ought to focus our attention not on epistemological worries about sources of knowledge in liberal philosophy, but on whether liberalism is *workable* as a social doctrine. However elegant liberalism may be as a political philosophy, it is nonetheless vexed by concerns about its practicability. Specifically, practical questions for liberals take the following form: Can liberal theory generate sentiments to inspire citizens to attach themselves to liberal institutions shaped by what Rawls calls "justice as fairness," the ruling criterion of a "well-ordered society"?[17] Would being a good person in a liberal society also be good for that person? Can liberal theory successfully join the right with the good, persuading us that its account of justice will contribute to our well-being? How could a society shaped along the lines of liberal theory generate dispositions that would be good for the agents in such a society?

Questions about motivation, in turn, bear directly on practical matters of civil order and civic loyalty: Can liberal theory, with its emphasis on individual freedom, generate motives that will lead to political allegiance, that is, to the commitment to contribute to the continuation and improvement of a liberal polity? Given what we know of human propensities and weaknesses, could a liberal society induce sentiments that would lead its members to approve of liberal institutions as praiseworthy? Without such sentiments, citizens may act to undermine liberal institutions through rebellion or, inadvertently, through various forms of apathy or antisocial behavior.

A liberal polity infected by resentment or anomie, in other words, may lack the conditions for political allegiance, the *sine qua non* of social stability in a society that places a premium on individual freedom. Hence we do well to view practical problems surrounding liberalism as a political case of conscience, generated by a potential conflict between the demand of freedom on the one hand and the need for social stability on the other. Indeed, if liberal institutions lack social stability, they are seriously deficient from the point of view of liberalism itself, seeking as it does to craft a theory that is both just and realistic.

Here I want to address concerns of motivation and stability by focusing first on Rawls's *A Theory of Justice*, since it is with Rawls that these concerns are most pronounced among liberal philosophers.[18] In particular I want to put considerations of realism to critical scrutiny in light of the kinds of questions posed by communitarians. We must then turn to Rawls's more recent arguments, especially his attempts to modify the main tenets of his theory in the wake of various philosophical complaints. In making these adjustments Rawls has set out to moderate the applicability of his earlier views, limiting his theory to the context of modern Western democracy. One thing that we will discover, I propose, is that Rawls's moderated liberalism has developed several lines of argument that falter when it comes to the question of motivation and the corresponding issue of stability. Indeed, by contextualizing his theory, Rawls develops a position in which liberalism's feasibility is presupposed more than it is proven.

This does not mean, however, that liberalism is wholly untenable from the point of view of stability. It means only that Rawls must chart another path if his liberalism is to commend itself in motivational terms. And he may do so, I want to argue, by way of another liberal tenet, one that found brief expression in the early stages of his philosophy: the good of pluralism. If liberals are to succeed in crafting a practicable theory, they would be wise to identify the emancipating breezes of a pluralist culture, one in which diversity offers liberation from what would undoubtedly be the claustrophobic sameness of a communitarian society.

Fairness and Feasibility

In *A Theory of Justice* Rawls notes that his argument proceeds by way of a two-step method. The first step, the bulk of his argument, develops the ideal of justice as fairness, premised on what he calls the principle of equal liberty and the difference principle. According to the first principle, "Each person has an equal right to the most extensive scheme of equal basic liberties compatible with a similar scheme of liberties for all." The second principle holds that "social and economic inequalities are to satisfy two conditions: they must be (a) to the greatest benefit of the least advantaged members of society; and (b) attached to offices and positions open to all under conditions of fair equality of opportunity." The first principle has priority over the second; in the second principle, part (b) has priority over part (a).[19]

The merits of these two principles have been the subject of prolific commentary, the effect of which is to infuse secular philosophy with the dizzying notion that it can address real-life issues. It is not my purpose to add to that commentary here. A second step in Rawls's argument has been generally ignored, and it is to this feature of liberalism that I want to direct my discussion. It concerns what I have called the realist dimension in his theory, the part of his argument where he tries to show that liberalism can commend itself as good, given what we know of human beings and their propensities.

Rawls begins the second step in his argument by asking whether the society corresponding to the ideal conception will actually generate "patterns of psychological attitudes that will undermine the arrangements it counts to be just."[20] He writes,

> It is . . . a consideration against a conception of justice that, in view of the laws of moral psychology, men would not acquire a desire to act upon it even when the institutions of their society satisfied it. For in this case there would be difficulty in securing the stability of social cooperation. *It is an important feature of a conception of justice that it should generate its own support.* That is, its principles should be such that when they are embodied in the basic structure of society men tend to acquire the corresponding sense of justice.[21]

Rawls does not mean simply that a conception of justice should generate its own support from those who have been inhabiting a society over time, individuals who have been subject to the arrangements of justice as fairness. Stability is not contingent on the effects of time and adaptation to liberal society. Rawls's quest for feasibility aspires to prove more. The true test of stability is whether supportive moral attitudes "are desirable from the standpoint of rational persons who have them when they assess their situation *independently from the constraints of justice.*"[22] The task that Rawls sets for himself, then, is to show that justice as fairness can commend itself as a moral doctrine to rational persons who are neutral to the doctrine in question.

The attempt to prove this point in *A Theory of Justice* moves along six lines, which combine several empirical, philosophical, and psychological considerations. The first four are minimalist: Rawls argues that his theory neither will generate socially undesirable behavior nor will be onerous for those who reside in a society shaped by his liberal tenets. The last two are more expansive; here Rawls asserts that a well-ordered liberal society would in fact inspire us to approve of its institutions, given the fact that the governing principles would conform to our nature as autonomous, rational agents, or would enable us partially to overcome our human limitations. Let us consider each of these arguments in turn.[23]

First, Rawls argues, justice as fairness is not overly burdensome, especially when it is compared with utilitarian doctrine. Utilitarianism requires "strong and lasting benevolent impulses," since it requires an individual "to acquiesce in an enduring loss for himself in order to bring about a greater net balance of satisfaction." Without such impulses "a rational man would not accept a basic structure merely because it maximized the algebraic sum of advantages irrespective of its permanent effects on his own basic rights and interests."[24] Rawls's social contract has advantages; it protects individual freedom from the collective will, and promises mutual advantage and reciprocity. The difference principle, in particular, allows for representative persons to advance their interests without requiring others to make sacrifices. It permits those who have been favored by nature or contingency to "gain from their good fortune only on terms that improve the situation of those who have lost out."[25] Thus, those at the bottom of the social ladder are not asked to tolerate the increased welfare of others simply because such an increase is better for the social whole.[26] Rather, they see that their destiny is caught up with the destiny of those better off, that the advantages of the fortunate may be improved only in ways that advance the prospects of the disadvantaged.

Moreover, those who are favored by nature or circumstance would be willing to tolerate a limit to their advantages should such benefits not favor the least advantaged, because, Rawls insists, "it is clear that the well-being of each depends on a scheme of social cooperation without which no one could have a satisfactory life."[27] We can ask for the cooperation of everyone only if the terms of the scheme are reasonable to all. It would be asking too much to expect the least fortunate to make sacrifices or tolerate social stagnation while those at the top of the social ladder become still better off. But if the terms promise to benefit the least advantaged, those more fortunate can reasonably expect others to collaborate with them.[28]

A scheme in which the difference principle operates, Rawls adds, can generate "active sentiments of love and friendship, and even the sense of justice." As members of such a society, we "agree to share one another's fate."[29] Thus, "we acquire attachments to persons and institutions according to how we perceive our good to be affected by them. The basic idea is one of reciprocity, a tendency to answer in kind."[30] As if to echo communitarian sentiments, Rawls invokes the metaphor of the family: Like those whose welfare is regulated by the difference principle, "members of a family commonly do not wish to gain unless they can do so in ways that further the interests of the rest."[31]

Second, owing to the bonds wrought by reciprocity, justice as fairness will mitigate the temptation of the weak-willed toward free-riderism. Those who may wish to cheat on their taxes or who may try to avoid doing their fair share of community work must remember that reciprocity brings bonds of affection and fellow-feeling, bonds that extend up and down the social and economic scale, given the demands of the difference principle. Free-riders, then, end up hurting everyone, "friends and associates along with the rest." Given the fact that bonds are extensive and that we cannot select who is to be hurt by our defections, "there are strong grounds for preserving one's sense of justice."[32]

Third, justice as fairness promises to be stable given that such a scheme will not deface our self-image or require self-abnegation; indeed, Rawls's well-ordered society will generate self-respect and self-esteem among its inhabitants. No one is to be instrumentalized. Rather, the advantaged are required to forgo gains that do not contribute to the welfare of the disadvantaged because in Rawls's scheme each person is to be regarded as an end in himself or herself. Further, insofar as our self-respect is contingent on the respect of others, justice as fairness can commend itself as conducive to individual self-esteem.[33]

In contrast, utilitarianism's requirement of self-sacrifice for the sake of a higher good tends to deprecate the worth of the individual. "The emptiness of the self," Rawls observes, "is to be overcome in the service of larger ends. This doctrine is likely to encourage self-hatred with its destructive consequences."[34] Although utilitarianism does not quite go to that extreme, "there is bound to be a similar effect which further weakens the capacity for sympathy and distorts the development of affective ties."[35] And it is important to recall that, in Rawls's mind, such ties are essential for the spirit of benevolence on which utilitarianism must rely.[36] For those in a society ruled by utilitarian principles, "surely it is natural to experience a loss of self-esteem, a weakening of our sense of the value of accomplishing our aims, when we must accept a lesser prospect of life for the sake of others."[37]

Fourth, general envy—the tendency of disadvantaged groups to resent economic disparities or to begrudge the more fortunate—is less likely to occur or to generate rancorous behavior in Rawls's well-ordered society. In the public forum, the principle of liberty guarantees that each individual, regardless of social location, is a "sovereign equal." Moreover, disparities between groups should be easier to accept for those on the bottom of the social scale, given that changes in welfare are constrained so as to benefit the worst off. The pluralism of association further mitigates sources of envy, because associations tend to divide society into many noncomparing groups, thus reducing the visibility of social or economic differences.[38]

Fifth, justice as fairness ought to commend itself because its basic dictates agree with our nature "as free and equal moral persons." Those who strive to abide by the principles wrought from the original position most fully realize their nature, understood in Kantian terms as prior to and independent of contingency and chance.[39] For Rawls, as for Kant, we express our nature as free from contingency by acting on principles of right and justice prior to all other aims. Our other goals can be achieved by a life plan that allows them to jockey for importance, requiring us to weigh and balance some aims against others. But justice is different. To weigh it off against other aims, to compromise justice on behalf of other goods, is to allow inclination to attenuate the dictates of autonomy. To compromise justice in this way "is not to achieve for the self free reign but to give way to the contingencies and accidents of the world."[40] In short, the principle of justice contains within itself its own priority. And in ranking it prior to the good, we reveal our natures as unconstrained by happenstance.

Finally, the pluralism of liberal society allows for talents to be developed by others in the social environment of diversity. However tempting it may be to suppose that everyone is, or ought to be, self-sufficient, "it is a feature of human sociability that we are by ourselves but parts of what we might be." Thus we must "look to others to attain the excellences that we must leave aside, or lack altogether."[41] Seen in this way, liberalism is well-suited to the conditions of finitude: Since we cannot realize all of our desires or even all of our endowments, it is salutary to reside in a culture in which others can realize their talents, which we can enjoy and even draw upon to develop our own skills. We may be natively tone deaf when playing the violin, but cultural pluralism allows musical prodigies to develop their respective skills, the fruits of which can be widely enjoyed. Echoing the apologist of pluralism, Emile Durkheim, Rawls writes, "It is as if others were bringing forth a part of ourselves that we have not been able to cultivate."[42]

Hermeneutical Liberalism

I rehearse these six arguments in part to highlight the contrast between *A Theory of Justice* and Rawls's subsequent refinements, especially as developed in *Political Liberalism,* which have been aimed largely at making methodological adjustments in his theory. Yet these adjustments pose difficulties when it comes to matters of feasibility.

85

Responding to the charge that *A Theory of Justice* is historically bound to and thus deeply implicated in the values of modern democracy,[43] Rawls has conceded that his theory has not been constructed in a historical or political vacuum. In this respect, Rawls has historicized himself.[44] He is not to be read as designing a theory that seeks to construct principles from an Archimedean point, removed from the effects of time or place. Rawls remarks,

> We are not trying to find a conception of justice suitable for all societies regardless of their particular social or historical circumstances. We want to settle a fundamental disagreement over the just form of basic institutions within a democratic society under modern conditions. We look to ourselves and to our future, and reflect on our disputes since, let's say, the Declaration of Independence.[45]

Central to such modern conditions, Rawls insists, is the fact that as a practical matter we have failed to arrive at a general moral conception on which to base a theory of justice. Any theory of justice, then, must begin by understanding that pluralism is an incorrigible feature of modernity. Although we cannot agree about what is true to an antecedent order, we can nonetheless agree about what is reasonable when it comes to constructing fair terms for coexisting in a pluralistic society.[46] Rawls's theory therefore begins by generalizing the idea of religious liberty, assigning to people's conception of the good a public status analogous to that of religion.[47] Accordingly, a theory of justice suited to the conditions of the modern nation-state "must allow for a diversity of doctrines and the plurality of conflicting, and indeed incommensurable, conceptions of the good affirmed by the members of existing democratic societies." Beginning in this way, we do not proceed in the abstract, but "from within a certain political tradition."[48]

This refinement requires Rawls to adjust the main lines of his method. His modified theory does not require us to reason from premises that are uncontroversial, premises that commend themselves to all rational people, ahistorically. Rather, we must understand Rawls's method as uncovering a common fund of values about which there is widespread agreement. The idea is to lay bare the "basic intuitive ideas that are embedded in the political institutions of a constitutional democratic regime and the public traditions of their interpretation."[49] Seen in this way, a theory of justice must begin interpretively, deciphering a set of common convictions from a diversity of views about the good.[50] Drawing on "a shared fund of implicitly recognized basic ideas and principles," Rawls expresses the hope "that these ideas and principles can be formulated clearly enough to be combined into a conception of political justice congenial to our most firmly held convictions."[51]

We are thus to understand Rawls's theory as "political, not metaphysical." Standing in a political tradition, facing the intractable fact of pluralism, liberals seek to craft a theory premised on the value of, and the need for, fair social cooperation. Liberals are able to do so, Rawls insists, without having to appeal to theories of human nature. All they need are certain "core conceptions" in order to fix ideas, namely, the idea of society as a system of fair social cooperation that serves the mutual advantage of all, and the idea of the individual citizen as a moral person.[52] In this way liberalism is able to remain "on the surface, philosophically speaking."[53] It prescinds from controversial tenets of metaphysics, applying the principle of toleration to philosophy itself.

On this revised account, social stability depends not on how well justice as fairness commends itself as practicable, given what we know of human inclinations and propensities. Rather, stability is a function of creating an "overlapping consensus," that is, a consensus that "consists of all the reasonable opposing religious, philosophical and moral doctrines likely to persist over generations and to gain a sizable body of adherents in a more or less just constitutional regime."[54] The idea is that each of the various comprehensive doctrines in a liberal society, "from within its own point of view, is led to accept the public reasons of justice specified by justice as fairness." The tenets of Rawlsian justice can be recognized "as theorems, as it were, at which . . . several views coincide."[55] Rival doctrines of the good (e.g., Catholicism, utilitarianism, egoism, and Kantianism) may coexist and compete for adherents in a liberal society, but they all converge on some basic moral beliefs (e.g., honesty, mutual trust, and social cooperation). It is equally plausible, Rawls argues, to think that such rival views might converge on the principles of justice as a public doctrine.

By this Rawls does not mean that societies with a smaller overlapping consensus will be less stable than those in which the consensus is considerable. Such a thesis would seem patently obvious, perhaps tautological. Instead, Rawls is saying that stability depends on the extent to which actual pursuits of the good in a democratic society *mirror* the tenets of liberal doctrine. The theory is likely to be stable, then, "if, among the admissible conceptions of the good, those which gain the widest support are ones which cohere with and sustain the conception of justice, for example by a certain compatibility between the ends and values of the prevalent conceptions of the good and the virtues required by justice."[56] And this can happen, Rawls argues, if liberalism sets out to satisfy three conditions of stability.

First, liberalism fixes the content of basic rights and freedoms, and establishes a basic priority, which, Rawls adds, takes those guarantees off the political agenda. The effect is to reduce the stakes of political controversy and decrease "the insecurity and hostility of public life."[57] Second, justice as fairness draws on a notion of free public reason, which avoids controversial philosophical claims, uses fundamental intuitive ideas, appeals to widely available evidence, proceeds by way of common sense, and places a premium on simplicity. Such a notion of reason thus avoids generating complexity and speculation, which "are bound to make citizens with conflicting interests highly suspicious of one another's arguments."[58] Third, and perhaps most important, liberalism encourages "the cooperative virtues of public life: the virtue of reasonableness and a sense of fairness, a spirit of compromise and a readiness to meet others halfway, all of which are connected with the willingness if not the desire to cooperate with others on political terms."[59] Societies whose diverse visions of the good place a premium on respect for persons, toleration of differences, and rules of fair play, for example, will have greater overall stability than societies in which these virtues are subordinate to, say, nonnegotiable ideologies or religious faiths.

Yet it is also true that, in Rawls's revised theory, stability is contingent upon the effects of liberal justice as it is experienced over time. In other words, feasibility depends on whether certain admissible conceptions of the good gain wide acceptance, namely those "which cohere with and sustain the conception of justice."[60] Whether such acceptance in fact occurs is scarcely guaranteed by Rawls's theory. Indeed, it is entirely a matter of chance whether such acceptance will occur, and even if it does, it may wax and wane over time.

Rawls admits that we must make certain sociological observations about the effects on social attitudes and practices that are likely to occur once we implement a political philosophy. We must accept as a fact of "common-sense political sociology," he argues, that "it is surely impossible for the basic structure of a just constitutional regime not to have important effects and influences on which comprehensive doctrines endure and gain adherents over time, and it is futile to try to counteract these effects and influences."[61] Justice as fairness is not designed to favor any particular comprehensive doctrine; in this respect Rawls's theory is neutral to rival views of the good. But it is wrong to think that justice as fairness can or must be neutral in its effects.

There is a difference, in short, between neutrality of design and neutrality of effect; effects are foreseeable, not intended, and liberalism should not be faulted for being nonneutral in this way. Nor is liberalism to be accused of favoring certain comprehensive doctrines if it happens that, over time, some pursuits of the good happen to die out. If interest in Christian Science, New Age religions, Catholicism, or pacifism ceases, there is no reason within liberal doctrine to lament the loss. Political liberalism can only be faulted for favoring certain doctrines, remarks Rawls, "if, say, individualistic ones alone can endure in a liberal society, or they so predominate that associations affirming the values of religion or community cannot flourish, and further, if the conditions leading to this outcome are themselves unjust, in view of present and foreseeable circumstances."[62] An individualistic ideology is unjust if it has been imposed by a regime with a comprehensive doctrine of the individualistic self. But an implemented liberal theory that prescinds from such a doctrine must be evaluated in other terms.

Rawls is thus able to defend his position by invoking various tools of casuistry. He may say that the outcomes of an implemented liberalism are unintended but foreseen, neutral in aim but not in effect. To this he may add that permitting an act differs from committing an action, the former being considerably less controversial than the latter. Rawls can say that permitting the foreseeable outcomes of an implemented liberalism in no way imposes liberalism on us as a comprehensive moral doctrine.[63] Given the fact that the sociological effects of implementing justice as fairness need not be neutral, justice as fairness can be acquitted of the charge that it is purposefully hegemonic.

From within the basic intuitive ideas of our culture, Rawls adds, we can extract and refine a theory of the moral person. He does not seek an overall philosophical anthropology or theory of human nature, as some might infer. Rather, he seeks to refine the theory of the person that coheres with his notion of justice as fairness, understood as a political morality. Here Rawls addresses the assumptions that lie behind the notion of citizen in liberal theory. Liberalism is not a doctrine about how we should view ourselves "from the inside"; it is rather about how we should want to be viewed by the state. Reference to a theory of the moral person is part of a moral theory that places limits on the actions of others or of the state, but it is not a comprehensive moral doctrine.[64] A theory of the *citoyen* as moral person, in short, does not require Rawls to commit himself to a theory in which the good is prior to the right.[65]

Citizens should be viewed, according to Rawls, "as fully cooperating members of society over a complete life, with moral powers that enable them to assume this role."[66] He thus identifies two "highest order interests," that is, interests to actualize two powers of moral personality: the capacity for a sense of right and justice (the ability to honor fair terms of social cooperation), and the capacity to embrace and revise a conception of the good.[67] Justice as fairness presupposes these powers as characteristic of citizens who make claims on the design of their political institutions. Without these interests citizens would lack sufficient motives to construct a society that is fair and ordered to protect their respective pursuits of the good.

This moral conception of the citizen allows Rawls to draw a clear distinction between public (or political) and nonpublic (or private) identity. Our public identity, the identity of the citizen, is not affected by changes that may occur in that individual's conceptions of the good. Those who convert from Mormonism to Catholicism, for example, "do not cease to be, for questions of political justice, the same persons they were before." They do not lose their public identity, "their identity as a matter of basic law."[68]

Our nonpublic identity, in contrast, refers to our personal affairs and associations, our attachment to ends without which it would be difficult if not impossible to interpret our experience. Such commitments, more intimate and controversial than our public commerce, are essential to how we understand "who we are." Nonpublic identity shapes and is shaped by one's pursuit of the good, guided by comprehensive philosophical, religious, or moral doctrines.

Nothing in liberal doctrine is designed to alter the way we pursue our private interests within the constraints of justice as fairness. Moreover, liberalism is a philosophy that holds, in theory, that our nonpublic allegiances are open to revision. Not only is liberalism neutral to rival visions of the good (within the limits of justice), it is also neutral to changes that people make in their visions of the good. Otherwise liberalism would be interfering with those more controversial beliefs from which it must prescind as a political morality.[69]

Rawls develops several claims about how justice as fairness can be viewed as stable in light of his theory of citizens and their highest-order interests. Central here is the fact that the well-ordered society of justice as fairness is experienced as good for individuals, for two reasons. In liberal society, Rawls writes,

> the exercise of the two moral powers is experienced as good. This is a consequence of the moral psychology used in justice as fairness. And that their exercise may be an important good, and will be one for many people, is clear from the central role of these powers in the political conception of citizens as persons.[70]

In this regard, he adds, "we might say that part of the essential nature of citizens (within the political conception) is their having the two moral powers that enable them to participate in fair social cooperation."[71]

Moreover, individuals will experience Rawls's well-ordered society as good because it secures citizens' fundamental needs, namely, "the equal basic rights and liberties, fair equality of opportunity, and the like."[72] Liberal society along Rawlsian lines, then, secures in the public forum the good of justice and the social bases of mutual self-respect. We may remain Catholics, Mormons, or atheists in the private realm, but if we do business with each other, we enter a realm in which our interest in the exercise of fairness can be realized. Persons with the capacity for a sense of justice, regardless of their private differences, will be attracted to a society in which commerce is regulated by the priority of the right.

Circularity and Doubtful Neutrality

Rawls's hermeneutical liberalism thus seeks to establish its feasibility by way of three claims: (1) justice as fairness can draw upon an overlapping consensus for its support; (2) a commonsense sociology shows that an implemented liberal doctrine will gain adherents over time; and (3) those who abide by the tenets of justice as fairness will satisfy their highest-order interests as citizens. What is noteworthy about each of these claims is that none of them echoes Rawls's discussion of stability in *A Theory of Justice*. Gone is the idea that the liberal doctrine can realize itself without being overly taxing, or that reciprocity wrought by the difference principle will mitigate the dangers of free-riderism, self-abnegation, and envy. For that matter, Rawls's modified theory entirely eschews these earlier claims, several of which rely on psychological assumptions. Nor are persons who are conscious of their limited talents and aspirations reminded of the good of pluralism. Also gone are claims that justice as fairness reveals our true natures, for Rawls's insistence that his theory is political—not metaphysical—undermines his fifth line of argument on behalf of feasibility in *A Theory of Justice*. To commend liberalism for revealing our true natures as autonomous and free from contingency would presuppose a metaphysic of the self, thereby suggesting that liberalism is a comprehensive moral doctrine.

Yet Rawls's modifications are problematic beyond the fact that they do not cohere with his earlier position. Consider Rawls's first line of argument, his interpretive turn and his appeal to an overlapping consensus. Not the least of Rawls's problems is his lack of ambition, at least from the point of view of *A Theory of Justice*. Recall that Rawls originally sought to provide an account of feasibility for parties who are neutral to his theory of justice as fairness, persons who have not adapted to life in a liberal society. The idea is to conceive of individuals who would assess the merits of a well-ordered society "independently from the constraints of justice."[73] But by relying on a method that excavates certain core conceptions from intuitive ideas in a democratic culture, Rawls's test of feasibility presupposes individuals who not only have adapted to liberalism, but are deeply implicated in the institutions and values of a modern democracy. To such individuals the tenets of liberalism have already commended themselves at some fundamental level of experience. There is no need to motivate us to accept the principles wrought behind the veil of ignorance; rather, prior allegiances have been assumed in developing the constraints that are to structure the original position. Indeed, given Rawls's appeal to a common fund of tradition, and given the salutary effects of having implemented liberal tenets over time (Rawls's "common-sense political sociology"), it is hard to imagine how a neutral vantage point, essential for an independent assessment, would be possible.

On this score Rawls might retort that he is abiding by the spirit but not the letter of his initial position regarding feasibility, namely, that his theory is not overly burdensome. In the revised doctrine, it appears that his theory remains feasible-as-not-onerous given that it derives from settled convictions that are widely shared. But achieving feasibility in this way only proves what has been presupposed. For Rawls, consensus is both necessary for principles of justice and a goal to be achieved for the stability of liberal doctrine. To excavate principles from intuitive ideas latent in the culture of a democratic society, and then to argue for the stability of the theory given its compatibility with widespread pursuits of the good, proceeds in a circular direction.

A similar problem plagues Rawls's more muted attempt to argue for stability on the basis of his conception of citizen as moral person. Rawls argues that a society ruled by his public conception of justice will be experienced as good because "the exercise of the two moral powers is experienced as good."[74] Yet it seems tautological to say that the exercise of one's highest-order interests would be experienced as good. Here, too, the circularity of Rawls's method generates difficulties. The idea that moral capacities, abstracted from individuals implicated in the shared institutions in liberal democracy, will be experienced as good in societies implementing a liberal theory is obviously self-fulfilling.

Rawls's idea of private life in relation to liberal tenets is likewise dubious. Liberalism is a philosophy that holds, in theory, that our nonpublic allegiances are open to revision. Yet, as he admits, we must absorb the virtues of liberalism into our visions of the good life in order for liberalism to work. The system's need for stability makes it incongruous to suggest that such virtues should be subject to revision in the same way that, say, religious convictions might be. We may be able to convert to Catholicism from Mormonism, but it is more desirable that we convert from Mormonism to a Kantian embrace of individualism and autonomy. And once we do, it would be unwise to leave such convictions open to revision—at least from the point of view of the stability of liberal theory.

One way Rawls might respond to this complaint is to argue that liberalism is not *designed* to penetrate our visions of the good. Liberalism can be seen as not *purposefully* hegemonic if we distinguish between what is intended and what is foreseeable when implementing Rawlsian liberalism: The sociological effects of justice as fairness upon our private allegiances are not intended, but over time they will inevitably shape the private self-interpretations of individuals residing in liberal polities. Adaptation to liberalism can thus be justified as foreseen but unintended.

Yet as I argued in chapter 2, this distinction between what is intended and what can be anticipated is clearer in theory than it may be in the realm of everyday life, at least psychologically speaking. To be sure, I do not want to abandon this distinction; it will be crucial to my attempt to address a case in medical ethics in chapter 6. But, as should become clearer in that argument, the distinction between effects that are intended and those that are only foreseen should be invoked with due attention to institutional mechanisms that can render the distinction viable in practice. When it comes to procedures in medical ethics, I will show that such mechanisms are already in place or are readily available. But the case is much different in the domain of political philosophy. Would a member of a liberal polity be satisfied in knowing that the progressive privileging of liberal tenets and the increased ideology of individualism is "foreseen but unintended"? Once Americans wake up and discover, as the authors of *Habits of the Heart*[75] have invited them to do, that a large number of them lack a vocabulary for naming their communal projects, how many persons would be satisfied by the retort that liberalism's hegemony on their moral imaginations was foreseeable but not intended by liberalism's architects? Those who find such a hegemony problematic because it distorts their participation in communal practices would be unlikely, I suspect, to be consoled by the claim that the ideology of individualism is merely a predictable accident of life in a liberal regime.

The Good(s) of Partial Memberships

One way that Rawls might avoid the problem of circularity or doubts about liberalism's neutrality is to reexamine an incorrigible feature of liberal life, namely, the fact of pluralism. In this context *pluralism* describes the situation of diversity produced when we tolerate religious and cultural differences. So understood, *pluralism* refers to the coexistence of different spheres of cultural activity, economic exchange, social influence, and political power, the experience of diversity along religious, cultural, economic, social, and political vectors. For liberals pluralism is a necessity; without a genuinely pluralist society, liberty and choice would be empty. Pluralism also means that we carry out lives of partial memberships, moving from one center of activity to another in a complex environment of diverse loyalties, needs, and tastes—with all their corresponding obligations. Members of a pluralist culture are thus able to occupy more than one sphere, juggling the demands of family, aesthetic needs, service organizations, local government, religious associations, labor unions, volunteer work, recreational teams, and friendly relaxation, to name but a few centers of activity available in a liberal setting.[76]

This experience of complexity is scarcely to be dreaded. For those active in a pluralist culture, partial memberships provide protection from the monochromatic sameness, limited self-definition, or tedium that would accrue to those committed to live in only one sphere in pursuit of communitarian solidarity. Indeed, the good(s) of partial memberships[77] can be traced along three related levels: the epistemic, the sociological, and the psychological.

At the epistemic level, partial memberships can remind us that in any one sphere our pursuit of truth is incomplete, that only through diverse forms of interaction can our own limited points of view find confirmation, correction, or growth. Our opinions are tested, challenged, and revised as we seek to apply them to the demands of different settings. In the process, we learn that certain truths have greater merit in some contexts than in others, or that some beliefs have limitations that we have not considered. To view partial memberships in these terms, then, is to embrace epistemic fallibilism, the idea that our views are vulnerable to limitation or error, that there is no omniscient point of view from which we may deliver ourselves from the possibility of contingency or distortion. Yet it is also to accept the idea that seeking omniscience is no self-evident desideratum, that we do better to rely on our practices in diverse spheres to broaden our horizons. As John Stuart Mill argued on behalf of the social benefits of tolerance, "since the general or prevailing opinion on any subject is rarely or never the whole truth, it is only by the collision of adverse opinions that the remainder of the truth has any chance of being supplied."[78] Life in a society composed of various memberships enables us to test our prejudices against those of others, seeking more adequate opinions than ours might provide.

These epistemic implications of pluralism require us to take an ironist stance toward ourselves. Individuals in a liberal culture must remain open to the possibility of being persuaded against their self-interpretations upon encountering an adversarial voice. Liberals are thus required to maintain a balanced tension between commitment and doubt. But to those who accept the implications of fallibilism, such an ironist stance does not entail skepticism or corrosively doubtful rationalism. Fallibilism is not unfriendly to self-constituting beliefs; it is more moderate. It means being open to revising one's convictions, perhaps converting to an alternative point of view. It also means that we should assume that self-constituting beliefs are not self-evident, that our identities depend in part on the *critical* appropriation of deeply held commitments. Ironism is not hostile to belief; it rather seeks to strengthen the bases on which beliefs are firmly held.

To this ironist outlook it might be objected that some commitments are surely unshakable, beyond challenge or improvement. But on this issue as well, the good of partial memberships must be recognized and developed, for sociological reasons. Among its benefits, diversity of opinion provides the antidote to petrification and what Mill calls the "deep slumber of decided opinion."[79] As Mill observes, the inevitable clash of perspectives in a liberal culture protects us from sterility and enfeeblement of belief, even those beliefs that seem beyond doubt. If our strongest belief "is not fully, frequently, and fearlessly discussed," says Mill, "it will be held as a dead dogma, not a living truth."[80] When a creed becomes hereditary, individuals tend "to give it a dull and torpid assent, as if accepting it on trust dispensed with the necessity of realizing it in consciousness, or testing it by personal experience, until it almost ceases to connect itself at all with the inner life of the human being."[81] Controversy and argument enable us to determine exactly why we hold to our beliefs, helping us to embrace them freely, as our own. Beliefs are freely chosen in the sense that they are professed openly in the context of ongoing dialogue with alternative self-interpretations and corresponding practices. Viewed in these sociological terms, pluralism is thus a catalyst of social vitality and freedom, requiring individuals to be responsible for understanding and appropriating their deeply held convictions. Where diversity reigns, society has greater insurance against blind faith.

The goods of partial memberships likewise promise psychological benefits. Partial memberships provide an opportunity for the self to develop within an array of relationships and within diverse contexts. In this way, as Nancy L. Rosenblum remarks, pluralism "mirrors the familiar sense of a luxuriously complex self that resists finitude and definition."[82] Committed to a variety of goods, moving in and out of diverse spheres, members of a liberal society can find self-enrichment without monotony. Diversity provides therapy for dreaded routine, restriction to one place, or identification with only one social role.

Transition from sphere to sphere thus emancipates any one role from having to carry the burden of satisfying the self's complex needs. Accordingly, the self can develop a manifold aesthetic in the quest for self-cultivation.[83]

The fact that in liberalism no single sphere must carry the burden of self-enrichment also means that liberalism can provide "limited liability."[84] Partial memberships protect us from excessive vulnerability to disappointment. Active in an array of spheres, we allow our vulnerabilities to be dispersed. The experience of defeat or disappointment in one context is likely to be balanced by achievements in other spheres. The stakes of success or failure in any one part of our lives are considerably reduced. Liberal philosophy, then, is not inimical to the communitarian idea of being vulnerable or being committed, only to the idea that our identity and vulnerability require singularity, understood as confinement to one social role or sphere of commitment. The liberal self resists exalting any one sphere to the exclusion of others as a means of self-definition, believing instead that by dividing the stakes we augment, rather than diminish, our sources of self-esteem.

Another Overlapping Consensus

It might be objected that these three benefits of pluralism nonetheless require us to embrace liberal tenets as more than a political morality—that fallibilism, the vitalization of belief, and individual self-enrichment are all implicated within a particular (liberal) view of the good. Such an argument for liberalism's feasibility, then, might point to evidence other than that invoked by Rawls, but it would be no less circular or biased in favor of liberalism (as a comprehensive moral doctrine) than his post-*Theory* arguments on behalf of stability.

To refute these charges it must be retorted that each of the benefits of pluralism I have mentioned finds resonances within a wide array of (nonliberal) religious and philosophical tenets. These resonances provide the possibility of an overlapping consensus about the good(s) of pluralism itself. The fact that nonliberal theories have reasons to endorse pluralism enables us to envision liberalism's potential for stability by uncovering a consensus in contemporary democratic culture about the advantages of pluralism. (I say the "good(s)" of pluralism to underscore the idea that the good in question is not a single, comprehensive good.) And, while a full discussion of such resonances merits a study in its own right, it is possible here to sketch how nonliberal visions in our culture might have reasons to embrace pluralism as a social good, thereby adding support to liberalism's claim for stability.

Perhaps the most comprehensive endorsement of pluralism outside of liberalism can be inferred from religions of radical monotheism, which affirm as a central tenet the sovereignty of God over all human endeavors. In such a frame of reference, the good(s) of pluralism converge with the prohibition, derived from radical monotheism, against absolutizing any relative commitment or practice. Radical monotheism, stated simply, affirms pluralism by relativizing the importance of various cultural pursuits of truth.[85] Embracing pluralism as a good, then, converges with radical monotheism's general resistance to the idea that we have a monopoly on truth or goodness in the realm of cultural affairs. Affirming the relative goodness of our diverse human practices underwrites the idea that we should allow individuals to pursue those goods in the diverse activities of our cultural life, within the limits required by fairness and order. In this way the sovereignty of God sanctions diverse cultural practices, practices that may be pursued according to the opportunities and constraints of partial memberships.

Consider as well how a natural law approach to religious freedom and its implied affirmation of religious pluralism might underwrite pluralism as a psychological good.[86] As it has been developed in official Catholic teaching, such an interpretation of the natural law begins by assuming that individuals "are both impelled by their nature and bound by a moral obligation to seek the truth, especially religious truth."[87] This duty entails the right to be free from coercion; otherwise the quest for truth would be inauthentic and insincere. To be immune from coercion, in turn, implies religious tolerance, the idea that "within due limits, nobody is forced to act against his convictions in religious matters in private or in public, alone or in association with others."[88]

Central to this endorsement of religious liberty is the idea, suggested by the psychological dimensions of pluralism I developed above, that religious belief is a matter of "personal assent." Individuals, we are told, need to form judgments of conscience that are "sincere and true,"[89] that is, uncoerced. The idea of human dignity, central to recent Catholic natural law morality, entails that individuals "should exercise fully their own judgment and a responsible freedom in their actions."[90] Of necessity, then, the state is forbidden to legislate religious beliefs. Natural law morality about religious liberty, in short, converges with the psychological good of pluralism by underscoring the importance of freedom as a condition for securing self-constituting beliefs, producing the requirement to tolerate religious (and, by implication, cultural) diversity.

The idea of epistemic fallibility likewise coheres with nonliberal philosophical and religious tenets that are now circulating in democratic culture. Catholic natural law teaching about pluralism, for example, makes an appeal for a dialogical approach to knowledge, claiming that "the search for truth . . . must be carried out in a manner that is appropriate to the dignity of the human person and his social nature, namely, by free inquiry with the help of teaching or instruction, communication and dialogue."[91] Here the ruling idea is that the pursuit of truth requires the free exchange of ideas. The official Catholic interpretation of the natural law thus suggests that knowledge relies on a process of interaction, that truth emerges from the interchange of finite points of view. At the very least, this social, dialogical approach to inquiry suggests that we cannot turn to any single agency—political or ecclesial—as the sole, monological source of truth and wisdom. Rather, we must place our trust in conversation, assuming that our visions will be aided by insights that emerge within the exchange of criticisms and conflicting beliefs.

Among philosophers, epistemic fallibilism coheres with various trends in historicism and hermeneutics, all of which eschew the attempt to secure a transcendental vantage point from which to view history and knowledge. Generally, these trends hold to a basic tenet in the sociology of knowledge, namely, that our modes of apprehension are culturally mediated. Philosophers as diverse as Hans-Georg Gadamer, Alasdair MacIntyre, Stephen Toulmin, Michael Walzer, and Richard Rorty have developed influential arguments to the effect that our commerce with the world is bound by the thought-forms and practices of our own particular contexts. Implied in this general idea is the claim that we are able to develop our knowledge by way of dialectical reasoning from within our own particular thought-forms, that by appealing to rival arguments or vocabularies we can overcome the limits of our own points of view. Given the conditions of finitude within which our knowledge develops, it is politically imperative to tolerate diverse beliefs.

This does not mean that various philosophies, religious beliefs, and natural law morality provide a *liberal* affirmation of pluralism. It means only that the goods of pluralism, which liberals affirm in order to secure a feasible, nonutopian doctrine, converge with ideas that can be extracted from comprehensive doctrines presently coexisting in our culture. Epistemic fallibilism and the socio-psychological benefits of pluralism include a set of "theorems," at which different comprehensive doctrines can converge from different starting points.[92] Accordingly, liberals can refer to these good(s) of pluralism and remain confident that their affirmation is neither hegemonic nor incommensurable with other, more comprehensive, beliefs in our democratic culture.[93]

The Return of the Repressed

By underwriting the good(s) of pluralism and partial memberships, liberalism is not hostile to communitarian sentiments, especially those that affirm the value of context, common goods, and self-constituting commitments. Indeed, by viewing liberalism as I have sought to do, we can see that the communitarian criticism resembles the return of the repressed, expressing sentiments that liberals, with their concern for formal structures and rational procedures, can too easily overlook.[94] If liberalism can somehow domesticate antiliberalism, it can protect itself from the charge that it is a doctrine of moral minimalism and mediocrity. Let us consider again those communitarian objections to liberalism.

First, against the allegation that liberalism fails to recognize our lives as embedded in and partially constituted by local commitments and shared projects, liberals can retort: Liberalism allows for a pluralism that is associational. Partial memberships provide space for identities to be shaped by common pursuits. Liberals do not oppose the idea of solidarity per se; rather, they oppose the idea that the good of community can generate a set of noncoercive political arrangements.

Second, to the charge that liberalism cannot work sociologically because its notion of detached selves breeds apathy and social fragmentation, we can rejoin: Liberals' pursuit of feasibility is synonymous with the need to generate loyalty and attachment. Indeed, the attempt to overcome the charge that liberalism cannot work is central to its nonutopian impulse. My discussion of the good(s) of partial memberships is an attempt to strengthen liberal political philosophy on precisely this point.

Third, in response to the idea that liberalism elevates justice to the highest virtue, failing to see that justice is required only when communal ties have broken down, liberals can retort that communitarians leave us with a false set of alternatives. Justice is the highest virtue in political morality because it must constrain our pursuits of the good, setting the boundaries outside which some of those pursuits are morally unacceptable. Justice is conceived in this way because our diverse communal ties fail to provide a single conception of the good that is sufficient for a theory of justice. Yet owing to the fact of pluralism, justice functions remedially in that it seeks to rectify a situation that would *otherwise* be left to arbitrary power or to utilitarian calculations. Liberals no less than communitarians can view justice as necessary in response to a situation of fragmentation and diversity. Conceived in this way—within the context of pluralism—liberal justice can be seen *both* as the highest virtue *and* in remedial terms.

Fourth, against the complaint that liberalism requires a strong state apparatus to protect human liberty, liberals can respond by insisting that the need for a strong state apparatus is even greater for comprehensive doctrines in communitarianism. Given what we know of human inclinations and propensities, how else could we guarantee the comprehensiveness of comprehensive notions of the good?

Fifth, in reply to the claim that liberalism's epistemology fails to recognize how our points of view are implicated in the traditions, thought-forms, and languages of a culture, Rawls can insist that he has developed a hermeneutical liberalism, extracting some core convictions from intuitive ideas in a democratic culture. These convictions serve as starting points for his political philosophy. In this way he eschews foundationalism, specifying his tradition, legacy, and political context.

Finally, against the idea that liberalism represses the voice of Romanticism, liberals can insist that Romanticism's quest for self-cultivation can be annexed if liberals develop the kind of endorsement of pluralism I have suggested above. Liberalism is not hostile to the Romantic goals of aestheticism and self-cultivation, only to the notion that such aspirations are to be pursued monochromatically.

Indirection and Ambivalence

Following the argument I have developed here, liberals who address the question of political and moral motivation can proceed in a way that is neither circular nor doubtfully neutral. The good(s) of pluralism do not provide a set of intuitions that are then refined into principles of justice. Thus, appealing to the good(s) of pluralism to secure liberalism's feasibility can avoid circularity. Nor is it necessary to argue that liberal values must shape our private self-interpretations in order for liberalism to be stable.

Yet it must be added that my approach to the questions of motivation and solidarity must be described as an indirect strategy. As a political morality, liberalism denies itself reference to a single, comprehensive moral doctrine by which we might be beckoned or to which we might attach ourselves. But this does not mean that Rawlsian liberalism lacks any strategy whatsoever when addressing matters of stability, only that it is without a direct, straightforward appeal to any single, all-encompassing vision. *Liberalism can inspire solidarity indirectly, calling attention to the beneficial effects of allowing diverse pursuits to exist beneath the umbrella of justice as fairness.* We can be moved to embrace liberalism, then, because liberal tenets ensure that our various interests and commitments have space to grow. If we accept the benefits of having a *diverse* set of pursuits, it becomes reasonable to expect denizens of a liberal polity to prefer liberalism to its reigning alternatives.

The good of liberalism is thus multivalent, requiring us to refer to the *good(s)* of partial memberships, not *the* good of partial memberships. The fact that pluralism is not a simple, single good does not mean that it cannot inspire, only that our political allegiances must direct themselves to the good(s) of diversity, the advantageous coexistence of our various visions and beliefs. Along the way our fallibility is recognized, our beliefs are tested and strengthened, and our individual complexity can find various avenues of self-expression and self-enrichment. And, as I have argued above, individuals who may prefer alternatives to liberalism as a comprehensive doctrine nonetheless have good reason to affirm contract doctrine as a political morality.

To be sure, arguments on behalf of the good(s) of pluralism point to epistemic, sociological, and psychological features of diversity, requiring arguments that Rawls generally sought to avoid when modifying his theory. Perhaps Rawls judged that reference to such features would be too controversial, contrary to his desire to remain "on the surface, philosophically speaking." But as I have sought to show, the various benefits of pluralism are compatible with several major nonliberal doctrines, *providing an overlapping consensus about the good(s) of pluralism itself.* Liberals can thus view pluralism not only in terms of a problem to be managed by political philosophy, but also in terms of the diverse, yet recognizable, good(s) of partial memberships. Viewing pluralism in this way, Rawls should be able to develop a case for liberalism as a practicable, nonutopian doctrine, one that commends itself as both fair and feasible.

Rawls's attempt to historicize himself—to create a hermeneutical liberalism—puts him within reach of more explicit efforts to join political philosophy, history, and experience with the tools of casuistry. Yet such efforts are more radically historicized than Rawls's modified theory. They express greater self-consciousness about the relativity of their points of view and less confidence in detached philosophical reflection. Seeking to interpret moral experience within our cultural practices, such approaches proceed more inductively. The overall goal is to decipher habits, experiences, and cultural meanings by using tools drawn from phenomenology and ethnography. For more radical historicists, practical reasoning ought to be unabashedly interpretive. We turn now to a discussion of the promise and the limits of one such effort.

CHAPTER FOUR

Romantic Casuistry, Holiness, and the Art of Separation

Rationality and Romanticism

Developed in a culture with many comprehensive moral doctrines, Rawls's social philosophy seeks to ensure that pluralism will not curdle into anarchy. With its roots in Hobbes, Locke, and Kant, contract theory invites us to construct principles of fair social cooperation by imagining what equal, disinterested persons would agree upon when placed behind the renowned "veil of ignorance."[1] One goal is to imagine a hypothetical situation—the "original position"—in which persons are unable to design principles that would favor any particular group once the veil is lifted. However complicated the specific features of the argument, its main tenets are well known: Assuming that rational deliberation is impartial, the theory asks us to infer what enlightened self-interest, constrained by rational consistency, would entail.

Yet contract theory is only one route toward a social philosophy in our culture, and its imaginary efforts have left many unsatisfied, owing to its (alleged) reliance on anemic, humorless rationality. A rival approach, with its roots in Romanticism, attempts to make manifest the social agreements that already shape our moral and political life. This rival proceeds less by way of logical argument than by way of symbolic description, seeking to illumine areas of consensus in our everyday affairs. Its images and metaphors are not used to create fictitious philosophical constructs; instead they work phenomenologically, colorfully describing commonplaces that furnish durable sources for moral principle and practice. The social contract is not *constructed* so much as *uncovered* from the customs, shared practices, and vitalities of history.

I shall call this the Romantic alternative to the Rawlsian approach I discussed in the previous chapter, and I want to examine its place in casuistry here by analyzing Michael Walzer's social philosophy. Of course, *Romanticism* is a dangerously broad term, leading some to doubt whether a unified category exists, while others have preferred to view it as a "sensibility" rather than as a distinct cultural movement.[2] Many of its main features are echoed in the communitarian criticisms of liberalism, which I rehearsed at the outset of chapter 3. But there I emphasized matters of identity and sources of moral knowledge, and we would do well to consider Romanticism's reaction to Enlightenment rationalism more expansively. At the risk of oversimplifying, this reaction might be summarized as follows:

1. Enlightenment rationalism produced the quest for "totalizing" knowledge, an omniscient point of view that produces either universal laws or an encyclopedic breadth of vision.[3] Such are the aspirations of crafting a "theory" or, in a more historical guise, a "metanarrative." The goal is to place the variety and particularity of our cultural practices under the hegemony of translucent, impersonal, detached reflection, *sub specie aeternitatis.*

Romanticism, in contrast, prizes local knowledge, knowledge that is rooted in, and relative to, specific times and places. It celebrates diversity and esteems not what is uniform, but what is rare, exceptional, incomparable, unique.

2. Enlightenment science aspires to isolate and quantify bits of data before erecting universal, rational laws. Part of its task is to break down the complexity of the natural realm into its simplest units, an undertaking premised on the predominantly Cartesian view of nature as a machine.

Romantics resist the quantification and atomization of experience, rejecting a mechanistic view of nature in favor of a dynamic, organic view. As Lilian Furst observes, "Nature [is] therefore envisaged no longer as a passive object, but as an animate being."[4] Seeking to capture the vitalities and organic interconnections of nature, Romantics integrate natural phenomena holistically. Wholes are prior to parts, and are perceived by way of a symbolic fusion or visionary gestalt.[5]

3. Enlightenment rationalism provides criteria to ensure that the mind is a clean mirror, one that perfectly reflects the natural order. Its language, appropriately, is meant to be designative, pointing with precision to the objects and movements of the "external" world.

Romantic writers appeal instead to the affections and the powers of the imagination, viewing the mind as a lamp rather than a mirror.[6] For Romantics, the intellect has creative power, imposing a certain

103

order onto reality. In this way, as Ashton Nichols remarks, "the ordinary is rendered remarkable by the imaginative transformation of experience," relying on the power of the imagination to produce significance out of the mundane.[7] This belief in the imagination, moreover, allows Romantics to view their mental powers as more projective than recollective, more original than reproductive. Accordingly, Romantics understand language not as designative but as expressive, figurative, and evocative, given the conviction that symbols have creative power. About such rhetoric Chaim Perelman observes,

> Romantics prefer discourses which seem most fitting to suggestion: poetry rather than prose; metaphor which brings together domains rather than comparison or allegory; word games which throw limits into disorder; better symbolic participation than causal relation; rather than the strategic, hypotactic Greco-Roman phrase they prefer the paratactic biblical phrase.[8]

Romantics view the image, like the natural world itself, vitalistically, bestowing on the artist a creative power not unlike God's.

This is not to say that Romanticism is averse to historical accuracy or descriptive precision, only that it is inclined to subordinate its descriptions to alternative visions. Romantic art and literature, as Charles Taylor remarks, are premised on the conviction that "manifesting reality involves the creation of new forms which give articulation to an inchoate vision, not simply the reproduction of forms already there."[9] Romantic art and letters were conceived "as a creation which reveals, or as a revelation which at the same time defines and completes what it makes manifest."[10] Gone, then, is the classical view of mimesis, with nature preceding image. Instead, as Earl Wasserman notes, "nature, which was once prior to the image and available for imitation, now shares with the image a common origin in the poet's creativity."[11]

4. Enlightenment intellectuals found Western religious traditions inadequate to address the needs of Europe after the Thirty Years War; to replace traditional religious and cultural authorities, many sought to craft a method that relies on reason alone, using as few controversial assumptions as possible. Such rationalist methods are typically abstract, speculative, and deductive, seeking to create neutral ground from which to develop moral and political legislation.

Relying instead on the particular and the concrete, Romantics open the door to the use of ethnographic tools to excavate from cultural data an understanding of goods that are internal to social practices. The alternative to Enlightenment abstractions is to proceed inductively and interpretively, culling from different cultures insights into human needs and their satisfaction. In effect, as George Stocking observes, Romanticism replaces the nomothetic with the idiographic.[12] And, in contrast with the Enlightenment suspicion of religion, many Romantics have celebrated the sociological value of religion, viewing it as the glue that holds societies together.

5. Enlightenment political morality that takes its bearings from Kant—as Rawls's theory illustrates—understands the right as prior to the good. Otherwise, the argument goes, our understanding of justice will be complicit with and relative to one particular vision of the good life. It will thus lack the distance necessary to judge our individual and institutional lives.

For Romantics, however, a more inductive, phenomenological, and/or ethnographic method requires us to view the good as prior to the right. By their account, we must interpret a community's concrete goods before we can craft principles that are appropriate to its particular form of life. For this reason Romantics are quick to criticize the dominant forms of Enlightenment politics as impersonal and legalistic, premised on rights and legal protections instead of shared loyalties and objects of fidelity.[13]

6. Political philosophy with Enlightenment roots is realistic insofar as it attempts to create a nonutopian ethic, one that is suited to the conditions of pluralism in the Western nation-state. Yet Romantics allege that they too are nonutopian in that they call attention to the moral importance of customs and practices, which testify to human motivations that are already in place. Romantics argue, in effect, that political or moral theories that rely on rationality alone are too demanding, and that it is unrealistic to expect such theories to find a sufficiently large following to be effective. Enlightenment rationalists ask us to accept their vision apart from appeals to human experience, affection, or love. But human agency, Romantics argue, is more complex than rationality alone. By proceeding inductively and ethnographically, Romantics allege, they have greater resources to appeal to the vitalities and motivational impulses of actual human beings— reasons of the heart—and that such appeals provide a more realistic method for crafting a social philosophy.[14]

At first glance it might seem odd to bring a discussion of Romanticism's distinctive features into a work devoted to casuistry. In the eighteenth century little if any cross-fertilization occurred between casuistical practice and Romantic developments in arts and letters. And even apart from historical circumstances, the two approaches would seem quite hostile to each other. Casuistry's ties to the obscure manualist tradition, the "outer voice" of the cleric in the confessional, and the durable dictates of divine law stand in stark contrast to Romanticism's affiliations with poetry, the inner voice of individual freedom, and epiphanic flights of emotion and imagination.[15]

Yet in Walzer's hands Romanticism and casuistry come together in ways that seem to defy history and logic. They do so by way of Walzer's use of historical cases in his account of justice, *Spheres of Justice: A Defense of Pluralism and Equality*.[16] Walzer eschews theory and metanarrative, preferring the use of cases to illustrate deeply held convictions and values, a method of philosophy that he himself has dubbed "casuistic."[17] It is important to understand how Walzer's use of the case method is inexorably connected with his latent Romantic sensibilities.

Interpretive Social Philosophy

Walzer's use of cases—vignettes from history and anthropology, abbreviated to illustrate a moral point—resonates deeply with each of the Romantic refrains I have mentioned. His inventory includes stories of Athens in the fifth and fourth centuries, Trobriand Islanders, Manchester in 1844, Macy's Department Store, the Israeli kibbutz, garbage collectors in San Francisco, and the history of holidays. These vignettes provide brief, often anecdotal stories of ourselves or other people, each of which is meant to sharpen the distinctive features of our own history and culture.

In this way Walzer's approach purports to be "radically particularist," premised on local knowledge. Instead of philosophizing by leaving Plato's cave to adopt an objective and universal standpoint, Walzer claims to "stand in the cave, in the city, on the ground." Distinguishing his method from that of Rawls, Walzer writes: "If a just society isn't already here—hidden, as it were, in our concepts and categories—we will never know it concretely or realize it in fact."[18] The use of the examples, then, "aim[s] to suggest the force of the things themselves or, rather, the force of our conceptions of the things."[19] Walzer provides a vision that is relevant not to all social worlds, only *our* social world, shaped by common understandings and their subtle meanings.

In Walzer's view, the task of the social philosopher is not to carry out "an integrated science, but an art of differentiation."[20] We are not asked to isolate some elementary principles of our social life, those uncontroversial rational maxims that might serve as building blocks for a grander theory. Rather, we must identify the various social wholes of our ordinary lives, what Walzer calls "spheres." *Sphere* refers to a set of social goods that money cannot buy, goods that are more or less bounded off from each other, about which we possess a "shared understanding": education, security and welfare, leisure, religion, work, office, power, and even the community itself.[21] In effect, our practical affairs move in and out of heterogeneous gestalts. To get an overview of these spheres, we must draw on the holistic skills of the cartographer, seeking not to invent the lines of society, but "to map out the entire social world."[22] This mapping must first chart the topography of goods and their meanings, providing an overview of how they define the contours of our everyday practices and motivations. The art of differentiation is premised not on fragmentary units of individual experience, but on the social wholes of collective life, producing a modest synthetic vision. Such a method requires neither the theoretical aspirations nor the atomistic science of Enlightenment rationality.

To proceed by way of local knowledge requires the social philosopher "to interpret to one's fellow citizens the world of meanings that we share."[23] In this respect Walzer's method recalls another feature of Romanticism: its hermeneutical orientation. We need neither to discover morality within the laws of revelation nor to invent it according to the dictates of Enlightenment reason. His own method "lends itself less to abstract modeling than to thick description. Moral argument in such a setting is interpretive in character, closely resembling the work of a lawyer or judge who struggles to find meaning in a morass of conflicting laws and precedents."[24] Genuinely effective morality must proceed from meanings that are shared and familiar, Walzer insists; it ought to mine our already existing moral customs and practices.

Proceeding interpretively, by way of local knowledge, requires Walzer to understand the good as prior to the right. The experience of one's community is, first and foremost, the experience of goods— objects of value that are shared, divided, and exchanged. Against the impulses of the Enlightenment to find a universal, rational principle, it is better, Walzer argues, to observe that in everyday experience we live not by one dominant good or organizing principle, but by many goods.

Consider, finally, the realistic impulse of Romantic philosophy: By drawing upon the stories and experiences of people in history, Walzer presents his vision as a nonutopian alternative to the dominant Enlightenment approach. Such a society, he writes, "lies within our own reach. It is a practical possibility here and now, latent already . . . in our shared understandings of social goods."[25] To proceed otherwise, deducing conclusions of rational individuals situated behind the veil of ignorance, would be to escape our social world, a move that, in his judgment, is needlessly abstract.[26] As a practical matter it is more productive to ask, "What would individuals like us choose, who are situated as we are, who share a culture and are determined to go on sharing it? . . . What choices have we already made in the course of our common life?"[27] Such choices are structured by a familiar morality, one that has already established its authority. Consequently, political programs premised on such authority are likelier to secure assent.

These distinctive features of Walzer's work can thus be seen as a moment within a wider cultural conversation, recalling Romanticism's rebellion against Enlightenment rationalism. But if this is true, it must include one enormous caveat: Walzer eschews the Romantic cult of the individual that we find, for example, in Blake or Rousseau.[28] And he does so out of deep—perhaps unconscious—religious reasons. Indeed, if Walzer is an ambassador of Romanticism, he must be understood as a Jewish attaché, socializing the Romantics' appeal to experience and uniqueness. In Walzer's vision, Romanticism's testimonies to the local and the incomparable are retained, but they are moderated by a Jewish desire to keep us faithful to our shared meanings and their history while maintaining clear boundaries between distinct spheres of life. Social philosophy, rooted in the particular and attentive to the exceptional, becomes covenantal and levitical, the grist for prophet and priest.[29]

This aversion to individualism means, among other things, that Walzer must modify the Romantics' celebration of the creative, projective imagination, which derives in large part from their cult of the hero and/or the genius. Rather, for Walzer the mind works as both mirror and lamp. He seeks simultaneously to describe the political world we already inhabit *and* to divine from our experience the materials for shaping an alternative, realizable political vision. For Walzer, such a vision is found in the tenets of a decentralized democratic socialism:

> A strong welfare state run, in part at least, by local and amateur officials; a constrained market; an open and demystified civil service; independent public schools; the sharing of hard work and free time; . . . workers' control of companies and factories; a politics of parties, movements, meetings, and public debate.[30]

This vision is meant to "bubble up" from Walzer's interpretations, emerging from within a "collective consciousness."[31] As if to suggest that we have been reading about ourselves *as* latent democratic socialists, Walzer introduces this program only at the conclusion of *Spheres of Justice*. And, it should be noted, Walzer brings us to this vision with a wide-ranging set of images, calling on numerous sources in the attempt to touch our imaginations and sensibilities. Indeed, as if to confirm Perelman's summary of Romanticism's rhetoric, Walzer recurrently recalls biblical figures and phrases, drawing freely from Deuteronomy, Amos, Exodus, and Jonah.

These (and other) Jewish refrains lie deep within Walzer's rendition of our shared meanings, and no understanding of his social philosophy is complete without reference to them. Yet the appeal to shared meanings and the duty to keep our spheres distinct generate considerable tensions in Walzer's casuistry, especially when we consider the illustrations on which he relies. For, as we shall see, it is by no means obvious that our shared meanings make for unity, or that keeping our spheres distinct is as possible (or as desirable) as Walzer suggests. In the world of practical affairs, the labors of prophets and priests do not always coincide.

Imagining Justice

If the idea of distinct spheres of social goods constitutes one feature of Walzer's theory, the second is the notion of "complex equality." Simple equality, the approach of Kantian, utilitarian, or natural law theory, produces a single standard by which to compare distributions to individuals. Complex equality, in contrast, requires us to understand the relativity of justice: Equality will be determined by *need*, or *desert*, or *freedom*, depending on which sphere of goods we are considering (or inhabiting). A member of the Senate may have his parking place reserved on the Capitol, but when vacationing at Martha's Vineyard he may not go to the front of the line at the movies. To invoke privileges appropriate to the exercise of power in the sphere of leisure, Walzer would have it, is unjust, a violation of boundaries. In the former sphere, goods are allocated (presumably) according to the principle of need; in the second, freedom reigns. Hence the distributive procedure, proscribing a foreign principle from becoming dominant in another sphere: "No social good x should be distributed to men and women who possess some other good y merely because they possess y without regard to the meaning of x."[32]

To this Walzer adds that "distributions are patterned in accordance with shared conceptions of what the goods are and what they are for."[33] Goods are social and historical: People (collectively) define themselves in relation to particular goods, and such relations have a cultural history. One key feature of a theory of distributive justice is to discover not only what goods are, but also what they *mean* to a particular society, for such meanings play a significant role in determining how various goods are to be allocated. For a culture devoted to the good of the body, health will be distributed according to principles that differ from those in cultures where esoteric or otherworldly goods are significantly more important than physical life. Americans now claim to believe in distributing health according to need, whereas the ancient Greeks allocated it on the marketplace, according to the principle of free exchange.[34]

The fact that distributions are patterned *within* a sphere of goods

109

and exchanges means that complex equality must assume a variety of distributive principles. The argument is thus premised on the claim that "the principles of justice are themselves pluralistic in form; that different social goods ought to be distributed for different reasons, in accordance with different procedures, by different agents; and that all these differences derive from different understandings of the social goods themselves—the inevitable product of historical and cultural particularism."[35] Consequently, we have a contextual account of social justice: "All distributions," Walzer insists, "are just or unjust relative to the social meanings of the goods at stake."[36] In our culture medicine and security are goods distributed according to need; punishment, public honors, and entrance into specialized schools are distributed according to desert; religion, wealth, and love are distributed according to free exchange. There is no single, uniform standard of distributive justice, only standards "for every social good and every distributive sphere in every particular society."[37]

Accordingly, the spheres of our social goods generate incomparable rules for practice. When the principles of one distributive sphere transgress those of another, a form of tyranny occurs: Our spheres become confused, our principles conflated. The task of a just society is not therefore to invent a uniform standard of distribution ("simple equality"), but to keep its heterogeneous spheres orderly and autonomous. In effect complex equality is premised on the domestic counterpart to the principle of nonintervention, placing a premium on self-determination in the spheres of social life.

Walzer's theory of justice is thus intended to correct not monopoly, but dominance. *Within* spheres, inequities may exist; injustice occurs only when the inequalities of one sphere translate into inequalities in another. Walzer is especially concerned with keeping money from interfering with the distribution of social goods; its appetite is voracious, and justice must be clear about what money can and cannot buy. Complex equality, then, produces a theory of "blocked exchanges," a series of barriers preventing money from affecting distributions in the spheres of political power, sex, divine grace, or kinship.[38] We have strong presumptions against nepotism, prostitution, simony, and spouses for purchase, and these presumptions reflect deeply shared beliefs about how money operates inappropriately.

Keeping money or other principles from transgressing their proper boundaries may seem to accord with the idea of human dignity and human rights, echoing the prohibition, found in Kantian or natural law theory, against instrumentalizing persons. But Walzer's account of justice owes less to a theory of human rights than to the way societies construct the meaning of (their) social goods. Reference to rights does "real work" in international disputes like war, Walzer notes, but in matters of domestic justice "to say of whatever we think people ought to have that they have a right to it is not to say very much." Rights "do not follow from our common humanity; they follow from shared conceptions of social goods; they are local and particular in character."[39] Indeed, for Walzer there is no family of humanity, if by *family* we mean a set of relationships that are constitutive of an individual's identity. Consequently, justice is relative to a society's goods, respecting rights (when appropriate) for "internal reasons." In domestic affairs, rights are not altogether jettisoned, but the duty to honor them is relative to certain spheres. Accordingly, there can be few transcultural standards for measuring one society against another, and those standards remain "thin," having bubbled up from their deeper ("thicker") meanings, which are a function of the specific causes and local contexts to which they pertain.[40] Emphasis falls on history and locale for ascertaining the concrete demands of social justice. So Walzer remarks: "A given society is just if its substantive life is lived in a way that is faithful to the shared understandings of its members."[41] Domestic justice is not a matter of principle, but of fidelity, of loyalty to local tradition and practice.

To ascertain which principles are to operate in which spheres, we must turn to our "shared understandings." Here Walzer is not referring merely to consensus or general agreement. Rather, he seeks to uncover "those deeper understandings of social goods which are not necessarily mirrored in the everyday practice of dominance and monopoly."[42] Accordingly, it may be more accurate to say for Walzer that he divines a collective *unconscious*, for he sets out to ascertain "those *deeper opinions* that are the reflections in individual minds, shaped also by individual thought, of the social meanings that constitute our common life."[43] In this way he is able to talk about a society of equals as "a practical possibility, *latent already* . . . in our shared understandings of social goods."[44] Consequently, Walzer insists, the fact that exemptions from the military service cannot be purchased in the United States reflects a "deep sense" that the duties of citizenship cannot be turned into a private transaction. Shared meanings are not obvious, and to find them we must have more than the results of an opinion poll. But they are so important that one use of political power is "to enforce the common understandings of what goods are and what they are for."[45] Such understandings call our attention to bonds that are unconsciously deep and constitutive, but not easily recognized.

Shared understandings not only authorize the principles internal to a sphere, *they also authorize the idea that our spheres should remain autonomous.* Walzer believes that his egalitarian vision is "hidden . . . in our concepts and categories," and adds that "our conceptions . . .

do tend steadily to proscribe the use of things for the purposes of domination."[46] So we have agreements *within* our various spheres concerning their principles of distribution and agreement *about* the fact that the spheres should remain separate. Walzer writes, "For us, and for the foreseeable future, [deeper] opinions make for autonomous distributions; and every form of dominance is therefore an act of disrespect."[47]

Walzer is well aware of dissent and disagreement in our culture, but his account of latency allows him to suggest that beneath our arguments a more basic unity is at work. In his book on war, for example, Walzer argues that disagreements between military realists and ethicists "are structured and organized by our underlying agreements, by the meanings we share."[48] Similarly, in *Spheres of Justice* Walzer holds to the idea that disagreements are nonetheless held together by an unconscious unity or common commitment, and that disagreement is a function of moral complexity. He writes, "A people's culture is always a joint, even if it isn't an entirely cooperative, production; and it is always a complex production."[49] Debates about welfare, for example, are, at the deepest level, interpretations of a basic social union.[50] Disagreements, then, are by no means evidence of disunity. Rather, Walzer adds, "when people disagree about the meaning of social goods, when understandings are controversial, then justice requires that the society be faithful to the disagreements, providing institutional channels for their expression, adjudicative mechanisms, and alternative distributions."[51] Dissent is a constitutive feature of our culture, a vital source of social criticism and renewal, and Walzer insists that we assign an important cultural role to dissonant voices.

Closely related, but by no means identical, to the idea of shared understandings is the value Walzer places on the good of community. Readers familiar with his work on war will recall that community is so important that he allows for the violation of basic moral principles to defend certain communities in a "supreme emergency."[52] Thus it was permissible, he argues, for British forces to violate the principle of noncombatant immunity by intentionally bombing German cities when the Allies had their backs to the wall during the early years of World War II. Nothing less than the future of civilized Europe was at stake, leaving the Allies to choose between the continuation of their common life and the rights of German civilians. Confronted with the dilemma of choosing between communal survival and individual rights, the British were justified in trading off the latter for the former. For Walzer, membership in a community is perhaps the greatest good, trumping rival goods in situations of extreme duress.[53]

Unfortunately, beyond these vague appeals to community Walzer fails to provide a clear conception of what a community is—a point to which I shall return. He is open to the charge, aptly expressed by Stephen Holmes, of invoking the idea of a "phantom community," an experience of solidarity the conditions of which are never defined.[54] At the very least, community for Walzer refers to a "bounded world within which distributions take place: a group of people committed to dividing, exchanging, and sharing social goods, first of all among themselves." One side of Walzer leads him to equate community with the nation-state; those who lack community are "stateless persons," at peril in a "condition of infinite danger."[55] But such states are not impersonal, legalistic associations; they are rather united by a social contract, which has almost salvific significance. Such a contract, Walzer remarks, is a "moral bond," connecting "the strong and the weak, the lucky and the unlucky, the rich and the poor, creating a union that transcends all differences of interest, drawing its strength from history, culture, religion, language and so on."[56] By restricting membership, states are able to produce "*communities of character,* historically stable, ongoing associations of men and women with some special commitment to one another and some special sense of their common life."[57] Communities establish boundaries between members and strangers, and no country can be loved that is not experienced in terms of some kind of kinship. Being a stranger, Walzer avows, is intolerable.[58]

Walzer's view of community, however vague, and his account of complex equality are directly related: Complex equality is a good not in and of itself, but for the sake of the social order. The autonomy of spheres "will spread the satisfaction of ruling more widely," generating mutual respect and shared self-respect.[59] In effect, the diversity of spheres paves the way for the experience of political diversity, the dispersal of sovereignty. By being neither masters nor slaves, citizens will be more motivated to participate in their own political self-determination.

Renewal, Purity, and Shalom

We have, then, three features of complex equality: shared meanings, community, and the duty to keep spheres distinct. The first two are prophetic, the third priestly. As I have suggested, Walzer's vision is formed by a profoundly Jewish appreciation for covenantal relations, shared history, and ancestral codes. These comprise a subtle set of religious attitudes, latent within his rendition of our shared meanings and social practices. Indeed, however odd such a reading of a political philosopher might seem, it renders intelligible some of Walzer's most distinctive claims.

Consider the prophetic strand: According to Walzer, meanings that emerge from the bonds of community provide resources for "connected criticism," a form of social critique that draws on an implied covenant. That covenant goes by the name of "community"; outside it, life is intolerable and genuine identity is impossible. In other words, Walzer's communitarian overtures can be read as blurring secular and religious discourse. Either *community* or *covenant* provides the metaphor for naming how citizens in our liberal culture are bound together by common projects and shared histories, through which they find meaning and identity.[60] It comes as no surprise, then, that the first good we find on the map of *Spheres of Justice* is that of membership. And membership is virtually impossible to sustain without shared rituals, codes, local heroes, and memories of sacrifice and travail. Indeed, for Walzer life-as-membership has almost redemptive implications.

Accordingly, prophetic social criticism must be viewed as contextual and intertextual, producing new wine from old wineskins. Prophets invoke the languages of their community—symbols, memories, heroes, moral codes, and ritual practices—to reawaken its members to their deeper values and commitments. Social criticism along these lines is possible because cultural languages create greater expectations than they can satisfy, leaving the disenfranchised with a set of unfulfilled promises *and* an idiom for expressing their dissatisfactions. Critics thus appeal to principles that are mocked more than mirrored in social life, contrasting the idealized picture of a community with its lived reality. Understood in this way, the task of social critics is to expose hypocrisy, and their criticism functions to redeem the community from within.[61] This task is but a version of prophetic discourse among the Israelites, for which Amos provides a clear illustration. For the prophets of the Hebrew Bible, social criticism pointed to unfulfilled dreams by recalling shared symbols and memories.

Yet, as we have seen, the shared understandings of our liberal culture not only operate within our separate spheres; they also authorize the commitment to *keep them separate.* This latter idea opens the door to Walzer's priestly strand, the desire to maintain clear boundaries between the spheres—or categories—of social life. As Mary Douglas notes in her anthropological study of Leviticus, this desire is essentially formed by religious rather than moral categories: Purity and danger have priority over categories of right and wrong. Leviticus, a text of the Israelite priesthood, is concerned with classifying clean and unclean animals for consumption. It forbids contact with animals that do not conform fully to their class (e.g., pigs and camels, which are not ruminants like other livestock). Those who make contact with such animals are disqualified from entering the Temple, the site of priestly worship and authority. Leviticus, like *Spheres of Justice*, must be read principally as a treatise against abominations. Each work is premised on a clear system of classification: The first pertains to a world that is made; the second to a world that a particular community has made. Both works respectively seek to establish order in the natural and social worlds inhabited by members of a particular group.

Viewing Walzer's work through a religious and anthropological lens allows us to see that domination is not merely a moral transgression in his thought; it is more fundamentally a form of pollution, the breakdown of an ordered social universe. The Romantic concern for the incomparable becomes, in Walzer's account, a prohibition against hybrids. One of the chief tasks of justice is to maintain an ordered quality to social life, preventing a monster like "desert/need" from becoming a distributive principle. In institutions where salaries are based on merit, we are impatient with colleagues who engage in special pleading about their financial needs just before the annual raise is determined. We rightly fear that the procedures for determining raises will be polluted by foreign principles. Similarly, we ought to feel uneasy about colleges or universities that link faculty salaries to the ability of faculty members to recruit and retain students. The obvious danger is that grading procedures will involve a conflict of interest, thereby generating disincentives to fail students.[62] Accordingly, for Walzer the heterogeneous spheres of justice must remain differentiated in order for society to remain whole.

This is but another way of saying that Walzer's justice works in the service of holiness, which, as Douglas points out, "is exemplified by completeness." Holiness is a matter of "keeping distinct the categories of creation," those spheres of life in which God's protective activity wards off the powers of chaos and death.[63] In a passage that could very well have been lifted directly from Walzer's argument, Douglas observes about the taboos of Leviticus that "morality does not conflict with holiness, but holiness is more a matter of separating that which should be separated than of protecting the rights of husbands and brothers."[64] Holiness does not require simply or chiefly an otherworldly gaze; rather, it is radically this-worldly, a form of hygiene. It involves "correct definition, discrimination and order," producing overall social health.[65] It functions in part to prevent the creation of monstrous doubles, those mongrels that blur one category with another.

It would be a mistake, then, to interpret *Spheres of Justice* as (only) secular political philosophy, and perhaps for this reason it has confounded its secular interpreters.[66] For the laws on which it relies have less to do with rational philosophy than with a historically contingent social order, whose prohibitions have parallels with ritual taboos. *Spheres of Justice* constitutes a vision of political purity, deeply informed by a religious imagination. Its goal is to keep the lines of our social life clearly drawn, hoping to prevent not only tyranny, but defilement. Walzer would be able to say quite literally that justice is concerned with the health of the political body.

In such a (social) universe, wrongful acts are chiefly the result not of intentional malice, but of wrongful contact. Morally corrupt deeds are tangible, almost physical. When political influence or academic talent is bought, Walzer would say, the sphere of power or knowledge has been corrupted, its integrity attenuated, by the good of money. Pollutions are objective evils and could very well be carried out with the best intentions. The best analogue for evil, then, is not secrecy or duplicity—a lack of integrity or strength of character—but illness, the breakdown of a healthy body. For Walzer social injustice has less to do with the ordering of our wills than with whether our contacts threaten to contaminate, thereby opening the door to chaos.[67] In Walzer's hands, the Romantic concern for holism becomes *shalom*, an orderly life of health, friendship, fidelity, and blessedness.

When understood in this way, Walzer's overtures to liberalism, like those he makes to the good of communal membership, are metaphorically ambivalent, blurring secular and religious discourse. At one level liberalism represents the "art of separation," the effort to create walls between various institutions of public life. The wall between church and state creates the sphere of religious liberty; similarly, the wall between state and university creates academic freedom. In both instances the lines of liberalism produce new forms of liberty. Yet at another level such walls should be understood in terms of order and purity. When seen in (latent) levitical terms, the walls of modern life set the boundaries of transgression, of trespass. To cross them, then, is to jeopardize not only liberty, but the health and history of the body politic.

Map Is Not Territory

As Romanticism's Jewish attaché, Walzer wears many hats: diviner, anthropologist, cartographer, storyteller, biblical exegete, prophet, and priest. He is less of a traditional political philosopher than a strong poet of political life, invoking images, metaphors, and histories to articulate his vision of our latent democratic socialism.[68] And as a strong poet, he provides an interpretive inventory that is, to say the least, bewildering in scope. But Walzer's argument has authority by virtue of the power of his writing, and we should not overlook the fact that he is first and foremost an author, sovereign over the terrain

he describes. It is, of course, Walzer's map we are reading, not necessarily our own, and his map is premised on his distinctive representations, judgments, and interpretive vantage point.[69] For, however
much he presumes to be "on the ground," he is nonetheless hovering
above the territory in order to map its contours.

Thus it is salutary to recall the adage made famous by Jonathan Z.
Smith: "Map is not territory."[70] Smith means that maps *themselves*
are particular constructions whose component parts are by no means
"simply out there." This is especially true, in Smith's mind, when it
comes to religious studies. Scholars of religion, he insists, must remember that "there is [*sic*] no data for religion. Religion is solely the
creation of the scholar's study."[71] As a scholar focuses on the various
practices of a culture, she works with a filtering process, sifting out
what counts as "religious" as opposed to what counts as "leisure" or
"exchange." *Religion* names a phenomenon that we cut out or isolate
from an array of data, like the butterfly in the Rorschach test or the
flying fish in the Escher drawing. It is by no means obvious in many
cultures that various domains of life can be cordoned off and called
"religious practice" as opposed to, say, "eating" or "politics."

In effect Smith is claiming that, for the Romantic at least, there is
no classical mimesis, wherein nature/territory precedes art/map. He
is interested in awakening scholars of religion to a higher level of self-
reflection about the fact that they interpret, but his point is applicable
to Walzer as well. We "discover" various features of a society with
the aid of constructs, which enable us to classify certain modes of behavior as, for instance, "ritual," or, in Walzer's case, "welfare" and "education." Walzer speaks as if these categories present themselves intuitively, absent any interpretive judgments, preunderstandings, or
filtering systems.

Yet Walzer's classification system is conditioned by quite contingent philosophical and political sympathies, and for those with divergent sympathies (or none at all), what is included and excluded on
his map is by no means obvious. Consider what is missing: Why is
education a sphere unto itself, while medicine is part of the sphere of
security and welfare? Why does he exclude one of our most hotly
pursued goods, information? (Journalists and media specialists who
turn to *Spheres of Justice* wondering whether information should be
subject to the market or regulated by political power will be disap-
pointed.)[72] Why is cultural expression not considered a good or a
sphere of goods? Is its absence from Walzer's map meant to suggest
that it is simply a good that money can buy? How then are we to
consider the proper content and allocation of cultural values in our
schools and publicly supported museums?

A further complication derives from the role of democratic social-

117

ism in Walzer's account. Why does our culture resist such a program, especially if its meanings are latent? Perhaps, Walzer's critic might argue, the fact that this agenda is repressed is *itself* a datum for political philosophy to consider. If shared understandings provide our source for social philosophy, the future of democratic socialism in the United States does not look hopeful. Democratic socialism may be more map than territory, constituting *the* place in Walzer's social philosophy where the Romantic impulse to express a creative vision goes beyond the confines of the reproductive imagination.

These observations about Walzer's topography boil down to one initial, critical point: In order for Walzer's map to be compelling, we must be able to locate ourselves on it. Otherwise his interpretations will not ring true, and his invocation of the word *we* will sound strained. But in several key areas I think that we are not reflected in his interpretations, that they simplify our complex, pluralistic lives. And in several other areas we have good reasons to wish not to be reflected on his map, if inclusion means that his sympathies are latent in our self-understandings. Four sets of issues come to mind.

One cluster of problems surrounds the *problem of contested meanings,* the idea that there are conflicting opinions about what goods mean and how they are to be allocated *within specific spheres.* Those who support public funding of abortion, for example, see abortion according to the principle of need, whereas opponents would leave abortions to those who can afford them, according to the principle of free exchange. How are we to handle deeply divided opinions about goods and exchanges in specific spheres?[73]

About this question Walzer is equivocal. On the one hand he tells us that justice requires us to be faithful to our disagreements and that we must provide institutional channels for their expression.[74] Yet on the other hand he tells us that one of the proper uses of political power is "to enforce the common understandings of what goods are and what they are for."[75] But this second claim hardly makes sense in light of the first. How can we be faithful to both our agreements and our disagreements, especially when the power of the state can be invoked to discourage the latter? If the state decides against the public funding of abortion, is it obligated to censor contrary opinions in order to enforce common understandings? If it does, then it is being unfaithful to disagreements. If it does not, then it is failing to abide by Walzer's account of one proper exercise of political power.

This practical problem aside, another question is analytical: If meanings are contested, in what sense are they shared? In his book on war Walzer claims that disagreements are structured by underlying agreements, by meanings we share.[76] One way to read him, then, is to infer the Davidsonian point about conceptual schemes, namely, that if our worlds were incommensurable then we could not even understand each other. If, by Davidson's argument, I say "Equity requires impartiality" and you hear "Basketball is a fine sport," then we do not have enough in common even to disagree about what equity requires. If, trying to clarify matters, I say "Yes, basketball is a fine sport" and you hear "Please make the pasta," then we lack what it takes to disagree about the merits of basketball (and, presumably, how to prepare fettuccine).[77] Relying on these Davidsonian premises, Walzer can say that highly polarized debates, like those about abortion in the United States, are held together by shared understandings. Davidson's treatment of incommensurability means that disagreement and disunity are by no means the same.

But this response to the problem of contested meanings will not get us very far. It is one thing to say that we speak the same language and quite another to say that we share some significant goods and values, that moral unity exists beneath heated cultural debates. The only morally relevant matter "shared" in arguments about abortion, to take an obvious example, is the right to free speech, which has little to do with adjudicating between those who defend the legality of abortion and those who wish to extinguish it. To suggest that a moral bond lies beneath the dogmatic impasse of the abortion debate is, to say the least, counterintuitive.

Another way that Walzer might approach shared meanings and their contestation is to have us consider psychological theories about latency. Shared meanings can be contested, Walzer might say, given the tension between what we think we believe and what we authentically, deeply, and unknowingly believe. Psychoanalysis provides a way to understand why some meanings are acknowledged and others are submerged, why some memories remain latent: They have been forgotten or repressed, but they have not disappeared entirely from the deep store of the unconscious. On this basis Walzer can say that shared meanings are contested because we are unclear about what we really view as good. The task of the social critic is thus to function therapeutically, releasing what we otherwise leave to latency or amnesia. Once we are clear about what our real meanings are, disputes will diminish.

Yet the appeal to latent values raises an enormously difficult psychological question for Walzer: How can we be faithful to what is unconscious? To ask us to trust meanings of which we are only dimly aware is to request the herculean. At the very least, Walzer asks us to anchor much of our social philosophy to the idea that our (apparent) shared understandings are dubious. The psychological strain of committing ourselves to a social vision premised on self-doubt would be more than a little demanding.

Assuming for the sake of argument that latent meanings are as reliable as Walzer suggests, it would seem appropriate to explain why certain images or memories have been submerged. Perhaps meanings are repressed because they are distasteful, repulsive, or embarrassing. But Walzer would have us overlook ethical questions surrounding the processes by which (latent) shared meanings have been secured. His historicism treats historical processes as benign, or at least as morally neutral. We are to remain faithful to latent meanings, which derive from the accumulated customs of historical experience. What if those customs are the products of pernicious forces and malevolent interests?

The point of this question is to suggest that Walzer provides no resources for addressing *dangerous memories,* stories about the loss of life and value for those whose customs did not find a place in history. For example, the fact that patriarchy has secured a place in the kinship system, Walzer concedes, means that distributions within the family will place special burdens on women. Yet Walzer provides no way to determine whether patriarchy has secured its privileges over the course of history in morally problematic ways. For members of a historically conscious, liberal society, sensitive to the experiences of marginal voices and cultures, Walzer's map seems two-dimensional, its distributive principles frozen in the present. It remains silent about the rivers of history—and the savagery of their currents—that have helped create our present social landscape.

Beyond these difficulties surrounding contested voices and shared meanings, a second cluster of problems concerns the *tension between what shared meanings might require and what it takes to sustain a community.* Readers familiar with *Habits of the Heart* know all too well that citizens in the United States have a deep, shared sense of individualism, which can be corrosive of communal ties. But Walzer's way of discussing spheres often seems ignorant of this tension.

Walzer's references to religion in America illustrate the problem. Although he obliquely acknowledges religion's sociological value, he is fond of saying that in liberal cultures all believers are "equally free to seek their own salvation."[78] In the United States, the disestablishment clause symbolizes the shared understanding about the proper relation between church and state. In effect, the wall creates the sphere of religious liberty, in which the good of grace is distributed according to the principle of freedom. Religion is thus a matter of private conscience, entirely immune from the "coercive power of political and ecclesiastical officials."[79] Grace is not a matter of communal provision or merit; it is an entirely private affair, a matter of individual choice.[80]

Walzer is surely correct in his account of religious freedom. But this shared understanding hardly coheres with the value he wishes to place on *community*. It seems doubtful that an individualistic approach to religious freedom can sit well with the importance of social solidarity. The former is avowedly private and discretionary; the latter enjoins communion and common beliefs. So long as religious freedom and diversity remain deeply shared values—*individualistic values*—it seems hard to imagine how we could stand together beneath the communitarian umbrella.

Religion is only one of the values having sociological importance that we esteem in highly individualistic terms. But it illustrates this second problem: Our shared understandings do not necessarily produce widespread covenantal unity. *In the United States we must face the paradox that appeals to shared understandings often lead toward atomism rather than community.*[81]

Third, a tension exists between *shared meanings and the requirement to keep spheres autonomous*. Walzer seems confident that we agree about those things money cannot buy, and we have a strong, if latent, aversion to domination in general. Yet what does he make of the idea that, as a matter of fact, our culture has a rather permissive attitude about the role of money in several spheres? For example, despite his claim that money cannot purchase sex, in fact prostitution is legal in Nevada. And, although money cannot purchase political power in any simple sense, it is still essential to mounting a political campaign. We tolerate the fact that few, if any, of our representatives are poor, and we generally find incredible the idea that presidential candidates will embark on fiscally austere political campaigns.

Yet this third problem goes beyond our attitudes about the power and influence of money. An additional difficulty is that Americans seem not to agree about the autonomy of spheres in several areas of social life. The experience of Charles E. Curran, former professor of moral theology at the Catholic University of America (CUA), is a case in point. In 1986 the Vatican began its attempt to remove Curran from the Department of Theology at CUA after a lengthy investigation into his positions on sexual ethics, divorce, and medical ethics. The inquiry concluded that his views were contrary to the official, noninfallible teaching of the church, and that he was "neither suitable nor eligible to exercise the function of Professor of Catholic Theology."[82] After a lengthy set of proceedings involving CUA's chancellor, an ad hoc faculty committee, the board of trustees, and Curran, in 1988 CUA insisted that Curran sign a statement that the Vatican's declaration was binding on him and that he could not teach theology at CUA. Curran refused to sign the statement and sued the university, arguing that the Vatican's investigation and CUA's subsequent action violated his academic freedom. In effect, he was arguing that matters pertinent to the sphere of grace were allowed to dominate in the

121

sphere of higher education, that the freedom of intellectual inquiry was being corrupted by this confusion of categories. Citing Walzer in support of his argument would seem to be easy. For Walzer, the sphere of higher education is protected against political or ecclesiastical coercion. Accordingly, walls between the state, the church, and the university leave "professors as free to profess as believers are to believe." In this way "students and professors . . . are, in principle at least, absolutely free in the sphere of knowledge."[83]

Yet the court decided against Curran. For all practical purposes, it concluded, a university's freedom of religious identity and self-definition, even with dogmatic strictures, trumps the good of academic freedom. Walzer offers little to help us with this case, or to justify any critique of the court's decision. The goods of each sphere—religion and higher education—are to be distributed, according to Walzer, on the basis of freedom. But when the principle of freedom in one sphere clashes with that in another, the conflict is impossible to adjudicate. Religious colleges and universities are precisely the kind of institution in which such conflicts regularly occur, though less dramatically than in Curran's case. In the experience of many educators today, it is counterintuitive to suggest that we have settled convictions about the autonomy of spheres.[84]

The Curran affair suggests a final problem for Walzer: His argument is confounded by the *problem of blurred spheres*. What do we make of instances when a boundary between spheres is not clear?

On this issue Walzer is again equivocal, suggesting that we should tolerate some instances in which spheres overlap. On the one hand, as I have indicated, Walzer expresses the priestly art of separation, keeping our spheres clear and distinct. Yet even an uncontroversial account of our social lives must include many examples in which spheres rightly overlap.

Education is one of those spheres, although Walzer's account makes it seem remarkably uncomplicated. For Walzer, this sphere involves allocating the goods of "teaching positions, student places, authority in the schools, grades and promotions, different sorts and levels of knowledge."[85] But perhaps more important, Walzer understands the role of schooling largely in political terms, so that "children learn to be citizens first—workers, managers, merchants, and professionals only afterward." Seen in this way, the primary role of education is to provide "the common currency of political and social life."[86] Within the context of democratic politics, the effects of education are as follows: "Everyone is taught the basic knowledge necessary for an active citizenship, and the great majority of students learn it."[87] Basic education is distinct from specialized schooling; the latter distributes ideas on the assumption that elementary skills are already in place.

With this account in mind, consider the enrollment of Michael at the local private elementary school. Michael suffers from a rare condition in which his body metabolizes certain amino acids into toxins. If undetected at an early stage, his condition will lead to neural degeneration, eventual mental retardation, and an early death. But Michael was diagnosed at birth and was given a special diet, preventing him from ingesting amino acids that resist normal metabolization. Accommodating his dietary and other needs generates special burdens for the school's staff, requiring them sometimes to overlook the less pressing but no less real needs of other children. Also, his diet requires an individual menu, for which the school cannot receive subvention from the state's food reimbursement program. Obviously the justice or injustice of Michael's special treatment must blur the goods peculiar to early childhood education and medical provision: learning, health, and self-image. Yet when we look at Walzer's map, such "blurring" is difficult to locate and assess. It is especially difficult to determine which distributive principles are to operate when settling problems at the margins.

While we might consider Michael's condition as exceptional, it is meant to highlight the fact that early childhood education distributes multiple goods: health, knowledge, and self-respect. Walzer discusses these goods in relation to the spheres of, respectively, welfare, education, and recognition. Perhaps we can separate these spheres, at least in theory. But as a practical matter it is difficult to imagine how we can block the exchange of goods associated with each of these spheres. In the education of children we allocate more than the essentials of knowledge, and no school today would be considered complete without mechanisms for empowering children to improve complex physical and interpersonal (as well as cognitive) skills. The case of education illustrates that our goods are too variable, our lives too multifaceted, for Walzer's map. When mapping a culture of pluralism, levitical impulses can tend to oversimplify.

On the other hand, Walzer tolerates some confusion of spheres, premised on the idea that spheres are only *relatively* autonomous.[88] But on this matter Walzer's own illustrative cases are not without problems. Consider again his views of women's roles in the family and in society at large. He has little to say about sexism in the family unit, or how patriarchy determines the allocation of labor and esteem at home. Indeed, his relativistic notion of justice requires him to accept the customary inequalities of domestic life, however oppressive for women. At the very most, he is able to say that the value of community has priority over shared meanings when these conflict in a family's experience: "Only when familial distributions undercut the promises of communal membership and welfare are interventions

123

required, as in the cases of neglected children, say, or of battered wives."[89] When such abuses occur, the value of community overrides the shared meanings of patriarchy, allowing for interventions to protect the innocent.

But short of such safeguards against being beaten or raped, women can enjoy few protections against inequitable treatment in the household.[90] In fact Walzer is less concerned with sexism in the family than with whether it extends into other social spheres. If women are barred from competition in business or schools, patriarchy has gone too far. Writing about women's liberation in China, Walzer remarks, "If women are to take the exams, then they must be allowed to prepare for them; they must be admitted to the schools, freed from concubinage, arranged marriages, foot binding, and so on. The family itself must be reformed so that its power no longer reaches into the sphere of office."[91]

Feminists might take solace in this suggestion. Walzer is aware that unless the distribution of work at home is reorganized, working women will be faced with double jeopardy: a job in the workforce and responsibility for most domestic chores. But what does Walzer's comment say about the autonomy of the domestic sphere? Reforming the family given the principles and exigencies of office would seem to be precisely the kind of tyranny (or defilement) against which he argues. In order to be consistent, we should treat sexism like money: restrict its power by confining it to its appropriate domain. But in the case of kinship Walzer suggests that we transform the family, rather than restrict its internal ethic. In some instances, blurring spheres may not be all that abominable if *relative* autonomy between them is the result.[92] Yet by the conclusion of *Spheres of Justice* it is by no means clear when the spheres of public life may be relatively autonomous and when they must be absolutely so. In places like the family, Walzer's casuistry seems lax, at least according to a strict construction of the priestly imperative to keep our spheres distinct.

Casuistry and Strong Poetry

Walzer's desire to use taxonomies, historical precedents, and cultural vocabularies is by no means unimportant for practical reasoning. As a casuist of political life, he is a strong poet par excellence, providing a countermethod to the more rationalistic tendencies of the Enlightenment. His goal is not to engage in lengthy methodological rebuttals of Enlightenment philosophy, but to outflank the efforts of philosophers like Rawls by proceeding directly into an alternative approach. Strong poets like Walzer are less concerned with extended methodological preambles than with articulating a vision that persuades by virtue of its interpretive perspicuity.

In this respect Walzer recalls several features of the Romantic rebellion against the Enlightenment's trust in detached rationality. Nevertheless, viewing him as a Romantic does not sufficiently reveal the religious dimensions of his social vision. Romanticism is customarily viewed as the attempt to repoeticize religion, to recast traditional religious symbols in secular terms.[93] In Walzer's case this relation has reversed itself: His account of justice is a religious poeticization of Romanticism, taking the Romantics' emphasis on experience and uniqueness, respectively, in covenantal and priestly directions. We cannot fully comprehend *Spheres of Justice* without developing a dual literacy, one that enables us to decode both the secular and religious resonances of Walzer's political map. Perhaps for this reason it seems futile to expect his account to abide by the expectations of contemporary philosophy, given the latter's propensity for nonrelative, ahistorical, secular principles.[94]

Yet even apart from such expectations, too many questions surround Walzer's vision of complex equality to render it workable as a social philosophy. To be sure, fidelity to our customs and the desire to end domination are no small virtues. But the diversity within our covenants and the untidiness of our social universe militate against his attempt to map our political life. In the final analysis, Walzer's complex equality is not complex enough.

Walzer's most acute problem is that in important areas—women in the family, for example—he fails to consider ethical questions about the force of history in shaping our shared understandings and self-interpretations. Histories are bearers of ideology, carrying particular interests and local tyrannies. A genuinely reflexive casuistry, then, must be informed not only by strong poetry, history, and an appreciation for interpretation, but also by a hermeneutics of suspicion. In this way we might be able to identify where morally questionable ideas of the past have sequestered themselves beneath the obvious meanings and cultural vocabularies that shape our self-interpretations. These are important matters for casuistry, given its (valuable) reliance on customs, conventions, and historical paradigms. The contribution of history to our present customs is not always or obviously benign, and to trust our conventions uncritically opens casuistry to the charge of moral innocence and naïveté. Our moral vocabularies are sometimes (perhaps often) congenital with a morally dubious history: a past of racial, sexual, and/or economic oppression. Casuistry that draws on the deposit of history, in other words, must be opened to ideological analysis and critique. As we now turn to casuistry and the body, I will attempt to show how such a reflexive analysis might be carried out.

125

PART THREE

Casuistry and the Body

CHAPTER FIVE

Popular Catholicism, *Humanae vitae,* and Ideology in Casuistry

Ethics and Cultural Criticism

History in casuistry is often used to suggest that ideas parading themselves as "natural" are in fact cultural, a product of what modern intellectuals often call "human constructs." Intellectuals like Walzer want to historicize moral values that seem to represent timeless absolutes, essential properties that are etched into "the way things are." Typically historicists hold, for example, that prohibitions against premarital sex have less to do with the "essence of human sexuality" than with culturally bound ideas about female honor and its connections with property rights. As our notions of female honor and women-as-property have changed, so too has the morality by which we often judge intercourse before marriage. What secularists did to religion in the late nineteenth century, historicists like Walzer wish to do in the late twentieth century: demystify our absolutes by showing how they vary across cultures or change over time. The point of identifying historical and cultural differences is to suggest that without such knowledge we would tend to regard our own values as timeless, essential, and/or universal—as good for everyone. For historicists, the rhetoric of "the natural" is often a ruse, concealing special interests, local knowledge, or the cabals of power in social institutions.

In this chapter I want to focus more carefully on the kinds of issues that Walzer calls to our attention, especially where he invites us to relativize those appeals to timeless essences in our practical affairs. In particular, I want to discuss an example of casuistry in which the "law of nature" represents a set of culturally determined attitudes, the result of ideological interests. Yet I want to take matters one step further than Walzer's historicism by showing how the categories of "nature" and "culture" *themselves* constitute a set of human constructs, a classification system for ordering the world of gender, procreation, and sexual morality. I know of no better place to study such a taxonomy than *Humanae vitae,* Pope Paul VI's notorious encyclical about parenthood, sexuality, and the regulation of birth.

The analysis that I wish to carry out here owes much to recent developments in literary theory, informed by deconstruction and psychoanalysis.[2] The idea is to call attention to the presence of a "subtext," a voice murmuring beneath the surface of an argument, discernible at symptomatic points of ambiguity, evasion, or overemphasis. A psychoanalytical approach to interpretation suggests that there is an "unconscious" of an argument or cultural work. Analyses of subtexts seek to uncover what is not explicitly said, given the conviction that what a cultural document represses may be as important as what it articulates, that what seems absent or marginal may provide a clue to the meaning of a work in its entirety. Hence the goal: To uncover the nexus between discourse and ideology, the way in which a work covertly expresses its own form of desire as it recommends a vision of social relations. In this view a cultural document is not only—or even primarily—a "text," with a literate "reader" at its behest. It is rather a concrete performance, a way of pleading, persuading, inciting, and exciting an audience, often with codes that are deeply hidden beneath the surface of a document's explicit message.

Within the guild of religious and philosophical ethics today, viewing cultural works in this way is rare; more articulate exponents are found in English and comparative literature departments. This is because ethics is typically conceived in terms of wrestling with arguments of one kind or another. Ethics today largely resembles what New Criticism represents in literary theory: the study of great writers and the verities (or questions) they have bequeathed for intellectual commentary and refinement. New Critics see in Marcel Proust a great writer of memory, image, association, and time, in Mark Twain a master of social irony and humanism; ethicists see in Aquinas an attempt to join theological and philosophical sources, in Mill a classic rendition of utilitarianism. Arguments (and authors) are often read in a cultural and historical vacuum, abstracted from the purposes and social relations in which they were originally embedded. In ethics, individuals who have been initiated into the academic guild are bestowed a kind of sixth sense, enabling them to carry out careful dissections of arguments and to analyze the great works that constitute the Western philosophical and theological tradition.

I confess to finding this attitude toward ethics attractive, having been trained to work in portions of the Plato through post-Nietzschean canon. But it nonetheless threatens to exempt ethical commentary from a wide gamut of cultural materials and social processes. I have already suggested the usefulness of a broader angle of vision for casuistry in my discussion of Walzer; in this chapter and in chapter 7 I want to gesture in my own way toward a casuistry that is informed by cultural theory and ideological analysis. Let us turn, then, to *Humanae vitae*.

Intrinsic and Extrinsic Arguments

When first released in 1968, *Humanae vitae* was a lightning rod for controversy in American Catholicism, generating widespread, open dissent among Catholics about the pope's interpretation of the natural law. In the United States that interpretation was found wanting, leading a vast majority of Catholics to ignore Paul VI's teaching.[3] On a more abstract plane, the encyclical raised doubts about the authority of noninfallible papal teaching, a subject of prolific commentary by Catholic theologians in Western Europe and North America.[4]

As if to prevent the document from retiring into permanent desuetude, Vatican officials have aroused concern once again, this time for those teaching in Catholic institutions of higher learning. A Vatican directive, issued in March 1989, requires scholars in Catholic colleges and universities to make a profession of faith, which includes the testimony, "I . . . firmly accept and hold each and every thing that is proposed by [the Church] definitively with regard to teaching concerning faith and morals."[5] Many have wondered about the kind of teaching to which the profession pertains. Attempting to clarify the directive on Vatican radio, Umberto Betti, consulter to the Holy Office, cited *Humanae vitae* as an example of the kind of teaching to which the profession refers.[6]

Humanae vitae is a clear example of casuistry about sex and procreation. Its main questions turn on the purposes of intercourse and, in particular, whether it is morally permissible to engage in sex without the intention to procreate. Given the natural connection between the generation of human life and coitus, do we act contrary to the designs of nature by engaging in sex for nonprocreative purposes? May married couples have intercourse in order to quench their desires or express their affections for each other without intending to procreate as well? If so, why? Which methods are acceptable? What kinds of justifications and limitations are appropriate to nonprocreative sex?

In response to these questions, Paul VI develops a highly qualified set of permissions regarding nonprocreative intercourse. His main argument permits "natural" methods and prohibits "artificial" methods of engaging in nonprocreative sex. The argument stands on two pillars. The first pillar supports a case for the *intrinsic* immorality of artificial contraception; the second makes an *extrinsic* appeal, based on the harmful effects of contraceptive practice.[7]

The first pillar attempts to defend the idea that artificial contraception is inherently immoral, regardless of the circumstances. It is premised on a specific interpretation of the natural law, which, Paul VI remarks, requires that "each and every marriage act must remain open to the transmission of life" (par. 11). Artificial contraception is wrong because "the conjugal act ... is deliberately made infecund and so is intrinsically dishonest (*intrinsece inhonestum*)" (par. 14). Accordingly, "natural" birth control, abstaining from intercourse during fertile periods, is the only morally acceptable way to regulate birth.[8]

The second pillar is developed in an argumentative digression and has gone virtually unnoticed in more than two decades of prolific commentary. This part of Paul VI's argument alludes to the harmful consequences of using artificial contraceptives and to the beneficial consequences of carrying out "ascetical practices" of "periodic continence." Near the conclusion of the encyclical, Paul VI asks us to consider "how wide and easy a road would thus be opened up towards conjugal infidelity and the general lowering of morality" where artificial contraception is permitted (par. 17). Those who are weak, he adds, must not be offered some easy means of eluding the dictates of the moral law. The practice of natural forms of birth control, in contrast, bestows "upon family life fruits of serenity and peace." Ascetical practice "favors attention for one's partner, helps both parties to drive out selfishness, the enemy of true love; and deepens their sense of responsibility." Paul VI adds, "This discipline which is proper to the purity of married couples, far from harming conjugal love, rather confers on it a higher human value" (par. 21).

By this latter account, we can look to empirical evidence to support judgments derived from the first pillar. The law of nature, Paul VI suggests, reveals its truth in more than one way, reinforcing from different perspectives the strength of his ban. Accordingly, appeals to ethical principles or cultural consequences lead to the same conclusion: Artificial contraception finds no ethical sanction. In appealing to cultural evidence, moreover, the encyclical voices a concern not only about individual morality, but also about the ethos of a sexually active culture. A contraceptive culture can all too easily promote sexual intercourse as "selfish enjoyment," leading us to overlook the "insurmountable limits to the possibility of our domination over the body and its functions"—limits that are defined by "the integrity of the human organism and its functions" (par. 17).

Herein lie the realist, nonutopian aspects of Paul VI's argument. According to *Humanae vitae*, a commitment to moral principle produces better outcomes than do rival ethical approaches. In effect, Paul VI seeks to join the right with the good, hoping to protect his argument against the charge that a commitment to a principled morality is overly taxing or idealistic, requiring too much of modern married couples. Rather, says Paul VI, those who practice natural methods of birth control will find that their lives are improved. Easy, artificial methods contribute to a lowering of morality and, in turn, a disrespect for the marriage partner. Even those motivated by self-interest, then, can find good reasons for refusing artificial contraception.[9]

In scholarly treatments of this encyclical, three criticisms have set the agenda for Catholic liberals, providing the conventional wisdom about the untenability of *Humanae vitae:* the logical critique, the physicalist critique, and the structural critique. The logical critique argues that Paul VI's several statements about the meaning of the conjugal act are incoherent, positing contradictory facts about the relation between intercourse and procreation. Because these facts are axiomatic to Paul VI's permission of only natural forms of birth control, his contradictory statements undermine the encyclical's argument from within. The physicalist critique argues that the "law of nature" to which the document tirelessly refers is only nature as physical matter, not "human nature" as rational and responsible. By appealing to such a highly reductive account of nature, Paul VI departs from a more holistic account of "the natural" as understood by Catholics throughout the past several centuries. A more personalistic and less physicalistic understanding of human nature would lead to different criteria for assessing contraceptive sexual intercourse, criteria that would include reference to parental responsibilities and personal goods as part of a fully human act. The structural critique examines the relationship between the intrinsic and extrinsic arguments and claims that, even if the intrinsic argument is valid, Paul VI's two pillars cannot support each other.

Each of these criticisms argues for greater freedom in nonprocreative sexuality. In my judgment, they are all unimpeachable. Together they show, as we shall see, that Paul VI's argument is both structurally flawed and incongruous with the Catholic tradition's view of natural law morality. But it is puzzling that two decades after *Humanae vitae* criticisms of Paul VI's encyclical have scarcely won the day. Instead, they have been interpreted as subversive, treacherous, petulant, and unfaithful to the ways of old.[10] To Catholic conservatives at least, *Humanae vitae* retains its grip. Could the encyclical be affirming something else that previous criticisms have missed?

The rest of this chapter is devoted to answering this question in the affirmative. However dubious the casuistry of *Humanae vitae* may be, its cultural appeal seems secure for a considerable segment of the Catholic right. That appeal lies in large part, I hope to show, in Paul VI's ideology of gender relations, especially his idiom about maleness and femaleness in *Humanae vitae*. Indeed, the encyclical has retained its power by expressing the phallocentric notion that the male is the source of freedom and action, in contrast to the female, whose connection with uncontrollable natural processes disenfranchises her from cultural agency. The appeal of such ideas can be discerned once we turn to popular literature of Catholic conservatism. There we will discover the "traditioning" of Paul VI's casuistry, especially where his ideas are taken up and elaborated in recent discussions of gender roles in a culture undergoing massive socioeconomic transformations.

In order to make this point, I will begin by retracing more thoroughly the logical, physicalist, and structural criticisms. All of these analyses approach the casuistry of *Humanae vitae* as if it resembled what Kuhn calls "normal science": Both normal science and casuistry use relatively stable conventions and paradigms—products of history—to solve puzzles or practical problems.[11] Essentially Catholic liberals argue that Paul VI uses deficient logical reasoning and an inadequate paradigm of natural law morality. But such prior analyses of the encyclical, I wish to show, do not go far enough in uncovering what is at work in Paul VI's argument. Specifically, they fail to discover the patriarchal dimensions of *Humanae vitae,* its ideology of gender relations. In contrast to prior treatments of the encyclical, I want to examine ways in which casuistry, by drawing on the products of history, can enshrine ideological interests—in this case, patriarchal interests. One of the tasks we shall embark on, then, is to open casuistry to ideological analysis and prophetic criticism. I will do so by attending less to the logical form and substance of the encyclical than to its subtext, hidden deep beneath the surface of its argument. In this way we will not only discover why *Humanae vitae* retains its cultural appeal. We will also learn that, despite various problems in the document, the intrinsic and extrinsic arguments in fact support each other—ideologically and subtextually—when sewn together by the thread of patriarchy.

Liberal Criticisms

THE LOGICAL CRITIQUE

The logical critique argues that Paul VI contradicts himself when citing two sets of facts to support his condemnation of artificial contraception. On the one hand, *Humanae vitae* rests on the notion that every conjugal act has an aptitude for procreation. According to Paul VI, Catholic teaching about birth control is premised on "*the inseparable connection,* willed by God and unable to be broken by man on his own initiative, between the two meanings of the conjugal act: the unitive meaning and the procreative meaning" (par. 12, emphasis mine). Intercourse unites husband and wife and "capacitates them for the generation of new lives" (par. 12). Any attempt to separate these two meanings contradicts the essence of intercourse, grounded in the facts of nature. We have only limited dominion over our bodies in general and over our "generative faculties as such, because of their intrinsic ordination towards raising up life, of which God is the principle" (par. 13). Because of these natural ordinations, Paul VI concludes, "each and every marriage act must remain open to the transmission of life" (par. 11).

On the other hand, *Humanae vitae* tells us that "not every conjugal act is followed by a new life. God has wisely disposed natural laws and rhythms of fecundity which, of themselves, cause a separation in the succession of births" (par. 11). In other words, not every act of intercourse, of natural necessity, leads to procreation. Hence, Paul VI argues, only natural forms of birth control—refraining from intercourse during fertile periods—are morally permissible, since they respect the "natural rhythms immanent in the generative functions" (par. 16). The regulation of birth is permissible, then, only by means of abstinence—a "grace of doing nothing" (or almost nothing) during times of fertility.

But if birth control can rely on the natural rhythms of *periodic* fertility, then it is impossible for each and every marriage act to retain an aptitude for procreation. Any destiny to procreation is obviously absent from intercourse during infertile periods. And if it is absent, then during infertile periods the unitive and procreative meanings of sexual intercourse are separable.[12] During periodic infertility, nature denies married couples the capacity "for the generation of new lives." Reference to natural facts, then, leaves *Humanae vitae* impaled on a discrepancy. Paul VI both asserts and denies the inseparability of the unitive and procreative aspects of sexual intercourse, referring to the law of nature to support each side of the contradiction.

Consider an analogous argument. Suppose that the specialist at the local natural food store told you that the "essence" of eating food must be understood in a certain way. By this she means that *consuming* food becomes *eating* food when two goals are achieved: nutrition and pleasure. Absent either of these goals, in other words, one's intake of food cannot be classified as *eating*. To this the nutritionist adds that the essence of eating is a design of God, and that any act of eating that separates these two goals violates the natural law. On this evidence you conclude that consuming vegetables, skim milk, and tofu counts as *eating* and is morally commendable, while consuming soda and popcorn at the movies is not. But as you share this conclusion with the nutritionist, you are informed that God has wisely disposed laws so that at times the ends of nutrition and pleasure in fact do not unite. Hence it is sometimes permissible to consume (now classified as *eating*) popcorn, complete with loads of butter and salt, and a large cup of caffeinated soda. The only requirement is somehow to remain "open" to the prospect of nutrition. Surely, one ought to conclude, the natural laws according to which this nutritionist is forming her judgments are incoherent.

THE PHYSICALIST CRITIQUE

Even apart from the logical problems of *Humanae vitae*, critics have alleged, reference to the so-called facts of nature reduces Paul VI's argument to purely physiological terms. Put simply, the charge is that his casuistry assesses the morality of action according to its material dimensions.[13] Nowhere else do we confine moral judgment to physiological facts alone. A more robust account of the "nature" of sexual intercourse, including its "human" dimension, is needed.

The physicalist critique focuses on Paul VI's account of the natural law, arguing that "nature" has been reduced to purely physiological processes. *Humanae vitae* determines the permissibility of the conjugal act solely in terms of its physical structure, however incoherent Paul VI's account of that structure may be. Since *nature* in this sense serves as the criterion for the morality of the conjugal act, a revised interpretation of *the natural* would lead to a different moral picture of sexual intercourse and the regulation of birth.

It is important to see how often the encyclical abides by a physicalist account of nature. When Paul VI first broaches the idea of competing views about the morality of contraception, for example, he clearly distinguishes between two approaches, the second of which is physicalist. He remarks, "It is . . . asked whether, in view of the increased sense of responsibility of modern people, the moment has not come for them to entrust to reason and will, rather than to the biological rhythms of the human organism, the task of regulating birth" (par.

3). Answering this question in the negative, Paul VI asserts that "it is licit to take into account the natural rhythms immanent in the generative functions" (par. 16). Sex during infertile periods as a means of birth control is permissible, whereas artificial contraception "as the use of means directly contrary to fecundation" is condemned as being always immoral. The argument continues: "In reality, there are essential differences between the two cases; in the former, the married couple make legitimate use of a natural disposition; in the latter, they impede the development of natural processes" (par. 16). Paul VI thus sees the moral difference between types of birth control *not* in terms of the partners' intention, since in each case the intention is nonprocreative. Rather, the moral difference turns on the distinction between natural and artificial, where "natural" is understood in terms of periodic fertility and infertility.

This appeal to the natural-as-physiological to sanction only certain forms of birth control marks a shift in the Catholic casuistry of sexuality and the regulation of birth. Prior to the nineteenth century, Catholic moral theology shared the widespread belief that the woman was simply the repository for the male seed, which needed nothing more for conception to occur. Catholicism also taught that each conjugal act was, by its very nature, procreative and could only accidentally fail to be so, that there was an "openness to the transmission of life" inherent in every sexual act, generally speaking.[14] Sex during sterility was permitted only for couples who believed they were acting to procreate. In this sense it was possible to speak of an "openness to the transmission of life" for sterile couples to designate their implicit or explicit intention. Bishops and theologians generally condoned sexual intercourse of sterile persons on the basis of the couple's desire for fertility. Where that desire was lacking, sexual intercourse was discouraged because it indicated a lack of self-control. Sexual acts *without* the intention to procreate were immoral, contrary to the design of nature. As Augustine remarks, "The intercourse necessary for generation is without fault and it alone belongs to marriage." Augustine cites the authority of St. Paul, saying "sexual intercourse that comes about through incontinence, not for the sake of procreation and at the time with no thought of procreation, . . . he grants as a pardon."[15] Accordingly, intercourse during pregnancy was a sin, as both Ambrose and Augustine argued.[16]

Medical discoveries in the nineteenth century revised the terms on which these traditional moral conclusions were based. In 1827 Karl Ernest von Baer verified the conjecture of J. L. Prevost and J. A. Dumas that the human ovum was located in the Graafian follicle. In 1845, Felix Archimedes Pouchet won the prize for experimental physiology of the French Royal Academy of Sciences for his report that conception in all mammals occurred only during menstruation and one to twelve days after menstruation. And in 1875 Oscar Hertwig demonstrated that the spermatozoon enters the ovum and that fertilization is accomplished by the union of the male and female pronuclei.[17]

These discoveries meant that Catholic moral theology would have to adjust its position concerning the immorality of intercourse during infertile periods.[18] Now it was impossible to see the woman as merely the repository of the male seed; further, sexual intercourse could no longer be viewed as only accidentally infecund. Consequently, the door was opened to the idea that intercourse with the intention *not* to procreate generally conformed to natural processes.

At the same time, however, Catholic moral theology retained the idea that sexual intercourse must remain "open to the transmission of life"—even intercourse with nonprocreative intent. Catholics were thus required to understand "openness" within a new discursive configuration. Now "openness" would have to refer not to the desire for fertility or procreation, since intercourse with the intention *not* to procreate by means of the rhythm method gained acceptance as a natural phenomenon.[19] *Humanae vitae* reflects this change. "Open to the transmission of life" is used in a new sense, designating "the natural laws of and rhythms of fecundity which, of themselves, cause a separation in the succession of births" (par. 11). As Bernard Häring has shown, in the new context malice does not lie in the unwillingness to propagate life while engaging in sexual intercourse, as it did for Ambrose and Augustine; rather, "it now lies in intercourse without absolute respect for 'the laws of the generative process.'"[20] *The moral problem thus shifts from the question of whether the intention is procreative to whether nonprocreative intention respects the biological laws of fertility and infertility.*

This change in Catholic teaching likewise entailed a subtle revision in its understanding of virtues in relation to sexuality. For Augustine, continence (understood as the virtue of self-control, or temperance) shapes the overall order of marital life. Incontinent couples have intercourse without the intention to procreate, succumbing to concupiscence and the pleasures of bodily desire. Pleasure is not forbidden but is to be subordinated to the rule of reason, which should order the conjugal act to the goal of procreation.[21] The shift in modern Catholic thought, permitting some intercourse with nonprocreative intent, suggests a notion of continence as the requirement to abstain from intercourse during fertile periods. While Augustine did not deny that continence included some forms of self-denial, he understood it in more holistic terms than is suggested by the notion of continence implied by the revised Catholic position. Within the new framework, continence refers not to ordering one's intention toward procreation and subordinating pleasure to the rule of reason, but simply to the ability to abstain periodically from intercourse. A physicalist understanding of the natural, in short, reduces the virtue of temperance to a set of negative duties.[22]

The laws on which the encyclical's casuistry relies refer only to those processes that humans share with other animals. Insofar as the morality of contraceptive means is determined according to such bodily phenomena, Paul VI's argument stands on an account of "the natural" that excludes human reason, rational purposes, and the goods of marriage itself—characteristics that distinguish humans from the rest of animal life.[23]

The physicalist critique is premised on the belief that the account of nature on which the encyclical relies is wrong, that *nature* ought to refer to human nature in a personalistic sense. So Richard McCormick insists that "the person is the criterion of the meaning of actions. . . . Physical objects as such have no relation to the moral order. Thus 'taking another's property' is only a physical act; it is not yet a moral object. Similarly 'uttering an untruth' is only a physical act or object." These acts attain moral significance in relation to personal goods or values. So McCormick argues, "If . . . 'taking another's property' contains an attack on persons or a person, it contains the malice of theft (and is an unloving act)."[24]

Without denying the biological dimensions of sexual intercourse, those who champion the physicalist critique argue that contraceptive practices must be viewed against the backdrop of the goods of marriage, personal goods.[25] The moral reality to be evaluated is not conformity with physical processes, but the relation between intercourse and "its finalization toward the goods which define marriage."[26] If those goods can be enhanced through artificial contraception, then such contraceptive practices are permissible. Here *nature* remains the criterion for judging the morality of the contraceptive act, but *nature* is expanded beyond biological processes to include reference to the goods of persons and marriage as a whole.[27]

This broader understanding of *nature* and its implications for sexuality enable personalists to conceive of virtue in more demanding terms than we find in the physicalist account. That is, temperance for personalists would require something other than abstaining from intercourse during fertile periods. Personalists could argue—although they have yet to do so—that the virtue of temperance requires couples to order their procreation in light of the goods of marriage, and perhaps in terms of global goods. Personalists would thereby furnish a new discursive formation for the language of virtue and vice in sexual relations. Couples who procreate prolifically because they

139

reject the use of artificial contraception would be seen not as abiding by the law of nature, but as incontinent, procreating with disordered passions.[28] Such couples would be open to the charge that they have acted irresponsibly, oblivious to the duties of domestic responsibility in a world of decreasing social and natural resources to sustain families with numerous offspring.[29]

THE STRUCTURAL CRITIQUE

Besides calling attention to the various difficulties in *Humanae vitae*, the logical and physicalist critiques require us to focus on a crucial distinction between natural birth control and artificial contraception in the intrinsic argument. The logical critique does so by attending to the kinds of facts cited in support of the rhythm method as a permissible means of controlling birth, namely, the so-called rhythms of fecundity. Similarly, the physicalist critique focuses our attention on the meaning of "the natural" as physical nature, with which "the artificial" is contrasted.

This distinction between "natural" and "artificial" is of no small importance since, as I have said, one of the encyclical's goals is to allow some ("natural") forms of nonprocreative intercourse. Yet if natural forms of birth control are morally acceptable, then a further difficulty emerges when we turn to Paul VI's extrinsic argument: If some forms of controlling birth are permissible, then it is not clear how we are to make sense of his fears of a contraceptive culture. Those fears are cited to support the argument against artificial contraception. But they are equally pertinent to cultures in which natural forms of birth control are widely and successfully practiced.[30]

Apologists for *Humanae vitae* might retort that Paul VI's warnings are appropriate to a culture practicing widespread artificial contraception, not natural birth control, because artificial methods are easier and more efficient. With more effective forms of birth control, in short, we have every reason to believe that a "wide and easy road would thus be opened up towards conjugal infidelity" (par. 17). The ethos of a culture with easy means—artificial means—of birth control corresponds to the one about which Paul VI warns.

Yet Paul VI undermines this line of defense when he enjoins scientists to demonstrate in their research that no contradiction exists between "divine laws pertaining to the transmission of life and those pertaining to the fostering of authentic conjugal love." One fruit of such research, he notes, is that medical science might "succeed in providing a sufficiently secure basis for a regulation of birth, founded on the observance of natural rhythms" (par. 24). In other words, Paul VI himself deems more efficient and effective means of *natural* birth control a cultural desideratum. Yet if such a desideratum were to be realized, then those fears that accompany already efficient forms of artificial birth control would haunt effective forms of natural birth control as well. As André Hellegers puts the question, "When absolute assurance of nonreproduction in an act of intercourse exists with the perfect rhythm method, why will the same dire consequences, predicted in paragraph 17 of the encyclical, not befall those who practice perfect rhythm?"[31]

Paul VI's intrinsic defense of natural birth control, part of the first pillar of *Humanae vitae,* and his fears about a contraceptive culture, his second pillar, thus conflict. Moral conclusions derived from principles and consequences fail to corroborate each other, since there are good reasons to believe that natural birth control, made more available and efficient by modern science, could have deleterious cultural effects.

The Gender Critique

Thus far I have rehearsed the idea that *Humanae vitae* is doomed to fail whether or not the intrinsic argument is valid. If it is valid and its implications are advanced—that is, if efficient natural birth control is both morally permissible *and* a cultural desideratum—then it conflicts with the extrinsic argument; if it is not valid, then the encyclical's central claims must be discarded.

Why, then, has *Humanae vitae* not been scrapped? Perhaps these three critiques miss the target, focusing too narrowly on the explicit argument rather than on its subtext. If we take another look at the document, its enduring appeal may emerge from beneath its obvious untenability. I want to suggest that the encyclical's appeal for a patriarchal culture lies in Paul VI's account of gender and its bifurcation in terms of nature and culture. To paraphrase Claude Lévi-Strauss: *Humanae vitae* will retain its appeal so long as we identify women with the raw and men with the cooks.

To illustrate, note two points to which the logical, physicalist, and structural criticisms direct our attention: (1) "nature" is described in terms of bodily processes, which are independent of human volition and which reflect the "design of God"; (2) intercourse in a contraceptive culture may produce a "lowering of morality." Previous critiques have failed to notice that each of these claims, central to the intrinsic and extrinsic arguments respectively, is troped by the language of gender, cast in patriarchal terms.

Consider, first, how "nature" as physical process is described in the intrinsic argument. God's laws are "rhythms of fecundity," says Paul VI; hence, natural birth control is commendable because it uses a "natural disposition," namely, the "natural rhythms immanent in the

141

generative functions." Further, scientists are enjoined to "succeed in providing a sufficiently secure basis for a regulation of birth, founded on the observance of natural rhythms" (par. 24). We must respect "the integrity of the human organism and its functions," which establish "insurmountable limits to the possibility of our domination over the body and its functions" (par. 17). In each of these points, the body in question is the woman's body. She alone furnishes the site of natural rhythm, so important to the distinction between natural birth control and artificial contraception. And in each such instance the female body is defined in terms of autonomous laws and ordinations, rooted in wider patterns and processes, designed by God.

This identification of the woman's body with nature, of course, has other important associations: blood, milk, birth, determinism, immanence, immediacy, repetition, lack of transcendence. The body is embedded in things as given, subject to their earthly regularities. As Mark Kline Taylor writes, "Women's connectedness to birthing and lactating calls forth the setting of women in relation to the mysteries of life's origins. In women's birthing and lactating, the mysteries of human origins are integrally bound up with processes of bodily conjoining and expelling, of blood, flesh, and fluid."[32] Seen in this light, the female body is raw, like other natural phenomena. It is the instrument for culture, the material stuff with which technology is created, meanings are formed, socialization becomes possible, and the future is envisioned. Culture in this sense transcends nature, superimposing abstract ideas and transpersonal values on indeterminate matter. It thus breaks the cycle of repetition presented by natural processes, enabling humans to structure their environment with values and commitments, and to transmit those values over time.[33]

Consider, second, the dangers of a contraceptive culture as described in the extrinsic argument. We should observe that paragraph 17, in which the harmful effects of widespread contraception are noted, is the *only* place where Paul VI's main argument uses the Latin *vir* (man) to the exclusion of *uxor* (wife, spouse) or *mulier* (woman).[34] And Paul VI does so with explicit reference to men as exerting power over women. The real danger of a contraceptive culture, he warns, is *not* merely that sex will become "selfish enjoyment," but that women will be the site of such enjoyment. Paul VI elaborates:

> It is also to be feared that men (*viri*), growing used to the employment of anticonceptive devices, may finally lose respect for the woman and, no longer caring for her physical and psychological equilibrium, may come to the point of considering her as a mere instrument of selfish enjoyment, and no longer as his respected and beloved companion (par. 17).

Note that Paul VI *does not fear that the woman might instrumentalize the male;* the woman alone is vulnerable to instrumentalization. The male transcends the possibility of instrumentalization, presenting the danger of domination and manipulation. The woman, in turn, poses no danger to the male. She cannot be an agent of domination, someone who takes advantage of the opposite sex. The woman is candidate for victim and victim only.

As a matter of fact, of course, sexual relations are potentially exploitive for both members of a heterosexual liaison. As Simone de Beauvoir asks at the conclusion of *The Second Sex,* Why should we assume that sexual intercourse is an act whereby the passive woman is dominated or controlled by the active male? In a context in which women assume power over their own lives and their reproductive capacities, roles might be reversed—for better or for worse. De Beauvoir thus enables us to ask, What prevents us from imagining the woman's role in intercourse as potentially exploitive of the male?[35]

Paul VI's *inability* to imagine such a role should come as no surprise given what we have seen about the attitudes toward gender that underlie his casuistry and his appeals to the law of nature. The woman is the site of natural rhythms, through which animal patterns and processes find lawful expression. She is passive material, raw stuff. Taken by herself, she is nothing more than the matter on which other agents may act, or over which they can have controlling power. The male's transgression depends on how he exercises his power of agency, his capacity to transcend the rhythms of natural forces.

This is not to suggest, however, that the woman is wholly unable to commit immoral acts. The woman's evil must be found elsewhere. Paul VI suggests that the man's malice lies in misdirected forms of "cultural" activity, namely, the selfish use of power. Yet it will become possible to infer, as we shall see, that the woman's malice lies not in misdirected uses of power, but in the very exercise of agency itself.

The language of gender, repressed within *Humanae vitae,* thus presents us with an argument that is both structural and allegorical: structural, because it distinguishes female and male in polar terms; allegorical, because these terms point to something else, namely, immanence and transcendence, or nature and culture. Within this subtext, a struggle ensues to ensure that femaleness (nature, matter, passivity) retains, at best, a subordinate value. Maleness (culture, design, activity) is assigned the power to instrumentalize, to structure matter according to some nonmaterial principles, to exert dominion by using raw stuff for opportunistic enjoyment.

More to the point, this allegory allows us to see how Paul VI's intrinsic and extrinsic arguments actually support rather than undermine each other. The intrinsic argument glosses the natural with

143

the image of the female body understood as passive, patterned process. The extrinsic argument then *augments* this notion by suggesting that females alone are possible victims of sexual exploitation and that males alone can be the agents of such exploitation. In both cases the woman's body is the site of objectification, depersonalized in the equation of physical nature, passivity, rhythm, and femininity.

To be sure, *Humanae vitae* is scarcely alone in its account of the female. The woman's body as the site of nature, periodic fecundity, and repetition was an important assumption during the nascent years of gynecological science, during the nineteenth century. In Great Britain, France, Germany, and the United States this was a time when the "female genital organs were subjected to minute analysis, and specialized areas were described in detail."[36] Newly devised or newly improved medical tools facilitated access to the womb and ovaries, providing doctors with an armamentarium: the vaginal speculum, the curette, the uterine sound, and graduated metal rods for dilating the cervix.[37] Ether and chloroform were introduced to relieve the pain of childbirth. Books like T. Gaillard Thomas's *A Practical Guide on the Diseases of Women*, Walter Channing's *The Irritable Uterus*, and Charles D. Meigs's *Woman: Her Diseases and Remedies* focused medical attention on the peculiar features of female illness and the obstacles to proper treatment.

By midcentury several new operations had been successfully carried out, putting gynecology on a par with other forms of surgery: the removal of ovarian cysts; the repair of vesico-vaginal fistulae; the hysterectomy; the removal of diseased Fallopian tubes; and surgery for ruptured ectopic pregnancies. Starting in 1835, clinics and hospitals devoted specifically to women's illnesses sprang up in New York, New England, Philadelphia, and Illinois.[38] As I have mentioned, the human ovum, periodic fertility, and the details of conception became scientific knowledge. Further, in 1845 James Henry Bennett first distinguished between benign and malignant uterine tumors.[39] Crude experimental practices emerged as well, including the placement of leeches on a diseased cervix, and the use of leeches on the gums of pregnant women with toothaches.[40] The century was marked, moreover, by an explosion of new language, an "incitement to discourse," as Michel Foucault has put it:[41] perineal body, diaphragmatic ligament, Mullerian tubes, anesthesia, blastoderm, Sims's (knee-chest) position.[42] The nineteenth century was a time, as Dr. Samuel D. Gross of Jefferson Medical College remarked in 1867, with "womb on the brain."[43]

In this respect the woman's body was very much an object of diagnosis and objectification, the site of new invasion, exploration, discovery, and description. What is noteworthy is that *Humanae vitae* appears to have absorbed the values implied by the gynecological "incitement to discourse," turning them into ideological beliefs. According to the intrinsic and extrinsic arguments, respectively, the woman is the site of periodic fertility and the material for use and instrumentalization. In this respect the woman is nothing more than she was while under gynecological inspection: the place of vacillating fecundity, the object for further probing, the specimen on which to practice. But with *Humanae vitae,* these are not just scientific assumptions. Instead, they are etched into the natural law, designating "the way things are." They thus become carved into stone, rationalizing assumptions about the nature of women and the relations between the sexes. Such assumptions are thus able to parade themselves as inscribed in the natural order, reflecting "the design of God."

We are left, then, not with contradictions in the subtext of the encyclical's casuistry, but with a double irony.

One irony lies in the fact that the text's standard of value—the law of nature—designates a devalued object, the female body. The rhythms of the woman's body provide both the norm to which sexual practice must adhere *and* that which is ineligible for power in a contraceptive culture. The woman remains mute, silenced by the fact that she is denied agency and left with nothing more than a passive, material role in intercourse and conception.

The second irony is that Paul VI's idiom of patriarchal ideology appears most baldly where he expresses his paternalistic concern about the well-being of women in a contraceptive culture, in paragraph 17. Warnings against harming women trade on language in which *harm finds ideological legitimation,* namely, the idiom of male-as-culture, the center of creative power over instrumental feminine processes. *Humanae vitae's* structural allegory unwittingly fosters the notion that transgression is a male phenomenon, that men alone are candidates for domination. In this way Paul VI's paternalistic warnings deconstruct, affirming precisely the values that support the practices he fears. Paul VI's argument thus implodes by simultaneously seeking to protect the female while underwriting the cultural ideology with which sexual exploitation and violence find legitimation.

Gender Relations and Popular Catholicism

Earlier I proposed that the subtext of *Humanae vitae* endorses a set of values close to the heart of the Catholic right, values that go beyond whatever may be the subject of liberal criticisms of Paul VI's argument. Those values include some firmly held beliefs about the nature of the sexes and their proper relationship. Indeed, a survey of popular literature shows that Paul VI's structural allegory and its corresponding ideology are firmly entrenched in the popular imagination of Catholic conservatives.

Consider, first, the deep and abiding appeal for gender differentiation in materials like the *Wanderer, 30 Days in the Church and in the World, Fidelity,* the *Homiletic and Pastoral Review,* and *Communio.* Throughout this literature, authors insist that women's nature, as Paul VI suggests, is essentially passive, in contrast to the active nature of males. Hanna Klaus of the Natural Family Planning Center in Washington, D.C., finds clues in Genesis. According to Klaus, "Men can only establish masculinity by overcoming another; in other words, the man must always be aggressive, whereas the woman comes into a situation which is already made and her existence is provided for. In the beginning, when Eve was created, Adam was already there."[44] This does not mean that femininity is altogether devoid of agency; considerations of agency may be calibrated to the natural role of woman as nurturing mother. So Klaus writes, "Mother is indeed powerful. When she possesses she can control for a while but ultimately the control prevents growth. . . . In giving up possessiveness which is necessary to attain womanliness, the woman comes into her own because possessiveness is actually an abiding threat to womanliness."[45]

The idea that women are devoid of agency (except for the duties of maternity) points to a further parallel between popular American Catholicism and *Humanae vitae,* namely, female/nature and male/culture. For Klaus this gender identification can be explained in terms of our biological endowments. She writes, "Women tend to be far more intuitive, gifted as they are by nature to nurture the preverbal child, while men tend to manage external space more easily." Hence men are more inclined to seek control of the material world. Such tendencies are linked for Klaus to our experiences of sexual intercourse. She adds, "Because men are used to looking outside of themselves, (after all, sex takes place outside a man's body, but inside a woman's) they tend to look for external causes and effects and think in what has been named a logical pattern."[46]

One gloss on the identification of women with nature appears in discussions of the aesthetics of contraception. The idea is that artificial contraception represents an invasion of technology—alien objects or chemicals—into sexual intercourse. So Paul Marx decries the fact that contraception "puts responsibility on gadgetry and chemicals rather than on cultivated human will."[47] Included in such complaints is the notion that the woman represents pristine terrain and her basic rhythms a larger natural harmony. Debates about contraception, then, echo concerns about environmental protection: Artificial contraception constitutes technological imperialism, violating women's "natural" sensibilities. So Marx adds, "I have often been told by Protestant friends how unesthetic [*sic*] and inhuman contraception is. On this subject the women are always more eloquent."[48]

Taking the male/culture and female/nature allegory one step further, Monica M. Migliorino seeks to elevate matters to a theological level. To find clues about the meaning of masculinity and femininity, Migliorino draws inferences from the order of creation. "Masculinity," she writes, "derives its meaning as a sacramental symbol of God who generates life—a begetting principle which, of course, is perpetually present in God the Father. God the Father never rejects his generative role as Father." The key to properly ordered sexuality, Migliorino adds, is for couples to imitate the patterns established by this paternal generation: "In imaging God to his creation the husband likewise needs to affirm and never reject or destroy his own God-given generative powers." This is not to suggest, however, that the woman plays no role whatsoever, although her role is largely as a seedbed of paternal generation. Migliorino continues: "Christ too possesses generative power in relation to the Church. Christ fills the Church with his presence—his word. The Church as his Bride truly *receives* him." Indeed, the church "joyfully receives him and gives herself to him—holding back nothing!" As if literally to deify pre–nineteenth century biology, Migliorino remarks, the church "thus *germinates* what has been given to her."[49]

As I suggested earlier, this ideology of woman/passive/nature does not eclipse the idea of female agency altogether. For that matter, neither does it rule out the role of technology in regulating birth. Indeed, the idea of women as passive/nature legitimates radical technological exploration of female anatomy. In this context we can discover how females can be seen as transgressive, namely, when they attempt to exert some measure of self-determination over their reproductive systems.

Consider, for example, the methods associated with the Ovutektor, a device for detecting periods of fertility and infertility so important to natural forms of birth control. As developed by Ian Donald, the Ovutektor is premised on the fact that ovulation normally occurs in one ovary; more blood flows to that ovary than to the other. Donald's hypothesis is that the onset of ovulation can be ascertained if one can identify the difference in blood flow to the two ovaries. His research led to the development of an instrument for detecting a difference in heat transference. If two identical heat-measuring devices are applied to the ovaries, the transfer of body heat to one device will be faster than to the other device during times of ovulation. At all other times, infertile times, the transfer of heat should be identical.

What is more important than Donald's hypothesis is the technology he created for exploring female anatomy in search of data about imminent ovulation. As described by John Tracy, the Ovutektor

consists of two pencil-thin acrylic probes which lie parallel to one another like two fingers, and which are hinged so that the tips can be
opened out to a pre-set distance from one another. If you hold out an
index finger and middle finger in a closed position and then open
them to their full extent, you will see quite clearly the mechanics of the
Ovutektor. In the tips of the probes are mounted matched thermistors,
which are a type of heat sensitive transistor. When the probes are in-
serted into the vagina and opened to a comfortable extent, the tips lie
automatically in close proximity to the ovaries.[50]

Original models of the Ovutektor include thermistors "balanced in a
simple electrical bridge circuit fed by a small torch battery. The circuit
becomes balanced in the event of any circulatory change on either
side, and the difference is registered on a microammeter."[51]

Whether the Ovutektor relies on "gadgetry" rather than on "cultivated human will," as Paul Marx would have it, is difficult to say, since
using such a device combines technology with an ethic of abstinence.
Yet it is clear that using the Ovutektor presupposes the woman as a
field of exploration and a site of ongoing, autonomous rhythms. The
Ovutektor is not a device with which a woman may control nature or
transcend its processes. Rather, it is used to ensure that if a woman
wishes to regulate procreation, she does so without attempting to exercise control over autonomous forces. The use of gadgets must be
limited to exploration and diagnosis, tracking internal physiological
occurrences. Soon thereafter, "cultivated human will," or abstinence,
must take over.

The real evil for a woman to commit, then, is not that of regulating birth or using technology to help her do so. Rather, it lies in attempting to regulate birth by exercising agency or power over rhyth-
mic forces. Dominion over such forces finally rests elsewhere. And
toward those who in fact seek such dominion, only the most vicious
animadversion is appropriate. Carol Jackson Robinson writes, for example, that those who seek sovereignty over their reproductive processes "are anti-nuns, claiming the right to be whores."[52] About those
who use artificial contraception, Marx asks us to recall "how the insightful Gandhi observed that contraception 'is mutual masturbation'
and that the difference between a prostitute and a married woman
using contraception is that one is getting paid and the other is not."[53]

The Aspiring Female

These last comments suggest that the sexism among Catholic conservatives is more overtly misogynistic than is *Humanae vitae*. Paul VI's
stated concern surrounds the possibility that women may violate the

natural law in seeking to regulate birth, that they may be unable to abstain from intercourse during periods of fertility and thus may resort to artificial means. His sexism consists in his notion of the female as passive matter; the observable evils of which he speaks are, for the most part, those of the opportunistic male will. In the woman's case, using artificial contraception puts her in an occasion of sin.[54] She can be guilty of cooperating with the male by using artificial contraception, but her agency can take her no further: She cannot sexually exploit her partner by means of her own autonomy or volition.

In the literature of conservative Catholicism, the notion of female as passive matter endures, but the evils are not those of the selfish male will or the compliant female. Rather, they concern women's liberation, especially women's regulation of birth as part of their aspiration to leave the domestic sphere. The *female* will, the will to enter the socioeconomic realm, has been the source of anxiety for the Catholic right during the past three decades. In the present context, women's desire to participate in the public sphere represents incontinence, concupiscence, and the inability to act within the conditions of finitude, not the inability to abstain from intercourse during periods of fertility.

Central to the conservative vision is the idea of gender complementarity, the joining of opposites in conjugal love. These opposites put the male in the role of power and authority, and the woman in the sphere of domestic security. This familiar gender identification essentializes sexual differences by insisting that gender-specific needs go unfulfilled if men and women choose to depart from clearly defined paths. The idea is that our social woes can be traced to women seeking work and to men who attempt to offset the effects of women's absence from the domestic sphere by assuming more responsibility at home. Of course this view is not meant to open the door to male tyranny and oppression of women. As Robinson remarks, it is rather to make available to women a "domestic and maternal sort of life, which was naturally theirs anyhow, and which the vast majority of them would have freely chosen."[55]

Instabilities arising from women entering the workforce are central to E. Michael Jones's account of "the clearly asymmetrical relationship between the sexes in marriage." For Jones, "the man needs authority, the woman security." The problem with today's society is that women seek roles of authority, thereby forcing men to take compensatory action to secure their sovereignty. Therein lie the origins of a self-perpetuating cycle of male selfishness and female petulance. Jones writes:

> Once the man can be made to feel that he is indeed the head of the family, he is more willing to make sacrifices for it without feeling that he is sacrificing his masculinity in the bargain. Once the woman is reassured that she will be taken care of for better or worse, in sickness and in health, etc. . . . she will be able to relinquish her economic fears and insecurity and concomitant counter-productive behavior, most notably her nagging. The more the man assumes authority in marriage, the more secure the woman feels. The more secure the wife feels, the more she gives authority to the man, and the more he becomes devoted to her, the stronger the family becomes as a unit.[56]

Here the woman is not only confined to the domestic sphere, protected against "the rabid careerism at the heart of feminism."[57] She is first and foremost the object to be protected against the travails of agency itself, someone to be provided for. Absent her need for agency, males remain unthreatened in their social and economic roles; otherwise, they are likely to "join gangs, become homosexuals, or cultivate forms of violence."[58]

The role of women in the military is especially symbolic of our culture's failure to recognize asymmetry. While acknowledging that women have the ability to carry out strenuous physical tasks, James G. Bruen, Jr., goes on to ask, Why would they want to when they could stay at home? Bruen observes that "millions of American mothers routinely abandon their children. Some put their children in day care; some leave them through divorce; others are assigned to Saudi Arabia. . . . These modern American women are prepared to do battle in the business world or in the Saudi desert; they'll live or die for the free market. But they are deserters in the battle between good and evil over the souls of their children."[59] In Bruen's mind, "the primary sacrifice those women make is the sacrifice of their children *on the altar of the women's choice to do something other than raise their children*. That's nothing to be proud of."[60] Ignoring unmarried women or women for whom heterosexual love is not a "vocation," Bruen concludes that "women have something better and more important to do than go off to war: bear and raise children."[61]

Speaking more generally, Sheldon Vanauken writes of "the iron law of home." According to Vanauken, feminism has produced "a girl who will not accept her ancient and primary vocation to be mother and homemaker."[62] The problem today is that women are guilty of incontinence; they aspire "to have it all: career, family, everything." Vanauken asserts: "They can't. . . . The homemaking function has shrunk by half [owing to technology] but not vanished. This is a *fact*." Here, too, the danger lies in women's freedom: "The iron law of home—that home requires a homemaker—cannot be violated without destroying home. Women who want home, for themselves, for their husbands, for their children, must accept the iron law. If they *don't* want home, if they want a career more, that's fine; *it is their choice.* But they can't have it all without botching their lives, and their husbands' and children's lives."[63]

Ruth Price puts the point even more polemically. For her, women seek work outside the home because they lack the strength to meet home's challenges. "How many women," she asks, "enjoy washing out a messy diaper? I can't think of one. It comes down to a question of the will, and the will is free for all women. Each and every one of them can either choose to or not to change diapers, wipe noses, etc., and not one of them is any more well-suited to choose than the other."[64] Those who choose work outside the domestic sphere are weak-willed, having exercised their freedom for less strenuous causes. Price insists, not unreasonably, that work in the home requires tremendous effort and imagination. But by her logic, women who use their talents in careers have chosen the less noble route: "I daresay that if any mother at home feels underutilized or unfulfilled it is due to a lack of imagination on her part or a failure to appreciate the magnitude of the task at hand. What other job could be more challenging, calls for more creativity, or has more flexibility than raising a child? On what other job can a women apply *all* her talents to the end product?" Once again the key is that women have made the choice to work outside the home, and herein lies the true moral evil. The question is not of capability, but of volition: "Once again we become involved in a question of the will. It's not that a women can't use her talents in the home situation, it's that she chooses not to."[65]

Women who use contraception to balance child-rearing with employment are often subject to special reproach. Bruen asks us to consider the parallel between working women who use contraception and the tale of Captain Hook in *Peter Pan*. Hook knew that a crocodile wanted to consume him, but fortunately the animal had swallowed a clock that warned of its approach with a loud "tick tick." In Bruen's judgment, working women using artificial birth control are like "Captain Hook in drag," afraid of hearing their biological clocks ticking down while devoting themselves to "competition and success in traditionally male careers." He adds, "As the crocodile consumed Hook, their careers will then consume them completely."[66]

For Klaus, Jones, Bruen, Robinson, Price, Paul Marx, Migliorino, and John Tracy the ethics of contraception is now situated within a more general set of cultural anxieties—*Kulturkampf*—about sexual politics and women in professional and leadership roles. None of these authors even considers the possibility that men might share domestic duties in order to distribute household tasks more equitably.

151

Their focus is more radical than the casuistry of the encyclical, situating the ideology of female as passive matter in a discourse about traditional values and the perils of women seeking careers. For these authors, *Humanae vitae* is less an "argument" than a symbol of conservative cultural politics, a standard bearer for those anxious about women entering the workforce and usurping traditional male roles.[67] What shapes their imagination is not Paul VI's textual claims about the case of contraception, but his subtext about the proper way to understand women in relation to cultural freedoms.

Ideological Suspicion and Common Sense

To grasp the enduring appeal of *Humanae vitae*, it is necessary to change the subject from its interpretation of the natural law to its attitudes toward gender. And we can do so, I have suggested here, by means of a gender critique. This critique is an example of ideological criticism, designed to trace the covert desires nestled beneath the surface of the encyclical's text. It is thus not one more criticism, to be placed alongside the logical, physicalist, and structural critiques. Rather, it proceeds by means of a hermeneutics of suspicion, calling into question the very terms repressed beneath the argument as a whole. As such, it is not meant to reveal the untenability of *Humanae vitae*; its goal is rather to emancipate us from the grip of Paul VI's moral vocabulary, enshrined in his structural allegory.

By this account, the encyclical's real flaw is that it lacks the capacity to resist the ideology of patriarchy. To find that flaw we must proceed under cover, privileging the repressed in our interpretations, tracing the subtext of "nature" and the tropes of gender. Perhaps then we can equip ourselves to proceed critically and self-reflexively. Such an approach would be aware that women are moral agents, that the meaning of their experience is mediated by cultural languages, and that efforts to shape those languages with patriarchal ideology may be both more tenacious and more elusive than they first appear.

Yet it remains to be asked, How is it possible to engage in such a hermeneutics of suspicion? On what epistemological grounds can we open casuistry to ideological critique? In this case we can best proceed by recalling that in the history of casuistry one of the most tenacious sources of criticism was common sense. Critics of casuistry, those who claimed that it provided the basis for being an "honest thief," developed their skepticism by alleging that many casuistical conclusions were counterintuitive, contrary to what we commonly know, practice, and believe in everyday experience. When it comes to ideological criticism today, the instructions of common sense are no less liberating. For those informed by feminist criticism—those for whom the prophetic army of feminist metaphors has now been literalized[68]—it is a commonplace to say that women have powers of cultural agency, that they deserve equal rather than paternalistic treatment, and that their right to participate in public life is incontestable. No less today than yesterday, the limits of casuistry can be exposed by drawing on sources of common sense, especially those voices that have equipped us to reflect carefully on patriarchal prejudices and unspoken interests.

Recalling those voices, we can remember that the distinction between culture and nature is *itself* a cultural phenomenon, part of a classification system that seeks to shape gender relations and our perception of women's roles in society. Seen in this way, the taxonomy of "nature and culture" is nothing more (or less) than a human construction, over which we possess the power of critical hermeneutics, illumination, and reform.

CHAPTER SIX

On Transplanting Human Fetal Tissue

The Problem of Novelty

"In truth, if you re-
ally want to make
sure about love in
yourself or in an-
other person, then
note how he relates
himself to one who
is dead."
— Søren
Kierkegaard[1]

Ethical and policy questions about fetal research, first debated in this country during
the 1970s, have returned to the public forum. Recent debates concern the therapeutic possibilities
of transplanting fetal tissue from human abortuses after seven to fourteen weeks of gestation.
The transplantation of cells from fetal bone marrow, thymus, liver, and pancreas has been inves-
tigated in the treatment of genetic defects in
the hematopoietic system, leukemia, and aplastic
anemia.[2] Neural, adrenal, and pancreatic cells
from fetuses have been used to ameliorate brain,
spinal, and diabetic disorders in adults. Mexican
scientists were the first to report treating Parkinson's disease with fetal tissue implants; scientists
from the United States, Great Britain, Sweden,
China, Cuba, and Poland have also reported some
success in transplanting fetal neural cells into patients with Parkinson's disease.[3] Fetal brain cells
are endowed with special chemicals that could restore lost substances in the brains of Parkinson's
patients and induce the regrowth of lost connections.[4] The use of fetal thymus for DiGeorge's
syndrome (congenital thymic aplasia) has been
recognized as an effective treatment for decades.[5]
Human fetal membranes are used as a temporary
covering for burn wounds.[6] Perhaps more familiar to the public was the use of fetal liver cells,
which generate bone marrow, in victims of radia-
tion sickness at Chernobyl.[7]

Fetal tissue has several advantages over its alternatives. It is less likely to be rejected by the
immune system than transplanted adult tissue.

154

Moreover, it has a greater developmental capacity than adult tissue, owing to the lack of differentiation in fetal tissue and its ability to grow rapidly after transplantation. Also, fetal tissue is in more abundant supply than adult organs needed for transplantation.[8]

In the late 1980s, medical researchers led by Dr. Irwin Koplin proposed to implant fetal brain tissue into the brains of patients with Parkinson's disease, seeking to correct the loss of neural tissue. These researchers submitted a request to the National Institutes of Health, which forwarded the request to the Department of Health and Human Services. In March 1988, Dr. Robert Windom, Assistant Secretary for Health at HHS, wrote to Dr. James Wyngaarden, director of NIH, declaring a moratorium on the use of federal funds for transplanting fetal tissue.[9] Despite congressional attempts to overturn this moratorium, President Bush kept it in force until he was replaced by President Clinton, who rescinded it three days after he took office in 1993.[10] In this chapter I will remark on several of the ethical and practical issues surrounding the transplantation of human fetal tissue, hoping to add intellectual credence to current government policy and the use of fetal tissue in general.

By way of introduction, two observations are in order. First, casuistry surrounding the use of fetal tissue turns, in some measure, on the value ascribed to the fetus. If the fetus is construed as nothing more than maternal tissue, there should be no objections to transplantation or other uses of fetal materials, given informed consent from the donor. I am assuming, following U.S. law and prior attempts to weigh the ethics of fetal research, that the fetus is of *some* value, however vague that may be, and that some protections are to be assigned to fetal life.

Second, the casuistry surrounding the transplantation of fetal tissue is somewhat novel, lacking a clear precedent in medical ethics. Although guidelines emerged in the 1970s for fetal experimentation,[11] the case of transplantation is different. The most important fact is that in transplantation the fetuses are dead and (obviously) do not further suffer from medical use. With experimentation, the fetus is vulnerable to suffering and harm, but it also may benefit from research carried out *in utero*.

If we are to address the case of transplanting fetal tissue, then, we need a place to start, which is not readily available. We are thus forced to look to familiar materials in ethics in order to build bridges to the strange or unprecedented. Paradigms help us in the task of bridge-building, providing examples in which moral vocabulary and logical procedures are relatively clear and well tested. As I indicated in the introduction, they are central to Kuhn's view of "normal science," shaping a way of seeing for scientific (or other) practitioners.[12] As

155

Kuhn writes, paradigms provide "models from which spring particular coherent traditions of . . . research." Without them our moral interpretations would be disorganized and ad hoc, like science when it lacks a paradigm for interpretation and problem-solving.[13]

Kuhn's point is true for casuistry as well: When paradigms are used as a means of approaching unfamiliar cases, they enable us to reason analogically. We can solve our cases by drawing parallels with previous case solutions, attending to relevant similarities between our starting point in tradition and new questions or problems. Casuists cannot press into uncharted terrain without verisimilitude. They seek to resolve a case by first seeing how it resembles a problem for which they have already crafted a clear and uncontroversial solution.[14] Casuistry is thereby able to move laterally, as Jonsen and Toulmin remark, "from clear and simple cases to the more complex and obscure ones."[15]

Casuistry for the ethics of transplanting fetal tissue is paradigm-based research in that it requires us to begin with accepted models of ethical analysis, standard approaches with which professional initiates will be familiar. My argument will develop two such analogies, or bridges, for moral reflection (and lateral movement). First, for a general ethical framework, I will draw analogies from the criteria of the just-war tradition. As I indicated in chapter 2, this tradition provides a justification, albeit with limitations, for using lethal force, overriding the moral presumption against violence.[16] Second, for the specific case of transplanting fetal tissue, bridges will be built from the paradigm of organ transplantation, or the use of cadaverous tissue. I will argue that the justification for transplanting fetal tissue begins by overriding the prima facie duty not to use others merely as means to ends. The limitations on the use of fetal tissue ought to parallel those that govern harvesting the dead. Central to such limitations are safeguards against conflicts of interest.

General Ethical Considerations

Moral discourse about war and, analogously, about transplanting fetal tissue might best be understood according to the logic of prima facie duties. In each case we begin with a strong moral presumption *against* the practice. In the case of war, we must begin with the prima facie duty of nonmaleficence, the duty not to harm, shed blood, or violate another person. In the case of transplanting fetal tissue, we must begin with the duty, widely held in religious and philosophical ethics and culture in general, not to use persons—dead or alive—merely as means to ends. This duty gives strong but not categorical weight to a basic proscription against instrumentalizing individuals.

It is compatible with a variety of cultural attitudes: respect for life, respect for the dead, noninterference, ethical personalism, bodily integrity, and human dignity, to name a few.

A theory of prima facie duties views the moral life as immersed in what Aristotle calls "the particulars."[17] According to this idea, human action cannot be understood apart from the constraints of contingency and variability. These constraints militate against the belief that morality can be regulated by absolute, unchanging rules, modeled on the ideal of mathematical fixity and certainty. Rather, ethics must build into itself the skill of discerning judgment, the virtue of prudence. Aristotle thus distinguishes between the theoretical and practical sciences, seeking in the latter reasonableness rather than exactness.[18]

For practical reasoning understood along such Aristotelian lines, prima facie duties give presumptive weight to values or duties that have stood the test of time. Such duties hold "generally and for the most part." A prima facie duty is one for which there are compelling reasons to act, all else being equal. It is our obligation to satisfy such a duty unless it conflicts with another within a carefully defined set of circumstances. Prima facie duties, then, are not absolute but place the burden of proof on those who wish to override them in light of conflicting demands. Presumptive duties may have to give way in instances in which generalities fail to cover the unusual or uncertain, with its attendant obligations.

For those who embrace just-war theory, war poses circumstances in which the duty not to harm conflicts with other important duties or values. According to the logic of prima facie duties, the duty not to harm may be overridden by the obligation to protect oneself or others from danger. In transplanting fetal tissue, analogously, moral justification can be construed in terms of conflicting duties. Overriding the duty not to use others merely as means to ends can be justified in cases in which other lives may be saved or great advances may be made in medical knowledge. The duty to the health of others—present or future, individuals or groups—may justify overriding the duty not to use or instrumentalize persons.

Here again it must be remembered that to override a prima facie duty is not to abandon it. Such duties continue to function in the situation or subsequent course of action, leaving "residual effects" or "moral traces." The overridden duty casts a shadow, affecting our action in pursuit of other duties or ends. In the context of war, such residual effects have both subjective and objective dimensions. At the subjective level, the subsequent course of action ought to entail not moral guilt, but at least regret about suffering and the loss of life. At the objective level, the duty of nonmaleficence exerts "pressure" on the conditions and methods of war, leading to a finely wrought set of moral criteria, the satisfaction of which constitutes a just war.

The objective moral traces that remain after overriding the duty of nonmaleficence are a function of two questions: the "whether" and the "how" questions. The first concerns whether recourse to lethal force is justified. Although I discussed these criteria in chapter 2, it may be useful to summarize them here:

Just cause: Defense of innocent victims of aggression, or sovereign territory.

Competent authority: The representative(s) of the community must declare war and marshal a defense.

Right intention: To reestablish the conditions of peace and fairness.

Last resort: All peaceful alternatives must be exhausted.

Reasonable hope for success: Rash or irrational resort to force is prohibited.

Relative justice: Neither side has a monopoly on absolute justice in defense of its cause or claims.

Proportionality: The foreseen risks must not outweigh the prospective benefits.

Whether resort to force is justified depends on the manner and extent to which these criteria can be satisfied.

The "how question" pertains to the morality of means: Which means are permissible in pursuit of a justified action? Raising the how question indicates that not all actions are appropriate in pursuit of one's goals, that the ends do not justify the means. The how question, then, implies a morality of limits, or limited means. With reference to this issue of means, two criteria shape our assessments of how war ought to be waged in defense of a just cause: discrimination and proportionality. The first prohibits any direct attack against noncombatants, while the second requires us to balance the foreseen, unintended damage against the values pursued in specific military tactics. Together these criteria form the *jus in bello.*

The details of these *in bello* criteria may not be directly transferable to the question of fetal tissue transplantation, beyond the obvious ethical requirement to be discriminate and proportionate in the operation itself. But the general thrust of these two criteria, and the how question to which they are addressed, have great ethical importance for our analogous case. These criteria define moral limits, creating barriers against the pressure of military necessity to justify using certain kinds of lethal force. The military imperative of efficiency must not "take over" the means of war; rather, that imperative must yield to the protections that surround civilians on the other side of battle. Thus, for example, the direct targeting of civilians is wrong, however much it might serve military interests by ending the war more quickly. Here, perhaps more than elsewhere in just-war criteria, the moral traces left by the duty of nonmaleficence show themselves. Whatever may serve military interests is nonetheless restricted by implications wrought from the overridden prima facie duty.

To the extent that these *ad bellum* and *in bello* criteria reflect the pressure of an overridden prima facie duty, they are paradigmatic for moral discourse about transplanting fetal tissue. In the case of war or fetal transplantation, the justification and limitation of the action may be understood as circumscribed by finely wrought moral standards. Using fetal tissue, however, requires additional information in order to specify exactly how the criteria, drawn from the just-war tradition, might take material shape. To that end it is necessary to build a second bridge, provided by our commonplace attitudes about care for the dead.

The Dead

To date all data indicate that fetal tissue for transplantation is provided by dead, not dying, fetuses. Thus, the ethical issues surrounding transplantation of fetal tissue differ from fetal experimentation with live, nonviable fetuses, or harvesting anencephalic babies, where questions about harm, criteria of death, etc. obtain. But the use of dead fetal tissue is not problem-free. The prima facie duty not to instrumentalize persons places presumptive weight against using even the dead merely as means to medically beneficial ends.

The duty not to instrumentalize persons who are alive seems to differ from duties surrounding the dead, if the former duty is conceived in light of Kant's proscription against treating others merely as means and not as ends, the second version of the categorical imperative.[19] Kantians conceive the duty not to instrumentalize live persons in light of the immunities that surround what it means to be an agent. Such immunities derive from the fact that others are agents of self-determination, ends in themselves. To use another person merely as a means violates his or her freedom and the corresponding protections that ought to surround rational autonomy.

But rational autonomy is obviously absent among the dead and never exists among fetuses. Those seeking to harmonize the duty not to instrumentalize the dead with Kantian philosophy might argue that the duty should be interpreted as an obligation not to treat persons against their rational, premortem wishes. In the cases of abortuses, rational premortem wishes would have to be presumed or hypothesized. Nonetheless, a problem remains: With human abortuses, it would be difficult to specify fetal wishes that would be violated by tissue transplantation when the main interest of the fetus,

159

the interest to survive, has already been extinguished. Does the decision to deny the main interest of the fetus exclude other duties toward the fetal dead?

This question actually has two parts: How, in practical terms, can fetal interests be represented? On what philosophical basis is it possible to speak of respecting fetal interests? The former question will be treated below under the heading of proxy. In response to the latter question, I would argue for the duty to respect fetal remains regardless of the cause of the death or its moral legitimacy. Respect would derive from the general respect for the dead, widely embraced and practiced in various ways in our culture. The dead are not treated merely as a means because a deep personal sentiment is virtually always attached to them. Owing to this sentiment, we do not discard the dead or treat them cavalierly, but with imputed dignity.[20] As Kierkegaard insists, remembering one who is dead is "a work of the most faithful love." For Kierkegaard, love of the dead furnishes a test for determining the depth of our generosity and compassion, for such love is unrequited.[21] At the very least, respect for dead fetuses might be seen as a natural concomitant to the prima facie duty of nonmaleficence, which derives in part from a more general attitude of regret about suffering and the loss of life.[22] Moreover, as I noted above, precedent already exists for respecting fetal life, however vague that respect may be. Respect for the fetal dead would be an extension of respect for fetal life and/or the imputed dignity of the dead. The prima facie duty not to instrumentalize the fetal dead can be construed as one expression of this virtue of respect.

If the presumption against instrumentalizing the fetal dead is to be overridden, competing or conflicting duties must be at stake. And, as I have pointed out, even the overridden duty must continue to shape the moral contours of the subsequent course of action. Drawing on the framework of just-war reasoning above, we can construct the justification for overriding the prima facie duty not to instrumentalize others, and the subsequent pressure exerted by that duty, as follows:

Just cause: The extraction of fetal tissue is permissible in order to confront a real and certain danger to others. The attempt to cure another patient can be construed as analogous with the effort to protect innocent persons from harm.

Competent authority: Proxy consent from the woman (discussed below).

Right intention: To cure the pathology for which the tissue has been extracted, and to gain knowledge about the prospects for curing future patients.

Last resort: All alternatives must be exhausted. Experiments with animals or with humans who may consent must have been found therapeutically deficient before fetal tissue is used. This criterion would also require researchers to examine alternatives such as genetically engineered cells that mimic fetal cells in animal research.[23]

Reasonable hope for success: Rash or irrational resort to research is prohibited. A review process is required with input from knowledgeable experts concerning the soundness of research design and assessment of risks.

Relative justice: Neither the researcher nor the fetus (or those representing the fetus) has a monopoly on absolute justice in defense of its claims. Rather, both are immersed in a situation of conflicting claims.[24]

Proportionality: The foreseen risks must not outweigh the anticipated benefits.

Satisfying these criteria, then, would justify recourse to fetal material for transplantation.

Yet justifying the use of others merely as means to ends does not justify all uses for socially beneficial ends, as I have suggested above. The pursuit of those ends, to continue the analogy, does not open the door to medical necessity or the imperative of medical efficiency. In this respect the moral problem of medical interest parallels that of military interest, but within a different set of institutional matrices. The question in the just-war context concerns the extent to which military interests subsume all justification of means in war. *In bello* criteria limit the extent to which such interests may prevail. In the case of using fetal tissue, the central question surrounding moral limits concerns the extent to which the interest of the researcher interferes with the abortion of the fetus. The question of limits and medical interest takes this material shape: To what extent has the woman's decision to abort been justified by the prospects of using fetal tissue in transplantation? To what extent has the medical imperative subsumed the justification to abort? To what extent are the medical decisions surrounding the woman complicated by a conflict of interest, especially the interest in procuring fetal tissue? Attempts to answer these questions would look for evidence about the circumstances under which the abortion occurred. Thus, an additional question arises: To what extent has the abortion procedure been altered by the imperative to procure fetal tissue?

These questions have important moral dimensions, given the prima facie duty not to instrumentalize others. If the abortion has been undertaken solely to provide fetal tissue for transplantation, then clearly the woman and/or fetus have been instrumentalized. Lying behind suspicions of conflict of interest, then, is the pressure exerted by the presumptive duty not to use other persons, dead or alive, merely as means to ends.

About this issue of conflicting interest, several canons have been developed to govern the use of cadavers under the Uniform Anatomical Gift Act (UAGA).[25] Fetal tissue is cadaverous tissue, and can be treated morally under already existing canons governing the procurement of tissue or organs from the dead.[26] Indeed, the UAGA includes dead fetuses within its provisions.[27] The existing safeguards surrounding the use of cadaverous tissue are likewise designed to prevent a conflict of interest, reflecting the prima facie duty not to use others merely as means to ends. When applied to the problem of how to limit the procurement of fetal tissue, those canons yield the following:

1. No financial exchange. This criterion would reduce incentives that subsume the abortion under the medical imperative to procure fetal tissue.

2. Clear separation, in timing and procedure, between the abortion decision and the decision about using fetal materials.

3. Someone other than those procuring tissue should determine the death of the fetus. Criteria for fetal death require specification.

Under the UAGA, however, it is permissible to donate an organ to a "designated individual." This provision would open the door to instrumentalizing women and/or fetuses in order to procure fetal tissue. For example, it would permit someone to conceive and abort in order to provide fetal tissue for a known recipient, perhaps a relative. To prevent such incentives, the three criteria above need the following amendment:

4. Anonymity between donor and recipient. That a woman may conceive in order to acquire fetal tissue for herself or a family member is not impossible, although the danger doubtless applies to relatively few pregnancies. Anonymity would safeguard against this possibility.

These four criteria reflect the pressure of the duty not to use others merely as means to ends, shaped in terms of barriers against conflicts of interest, the medical imperative. They are designed to ensure general consistency between using fetal and nonfetal cadavers (although criteria for death may differ owing to physiological and technological factors).[28] Such general consistency suggests that we ought not make a moral exception of fetal tissue, protecting it less than nonfetal cadavers against the medical imperative. Taken together, these criteria ought to answer the "how question" of procuring fetal tissue, developed under the shadow of the prima facie duty not to instrumentalize others merely as means to ends.

Incidentally, the groundbreaking Mexican transplantation of fetal tissue to a patient with Parkinson's disease followed the restrictions listed above: anonymity, written approval from a review board, consent of the woman, separation of the abortion from the transplantation. To ease anxieties about the source of the fetus, it should be noted that Mexican law forbids nontherapeutic abortions. The tissue was the result of a spontaneous abortion.[29] Moreover, the report made no mention of financial exchange. These facts approximate an ideal moral case.

Transplanting fetal tissue, as I have indicated, remains confined to the use of dead fetuses. Nevertheless, it is not entirely inconceivable that fetal tissue could be acquired from an intact fetus removed from the uterus by hysterotomy.[30] In this instance we could be dealing with a dying, nonviable—but not dead—fetus.

Canons governing the transplantation of tissue from dying fetuses ought to be consistent with those governing experimentation with nonviable fetuses under present NIH guidelines. Here again already existing canons can be extended to problems posed by new technological capabilities. The relevant question in this case would be whether such transplantation goes beyond the "minimal risk" allowed in pediatric research or other fetal research. The criteria listed above—justifying, yet limiting, fetal research—would likewise obtain.

The Complicity Question

The complicity question in its general form expresses moral reservations about the fact that fetal material is provided by induced abortions, some of which may be morally questionable. The almost ideal case of the Mexican transplantation would be difficult to repeat as a general rule, since most spontaneous abortions yield genetically or physically defective fetuses. Moreover, therapeutic abortions are doubtless too few in number to provide a reliable source of fetal tissue.

Questions about the reason for the HHS moratorium suggest that the morality of abortion may have been the actual subtext, the hidden agenda in the Reagan administration's policy. Questions arise because it is not clear why the request to transplant fetal tissue prompted a moratorium.

On the one hand, if HHS officials had moral reservations about fetal research per se, they did not need a request to transplant fetal tissue as the occasion to initiate legal and ethical inquiry, since fetuses were already being used in research. Events prior to Dr. Koplin's request, in short, were sufficient to raise questions about the use of fetuses per se. Thus, something other than this use must have been at stake. As the Windom memo makes clear in four of its ten questions,

163

the relationship between elective abortion and the procurement of fetal tissue was central.[31]

On the other hand, however, if abortion was the hidden agenda, then the HHS moratorium should have extended beyond the use of fetal tissue for transplantation to other fetal research, since the latter is doubtless allied with the practice of elective abortion. Since the moratorium did not extend beyond the issue of transplantation, then something other than abortion must have been at stake (assuming that HHS officials reasoned consistently about the connection between elective abortion and the use of fetal materials).

This second interpretation, however, seems the weaker of the two because it overlooks important political considerations. If a request for using fetal tissue for transplantation had occasioned a moratorium on *all* uses of fetal materials, then the Reagan administration's anxieties about the relationship between abortion and fetal research would have been transparently clear to the public. In all likelihood, then, the moratorium would have been assailed for carrying the weight of the abortion debate, perceived as policymakers' attempt to attack abortion laterally rather than frontally. Redirecting attention to the abortion issue while denying doctors permission to pursue a potentially therapeutic treatment would have been politically unwise.

Taken together, these two interpretations suggest that HHS may have sought to raise questions about the morality of abortion, but only covertly. If this inference is correct, the HHS moratorium represents another episode in the post–*Roe v. Wade* era, during which policymakers have sought to call attention to the morality of abortion, restrict payments for abortion, and generally qualify the liberalizing effect of decriminalized abortion.[32] Attention to the connection between abortion and the use of fetal tissue returns the debate about fetal research to the parameters of its initial (1970s) phase.[33] For these (and perhaps other) reasons, it is necessary to address moral issues about the relationship between elective abortion and the procurement of fetal tissue, the complicity question.

In its simplest form, the problem of complicity has been posed by Dr. John Willke of the National Right to Life Commission, who states, "You don't kill one patient to cure another, it's that simple. It is totally revolting, totally unacceptable."[34] It is also posed less polemically by the Roman Catholic Congregation of the Doctrine of the Faith, which, when speaking about the use of dead fetuses, remarks, "The moral requirements must be safeguarded that there be no complicity in deliberate abortion."[35] In the recent ethical debate about using fetal tissue the complicity question actually takes four forms, each of which has distinctive nuances and requires separate analysis.

The first form is fashioned most trenchantly by LeRoy Walters and focuses attention on the moral issue of *cooperation:*

> If a particular hospital became the beneficiary of an organized-homicide system which provided a regular supply of fresh cadavers, one would be justified in raising questions about the moral appropriateness of the hospital's continuing cooperation with the suppliers. . . . Ought one to make experimental use of the products of an abortion-system, when one would object on ethical grounds to many or most of the abortions performed within that system?[36]

Similarly, James Burtchaell writes, "Experimentation upon fetal tissue derived from elective abortion places the scientist in moral complicity with the abortionist. . . . The researcher is a confederate by resorting to the abortionist as a ready supplier of tissue from unborn humans who have been purposely destroyed." So, for Burtchaell, the association between elective abortion and fetal research "implies and engenders approbation that creates moral complicity."[37]

Cooperation as a moral term is used here inexactly, and a refinement of its meaning would eliminate the problem posed by Walters and Burtchaell. Strictly speaking, cooperation is done "by acting together with another in doing something that is morally wrong or by supplying another with what is helpful to him in doing something that is morally wrong."[38] Cooperation takes two forms: formal and material. Formal cooperation refers to active assistance, with an attitude of approval, in performing an immoral act. If the act is immoral, then formally cooperating is also immoral. Material cooperation, in contrast, refers to "that in which, without approving another's wrongdoing, one helps to perform his evil action by an act which is not of its nature morally wrong."[39] It may or may not be immoral, depending on extenuating circumstances, placed in a calculus of proportionate reasoning.

I submit that a hospital's use of "fresh cadavers" need not be either form of cooperation, since those procuring cadaverous tissue are not assisting in the deaths themselves. The killings are not occurring as a means to the end of research or transplantation. The criteria defined in the second and third sections of this chapter are designed to provide barriers against any cooperative connection between an "organized homicide system" and the procurement and use of cadaverous tissue. Applied to Walters's example of a hospital benefiting from organized homicides, those criteria would take the following form:

1. The suppliers would not know the identities of the recipients of cadaverous tissue. They would not be able to kill an individual in

order to guarantee cadaverous tissue for a relative, given the criterion of anonymity of the recipient.

2. The suppliers would not be paid by the hospital or profit in any other way.

3. Those carrying out the killings would not become the researchers.

4. The dead would undergo various procedures reflecting respect. Those who declare the victims dead would not be researchers.

5. Consent would be provided by the victim (obviously in advance) or by next of kin.

The goal of such safeguards is to prevent any intentional collusion between "the system" and the hospital. Those working in the hospital may be able to foresee that some of their subjects will be victims of unjustifiable acts. But foreseeing is neither willing nor intending. Absent will or intent, the hospital workers (or, analogously, those transplanting fetal tissue) are not necessarily implicated in a system toward which they may feel moral opprobrium. Thus, it is a matter of proportionate reason whether this foreseeable harm may be a component of medical care, even for those who object to the source of the material. In the case of transplanting fetal tissue, the benefits promised are proportionate to the use of fetuses from elective abortion at this experimental stage. That judgment is subject to revision should it become clear that transplantation offers no significant therapeutic benefit.

Of course, some persons may indeed approve of (or at least tolerate) morally questionable abortions. But the point here addresses those who do not: They need not be implicated in the system. Individuals involved in transplantation may (and from a moral point of view probably should) feel remorse or regret. But they are not objectively guilty of cooperation in a system about which they may have moral questions, since they are not assisting in abortions. Indeed, those who insist that persons transplanting fetal tissue are moral confederates in elective abortion would have to hold, as a matter of consistency, that plans to use murder victims for research or organ donation entail immoral cooperation, tainting such plans with association and implied approbation. Such a view fails to recognize the important distinction between foreseen and intended aspects of a human act.[40]

Those addressing the problem of cooperation often hold that the use of fetal tissue from elective abortions is analogous with Nazi experimentation on prisoners in the death camps. So Burtchaell argues:

The physicians who experimented upon the Nazi victims argued that they played absolutely no part in the decisions to imprison, torment, and exterminate those subjects. That would have happened with or without their participation. The response of the witnessing world was that their professional presence offered endorsement and legitimacy to the victimizers, and established them as accomplices in the exploitation of the helpless. . . . The doctors had entered fully into collusion with the SS by accepting their victims as experimental subjects.[41]

Insofar as Burtchaell's analogy is designed to underscore the importance of informed consent in the use of others, his point is surely correct. As an argument about cooperation, however, the analogy fails. As I have argued above, current researchers may override the prima facie duty not to use others merely as means to ends given the criteria developed. Nazi experimentation is reprehensible *not* first and foremost because it represents an act of cooperation, but because as *a form of experimentation* it failed to satisfy initial criteria for justification. As Burtchaell himself acknowledges using the language of consent, Nazi experimentation lacked competent authority insofar as it lacked informed consent. Indeed, it is difficult to imagine how such a criterion could have been satisfied, given the environment and the alternatives for the prisoners.

At the level of policy, the question of cooperation is reducible to the problem of a conflict of interest. In both cases the goal is to ensure that researchers neither will, nor have the incentive to will, elective abortion, even if they can foresee that such abortions will occur.

With the appropriate safeguards, like those listed above, this distinction between willing and foreseeing can be institutionalized. Such safeguards are designed to prevent a conflict of interest about foreseeable events. Without such a conflict, the moral problem of cooperation can be addressed at the level of policy, by seeking to ensure that researchers can permit an action without having to consent to it.[42]

The second form of the complicity question addresses the problem of *encouraging abortion,* the idea that the use of fetal tissue might make abortion more attractive to those who are considering it. Commenting on the breakthroughs promised by tissue transplantation, Mary B. Mahowald writes, "Even among those who endorse its legality, few if any would want to see abortion encouraged through the use of the new technique."[43] There is a moral difference between societies in which abortion is tolerated and those in which it is welcome.

The safeguards listed above are designed to remove any incentive for women to abort for purposes of gain, financial or otherwise. Such safeguards, especially those separating the decision to abort from decisions about the subsequent use of fetal tissue, are designed to remove the incentive to abort for reasons beyond maternal well-being. Without such safeguards, the woman's decision to abort is open to the possibility of either self-instrumentalization or a premeditated in-strumentalization of the fetus.

The third version of the complicity question is expressed by Rich-ard McCormick:

> If one objects to most abortions being performed in our society as immoral, is it morally proper to derive experimental profit from the products of such an abortion system? Is the progress achieved through such experimentation not likely to blunt the sensitivities of Americans to the immorality (injustice) of the procedure that made such advance possible, and thereby entrench attitudes injurious and unjust to na-scent life? This is, in my judgment, a serious moral objection to experi-mentation on the products of most induced abortions.[44]

The first question is a version of the cooperation question, and my answer to Walters applies to McCormick. McCormick's second ques-tion, however, is slightly different. It focuses our attention on the rela-tionship between procuring fetal tissue from elective abortions and *cultural attitudes* about nascent life, and it deserves a separate reply.

Whether medical progress would entrench attitudes injurious and unjust to nascent life is a difficult judgment to make. But more to the point, decisions about procuring fetal tissue are not the place to ad-dress such questions. If, indeed, attitudes toward nascent life are to be addressed and potentially reversed through policy, such attitudes should be addressed frontally. Policy about research and transplan-tation ought not carry the weight of policymakers' attitudes about abortion. If cultural attitudes are the question, in short, then re-stricting research and transplantation is the wrong way to develop policy. Rather, the appropriate topic for debate should be the legality and morality of abortion. And, as McCormick observes, our culture manifests profound disagreement about the issue of abortion. Thus, if policy is to reflect the deepest moral perceptions of the majority, or at least principles the majority is reluctant to modify, then policy decisions about procuring fetal tissue ought to prescind from the task of revising cultural attitudes about abortion.[45]

The final version of the complicity question raises the question of *scandal.* In its brief discussion of using dead fetal material, for ex-ample, the Congregation of the Doctrine of the Faith requires that "the risk of scandal be avoided," although it fails to specify factors that pertain to scandal.[46] Traditionally, scandal concerns the occa-sioning of a misdeed or the weakening of moral integrity; it is espe-cially pertinent where the performance of some actions is associated with questionable deeds of others. The question of scandal includes reference to public perceptions and the public trust. Even when one is not formally or materially cooperating, does the "taint" of certain

actions by some persons lower the moral integrity of others associated with those actions, or lower the moral attitudes of society in
general? The issue of scandal is a variation of the Pauline dictum,
"'All things are lawful,' but not all things are helpful" (I Cor 10: 23).

The question of scandal, with its roots in biblical and Catholic
thought, was briefly resurrected by Sissela Bok during an earlier
debate about fetal research. Bok asked whether killing or harming
young fetuses had a dehumanizing effect on the agents of abortion
and subsequent research.[47] In the present context, the question would
take the following form: Does collection, dissection, and transplantation of fetal tissue brutalize the women and men who perform these
procedures, lowering their respect for life? Does the taint of abortion
deleteriously affect wider cultural perceptions and moral expectations surrounding biomedical research? Does association, as Burtchaell suggests, imply approval?[48]

Here again, refining a technical moral term should eliminate the
problem. Scandal, strictly speaking, concerns acts or omissions that
induce another to sin. It takes two forms: direct and indirect. Direct
scandal is a malicious act in which one person deliberately tries to
corrupt another. Direct scandal thus does not pertain to transplanting fetal tissue. Indirect scandal "is that in which another's sin is
foreseen but not wished."[49] It is immoral if the act following upon the
foreseen sin is morally wrong, or if that act is not morally wrong but
lacks sufficient reason. Indirect scandal is thus morally acceptable if
it has sufficient reason, that is, if great goods would be gained by
continuing the practice.

Of course, whether the alliance between abortion and the procurement of fetal tissue diminishes the integrity of the researchers, or our
attitudes toward biomedical research, can only be settled empirically.
But as I indicated in discussing cooperation, for those who object to
elective abortions, the evil involved in using fetal tissue may be foreseen but neither wished nor intended. Foreseeing an evil caused by
another hardly implies approval. Transplanting fetal tissue is an instance, at most, of indirect scandal in a culture in which abortion
remains a highly emotional and controversial issue. Given the puta-
tive benefits of transplanting fetal tissue, at least at the experimental
stage, the alliance between abortion and procuring fetal materials
would seem justified by proportionate reason.[50] The problem of scandal suggests that fetal transplantation ought to be carried out not in
secrecy, but with discretion and careful oversight. It also suggests that
fetal research and tissue transplantation should be a matter of public
education and discussion in schools, policy hearings, meetings of
professional medical and ethical societies, and the media. Evidence
drawn from these contexts would prevent the accusation of scandal

from being purely speculative; moreover, debate within these contexts would reduce the possibility that it would occur, or increase.

Proxy

Questions have been raised about whether the woman is an appropriate proxy for the fetus.[51] Proxy consent is premised on the fact that proxies represent the best interests of the child (here the fetus). Yet this form of representation is difficult to apply to cases in which the woman elects abortion. The decision to abort for nontherapeutic reasons seems to disqualify the woman from the position of competent authority, one of the key criteria necessary to override the prima facie duty not to use others merely as means to ends. However, a justified (spontaneous or therapeutic) abortion does not disqualify the woman. My response to these observations has two parts.

On the one hand, even if a woman has the right to decide the fate of the fetus, she does not necessarily have the right to determine what may be done to the fetus before, during, or after abortion. Her constitutional protections are confined to the decision to abort. Thus, she has no monopoly over the decisions about how to treat the fetus.

On the other hand, the morality of abortion remains too controversial in the public realm to determine, as a matter of policy, that the woman's eligibility as proxy is contingent upon the morality of her decision to abort. The factors entering into a woman's judgments are various and complex. Individual abortions can be objectively wrong from the point of view of many along the wide spectrum of opinions about the morality of abortion; accepting the legality of abortion does not entail that all elective abortions are morally acceptable. But an objectively unjustified abortion does not mean that the decision to abort was subjectively capricious, unreflective, without seriousness or psychological complexity.[52] A policy that disqualifies as proxies *all* women having elective abortions seems overly restrictive, perhaps moralistic.

The complexity of abortion as it pertains to proxy is particularly relevant to those for whom therapeutic abortions are justifiable. A justified abortion would not disqualify the woman from serving as proxy in decisions about the use of fetal tissue, if eligibility as proxy is contingent upon the morality of her decision to abort. But are we absolutely sure what ought to count as a therapeutic abortion? Might we, at some later time, consider as therapeutic many abortions now considered nontherapeutic, for example, abortions for reasons of social, psychological, or economic well-being?[53] If so, can we securely anchor proxy to the condition that the woman's decision must be morally acceptable? The morality of abortion, especially the vagaries surrounding the meaning of a therapeutic abortion, would suggest not.

Here we must walk the line between morality and policy. Given the ethical complexity of abortion, a certain measure of agnosticism about the morality of abortion seems appropriate for identifying the proxy. Since the woman must bear the weight of her decision about abortion, she should have the first say about procedures involving the fetus subsequent to her decision. She constitutes, then, the competent authority responsible for deciding whether the duty not to instrumentalize the dead fetus may be overridden on behalf of medical goals.

Conclusion

When considering the ethics of transplanting human fetal tissue, we must change the subject from the problem of complicity in abortion to the question of justification, authority, and limited means. Otherwise the controverted politics of abortion will distort our moral vision and obscure the real problem at hand. Indeed, casuistry about using fetal tissue illustrates an important methodological point: If we put aside doctrinal debates and absolutist positions we can focus evenhandedly on a separate case. We must eschew, in other words, the tyranny of principles that clash in abortion debates, pitting advocates of a "right to life" against defenders of the "right to choose." Dislodging the case of fetal tissue transplantation from the case of abortion allows us to get beyond an intractable cultural war and consider the ethics of fetal tissue transplantation afresh.[54]

Accordingly, the first problem confronting us in the casuistry of transplanting fetal tissue is how to name its ethical dimensions accurately. In order to do so, we must meet this unusual case with some foothold on more familiar moral terrain. Casuistry as a form of paradigm-based research enables us to move to the new and the strange from a series of analogous benchmarks that have stood the test of time. Approached in this way, the problems posed by transplanting fetal tissue are not wholly novel, given existing models for casuistry about conflict situations and the care of the dead. An ethical framework designed for this problem would have four features.

First, the general framework for justifying, yet limiting, the use of fetal tissue for transplantation should draw from the paradigmatic structure of just-war reasoning. Both begin by overriding a strong presumption against the practices, respectively, of war and transplanting fetal tissue, given a situation in which duties conflict. In the case of fetal research we begin with the prima facie duty, widely held in our culture, not to use others merely as means to ends. An overridden prima facie duty nonetheless shapes the moral contours of the subsequent course of action.

Second, using dead fetuses should be governed by the same canons that govern the use of cadaverous tissue, with safeguards to eliminate conflicts of interest. Respect for abortuses, while apparently incongruous from the point of view of Kantian ethics, is nonetheless intelligible as an extension of the respect for fetal life and respect for the nonfetal dead. Respect for dead fetuses may be seen in light of the prima facie duty of nonmaleficence, requiring attitudes of regret about suffering and the loss of life.

Third, questions about cooperation with, encouragement of, or attitudes about abortion are separable from the use of dead fetal tissue. The death of nascent life is foreseen but not necessarily intended by those engaged in using fetal tissue. Safeguards against conflict of interest are sufficient for institutionalizing the separation between anticipating and intending elective abortions.

Fourth, proxy should not be made contingent upon the morality of the woman's decision to abort, given vagaries surrounding the moral terms on which abortions are sometimes justified. Hence, the woman should not be denied proxy status.

Seen in this way, a justification for the limited procurement of fetal tissue can draw on familiar canons in medical ethics. This case of instrumentalizing the dead can thus be annexed into our moral repertoire by way of analogical reasoning. Remembering the dead can thereby remain what Kierkegaard understood to be a faithful work of love, a work that is structured by a conflict of duties and an ordering of charity.

CHAPTER SEVEN

The Case of Violent Pornography: Mimetic Nihilism and the Eclipse of Differences

Bondage and Discipline

The truth is that one should not try to find an efficient cause for a wrong choice. It is not a matter of efficiency, but of deficiency; the evil will itself is not effective but defective. . . . To try to discover the causes of such defection — deficient, not efficient causes — is like trying to see darkness or to hear silence. Yet we are familiar with darkness and silence, and we can only be aware of them by means of eyes and ears, but this is not by perception but by absence of perception.
— Augustine[1]

There are at least three points where chaos — a tumult of events which lack not just interpretations but *interpretability* — threatens to break in upon man: at the limits of his analytic capacities, at the limits of his powers of endurance, and at the limits of his moral insight.
— Clifford Geertz[2]

In recent decades the graphic depiction of sex and violence in popular culture has generated various academic studies, legislative proposals, and governmentally sponsored inquiries into the pornography industry. This attention culminated in the report by the Attorney General's Commission on Pornography in 1986, which argued that violent pornography was causally related to violence against women, and called for a moral crusade against the pornography industry.[3] Many intellectuals who may be disinclined to associate themselves with the conservative politics of this report nonetheless hold that pornography is in effect a reprehensible epistemology—a way of knowing women as objects for male domination and pleasure. There is the general fear that pornography instrumentalizes persons, reducing them to a mere means of consumer gratification. Or, to be more precise, if instrumentalizing persons is presumptively wrong (as I argued in chapter 6), then it would seem that literature depicting the instrumentalization of persons is presumptively bad. In a culture that prizes freedom, however, such presumptive judgments seem needlessly censorious, perhaps overly scrupulous or prudish. At the very least, they threaten to jeopardize freedom of expression and sexual pleasure. Accordingly, pornography (especially when it includes violence) has become a test case for political attitudes toward censorship, representations of women, sexual tolerance (and deviance), definitions of art, and the effects of mass culture on social mores.

173

Yet it may surprise many to know that violent pornography has produced little commentary in religious or philosophical ethics. In contrast to social activists, literary critics, film critics, sociologists, historians, journalists, and legal scholars, ethicists have been virtually silent about the kinds of cultural anxieties generated by violent pornography.[4] One reason for this lack of attention, as I suggested in chapter 5, is the general aversion in academic ethics to issues in mass culture. Violent pornography is widely perceived by ethicists as "lowbrow"—to be contrasted to what is the equivalent of "high art" in the guild of ethics today: Kantianism, utilitarianism, narrative ethics, liberation ethics, natural law morality, comparative religious ethics, hermeneutical theory, social and political theory, professional and applied ethics, etc.

In this chapter I want to depart from this prejudice surrounding mass culture in general and violent pornography in particular. My goal is not to end the silence about violent pornography, but to show that there are good reasons—beyond intellectual snobbishness—for being silent. For, if I am correct about the truth of violent pornography, silence should not derive from academic prejudice; it should follow from a profound sense of what violent pornography actually depicts. To analyze violent pornography with finely wrought ethical distinctions is to be lured into and trapped by the ruses of the medium itself. Casuistry that is reflexive about this form of mass culture, in other words, must resist violent pornography's attempts to "bind and discipline" yet another unsuspecting victim.

In order to prepare for this point it might be helpful to sketch the landscape of violent pornography. To this end I introduce here images and episodes from the film and print media collection of the Kinsey Institute for Research in Sex, Gender, and Reproduction at Indiana University. In order to impose manageable limits on these materials, I will confine my discussion to visual materials that depict nonconsensual, violent acts carried out against women, or between (mostly) adult heterosexual actors. I will leave to others to determine whether the conclusions of this chapter extend to consensual, heterosexual, violent pornography (sadomasochistic pornography); consensual, heterosexual, nonviolent pornography ("hard-core" and "soft-core" pornography); gay and lesbian pornography (consensual or nonconsensual, violent or nonviolent);[5] and child pornography. I will also leave aside depictions of sex and violence against women in pulp fiction and video games.

Iconography of the subjugated, eroticized female in magazines like *Shaved and Bound, Rope Burn, Slaves of the Dungeonmaster, Tied and True, Punished!, Kidnapped, Rope, Strict!, Shackled, Glamour in Bondage, Roped and Rewarded, Bondage Digest,* and *Stocks and Bonds* more or less combine the following features: Ropes are tied around a woman's arms, torso, hands, buttocks and feet, and at least one rope is almost always brought up through her crotch and into a series of knots or pulleys. Often the victim has her hands tied above her head and is hung down from a ceiling, or her feet are tied to ropes that drop from a ceiling so that she can be hung upside down. Not infrequently the victim wears high heels throughout the torture "ceremony." At times ropes tightly encircle a woman's entire breast, forcing it into a football shape. Sooner or later a muzzle is put over the victim's mouth, with a ball gag placed in the teeth. Collars and leashes are often used. The depictions include familiar domestic symbolism: the ubiquitous chair, bed, shower stall, bathtub, or desk. Brooms are lodged in vaginas, and women are frequently bent over chairs or school desks. In one scene from the magazine *Obedience!*, a female "slave" is photographed pushing a vacuum cleaner with her ankles manacled. In another instance a ball gag is made out of what appears to be a bathtub drain stopper with a chain, centered in a strap of leather, which is tied around the model's jaw. Victims are clad, semi-clad, and nude. In some glossier magazines, women are depicted as punishing other women. Virtually all of the women are Caucasian, although *Rope* uses Asian models.

When scenes include a man it is not the case that his orgasm (the "money shot") is always the central or defining part of the account, even if he is the main protagonist. In the film *Making Danielle Talk!* (Bon-Vue, 1990), for example, John puts Danielle through a sequence of tortures without ever expressing sexual arousal, taking off his clothes, or inquiring into her pain. Virtually all of John's speech—delivered in a insipidly cheerful, Mr. Rogers-like tone—describes how he is going to change Danielle's bondage apparatus. Similarly, in the magazines I surveyed men are typically photographed with their backs to the camera or wearing executioner-like masks, and their chief role is to arrange or rearrange bondage mechanisms. Rarely are males photographed fondling the exposed body of the woman, but she is typically in a position to be ravished. Victims are occasionally placed in front of a mirror to witness the extent of their subjugation, which often (allegedly) intensifies their arousal. Occasionally, but not frequently, rings or clips are placed through a woman's nipples; the rings are sometimes tied to ropes that stretch the breasts out and up toward the ceiling. In those instances in which sex is coerced, the woman almost always announces her pleasure, as if to vindicate her aggressor.

Within films and magazines, these generic features are situated within a brief narrative or some simulation of a story. Consider the following:

• In an issue of *Roped and Raped,* Lois sets out to blackmail her male friend about their prior trysts. The male, unnamed, is soon to be married and wishes to keep his prior relationship with Lois a secret. After she arrives at his office and announces her threat, he forces her to strip and then takes her out to a studio. The author's description (with accompanying photographs) provides a somewhat standard depiction of the victim: "She was so nasty that I had to strap her mouth. I tied a rope around her waist and ran it through her crotch to a pulley. A line hoisting her arms up completed the set and she felt the strain on her back and shoulder muscles." The rope is arranged so as to rub against her labia as she breathes.

• Not infrequently, bondage and discipline are meant to provide a compensation, or corrective, for prior unsatisfying sexual relations. Another story from the same issue reports: "She wondered what it would be like to be actually raped while bound! Sex had been a real strikeout in her life. Premarital experiments had been uncomfortable, marriage sex had been a disappointment and a bore. Her husband, Will, never seemed to get involved enough for her to really enjoy him." (In this instance the woman sets out to find a real "will" to which she can submit.) After being tied, gagged, and mounted on a makeshift wooden saddle "that dug into her cooze in a sharp painful way," she is hung upside down, which gives her "some of the most ecstatic feelings she had ever had." Finally she is let down and begins to masturbate. But her fingers are quickly brushed aside as the male engages her in coitus.

• Consensual relations can turn into nonconsensual ones. In "Pubic Rope Burns," also in *Roped and Raped,* Donna and a man engage in a housewarming tryst that first suggests a consensual affair. She arrives dressed in hotpants and boots to arouse her friend. "Let's play capture," she urges. She soon finds herself tied up on the bed, lying on her stomach. The author writes, "Her rounded fundament looked so inviting I got behind her to use a little of it." She is then gagged and sodomized.

• Often these accounts are presented with a veneer of justice, producing the theme of vigilante sex (retribution for a transgression). The story "Hung Out to Dry" in *Stalked* tells of a wife who is punished for her infidelity as a truck-stop waitress. She is tied and bound with a noose around her neck—an unusual pose in the magazines I surveyed. The narrator remarks: "Sandy was a sacrifice. She was here to pay for her sins against fidelity, and against their relationship. She was going to be hung out to dry, forced to see her mistake. He started to educate her with the belt." The ropes that rise up through her labia arouse her, and the story ends with wife and husband in coitus.

- An edition of *Stocks and Bonds* ends with Joan on the bondage cross, in which she is photographed in a variety of positions resembling Christ's crucifixion, naked with the exception of a loin cover.

- An issue of *Torment* combines the theme of vigilante sex with the theme of compensatory or corrective pleasure. In "Spare the Rod," an extended narrative (highly unusual for magazines), we are told of Samantha, orphaned to her Aunt Sarah and Uncle Henry, caught in her bedroom with Randy. Samantha tells us, among other things, that Randy was not terribly good in this, her first sexual act. As punishment for her transgression, Uncle Henry enrolls Samantha in the Traynor Academy for Women. (The copy of the story is interspersed with numerous shots of different women bound and chained in a cellar, in fairly standard bondage and discipline poses.) Traynor is dull and drab—with strict hours, a dress code, and no rock 'n' roll. Unable to comply with Traynor's regimen of discipline, Samantha is eventually led, against her will, into the school's basement, where the Dean of Students gags her, fastens a dog leash around her neck, and ties the leash to a ring in the floor. Uncle Henry soon appears. Aroused, both he and the dean tie her hands behind her back. She is then whipped: "Each blow jerked a horrified screech of pain from the helpless girl, and each strike of pain lashed the flame higher in her body. . . . She wept for pity—uselessly. They were in full control of her helpless body, and they used their control cruelly. The whipping continued, turning her welted ass an angry, tomatoey red before it crept higher and higher over the arched small of her back and the straining muscles of her firm thighs."

Yet, predictably, the pain soon leads to "a simmering eroticism her single early sexual experience had not approached. . . . In the midst of her desperate struggles, a corner of her whirling brain noted the fire burning in her loins and wondered at it." Fondled by the dean, she soon experiences multiple orgasms. Then she is vaginally raped by her uncle, followed up by anal intercourse and forced fellatio. She finally acknowledges that "she had been conquered" and "would do whatever her uncle wanted in the hope that he would repeat the performance—yes, even the whipping—again and again."

- The June 1990 edition of *Hustler* features a three-page entry titled "Pictures of Murder" that is strikingly macabre. The first page contains pictures of faces, two of which appear to be men's. These pictures are held down by razor blades to what appears to be a piece of skin. A bloody mouth and strings of hair attached to a piece of scalp are positioned on the backdrop. On the second page there are four pictures of battered human faces, accompanied by a picture of some internal body part. Once again the pictures are held down at each corner by razor blades. A slice of an ear and other bloody body parts are situated against a backdrop of bloody flesh. On the third page four pictures of women's bodies are placed against the same background of bloody skin. Clitorises and nipples are also attached to the skin with fish hooks and safety pins. Some of the skin appears to be burned. The top picture depicts a woman without head or hands, and the middle picture shows a woman with a missing left leg and a torso that is ripped open. The third picture is splattered with blood and depicts a dead woman lying by a toilet. The bottom picture shows the trunk of a woman whose legs are amputated below the knees.

• A photograph from *Hustler* shows a naked woman on the floor with legs spread. Over her stands a man (no face), dressed in an undershirt and jeans, forcing a jackhammer into her vagina. The caption reads, "A Simple Cure for Frigidity."

• One copy of the *Bondage and Discipline Quarterly* includes a ten-page section in which Cathy ties, handcuffs, and strips David and puts him on a leash. The last picture shows her, semiclad, riding him, his face covered with a leather muzzle. One caption in the section reads, "Bound with ropes and hung from the rafters, her cat stings his flesh. Screams for mercy go un-heeded."

• The film *Ilsa, the Wicked Warden* (Jess Franco, n.d.) is about an institution that operates as a clinic for women with "female disorders" (identified as nymphomania and prostitution) and as a penal colony for female political prisoners. The first group of women is housed in a dormitory, the second in separate torture chambers. Most of the women wear only short-sleeved shirts and are often shown showering or lying naked in bed. The prisoners are whipped and given shock treatment at various points in the film; they are all disfigured.

The plot of the film turns on the character of Abby, who is seeking to find the whereabouts of her sister, Rosa, in the institution. With the help of a local doctor, Abby is able to secure admission on the pretext of being a child molester. She is soon befriended by Juanna, one of the leaders in the dormitory and a lover of Ilsa, the institution's warden. Ilsa engages in sadomasochistic trysts with Juanna, which include placing needles in Juanna's breasts and abdomen and then lying forcefully on top of Juanna to kiss her.

From the minute Abby arrives, Juanna expresses sexual interest in her. But her overtures toward Abby are unsuccessful, and soon she turns vindictive. To show her displeasure, Juanna frequently harasses Abby and at one point forces her to lick between her buttocks after defecating.

That scene is followed by one in which male ex-convicts are brought to the clinic. The audience is told that the men haven't seen a woman in years. Women from the dormitory and torture rooms are brought into a room with the men and are told that they will soon add to medical knowledge. The door to the room is locked and the men are given permission to fall upon the women and rape them as the female guards watch. A hidden camera, operated by one of Ilsa's henchmen, films the scene. Later we learn that he is selling the film on the side to a distributor of pornography. The buyer specifies that for his next purchase he wants something with death in it.

Eventually Abby is led into a room to find her sister, who is blind, disfigured from previous torture, and tied to a bed. Ilsa suffocates Rosa as Abby watches in horror. Afterwards Abby is taken off to be tortured by Ilsa's guards.

Then, inexplicably, several ministers of police come looking for Abby. Ilsa releases Abby, delirious from shock treatment, to their custody, as Juanna looks on in despair and jealousy.

For the film's conclusion, Juanna sets out to take revenge for Ilsa's treatment of Abby. She releases several prisoners into Ilsa's room. They stare at Ilsa with disfigured faces and shake uncontrollably. They then descend upon her and literally devour her in a long scene that crosscuts with close-up pictures of a lioness eating her prey. The movie ends with Ilsa's henchman secretly filming the scene as Juanna and the prisoners cannibalize Ilsa alive.

• Alex deRenzy's *Femmes DeSade* (n.d.) follows the trail of Rocky, recently released from prison. Rocky begins his exploits by hitching a ride with another recently released convict, Joey, who is picked up by his girlfriend outside the jail. After Joey and his girl retreat to have sex, Rocky enters their cabin, beats up Joey, and proceeds to rape and sodomize the (unnamed) woman. Joey returns to defend his girlfriend, who by that point is sufficiently aroused to call Joey off the scene.

The next several scenes shift to a porn-and-sexual-aids store run by Johnny, who is subject to various sexual fantasies. Johnny's girlfriend, Royce, is one of many prostitutes who frequent his store, along with daily customers and some of Johnny's friends. After introducing Johnny, the narrative dissolves into his fantasy about being a gynecologist who treats one of his customers from the porn shop (Marge). With the help of one of his nurse/prostitutes, Johnny spreads Marge's legs as she looks on expectantly; he then cuts her stockings open by pushing a knife between her legs and proceeds to inspect her vagina. After inserting and removing a dildo Johnny has coitus with Marge as the nurse fondles Marge's breasts.

The story returns us to the porn district, where Rocky picks up a prostitute and departs for a hotel room. The tryst is somewhat unsuccessful: Rocky's penis is too big to enter her, so she proceeds to fellate him, after which he bends over to fellate himself. Rocky then makes her stimulate herself orally by violently forcing her head down between her legs.

Later Rocky enters Johnny's shop to see a porn movie. He is followed by Andy, who is carrying a poster for "THE BALL: Blood and Mother's Milk." Seeing the advertisement, Rocky brusquely grabs an invitation to the party. After leaving the shop, Rocky meets Royce and they go off to do a trick.

In their room Royce unzips his pants and fellates him. He then asks her to put on a collar, to which she agrees under the condition that he does not get rough. He snaps on the collar painfully, puts Royce on a leash, and enters her vagina from the rear. Rocky then burns her breasts with a cigarette butt and starts to beat her. He ends the session by putting a glass bottle up her anus. She is left on the bed looking dead.

In the next scene Johnny comes home to find Royce in a state of shock. Johnny recognizes Rocky from her description, and they put out a call to warn the other girls. Royce's friend Blossom tells her of another prostitute who was also beaten up recently. They surmise that Rocky was the culprit in that beating as well.

Johnny and Royce then plot to meet Rocky at the ball and carry out revenge. The film's conclusion, the S and M ball, begins with a carnivalesque, orgiastic scene. One woman hangs upside down at the ball's entrance, another is beaten with a hot poker. Semiclad singers and dancers hover in the background as numerous individuals combine to carry out sexual tricks in countless positions.

Eventually Rocky enters the room and is recognized. The colossal orgy comes to a halt as Johnny and a woman engage in a whipping fight. She puts a whip and a collar around Joey, and then sets out to seduce him. As they kiss, the rest of the group walks around them, including Royce. Other women begin to draw Rocky into the orgiastic fray. He is slowly chained up as he is fellated, brought to the ground, and shackled. He begins to fight himself free as the group uses a dildo to sodomize him. Afterwards everyone dances around him and sings a farewell song: "Bye, Rocky, you're full of shit; Bye, Rocky, that's what you get." Several girls then defecate on his abdomen, and Rocky's previous victims disclose themselves to him: Joey, his girlfriend, Johnny, and Royce. The movie ends with the camera focusing on Rocky's corpse in the now empty room.

• Joseph Davia's *The Night of Submission* combines themes of religion, degradation, and compensatory sex. It focuses on an editor who sets out to infiltrate a voodoo-sex cult after pictures of the sect taken by Sandy, one of his photographers, mysteriously fail to develop in the darkroom. But the audience is not denied the details of Sandy's gaze. We first see a line of people who carry a woman into a room and lay her on a bed. The woman is being initiated as a "virgin" into the cult and promises to do whatever she is commanded by the priest. The priest then puts pins in a doll, after which the victim is beaten across her abdomen and stroked with a feather by members of the group. Ointment is poured over her and her nipples rise. She is slowly turned over, after which her buttocks are whipped and her arms tied up. Then a dildo is placed in her vagina. Afterwards she is brought onto a bed where she has a number with three men.

In the next scene we are brought back to the editor, who tells his lover that the violent voodoo group is devoted to "ritual destruction." After she announces interest in the group, the editor says he's already promised to take his wife to the cult, remarking, "She's one bitch I'd love to beat the shit out of."

Soon the editor and his wife infiltrate a voodoo ritual. They first encounter a woman shouting in pain as her nipples are tweaked by clips. The woman then fellates the voodoo priest and a huge orgy ensues. The editor proceeds to chain up his wife and engages in what is presented as pleasurable coitus with her.

In the final scene the narrative shifts to the editor's office, where he is finishing his story about the cult at the typewriter. But as he puts his pages together, we see that all the ink—like Sandy's photographs—has disappeared.

As these examples show, violent pornography does not always include the display of exposed genitalia or sexual exchanges. Instead, these materials feature images of people, usually but not always women, humiliated, bound, beaten, raped, tortured, or murdered for entertainment or profit. Violent pornography suggests that the willful and deliberate brutalization of another can be the source of entertainment and sexual pleasure, condoning for viewing amusement the gratuitous, wanton victimization of others. And, while these materials appear to blur the genres of pornography and horror, it is important to note, as Carol J. Clover writes, that "rape is practically nonexistent in the slasher film, evidently on the premise . . . that violence and sex are not concomitants but alternatives."[6] With violent pornography, in contrast, sex and violence are allies, the latter often serving to prepare a victim for rape and further victimization.

Aesthetic and Hermeneutical Ambiguities

Efforts to assess violent pornographic materials are beset by several vexations, which cluster into three groups. The first cluster concerns the *aesthetic and hermeneutical ambiguity* of pornographic materials. Is pornography best understood as a visual medium whose proper domain for analysis is aesthetics? If violent pornography is an aesthetic medium, should we confine its study to a consideration of its phenomenal properties, its use of figures and forms, the relation between surface and depth, and the structural configuration of parts within a totality of a bounded perceptual field? Should we focus on texture, balance, unity, and theme in order to appreciate the work of pornography? Or is pornography best conceived as a mode of discourse, a speech-act in which certain forms of behavior are suggested if not implicitly commanded?[7] If pornography is a mode of discourse, then is the proper domain for analysis hermeneutics rather than aesthetics? What tools are most appropriate for deciphering the signs and structures of pornographic works, when construed as modes of discourse? Or is the distinction between aesthetics and hermeneutics implied in these questions untenable, given the curious phenomenon under consideration? Is the first real vexation of pornography the fact that it defies the commonplace distinction between aesthetics and hermeneutics?[8]

An affirmative answer to these last two questions seems to suggest itself. Pornography blurs the distinction between aesthetics and hermeneutics because it recommends certain forms of human behavior (a discursive act) by means of suggestive symbols and images within a bounded perceptual field from which the observer is to derive enjoyment or sensual pleasure (an aesthetic act). Pornographic media use suggestive images that appeal to affections and sensual pleasures; they are also speech-acts in that they bid their patrons to assent to judgments demanded by the medium.

Yet if pornography is in part a discursive act, then it is not clear how we can classify its rhetorical strategies according to conventional terms or categories. Is pornography oral or written discourse? How can it be either? Efforts to think about the role of mass media (of which pornography is a part) in technological societies seem to furnish a clue to this problem. In his work on symbol systems in modern culture, Richard Stivers argues that mass media exhibit the same characteristics commonly attributed to oral discourse of myth and ritual in pretechnological or so-called primitive societies: Like primitive oral cultures, mass media form a closed and separate system, and repeat commonplaces and clichés in a highly stylized manner. The system remains closed and separate insofar as viewers fail to submit its messages to reflective criticism, disbelief, or empirical verification. The strategy of mass media in contemporary society is to deny the viewer the freedom that is a condition for criticism by creating an altogether different sense of freedom, that is, freedom understood as an abundance of choices. The strategy is not simply to construct a world of seemingly unlimited possibilities as an end in itself, however, but to entice the reader with the suggestion that such a world is the real world. The system remains closed and separate because its authority—like the authority of myth and ritual in pretechnological societies—does not rest on a "reality check." Rather, the converse holds: "Reality" is measured by the images created in the media.[9]

Pornography, as an item of mass media, operates according to roughly the same strategies of closed and separate systems. Pornographic messages are not subject to a "reality check" but bid us to gauge or imagine our own experience according to the images promoted in the medium. Pornographic images ask us to suspend critical reflection, and in the place of such reflection pornography substitutes a plethora of sexual choices: body shapes, settings, orifices, garments, participants, contexts, ages, liquids, sizes, positions, durations, paraphernalia, and moods. The "freedom of choice" extolled by the mass media is refined in sexual terms by pornographic media, but this freedom is a necessary condition for keeping the system closed and separate. Following Stivers's lead, then, we can say that pornography does not substitute freedom for restraint, prudery, or repression, but one form of freedom (the fantasy of unfettered choice) for another (rational criticism and suspicion).

A second current operates in mass media in general, and violent pornography in particular, which runs contrary to the celebration of sexual freedom mentioned above. Clichés and stereotypes are manufactured by the media and are refined in pornography, leaving the viewer with a strange sense of familiarity, perhaps déjà vu. Pornography has no original, no Ur-text, but only ongoing variants.[10] Like much of the American landscape today—its shopping plazas, fast-food eateries, convenience stores, strip malls, and highway interchanges—pornography is remarkably generic. It is one more instance of the leveling effects of modernity in America, producing for many a kind of cultural claustrophobia. Commenting on the highly repetitive and predictable patterns in pornography, George Steiner argues that its essence is boredom because it leaves little leeway to the creative workings of the imagination.[11] Differences between persons or situations are generally negligible in pornography; patterns have become fixed, the activity routinized. The system remains closed, then, not only because we must suspend our criticism, but also because the grist for fantasy has been reduced to highly conventionalized formulas. The sexual freedom associated with pornography coexists in an uneasy tension with predictable patterns, fixed settings, and pseudo-individuals. Insofar as pornographic models are objectified and stereotyped, individual details are effaced. Pornography's success rests in large part on its ability to deliver a cliché. This effacement of detail is particularly true of violent pornography, which seeks to erase differences not only between the models themselves, but also between models, animals, and other physical objects. In fact, the distinctive feature of violent pornography is not simply that violence is more pronounced than in soft-core and hard-core porn, but also that, as a precondition of violence, *differences must be eliminated.*

Indeed, within this first cluster of considerations the elimination of differences seems to be what violent pornography is all about: Violent pornography is both aesthetic and discursive; as a discursive act, it is both free and fixed; fixed patterns, especially within violent pornography, resist any distinction among victims or between victims and other objects; and pornography's freedom, in turn, eclipses freedom of another sort.

Social and Ethical Ambiguities

While the vexations of violent pornography exemplify many of the characteristics of mass media in general, several peculiar features of violent pornography can be sharpened if we turn to a second cluster of problems, which concern its *social and ethical ambiguities.* Two widely divergent models are frequently invoked to assess the effects of viewing pornography on human character and conduct: the "purgative" and the "exemplary." The former argues for the benign if not beneficial effects of viewing pornography, which generates an aesthetic distanciation between text and viewer, a distanciation that in turn causes a discharge of sexual or emotional tension. By directly appealing to the libidinous, pornography purges the viewer of negative affections or transforms them into less harmful passions. Implicit in this account is the claim that pornography, however graphic and otiose, is essentially a fictional mode of representation, creating another world in which the viewer may privately and vicariously participate. Left without such useful fictions, unable to be transported to the private world of fantasy, viewers of pornography (especially violent pornography) may seek more harmful outlets for their frustrations or anxieties.

According to the purgative theory, society clearly benefits from the open sale of pornographic materials; the social order remains relatively stable because of, not despite, the transgressions vicariously enjoyed by viewers of pornography. Real transgressions are supplanted by imaginary ones, and pornography thus plays a positive social function.

Something of this approach can be found in Joseph Slade's semi-autobiographical depiction of sex-film regulars in New York City.[12] Although he recognizes the potentially damaging and dehumanizing aspects of pornography, Slade finally embraces the notion that peep shows and stag films are relatively benign, that they can be confined to the realm of private fantasy even if the fantasy is regressive and adolescent. Pornographic fantasies may not supplant real sex, but such fantasies have positive effects in that they "permit mental adultery while preserving monogamy." Sex-film regulars are by and large not psychotics but are "our own next door neighbors and not certifiably insane." Moreover, pornography is not only sexual in its appeal; it also "caters to the voyeurism inherent in most of us." Questions about morality, art, or taste in pornography may be interesting, but they are generally beside the point. Rather, the "patrons know that what they are watching is artifice and illusion, that real sex involves responsibilities, respect for others, and emotional and intellectual involvement. They have fled those bonds in coming to the theaters, and they know that they will return to them."[13]

Slade's account was written in 1971, before the proliferation of the kinds of violent pornography described above. I cite his article because it exemplifies a more general attitude, namely, that pornography is essentially a private, fictional, humorous medium whose dehumanizing suggestions are left at the door once one leaves the theater (or closes the magazine). In fact, Slade gives us no reason to believe that his humorous account of pornography would not apply *a fortiori* to more violent forms. He suggests as much when he takes up the issue of violence. By Slade's account, "overt sadism, masochism and bestiality are rare. . . . This picture could change, of course, contingent primarily on the ingenuity of the Californians."[14] If we follow this treatment of pornography, the fitting response to its iconography is not disbelief or suspicion, but laughter. Concluding his discussion of pornographic theaters, Slade quotes a fellow patron who remarks (after watching two hours of predominantly long-haired performers in a stag film), "At least you can tell the boys from the girls."[15]

The exemplary model, in contrast, would hold that pornography depicts behavior that the viewer positively identifies as a model for sexual activity. Pornography generates not aesthetic distanciation but behavioral approximation or identification between text and viewer. Understood in this way, pornography is promotional, not just imaginary; it bids the viewer to accede to judgments demanded by the text. The effect of viewing violent pornography, then, is to intensify, not to purge, sexual tensions and to bring the viewer even closer to the need for a violent outlet. By this account, we distort the true nature of pornography if we confine it to a private, imaginary, and harmless realm. Rather, pornography has genuine effects in people's lives. We must "plot" the story of pornography and its viewers within the wider narratives of social violence, and contemporary social scientists are clamoring to present data that reveal a direct correlation between

185

viewing violent pornography and increasing permissiveness about violence against women.[16]

Despite the seeming differences between the purgative and exemplary approaches, we would be mistaken if we overlooked their common assumptions. Each approach either establishes or denies a moral justification for pornography on the basis of its social effects. Whether pornography "permit[s] mental adultery while preserving monogamy" or intensifies sexual desires, social consequence is the ruling consideration. In other words, the differences between the purgative and exemplary models are effaced by the fact that each is firmly rooted in the soil of consequentialism. And, however plausible either model might seem, both are subject to the limits commonly associated with consequentialist reasoning: How are social effects properly measured? Within what time frame? What other factors must be present (e.g., anger) for violent pornography to elicit an antisocial response? Is mere exposure to such pornography, considered apart from other contingencies, necessary *and* sufficient for generating violent responses? Does a growing tolerance of violence in other media contribute to or diminish the seeming ill effects of violent pornography? Although current research indicates a strong correlation between viewing pornography and sexual aggression, "proof" of this conclusion remains subject to doubt and, in any event, places a moral verdict on the shifting sands of contingent data.[17]

An alternative effort to weigh the moral issues surrounding pornography would focus on principles, rights, or moral laws, irrespective of social effects. One such approach, as developed by Harold Gardiner, S.J., attempts to define "the obscene" in order to determine a special class of materials whose content is intrinsically immoral. Invoking the authority of Aquinas, Gardiner defines the obscene as any material that "rouses to genital commotion." Media whose chief objective is to arouse such commotion must fall under the censure of canon law and of reasoned individuals. The argument here illustrates a form of Roman Catholic moral theology, which defines the essence of an act by examining its orientation toward a telos. Acts ordered away from natural ends or inclinations run contrary to the natural law and are thus intrinsically immoral. Venereal pleasure enjoyed as an end in itself, divorced from the conjugal act in valid marriage, is unnatural and therefore immoral; such pleasure is ordered to improper ends.[18] Materials that promote this form of pleasure fall under the same general condemnation.

Yet it is doubtful that Gardiner's in-principled approach marks a genuine advance for critics of pornography. The most problematic feature of his argument lies in its appeal to principles without reference to those commonly depicted in pornographic literature—

women. Like the pornography he wishes to assail, Gardiner's argument is pitched in the direction of a male audience, is cast in terms of male libidinous affections, and is ignorant of the status of the female as stereotyped and abused in the pornographic text.[19] Gardiner's analysis assumes that it is sufficient for moral evaluation to attend to the adverse effects of pornography on the male viewer; the boundaries of Gardiner's approach, like Slade's, are thus defined by the location and vantage point of the male in the pornographic speech-act. Rather than providing any critical moral distance on pornography, then, Gardiner's account actually falls prey to the seduction of the pornographic text in that both define their speech-acts in terms of male attitudes and experience. The place of the male viewer is sufficient for Gardiner's moral evaluation; his argument shares more in common with pornography than his criticisms might suggest. Hence, and most important, the common ground between Gardiner and his adversaries leaves us with yet another pornographic vexation: Again differences disappear, this time between text and conservative critic.

An in-principled alternative to Gardiner's approach might focus on the rights and dignity of women. Is pornography not defamatory literature? Is it not akin to other forms of hate literature, such as racist or anti-Semitic materials? Do not such materials bid us to assent to degrading images and stereotypes?

Arguing that the answer to all of these questions is yes, Eva Feder Kittay invokes a "universal moral imperative" to censure violent pornography, and the acts depicted therein, as intrinsically immoral. The chief pillar of her argument is the Kantian imperative to treat persons as ends, never as means only—an imperative that holds regardless of the historical, social, or cultural particularities of any specific sex/gender system. One may not use other persons merely as means to one's own ends, but must respect others as equals, as ends in themselves. Implicit in this Kantian approach is the claim that each moral agent acts as an autonomous subject, an end in itself, and to treat other moral agents merely as means to one's own ends is to violate the claim that such agents have to freedom from instrumentalization. To act for one's self-chosen ends, while treating other agents merely as means, is to make an exception of oneself, privileging one's own freedom above that of other autonomous agents.

It follows that to exploit, degrade, or abuse others is to trespass inviolable claims that derive from their autonomy. On moral grounds, then, Kittay argues that some violent sexual acts are illegitimate—"illegitimate by virtue of the moral impermissibility of harming another person and particularly for the purpose of obtaining pleasure or other benefit from the harm another incurs."[20] Violent pornography, whose intent is to cause harm to innocent persons, is hate literature and should be morally censured as intrinsically illegitimate, regardless of the social benefits that might accrue. The inviolable moral rights of women are infringed by violent pornography insofar as such literature depicts women in instrumentalized, humiliated roles.

But to focus exclusively on rights and principles, for Kittay, is to overlook a wider constellation of morally relevant aspects of violent pornography. Accordingly, she insists that the harm of violent pornography extends well beyond individuals thus depicted, that "society as a whole is harmed in its moral fiber when the moral status of all its members is not considered of equal worth by all the members of the society." A healthy social order and the morality requisite for such an order are clearly jeopardized by the proliferation of defamatory literature. Violent pornography represents "a brutalization which causes a breakdown in our moral imagination, the source of that imaginative possibility by which we can identify with others and hence form maxims having a universal validity."[21]

To Kittay it thus seems counterintuitive to suggest that the dignity of women can be disfigured without widespread social consequences. However benign it might seem, violent pornography nonetheless trades in the currency of domination and subordination. Those who justify pornography according to its purgative benefits fail to question the terms on which their understanding of social benefits depends; to say that the social organism remains relatively stable when pornography is allowed to flourish presupposes that the organism's conditions are essentially healthy. But this presumption is precisely what Kittay and other feminist critics of violent pornography want to question. At the heart of the social order is a structure of male domination and female subordination that is stabilized through various strategies, including images and impressions like those promoted in pornography.

In Kittay's mind, then, violent pornography not only "causes a breakdown in our moral imagination," it is also symptomatic of wider patterns of social interaction and exchange.[22] The brutalization of women in violent pornography reflects already pernicious social structures. Hence, violent pornography is as much a product as it is a cause of moral and social breakdown. One implication of Kittay's claims, although she does not draw it, is that such literature is self-enclosed; as a cause of social breakdown, it feeds on the pathologies of which it is a product.

Kittay's argument is an important one, for beneath her trenchant criticisms we find another set of false dichotomies and an elimination of differences. It does not matter whether one begins with a study of the strategies of the media in society (Stivers) or with the social mechanisms that are reflected in the media (Kittay): Violent pornography is a self-enclosed and separate system. Moreover, with Kittay the differences between symptoms and causes, and rights and consequences disappear: The inviolable claims of women-as-persons and the health of the social order are correlatively at risk. Unlike our previous arguments, however, Kittay's appeal to rights and social effects produces a twofold critique of violent pornography.

Indeed, the elimination of differences within this second cluster of considerations runs parallel to that within the first. Dichotomous forms of moral discourse are hardly dichotomous at all. Purgative and exemplary models both operate according to canons of consequentialist reasoning; an in-principled approach of one conservative critic operates within, not apart from, the masculine lure of the pornographic speech-act; and feminist analyses of rights bear directly upon considerations of social effects. The world of violent pornography seems to blur our conventional boundaries; it vexes our commonplace distinctions. It seems that the chief transgression committed by violent pornography is to violate such boundaries—not boundaries *within* our moral discourse, but those more fundamental boundaries that provide the conventional structures, the basic conditions, *for* moral discourse. The transgressive act of violent pornography is not to violate our conventions, nor is it simply to ignore them; rather, it is to *annihilate* them.

The Secret of Nihilism

A third set of vexations concerns the *relationship* between the first cluster of ideas (hermeneutics and aesthetics) and the second cluster (social and ethical) mentioned above. The issues pertinent to each pair seem to move without much reference to the other, as if they proceeded on divergent tracks, with no point of intersection or common ground. Although considerations of pornography tend to efface distinctions within each cluster, the division *between* clusters seems unbridgeable. There is a strange feeling that by bridging the gap between these two clusters we are taking pornography *too* seriously— and seriousness, as Slade suggests, is not what pornography is about. Our seriousness fails to follow pornography's bid to suspend our concern for social criticism and to enter into its separate and closed realm of the imaginary.

Violent pornography reinforces the division of labor between these two clusters—indeed, it depends on that division—insofar as it operates within a closed and separate system where disbelief or suspicion cannot freely operate. As an enclosed and insular system, pornography is designed to resist the invasion of considerations from

189

seemingly foreign regions of thought. It would seem that pornography would be hostile to interdisciplinary analysis, preferring instead to endorse the fragmentation of inquiry that frequently characterizes specialized knowledge in the humanities today. The critic of violent pornography must reckon with the problem that the conditions necessary for criticism are denied as an essential condition of the pornographic speech-act, that one is doing violence to the violent pornographic text by submitting it to critical scrutiny. There is a danger that if the images are removed from their pornographic setting, they will—like Sandy's photographs—disappear. Thus, another set of vexations: If we assess violent pornography according to criteria of social thought and ethics, we fail to accomplish much, because pornography is designed to subvert, or at least ridicule, conventional moral attitudes and assumptions. If we bridge the division between these two clusters, then, we either belabor the obvious or force pornography as pornography to disappear under the light of normative criteria, introduced from a foreign domain.

We might bridge this gap without forcing violent pornography to disappear under the light of critical seriousness if we begin with the notion that pornography, as an aesthetic and discursive phenomenon, is essentially a *mimetic* form of representation. The term *mimēsis* has a long and checkered history in Western philosophy.[23] *Mimēsis* in the arts, disparaged by Plato, finds a positive expression in Aristotle's *Poetics*. Aristotle understood poetry as exercising a mimetic function, by which he meant a creative imitation or representation of a world of human actions that already exists.[24] A mimetic work is not a copy of reality—it is not simply a photographic duplication—but a poetic construction that is the product of creative genius. The success of a mimetic work lies in its ability to imitate the logical structure, the meaning, of events. For Aristotle, moreover, a work of *mimēsis* imitates human affairs not only by capturing their structure, but by making them appear better or more noble than they would otherwise be. Amplifying Aristotle's ideas, Paul Ricoeur defines *mimēsis* as a "disclosure of a world," a world that constitutes a creative possibility for the viewer (or reader).[25] As a creative imitation of action, *mimēsis* designates what Ricoeur, following François Dagognet, calls an "iconic augmentation" of a world of human activity, a refiguring of events in which their meaning or essential structure is displayed.[26]

One problem with violent pornography, however, is that it seems to lack an ennobling function, understood in a moral or valorizing sense. If it lacks such a function, can we say that it includes an augmentation, especially an iconic augmentation?

Pornography is iconic insofar as it uses images and symbols to disclose a world, or a possible world, in which patterns and structures of human activity are figured for the receptive viewer. Violent pornography includes an augmentative function not because it ennobles human activity in any heroic sense, but because it depicts violence and degradation in a positive light, as a source of pleasure and entertainment. As I have remarked, it bids us to assent to the judgments that are implied in its depiction of persons and the responses those depictions are meant to produce. In this sense, then, we can speak of an "augmentation" occurring in the *mimēsis* of violent pornography and thus, following Ricoeur, we can speak of such pornography as "disclosing a world."

But settling the augmentative function of pornography raises a second problem: What is the subject matter that is iconically augmented, or the world that is disclosed, in the violent pornographic text? We might say that the subject matter of violent pornography is sexually suggestive images, images of domination and subordination, or subjects that have been reduced to brute and brutalized objects. But these candidates, and there could be several more, are deceptive because they presume that this problem of "subject matter" is based on sound terms. I will resist this presumption and will offer a different candidate as the subject of violent pornography—namely, that it is nothing. I do not mean that nothing or no one is represented, that images and ink disappear once we finish recording our perceptions at the typewriter or computer. Nor do I mean that violent pornography's subject matter is indeterminate, or trivial, or beyond critical scrutiny. Rather, I mean to follow the lead implied by *mimēsis*, where one is not to look at the acts that are imaged but at the meaning and structure of acts that are figured in the representation. My simple point is that the acts that are imaged may be acts of violence, but their very structure is nihilistic. Indeed, violent pornography is an iconic augmentation of nothingness, a celebration of the surd of death and destruction. Moreover—and this point is crucial—the nihilism of violent pornography provides a clue, indeed *the* clue, to its vexing, transgressive nature.

Violent pornography is essentially nihilistic not simply because it suggests a flagrant violation of customary attitudes and practices. The Dionysian festival also celebrates moral and social anarchy, but the difference between the festival and the violent pornographic speech-act lies in the fact that the former, at its core, celebrates fertility, life, and perhaps even the pursuit of immortality, while the latter refigures structures of servility and death—fatality as an end in itself. This difference constitutes a difference in kind, not degree, between the Dionysian festival and the world of violent pornography. The former represents a furious violation of conventions within life, while the latter denies the *conditions* for boundaries themselves.[27]

This distinction also suggests a distinction within the genre of pornography itself. Violent pornography is thanatic, whereas erotica—nonviolent, consensual pornography—more closely resembles the festive anarchy of the Dionysian orgy. As Rosemarie Tong argues, erotica depicts pleasure, enjoyment, and, on some occasions, intimations of love.[28] Sexual exchanges include self-respect and mutuality. Even though some pain may be depicted, it is not inflicted as an exercise of domination or proof of one's superiority over another. Thanatica, in contrast, "not only depicts but celebrates . . . and encourages either the callous frustration of one's own or someone else's preferences as a sexual being or, worse, the intentional violation of one's own or someone else's rights as a sexual being."[29] In its most extreme form, thanatica depicts the annihilation of others and "elevates" such nihilist visions by suggesting that the death of another can be a source of amusement. Thus, the paradigm of thanatica must be distinguished from that of erotica because the death celebrated therein represents an annihilation of the conditions for enjoyment, pleasure, or intimations of care. The world of violent pornography is radically nihilistic because the death it celebrates denies the conditions for boundaries, which are necessary for structuring a moral universe.

Violent pornography thus understood discloses a nonworld, an antiworld, a world in which conventions, boundaries, and distinctions become mute—not a utopian world of private fantasy, but a dystopia, a world designed to level the conditions for utopian imaginings and fictive possibilities. Violent pornography has a surdlike quality; it establishes an antiworld of violence to which one's initial response is neither laughter nor vocal disdain, but silence. Indeed, the silence that follows the disclosure of violent pornography is but a symptom of its nihilistic, surdlike character; it denies the conditions in which speech, as either laughter or derision, is appropriate. Violent pornography resists the dominion of speech because its surdlike quality denies the conventions on which speech depends and to which it contributes.

Consider, more specifically, the symbolism of violent pornography, and how it reverses the conventions and institutions of everyday life: the home (broom, bed, bathtub, household cleaning), education (school desk), religion (voodoo cult, crucifix), law/justice (the penal colony in *Ilsa;* recurrent vigilantism in magazines), and medicine (Johnny the gynecologist, the "medical knowledge" as pretext for rape in *Ilsa*). These institutional fixtures, and the world they constitute, are used to *unmake* the world for the victims in violent pornography: *The social units of shelter, culture, fairness, order, and health—institutions that enable us to expand our world, to protect and augment our being—are brought down on the victim's body, reducing her world to painful sensations.* In many respects violent pornography mimics the paradigm of torture, as described by Elaine Scarry:

> Civilization is brought to the prisoner and in [her] presence annihilated in the very process by which it is being made to annihilate [her]. Civilization itself in its language and its literature records the path that torture in its unconscious miming of the deconstruction of civilization follows in reverse: the protective, healing, expansive acts implicit in "host" and "hostel" and "hospitable" and "hospital" all converge back in "hospes," which in turn moves back to the root "hos" meaning house, shelter, or refuge; but once back at "hos," its generosity can be undone by an alternative movement forward into "hostis," the source of "hostility" and "hostage" and "host"—not the host that willfully abandons the ground of his power in acts of reciprocity and equality but the "host" deprived of all ground, the host of the eucharist, the sacrificial victim.[30]

What Scarry traces in her phenomenology of torture echoes the subversive, leveling undercurrent of violent pornography: Symbols of health and order are turned against those whom they might otherwise serve. The fixtures of shelter become a menace, a dystopia, insofar as the weapons of torture (and violent pornography) draw from symbols of domesticity. These weapons are used to reduce their subjects to what Scarry calls "corporeal engulfment,"[31] causing the world to dissolve into pain and subjugation, thereby subverting the conditions of human well-being. Accordingly, in torture and violent pornography the body becomes all and nothing at once.

For this reason it is appropriate to speak of the *radical* evil of violent pornography. As I have insisted, the iconography of sex and violence does not represent merely the violation of ethical codes within an otherwise orderly world. Violent pornography is not easily domesticated by our conventional canons and mores. Instead, it is beyond good and evil insofar as its representations deny the conditions for the possibility of a world at all. Scarry's words about torture pertain to violent pornography as well: "The unmaking of civilization inevitably requires a return to and mutilation of the domestic, the ground of all making."[32] This is how violent pornography "unmakes" a world: It subverts the terms and conventions according to which it is possible to have a world in which good and evil exist.

The claim that, by analogy with torture, violent pornography is a representation of nihilism, a deconstruction or unmaking of the world, can account for its several aesthetic and hermeneutical vexations—puzzlements about commonplace categories and the distinctions therein, of perception and promotion, kinds of freedom, and

193

degrees of freedom experienced by the viewer. The symbolic speech-act of violent pornography is antispeech, an endeavor to annihilate the premises according to which symbols and language can signify a world. Commonplace categories and distinctions are thus blurred within our first cluster of ideas, and, insofar as discursive practices rely on verbal distinctions, the eclipse of differences wrought by violent pornography is not without important implications for aesthetics and hermeneutics. But the eclipse of differences should come as no surprise once the leveling strategies of violent pornography are brought into view.

The same observations can be made about the eclipse of differences when we turn to the social and ethical aspects of violent pornography, drawing upon commonplace categories of positive and negative consequences, essential acts, rights, and social order. Here the question is not simply whether violent pornography is "moral" or "immoral." The question is more radical: It is whether a moral world, with its categories and distinctions, is possible at all in the iconography of sex and violence. My answer is that it is not. Drawing on the idea of representation as *mimēsis,* we can relegate violent pornography to the objectional status ascribed to other surds, other nihilistic endeavors, other versions of thanatica in human experience. Thus it is unnecessary to develop an elaborate casuistry of violent pornography, or to fashion something like a set of criteria for "just violent pornography." There is not, nor ever need be, a "just violent pornography doctrine," justifying the limited use of violent pornography. To do so would be to overlook the radical evil of violent pornography, the fact that it lies beyond the terms, conventions, and assumptions within which moral discourse typically finds its meaning.

The Irrationality of Cruelty

The relationship between violence, nihilism, and distinctions lies at the heart of my analysis of violent pornography's many vexations. It may be instructive to conclude by distinguishing my account from a seemingly similar treatment of violence, distinctions, and social order developed by René Girard. Girard locates the eruption of violent acts in premodern myths and cultures in the eclipse of differences, differences that generally contribute to the internal structuring of society. For example, Girard points out, in premodern myths twins must be sacrificed lest their patrilineal heritage be confused; Oedipus must be banished because his fate has nullified the kinship distinctions between father, son, mother, and wife; incest must be prohibited because it obscures the distinction between parent and child. Each of these examples represents an eclipse of differences, the emergence of a "monstrous double" whose presence must be eliminated. Sacrificial rites grow out of cultural crises; in response to the eclipse of differences, a surrogate victim is ritually sacrificed. The community institutionalizes ritual practices in its recurring efforts to maintain and renew social distinctions, which are essential to the health of the community. The threat of violence permeates the primitive community, and ritual practices function to restrain the force of violence, especially reciprocal violence, from destroying the community from within. Ritual practices are cultural mechanisms by which the community is able to channel archaic, subterranean currents of violence.[33]

The sacrifice of scapegoats, according to Girard, is the most effective mechanism by which the perpetual danger of communal violence is tamed and humanized. Scapegoats are commonly drawn from the margins of the community—slaves, children, and livestock.[34] Distinctions are maintained or restored by sacrificing some facsimile (but not an exact replica) of that which originally wrought an eclipse of differences. By Girard's account, ritual practices are prompted by some past, historic crisis. However strange the practice may appear to later ethnographers, it has its source in some primal catastrophic event.[35] Thus, the rite has a logic, however vexing it may be to outside interpreters.[36]

Girard's provocative argument, summarized all too briefly here, seems to provide an explanation for violent pornography in contemporary society. One might argue that the feminist movement has reduced or eclipsed patriarchal distinctions and that violent pornography is a response to the emergence of a new "monstrous double": the liberated woman, a female with agency. Violent pornography provides surrogate victims whose sacrifice restores a clear differentiation of sex roles and a patriarchal ordering of male-female relations. Like the sacrificial rites of primitive society, violent pornography provides a cathartic outlet for tensions created by social change and newfound freedoms. Confirmation of this thesis lies in the fact that violent pornography seems to have increased in direct proportion to the advance of the women's movement. Efforts to restore patriarchal distinctions can be correlated directly with growing equality.[37] Similarly, the emergence of child pornography, the depiction of master-slave relations, and the reduction of women to animal-like status all parallel the use of "marginal" surrogates in primitive societies.

Although this extension of Girard's argument seems highly plausible, it nonetheless contains a flaw from which his general theory suffers. That flaw is the notion that cruelty is logical and that violence lies, almost ontologically, within the deepest structures of the social order. Girard fails to consider violence as a possible surd because his argument is premised on the ontology of violence—a premise that excludes nihilism and irrationality from consideration. Girard's presentation, and its extension here, insists that violence must have some rational explanation; his account fails to consider the possibility of wanton violence, violence that is expressed purely for its own sake, with unqualified malicious delight, without reference to social disturbance or social change.

Furthermore, an extension of Girard's argument is unable to account for the emergence of *female* domination and *male* subordination in some versions of violent pornography (like those mentioned above), since the argument must confine itself to explaining why women are surrogate victims. If we explain the emergence of violent pornography as a backlash against women's equality, then this role reversal appears anomalous. On the other hand, if we understand it as nihilistic, then role reversal can be seen as yet another eclipse of differences. Indeed, one can interpret role reversal as a clear outcome of the leveling tendency of violent pornography because now the violent protagonists imitate each other. Violent pornography is indiscriminate in its potential for degradation.

If the secret of nihilism enables us to account for the several vexations within our first two clusters of ideas (aesthetic-hermeneutical, social-ethical), then perhaps it permits us to draw the two together without forcing violent pornography to disappear under the light of reflective scrutiny. Success in this task rests on our ability to recognize the dystopian, nihilistic strategy of violent pornography. In assessing the aesthetic, hermeneutical, social, and ethical aspects of the violent pornographic world, and in attempting to build bridges between these clusters of ideas, we must recognize that the world disclosed by violent pornography is not a world, but an antiworld. Only under this light, or within this darkness, does violent pornography refuse to disappear. But that is only fitting for the iconography of sex and violence, for it is in darkness that distinctions become indistinguishable.

PART FOUR

Casuistry and Method

CHAPTER EIGHT

On Not Keeping Religious Studies Pure

Purity, Danger, and Theology

Looming large on the agenda of Religious Studies today is an agonizing case of conscience. It concerns the widespread doubt that theology deserves a place within the academic study of religion, doubt premised on ambiguity about the meaning of the term *religion* and the proper modes of its investigation.[1] The divisions between religionists and theologians have become virtually intractable—the former viewing religion as "an attribute of social groups, comprising a component part of their cultural heritage,"[2] the latter viewing religion as providing the material for second-order truth claims. If understood as part of culture, religion is easily domesticated within the wider study of the humanities and the social sciences (largely descriptive and explanatory), drawing on methods familiar to anthropologists, historians, sociologists, and psychologists. But theology is different. Owing to its association with faith communities, theology has had a more difficult time immigrating and assimilating into the humanities, especially in large, secular universities. To many, theology appears parochial, sectarian, or prone to special pleading. The main concern is that theology often relies on modes of reasoning that invoke nonverifiable data. Put simply, the complaint is that theology depends on faith, whereas the study of religion relies on widely shared (although not uncontroversial) canons of reason.

Yet it would seem strange to exile theology altogether from the study of religion, given its historic associations with religious life and its place in the experience of most religious traditions. Indeed, studying a religious tradition or symbolic system without reference to its theological self-understanding seems counterintuitive. Moreover, many would argue, even if we were to view the study of religion as part of a wider examination of culture, it would be impossible to understand most cultures without an acquaintance with their theological heritages. Could a student of Western culture claim basic literacy without having studied Augustine's *Confessions?*

This ambivalent relationship between theology and religion has produced a need for the study of religion to produce a metadisciplinary account of itself. To that end I want to defend the idea that theology—or at least some theology—owns a rightful place in Religious Studies. It is my view that debates about theology within the study of religion are pointless because they presuppose an essentialist rendering of "Religious Studies." This essentialism seeks to keep the study of religion pure in two ways: First, by availing us of a crystalline definition of *the essence of religion* or *Religious Studies;* second, by keeping Religious Studies from being contaminated by the impurities of normative, theological inquiry. The idea is to develop a clean, clear, objective method for studying religion that will ensure a scientific approach, explaining religious phenomena according to their genetic causes and/or invoking canons of detached objectivity.

My main worry is that this quest for scientific purity is antiliberal, seeking to impose a criterion for Religious Studies that would in effect censor much of the current activity in the academy of religion. The impact of such approaches, if they were put into practice, would be to eliminate the rich, experimental, pluralistic study of religion that we now enjoy. The problem echoes liberalism's complaints about communitarian philosophy: The quest for purity seeks to impose a comprehensive vision of the discipline, but as a practical matter a single vision of "Religious Studies" is too contested to function as a basis for coordinating our intellectual life.[3] I am less concerned, in other words, with the metaphysical differences between theologians and religionists than with the practical and political fallout of letting the latter group establish the methodological rules for studying religion. Debates about method in Religious Studies are political, not metaphysical. We risk losing our pluralism and intellectual freedom in the quest for purity—no small price to pay in academic life.

As an alternative, I want to defend the present diversity within Religious Studies—diversity that creates room for theology—by developing what I will call a "poetic" as opposed to a "theoretical" approach to the study of religion. A theoretical approach attempts to define *religion* or *Religious Studies* and then asks whether various forms of research operate within the terms implied by the definition.

A neutral, objective definition allows scholars to operate according to the ideals of scientific rigor. Scholarship that is associated with non-scientific research is considered impure; it transgresses a definitional taboo.

A poetic approach, in contrast, is inductive and interpretive. It asks us to view Religious Studies as the attempt to ascertain complex meanings within a discrete set of problems, cases, symbols, or ethnographic encounters—absent the need for methodological orthodoxy or a comprehensive vision of the discipline's identity. Following Ludwig Wittgenstein and Clifford Geertz, this alternative is topical and eclectic, aiming to examine discrete cases that regularly present themselves in the ongoing life of a people. It will thus provide scholars the space necessary to try out new ideas, draw on a variety of hermeneutical tools, and explore uncharted terrain. We should understand philosophers of religion, historians of religion, comparativists, anthropologists, psychologists of religion, theologians, philologists, religious ethicists, and religious feminists as working within a series of concrete cases or areas of inquiry. Following Wittgenstein, I want to show that all we need to classify specialized modes of investigation as "Religious Studies" is a family resemblance among various subdisciplines in the field. Seen in this way, the study of religion can be understood as requiring only an overlapping consensus of diverse spheres of investigation, not methodological uniformity or a comprehensive definitional consensus about what counts as the subject matter of religion.

What is more important for the study of religion than a common subject matter or scientific mandate is whether teachers of religion are able to cultivate a sophisticated set of hermeneutical skills. It is here that the idea of Religious Studies as a poetic practice is most apparent. Scholars of religion will be identifiable—with their own address and zip code, as it were—not because their subject matter or modes of inquiry are all the same, but because their theories, conventions, vocabularies, and interpretive expertise enable them to talk to each other as well as to other faculty members and intellectuals in the humanities. Their citizenship in the humanities will be stable, in other words, not because of *what* they study but because of *how* they study it—provided they carry out their work with hermeneutical perspicuity.

No doubt a defense of Religious Studies in these terms seems strange. To be sure, what I am calling an issue of academic conscience presents a different kind of case than those addressed in the first three parts of this book. But debates about method lie at the heart of assessments that scholars regularly make about the practical value of their colleagues' work in the study of religion. It is no exaggeration to say that the divisions between religionists and theologians involve deep-seated judgments about the intellectual merits of their respective endeavors. Metadisciplinary controversy is not "merely academic." Indeed, as the pilot study by Ray Hart indicates, the relationship between theology and Religious Studies represents the most agonizing case in the American Academy of Religion today.[4] It strikes at the heart of a young, often insecure field of inquiry, and plays a significant role in job searches, annual evaluations, graduate recruitment, advising, and judgments about the intellectual value of our peers' ongoing work. For this reason we do well to view this metadisciplinary issue as involving a case of professional conscience. As J. Samuel Preus writes, "The stakes are enormous, because basic decisions are involved about how the next generation of scholar-teachers ought to be trained, and such decisions are in turn informed by fundamental ideas about what liberal education is about, as well as notions about the future of religion."[5]

Simple and Complex Ascriptions

The current debate about theology has familiar historical parallels. To state it broadly, we have moved from the nineteenth-century quest for *the essence of Christianity* (voiced by Harnack and Ritschl) to the desire to define *the essence of religion* (voiced by historians and social scientists).[6] Harnack's work sought to distinguish the core of Christianity from its subsequent doctrinal accretions. Today's efforts are metacritical, attempting to determine the phenomena to which the term *religion* ought to apply. The goal is to provide a basis for distinguishing the proper subject matter for the academic study of religion from its unscientific impostors. In other words, defining *religion* is a metadisciplinary endeavor, providing the first step toward determining what ought to be the essential subject matter of Religious Studies. If we are able to define religion as, say, "xy@ˆz," it seems to follow that "Religious Studies" ought to subsume those inquiries directly devoted to studying xy@ˆz. Having a clear definition of religion provides the basis for drawing boundaries around the discipline. It thereby enables scholars of religion to volunteer part of their time for border patrol.

All of such pursuits are pointless insofar as they remain linked with essentialism. Yet the enduring traces of essentialism are quite paradoxical, situated as they often are in social scientific approaches that purport to be antimetaphysical and antiessentialist. But social scientists' attempt to avoid metaphysical pursuits in the study of religion have failed to take the Wittgensteinian critique of essentialism to heart. As a result, social scientific discussions of "the essence of religion" (and, by implication, "Religious Studies") lead to an intellectual cul-de-sac. The best therapy is not merely to criticize such essentialisms, but also to dissolve them. I shall do so momentarily.

One can only speculate about the circumstances and anxieties that energize this pursuit of an essential definition. One likely factor is that the disciplinary cohesion of Religious Studies is, at best, in doubt. Disciplines congeal, Stephen Toulmin argues, when they have a common ideal or goal, around which problem-solving endeavors are clearly structured. Yet not all disciplines or areas of inquiry are equally well developed. Toulmin distinguishes "compact," "diffuse," and "would-be" disciplines. The ideal—a compact discipline—has five characteristics:

> (1) the activities involved are organized around and directed towards a specific and realistic set of agreed collective ideals. (2) These collective ideals impose corresponding demands on all who commit themselves to the professional pursuit of the activities concerned. (3) The resulting discussions provide disciplinary loci for the production of "reasons," in the context of justificatory arguments whose function is to show how far procedural innovations measure up to these collective demands, and so improve the current repertory of concepts or techniques. (4) For this purpose, professional forums are developed, within which recognized "reason-producing" procedures are employed to justify the collective acceptance of novel procedures. (5) Finally, the same collective ideals determine the criteria of adequacy by appeal to which the arguments produced in support of those innovations are judged.[7]

Compact disciplines, Toulmin writes, are capable of being exposed at every stage "to critical reappraisal by qualified judges." Diffuse disciplines conform only loosely to these requirements, and would-be disciplines have the potential to become areas of disciplinary cultivation, but have yet to do so.

Generally a field falls short of the ideal because it lacks a common goal or because its institutional mechanisms are undeveloped. When disciplines lack a clearly defined reservoir of problems, "conceptual innovations within them face no consistent critical tests and lack any continuing rational direction."[8] Indeed, without a common goal, diffuse or would-be disciplines lack agreement about "standards for deciding what constitutes a genuine problem, a valid explanation, or a sound theory." The immediate result, Toulmin observes, is that "theoretical debate . . . becomes largely—and unintentionally—methodological and philosophical; inevitably, it is directed less at interpreting particular empirical findings than at debating the general acceptability (or unacceptability) of rival approaches, patterns of explanation, and standards of judgment."[9]

Religious Studies is clearly a diffuse discipline. Although its institutional mechanisms—professional societies, annual meetings, academic journals, fellowship and grant opportunities, refereeing procedures, and prestigious publishing houses—are securely in place, it lacks a sufficiently agreed-upon goal in terms of which common problems can be identified and tackled. For this reason the study of religion is conspicuously unscientific. Yet if we arrive at a definition of religion, it is alleged, we might be able to overcome this difficulty. As Hans Penner and Edward Yonan remark: "Without valid definitions and theories, a science of religion is impossible."[10] Science succeeds by defining its terms and the scope of its data, and we should expect no less in the quest for a science of religion. In a separate essay, Penner writes: "The first challenge is to present a well-formed theory which will define and describe the object of religion. . . . The goal . . . would be nothing short of a theoretical description of the universal structure of religion."[11] In effect, Penner and Yonan want to move the study of religion from its status as a diffuse discipline to something closer to a compact discipline, with a clear set of terms and objectives. They thus set out to define what constitutes a definition and insist that efforts by scholars to define religion must meet a series of formal conditions.[12] (Definitions should not be circular, should not use vague or general terms, should cohere with our shared understandings, etc.) Their goal is to specify the logic of a definition, providing rules that will advance the theoretical and scientific status of the study of religion. As it is, Religious Studies remains "theory-shy," frustrated by terminological imprecision about its proper phenomena.[13]

In a similar vein, Frederick Ferré argues that defining religion is the first step toward eliminating "the present state of conceptual chaos engulfing studies about religion."[14] The idea, once again, is to recall the model of the sciences, which proceed with great efficiency once tendentious terminological claims are resolved. He thus calls to our attention the "shameful disparity between the conceptual order from which our scientific colleagues are capable of profiting at ever accelerating rates and the conceptual shambles within which students of religion are obliged to make their halting way."[15] To reduce this disparity we should establish a definition, understood "as a minimum set of characteristics that are laid down as both necessary and sufficient for the application of the term to whatever possesses them." (Religion, Ferré argues, is "one's way of valuing most intensively and comprehensively.") Essences are not ghostly things but provide logical tools, "sharpening our discrimination among particular things and aiding our conceptual ordering of the world of experience into groups of things that are similar in important respects."[16]

I have suggested that Wittgenstein provides an alternative view of what constitutes a definition, freeing us from the need for strict, formal conditions and theoretical purity. Conceiving of definitions in essentialist terms, Wittgenstein would say, presupposes a nounlike, designative understanding of how ascriptions work.[17] That is, essentialism invites us to conceive of definitions along the model of a word pointing to an object, as the word *chair* designates the object on which I am sitting. Essentialists abstract from that object some enduring qualities—the essence of "chairness"—and then map the rest of the objects of the room by ascertaining which of them satisfies the terms implied by the abstraction. The goal, then, would be to produce something like a theoretical description of the universal structure of chairs. The method works abstractly and deductively, first by arriving at an essentialist rendering of chairness and then applying that essence to the phenomena that present themselves in the room. The overhead device moving air in my study is clearly not a chair, since it lacks legs, cannot be sat on, provides no back support, etc. It is a ceiling fan, which calls for a different kind of definitional representation.

However helpful this approach may be for understanding how some ascriptions work, it is unhelpful as a model for the vast majority of things to be designated. It is rather the case, as Wittgenstein argues, that we assign definitions to some objects because we find sufficient likenesses among those objects to ascribe to them the same term:

> Why do we call something a "number"? Well, perhaps because it has a—direct—relationship with several things that have hitherto been called number; and this can be said to give it an indirect relationship to other things we call the same name. And we extend our concept of number as in spinning a thread we twist fibre on fibre. And the strength of the thread does not reside in the fact that some one fibre runs through its whole length, but in the overlapping of many fibres.[18]

Whereas essentialist theories aspire to produce simple, straightforward definitions, Wittgenstein's approach requires us to conceive of definitions in complex terms, as "family resemblances." Such resemblances are complex insofar as they require us to see how terms emerge from overlapping phenomena. The items to which an ascription applies share similarity, not uniformity or identity. Members in a family are recognizable not because they all possess the same characteristics, but because they all possess some common characteristics—like a chain of overlapping circles. Some members of the Jones family have long noses, many freckles, and curly hair, while others have long noses, large eyes, and a few freckles. Consider Wittgenstein's famous example of how we assign the word *games:*

> I mean board-games, card-games, ball-games, Olympic games, and so on. What is common to them all?—Don't say: "There *must* be something in common, or they would not be called 'games'"—but *look and see* whether there is anything common to all.—For if you look at them you will not see something that is common to *all,* but similarities, relationships, and a whole series of them at that. To repeat: don't think, but look!—Look for example at board-games, with their multifarious relationships. Now pass to card-games; here you find many correspondences with the first group, but many common features drop out, and others appear. When we pass next to ball-games, much that is common is retained, but much is lost.—Are they all "amusing"? Compare chess with noughts and crosses. Or is there always winning and losing, or competition between players? . . . In ball games there is winning and losing; but when a child throws his ball at the wall and catches it again, this feature has disappeared.[19]

Similarly, members of the family of "Religious Studies" can overlap because some of them deal with historical change, symbolic worlds, and religious institutions; some with ethnographic reports about symbolic worlds, social legitimation, and ritual practice; others with problems concerning religio-philosophical treatises and modes of social legitimation; some with worries about the crisis of authority and power in religious institutions; others with interests in moral or philosophical reasoning in religious discourses that inform religious authority; some with interests in literary conventions, symbolic formulae, and the social circumstances of religious writings.

The key point is that some of these family members raise issues that move them into conversation with other members to such a degree that they recognize themselves as related to each other in a complex intellectual kinship system. Historians of symbolic systems and religious institutions draw upon the tools developed by phenomenologists, who learn from the data of anthropologists, who concern themselves with power and the symbolic reinforcement of authority, along with its past historical manifestations. Those interested in the literary forms and social contexts of religious writings draw upon tools provided by social scientists of religion, who help us track the effects of social change on thought and writing. Ethicists and philosophers consider the normative implications of such findings, raising questions about the propriety of one or another symbolic world.

In any event, herein lies the complex understanding of how the same term (*Religious Studies*) can serve as a definition: The phenomena it includes need only provide enough similarity for the defining term to operate ascriptively. Such is the Wittgensteinian understanding of how a term functions to join together various phenomena. Religious Studies will retain its strength not if it finds some essential core, but if it is woven together by a series of overlapping and mutually reinforcing conversations that constitute the fibers of its enterprise.

Avoiding the kind of simplicity implied by an essentialist approach to definitions in no way derives from a fear of theory—Penner and Yonan's assertions notwithstanding. It rather derives from a philosophical awareness that the pursuit of simplicity and purity leads nowhere. That is, what is wrong in debates about the study of religion is not that we lack an ascription like *religion* or *Religious Studies,* but that we lack a philosophically adequate understanding *of a definition.*[20]

Objective Science or Genre Bending?

Penner's quest for "a well-formed theory" is part of a larger and more ambitious aspiration to craft a science of religion, complete with scientific protocols of explanation and criticism. Its vision of rationality purports to be "objective": neutral, shareable, omniscient, impartial, dispassionate, and verifiable though observation. The goal is to apply to religion, in the words of Donald Wiebe, "the ordinary obligations of neutrality and objectivity that attend our other academic activities."[21] Its adherents are therefore suspicious about appeals to tradition and memory, which occlude analytical vision. The special pleading that is (allegedly) typical of theology, Wiebe writes, "can only lead to the infection of Religious Studies by religion itself," thereby placing in question "the objectivity of the results of the research undertaken."[22]

The clearest example of this line of reasoning appears in the important study by J. Samuel Preus, *Explaining Religion: Criticism and Theory from Bodin to Freud.* Preus traces the emergence of the naturalistic paradigm for studying religion, a paradigm that turned from theological explanations to social or psychological explanations for the origins and persistence of religious belief and practice. Why does religion continue to exist in society and culture? What ongoing needs does religion meet? The naturalistic approach holds that conscious reasons for belief and action are insufficiently explanatory, that behind the explicitly stated, conscious reasons identified by believers lie forces or impulses of which they may be unaware. Its goal is to provide alternatives "to the explanations that the *religious* offer for religion,"[23] laying bare the hidden motives for religious belief. Naturalistic inquiry developed with the conviction that explanatory procedures that seemed fruitful in the realms of nature and social institutions could be applied to religion as well. Its modern exponents—Hume, Comte, Tylor, Durkheim, and Freud—thus set the terms for "a coherent research tradition that produced a new paradigm for studying religion."[24] Remarks Preus, "Only on such an assumption could the modern study of religion build."[25]

Taken together, the arguments on behalf of a scientific or explanatory paradigm—and against theology—are many and varied. One concern, as I have mentioned, stems from the perception that theology's modes of reasoning are "nonpublic." As Preus remarks, theology "devotes its energy primarily to the interpretations of religious experience from within."[26] In contrast, the scientific, humanistic study of religion adopts a mode of rationality that

> challenges the popular notion that the only proper approach to religion is "from inside" . . . ; it argues that a clear distinction between a naturalistic approach—with its own explanatory apparatus—and religious approaches is necessary to achieve a coherent conception of what the study of religion is all about; and, negatively, that such a distinction is needed in order to clarify the difference between study of religion in the framework of the humanities and human sciences and often hidden apologetic intentions that inform much contemporary writing and teaching about religion.[27]

Hence the allegation: Theology is "apologetical," creating barriers to explanatory modes of inquiry. That is, theology provides an account of religion and religious experience that exempts religion from the kinds of questions that we put to other realms of human life.

One problem with this complaint is that it fails to distinguish confessional theology from apologetics in the study of religion. The terms are not synonymous, and it is by no means obvious that antitheological opprobrium applies equally to both. Confessional theology is credal, seeking to articulate the meaning and implications of an ostensive religion's beliefs. Typically, confessional theologians care little about whether they make sense to a wider public. But apologetical discourse is different: It attempts to defend religion according to wider canons of experience and rationality. Indeed, confessional theology would hardly understand itself to be apologetical. Echoing Karl Barth, those now developing confessional theology (e.g., George Lindbeck, John Howard Yoder, William Placher, and John Milbank) overtly or covertly reject the requirements of public argument that are typically associated with apologetics.[28] Insofar as confessionalists seek only to develop their truth claims from within the practices and beliefs of a particular religion, religionists have it right: Confessionalists seem to disavow canons of inquiry that might be shared by the nonbeliever, and so develop claims that are wholly "from the inside."

Complaints about apologetics must turn elsewhere, and usually show up in discussions of Mircea Eliade's phenomenology. Indeed, Eliade is a favorite whipping boy for exponents of a scientific method. In Eliade-like phenomenology, Wiebe writes, "religion is a *sui generis* phenomenon . . . that can only be properly treated 'on its own terms.' To understand the 'religions' as a psychological or sociological phenomenon, therefore, is simply not 'taking religion seriously.'" The descriptive impulses that follow from phenomenological procedures insist

> *that the study of religion remain free of theory and forego any explanation of religious phenomena.* To explain, it is argued, is to assume either that such phenomena are, in some sense or other, illusory or veridical and so to invoke the very category of truth that the principle of the *epoché* banished in its attempt to achieve a neutrality that could ground an academic study of religion. "To explain" is taken to mean "to explain away" . . . which implies, I suggest, an ontological reality of religion that it may not really have.[29]

In Wiebe's mind this acceptance of the autonomy of religion protects it from the kinds of critical questions put forward by scientific methods. Phenomenology thus produces "an implicit but . . . unconscious and unintended theological agenda in the academic study of religion."[30]

Yet the idea that phenomenology is covertly theological is, to say the least, odd. Its famous methodological *epoché* brackets *confessional* truth claims of religious traditions as a first step toward uncovering their formal properties and adopting generic frameworks for analysis.[31] Phenomenological methods begin by announcing neutrality toward the *credal* claims to truth made by religious practitioners, the "first order language" of religious belief and practice. In this way phenomenologists attempt to examine a religion's construction of time, communal life, space, pilgrimage, rites of passage, or place by using an alternative, nonconfessional framework for interpretation and comparison. Having uncovered some basic properties in one religion, the phenomenologist can then move on to compare one religion's attitudes toward various phenomena—e.g., time—with another religion's. But for those seeking to explain, this announcement of neutrality is not only insufficient for the academic study of religion, it is a methodological smokescreen, concealing covert apologetical interests. Whatever pretensions it may have about neutrality, phenomenology nonetheless fails to produce a *naturalistic* explanation for religion.

209

The idea that, lacking a naturalistic paradigm, scholars are guilty of what Wiebe calls "crypto-theology" of course begs the question, Why are nonnatural approaches *religious* or *apologetical?* Indeed, it appears that in a naturalistic account *all ideas* have dubious status. The metaphysical materialism of much naturalistic theory has yet to be accounted for. Yet the strictures it would impose are clear. For example, the naturalistic paradigm would render inadmissible the language I used in the last chapter about "radical evil." Naturalists provide no room for such language, given that it is unverifiable according to basic canons of so-called objective, scientific inquiry. Similarly, my earlier discussion of why Western religion has an interest in pluralism is methodologically heretical, given the fact that I eschew discussion of genetic causes or unconscious motives of any religion's interest in civic order or public life.[32] But to assert that this treatment of religion or religious terminology is nonnatural and therefore apologetical is, of course, absurd. Naturalistic theory proves too much, leaving a vast chasm between inquiry into genetic causes on the one hand and apologetical interests on the other. Surely much terrain lies between. For scholars of religion to provide, for example, an account of medieval Confucian attitudes toward the body and medical practice scarcely means that they are engaged in apologetical or crypto-theological discourse. Nor is it obvious that their inquiry lacks objectivity. To identify it as confessional or apologetical is to overlook the obvious distinction between interpreting the meaning of events *to* practitioners and interpreting the meaning of events *about* practitioners. Religionists can easily carry out the latter in nonnaturalistic terms without the slightest hint of apologetics or confessionalism.

It is not obvious, in other words, that relying on nonnatural methods is tantamount to producing a defense of theological inquiry. Nonnaturalistic approaches to religion are no more controversial than the claim that a work of art cannot be understood solely in social scientific categories. That is, we regularly (and uncontroversially) inquire into the works of Beethoven, Matisse, Bob Dylan, or Toni Morrison in terms that cannot be captured fully by explanatory interrogation. Nonnaturalistic discourse is scarcely unique to the study of religion. And, most important, within the humanities we scarcely consider it methodologically heretical to say so. To suggest that a scientific or naturalistic approach to human experience is sufficient to justify a place for the study of religion within the humanities is premised on counterintuitive perceptions about what is going on in colleges and universities today.

What is at stake in the argument against naturalism as the dominant paradigm for the study of religion? It is not, as Wiebe tirelessly asserts, the desire to protect the autonomy of religion or to smuggle theological agendas into the classroom. It is rather the idea—evident in the works of Weber and Troeltsch—that religious belief can have a causal effect on social behavior. Naturalism is problematic, in other words, not because it might "explain religion away" and thus disappoint religious devotees, but because paradigmatic studies have shown that religion can be as much a cause as an effect in social life. Moreover, it seems improbable that we can understand how a religious tradition can have particular historical effects without knowing how its symbol system works "from the inside."

The desire to resist the totalizing aspirations of naturalism, then, is driven by works indicating the powerful force that religious belief can exert in social movements. *The Protestant Ethic and the Spirit of Capitalism* and *The Social Teaching of the Christian Churches* argue on behalf of a dialectical, interactive relationship between religion and social practices. They were self-consciously developed by Weber and Troeltsch to correct naturalism's monocausal, unilateral understanding of human motives in relation to religion.[33]

Related to naturalism's suspicions of phenomenology is the claim that Religious Studies needs the naturalistic or scientific paradigm in order to secure a place on the cutting edge of contemporary scholarship. If scholars of religion want to develop new insights and problems for investigation, it is alleged, they should wed their methods to explanatory theories in the social sciences. In this way the study of religion can free itself from the parochial needs of religious denominations and turn to issues that are on the frontiers of humanistic inquiry. If, however, we allow theology a place in the study of religion, Wiebe warns, we "will set the academic/scientific study of religion back 100 years or more."[34]

Yet even a cursory glance would reveal that the naturalistic paradigm is scarcely queen of the social sciences, or that explanation constitutes the chief goal of cutting-edge social scientific work. It is rather the case, as Geertz argues, that the social sciences are currently undergoing an enormous amount of "genre mixing," leading to new, complex reconfigurations in social thought. We are now in the throes of "blurred genres," Geertz writes, in which the lines joining and dividing intellectual inquiry are "running at some highly eccentric angles."[35] (Who is Richard Rorty, anyway—philosopher, political theorist, cultural critic, literary theorist? Who is Edward Said—advocate, ideologue, historian, literary critic? What is *Writing Culture*—history, historiography, anthropology, cultural studies, literary criticism?) In a similar vein, James Clifford speaks of the "inventive syncretism" apparent in recent ethnographic writing, which bridges the disciplines of anthropology, literary criticism, and hermeneutical theory.[36] Social scientists are drawing on a wide, eclectic range of tools to decipher social behavior, and the stock of finding determinants of human action has decreased in value. The present goal is to ascertain the meaning, not the causes, of action, leading social scientists to embark on inquiries "closer to what a critic does to a poem than what an astronomer does to account for a star."[37]

While not aimed directly at religionists, Geertz's comments are nonetheless instructive: If Religious Studies hopes to break new ground, it will scarcely find itself on the frontier of the social sciences if the latter means "explanatory theory." Geertz rather suggests that the social sciences are better conceived pluralistically and hermeneutically, drawing on cultural, historical, literary, sociological, legal, and philosophical tools to ascertain not why actions occurred or what laws of behavior were illustrated, but what those actions mean for the rest of us. Geertz remarks, "Many social scientists have turned away from a laws and instances ideal of explanation toward a cases and interpretations one, looking less for the sort of thing that connects planets and pendulums and more for the sort that connects chrysanthemums and swords."[38]

This is not to say that theologians can easily join cause with cultural anthropologists. In fact, many religionists who accept some of Geertz's claims insist nonetheless on the importance of comparative or cross-cultural studies as an antidote to theology. The main idea is that comparison ensures that one religion's claims to truth will be relativized when parallels are shown in other traditions. Comparison all but guarantees that the uniqueness of any one religion—and the claims that it makes on behalf of its uniqueness—will be deflated. This "comparative imperative," as I will call it, fears that a student's appreciation of one religion will be confessional or parochial unless it is developed within a comparative framework. The popular form of this imperative is the aphorism, "You don't know one religion until you know two," or "You don't know *religion* until you know two religions."[39] To prevent confessionalism, many Religious Studies departments require students to study at least one religion outside their primary interest. Summarizing the views of the American Academy of Religion Task Force in "The Religion Major: A Report," Stephen D. Crites writes, "Studies in depth in religion are intrinsically multicultural, directed to more than one religious tradition. . . . To study any one religion in depth the student should expect to study more than one."[40]

No doubt comparative work has the beneficial effect of showing that many claims that religions make on their own behalf are exaggerated or historically naive. Religions are infamous for privileging their own beliefs, folklore, history, or practices, as if there were no parallels in other religions or realms of human experience. A final vocabulary seems less than final—but often more human and humane—when juxtaposed with other religious vocabularies in comparative religious discourse.[41]

But however edifying comparisons are, the cash value for the study of religion can be confused or overstated. Works like Geertz's *Islam Observed*,[42] comparing the politics of Moroccan and Indonesian Islam, are widely heralded as exemplary for those interested in multicultural, comparative work, but Geertz never compares Islam with another religion. His failure to put Islam in dialogue with another religion scarcely means that he is an apologist or confessionalist for Islam, or that his work lacks "objectivity."

Moreover, even if we adopt more modest expectations about what comparisons require (or produce), it is not clear that comparative inquiries are sufficient for securing a place for Religious Studies within the wider study of the humanities. Nor is it obvious that they ought to. In the study of English, for example, scholars certainly do not argue that "you don't know one genre of literature until you know two." Rarely if ever do we find scholars in Comparative Literature parading their skills as superior to or as a corrective for the kinds of skills developed in English departments. Nor do political scientists hold, as a methodological axiom, that students will not know what "political science" is unless they study comparative politics. For that matter, comparative economics is, at best, a subfield in economics departments. Yet English, Political Science, and Economics departments are secure in granting minors, majors, and graduate degrees without making comparison central to their inquiry. Religionists' insistence upon comparison as sufficient for establishing methodological sophistication in the study of religion is premised on a highly truncated vision of scholarship and teaching in other realms of the human sciences. We are left with the idea that religionists' impressions of other intellectual enterprises are seriously limited, perhaps wishfully so. But whatever its motives, the suggestion that naturalism or comparative inquiries get to the heart of activity in other fields in the modern college or university is counterintuitive.

It is interesting to note that within this discussion religious ethics does not generate the kinds of suspicions that surround theology. Consider, once again, comments from the Hart report. In the study of religion today, the report observes,

> the most often cited, clearly discernible trend in the sample is a preoccupation with issues under the rubric of ethics. . . . A by no means complete list of specific ethical issues includes the following: the ever-widening gap between rich and poor worldwide; population growth and distribution; the exhaustion of natural resources; "apocalyptic

213

consciousness"; environmental pollution; the threat of nuclear war; family structures; teen-age parenting; . . . the growing aging segment in the American populace; . . . homelessness; biomedical ethical issues; ethics of the professions; religion and "conflict."[43]

What many of these issues have to do with religion, especially as it is conceived within the scientific paradigm, is unclear. Yet the acids of naturalism would be as damaging for ethics as they are for theology, given that the former no less than the latter presumes (in the words of Wiebe) to put "persons in contact with what is ultimately real, true, and good."[44] The Hart report suggests that, in areas that are not obviously theological, those who teach religion in American higher education seem unconcerned about the place of normative inquiry per se. Theology may be on the ropes, but ethics (and feminism, another realm of inquiry with clear normative implications) remains in the center of the ring. Strangely, religious ethics and feminism have remained virtually untouched by the quest for purity and naturalism in the study of religion. The reasons for this discrepancy are, at best, mysterious.[45]

Religion and the Humanities

The status of Religious Studies as a diffuse discipline suggests that the attempt to establish objectivity in Religious Studies is symptomatic of a grave inferiority complex in the field. This complex is energized in part by doubts about whether those who study religion are as sophisticated methodologically as their colleagues in the humanities. Hence the desire to draw parallels between the study of religion and other disciplines. According to Preus, the naturalistic paradigm for studying religion—as distinct from a theological approach—was institutionalized with "Tylor gaining a university post in anthropology, Durkheim a first university chair in sociology, and Freud founding the International Psychoanalytic Association."[46] In a similar vein, Jonathan Z. Smith remarks, "Religious Studies are most appropriately described in relation to the Humanities and the Human Sciences, in relation to Anthropology rather than Theology."[47]

It is tempting to speak as if there were huge Platonic Forms hovering over colleges and universities, Forms like "History," "Folklore," "Philosophy," or "Anthropology." If that were the case, then we could clearly organize the intellectual departments of a university and differentiate one unit from another. Unfortunately, however, there are no such essences to constitute disciplinary boundaries, to guide budgetary decisions, to structure departmental appointments, to shape curricular judgments, or to justify tenure decisions. There are only history departments, folklore departments, philosophy departments, psychology departments, anthropology departments, and so on, which are nothing more than highly contingent and fluid human constructs, occupied by scholars whose methods and interests overlap, more or less.[48] We should therefore demystify appeals to disciplinary Forms and reduce them to the pragmatic aphorism (or wish) that people who label themselves "religionists" will probably sit on more dissertation committees or schedule more lunches with anthropologists, folklorists, or historians than with theologians or scholars of hermeneutics. Seen as anything more than such an aphorism (or wish), parallels between Religious Studies and "Anthropology" or "Psychology" become one more set of academic interests seeking legitimation by appealing to what purport to be abstract essences.

The desire to envision the study of religion along the lines of other humanistic disciplines is premised on the misguided notion that other fields have congealed, that they have achieved the status of compact disciplines. But there is no more reason to worry about the disciplinary coherence of a Religious Studies department comprising a scholar of modern Japanese religion, a psychologist of religion, a specialist in hermeneutics, an intellectual historian of Christianity, a Talmudic scholar, a historian of Sufism, a biblical exegete, a scholar of Chinese religious syncretism, a religious ethicist, a scholar of Tantric Buddhism, and a specialist in the Pali canon than there is to worry about English departments that teach Chaucer, Wordsworth, Twain, Proust, Achebe, New Criticism, Lacanian theory, feminism, Derrida, the ethics of fiction, rhetorical theory, creative writing, film theory, and introductory composition. Once again, anxieties about intellectual heresies in the study of religion might be significantly mitigated if we consider the pluralism that enriches other departments in the modern college or university. Religious Studies should remain content about its status as a diffuse discipline. It would then have no more reason to worry about its intellectual rigors than do most other disciplines in the humanities today.

As I mentioned earlier, how and where departments of religion are located in relation to other disciplines (or departments) is less important than the problem of essentializing the study of religion, or relying on an essentialism that imputes to other fields some timeless Form. The essentialist temptation can easily lead scholars to model the study of religion on idealized visions of other disciplines, with strict boundaries and an orderly system of classifying who ought to be "in" and who should be "out." With this quest for purity comes the desire to exercise power by controlling membership in (and assigning rewards within) the research community. A poetic approach to the study of religion, in contrast, ensures that power is diffused across a spectrum of scholarly approaches and perspectives. Thus it seems

215

wise to maintain a pluralistic view of the profession, if only to distribute power more democratically across subfields.

It is ironic that scholars of religion—those who have done much to call attention to the contingency of human thought and practice—seek to cloak their methods in the language of purity and danger. This irony is compounded by the fact that religionists not infrequently call attention to the potentially alarming affinities between knowledge and power in various formations of social life. Having demystified religion, the pursuit of purity in the study of religion would do well to demystify itself. Unfortunately, such self-reflexivity in the American Academy of Religion is conspicuously lacking.[49]

One result of this essentializing tendency is that attempts to fashion Religious Studies along the lines of other humanistic disciplines seldom make reference to the recent history of other cognate fields. On this score it is instructive to consider what has happened in departments of philosophy in the United States since World War II. As Rorty indicates, academic philosophy during this time has gone in hot pursuit of methodological orthodoxy, shaped in large part by the kinds of rational ideals represented by science.[50] What many of us (still) consider to be philosophy—the study of the Greeks, the Stoics, medieval scholastics, idealism and empiricism, modern political theory, phenomenology, pragmatism, etc.—has fallen on extraordinarily hard times. In many circles of American philosophy today, Rorty writes, "one can still cleave to the view that philosophy began as natural science's account of itself, that attempts to claim knowledge outside of the natural sciences are to be measured against the procedures used within them, and that philosophy has recently become scientific and rigorous."[51]

As a result, philosophers have entered the "Age of Analysis," training for which has often led them "to despise the sort of person who was interested in the history of philosophy, or more generally the history of thought, rather than in solving philosophical problems."[52] Many of those who have been trained in the history of ideas are still hoping to fight their way back into the halls of power in the American academy of philosophy. Some have found asylum in comparative literature departments, political science departments, and professional ethics congeries. In departments of philosophy today, the hegemony of analytical philosophy is well known—as are the dissatisfactions of undergraduates who have the untutored hunch that philosophy is a strange consort of computer science or artificial intelligence, two cognate disciplines of analytical philosophy. Ironically, the attempt to fashion philosophy along the ideals of science did little to join philosophy departments to other departments in the humanities—quite the contrary. But few of these problems seem to have made an impression on religionists who seek to impose a similar standard of purity. Refusing to heed the experience of philosophers, many modern scholars of religion seem determined to repeat the same mistake.

Skills, Not Content

Seeking to understand Religious Studies as a kinship system instead of a simple ascription does not necessarily mean that all forms of theology automatically deserve admission to the field. It only means that theology's immigration and subsequent membership in the humanities cannot be ruled out *a priori*, or that admission standards are to be settled abstractly and deductively. Whether theology overlaps sufficiently with other interests in the field will depend on how that theology is developed. Theological inquiry that abdicates the canons of scholarly inquiry—broad as these canons may be—absents itself from full membership. Strident confessionalists may wish to play by other rules, but they may not have it both ways: enjoying membership in Religious Studies while renouncing the general terms according to which the modern study of religion is carried out.[53]

The task of scholars of religion today is not to determine whether theology, conceived in the abstract, belongs in Religious Studies. Their task is rather to determine *which* forms of theology are appropriate to the study of religion, and why. Figuring out where and to what extent theology overlaps with other areas in the field, I am suggesting, will determine the proper places to draw distinctions. That is, we can begin distinguishing between theology that is friendly and theology that remains hostile to Religious Studies by discerning the extent to which specific examples of theological discourse overlap with other modes of inquiry in the study of religion.

Of course, defending a place for theology within Religious Studies does not mean that theologians ought to abandon the seminary setting or church-related theology departments and emigrate to a secular university. This is especially true of Christian systematic theologians, for whom excellent resources already exist in several North American divinity schools and theology departments. As Van Harvey recognized over twenty years ago, "the seminaries will always have a legitimate interest in Christian theology and, by and large, will be able to provide the best context for it. The seminaries can provide a range of supporting disciplines with which secular departments of religion cannot compete."[54] Theologians who prefer a Religious Studies department to a seminary, divinity school, or theology department as a more desirable location for carrying out research and teaching elect that option at some risk.

In any event, attempts to ascertain where and to what extent a theological program can find family resemblances in Religious Studies is finally a matter of judgment. No short formula, no laundry list of characteristics, can be specified in advance. Family resemblances enable us to understand Religious Studies "from below," from on the ground, not from the Olympian clouds of theory, simple ascriptions, and essentialist rationality. It is ironic that many historians of religion wish to settle this issue abstractly and deductively rather than inductively. An inductive approach would ask us to begin by probing the actual practices, experiences, customs, and choices within the academy of religion. It thus requires a more intimate knowledge of theology than is evident in most antitheological writings today.[55]

Embarking upon an inductive route means that we need not settle tendentious metaphysical arguments about naturalism versus supernaturalism, explanation and interpretation, or reason in relation to faith. All that is necessary to ascertain the "study of religion" is enough common ground among various modes of inquiry to establish an overlapping consensus. An inductive approach frees us from having to construct a strict (definitional) consensus about what counts as the subject matter of "religion." Following Wittgenstein, definitions that are essentialist, premised on the notion that language is merely designative, are overly restrictive, failing to account sufficiently for diversity.

Whether and where an overlap occurs, I have suggested, is a matter of judgment, which must occur prior to any ascription or definition. Judgments require us to ascertain how distinct phenomena overlap, and where similarities end or are only trivially interesting. For example, we use *mysticism* not to name *exactly* the same phenomenon in more than one religion (Sufism/Kabbalah). Instead, we say that sufficient similarity exists between Sufism and Kabbalah to warrant for both the ascription *mysticism*. As I have suggested, the same method should shape our ascription *Religious Studies*.

One possible rejoinder to this Wittgensteinian approach might claim that reliance on our customs and practices in the study of religion nonetheless betrays the promise to produce a new angle of vision for studying religion in the modern university. The fear is that after finding a place within the academy by promising to be scientific, Religious Studies has nonetheless failed to purge itself of the vestigial remains of theological discourse. As Wiebe argues, to allow theology to remain in Religious Studies constitutes a "failure of nerve" among scholars to keep the study of religion independent of confessional or apologetical interests. Tolerating theology is tantamount to betraying the "original intention" of the founding fathers of Religious Studies, namely, to study religion in nontheological terms.[56]

Yet it is hardly apparent that the place of theology in the academy of religion today is the result of bad faith. Rather, the study of theology is often driven by a larger commitment to moral and religious literacy, introducing students to the thought-forms, beliefs, and arguments that shape various religious traditions and philosophical inquiry. Reference to theology in this sense is scarcely confessional or apologetical. Indeed, even a cursory glance at contemporary theology would reveal that much of it is acutely conscious of the challenges posed by Kant, Marx, Nietzsche, and Freud, and that it is keenly aware of the winds of modernity. For that matter, virtually all of the leaders of contemporary theology in Europe and the Americas are conversant with Wittgenstein, Heidegger, Ricoeur, Gadamer, Habermas, Foucault, and Rorty. To worry that theology is tied to an established canon, or that it is engaged in something akin to defending the Synod of Dort, is woefully anachronistic. Quite the contrary: If the leading theologians of the American Academy of Religion have a problem today, it is that little of their work seems directly to address an ostensive denominational community.[57] It is hardly the case that their theology is tied to a parochial audience.

A quite different concern consists in the idea that granting (some) theologians their green cards according to the reasons I have provided nonetheless poses the danger that Religious Studies will lack a methodological center.[58] The quest for an overlapping consensus between different areas threatens to produce intellectual balkanization, leaving the study of religion to ad hoc modes of inquiry.

But so long as various spheres of inquiry overlap sufficiently, this danger is negligible. Indeed, a curriculum established along the lines I have sketched—one that eschews essentialism and embraces complexity and pluralism—would produce sophisticated interpreters of religious phenomena. They would have a wide, eclectic range of tools with which to exercise their interpretive and religious literacy.

What kind of literacy would this vision produce? What kind of pedagogy would these notions require? Consider, for example, how we might teach Augustine's *Confessions*—a not unlikely topic in Religious Studies and Theology departments today. Undergraduate teaching aimed at literacy in the study of religion—including theological literacy—could combine several possible lines of inquiry. One obvious route would be to draw on sources in intellectual history. Here the purpose would be to inform students of Augustine's ideas about God, creation, and time, and to relate those ideas to the views of Manichaeans, Stoics, and neo-Platonists. Supplementary readings could draw from secondary sources that would fill out the intellectual backdrop of Augustine's narrative. Selections from Peter Brown's *Augustine of Hippo* and John Rist's *Augustine: Ancient Thought Baptized* would be essential reading.[59] Another route—more in keeping with an explanatory agenda—would be to draw on the writings of Freud to examine the psychological dynamics of Augustine's introspection, his relationship to his parents, his sexual imagery, his development from infancy through adolescence and adulthood, and his experience of God. Here *Confessions* would be supplemented with readings from *Three Essays on the Theory of Sexuality, The Ego and the Id, The Future of an Illusion, Civilization and Its Discontents,* and Freud's work on religion and obsessional neurosis.[60]

But surely there is more to learn from Augustine. Consider other routes: We could inquire into accounts of how the self is constituted by its self-interpretations, adopting a hermeneutical and ethical set of categories that could link up with other autobiographical literature—say Rousseau and Merton. Supplementary readings could develop insights from Charles Taylor and Rorty. In a related vein, students could explore Augustine's notion of agency and could ask whether it is primarily voluntarist or cognitive.[61] Or one could interrogate Augustine's notions of evil and his struggle with the issue of theodicy. On this topic, readings could draw from philosophical commentary on evil and human experience.[62] Or one could relate Augustine to other "crisis religion," with readings from John Bunyan or Jonathan Edwards and with screenings that capture the paroxysms of Protestant televangelism.

Whichever route or routes are pursued, the point is obvious: Augustine's *Confessions* calls for a considerably richer and more fruitful range of interrogation than a scientific paradigm would permit. An approach aimed at deepening students' interpretive perspicuity invites a self-consciously genre-bending method, devoted to poetics rather than genetics. Explanatory knowledge fails to tell us everything we want to know, and for this reason it will never suffice as a cultural idiom. Moreover, pedagogy along these lines could just as easily occur in a Religious Studies department as in a Theology department. The goal would be not to produce Augustinians, but to indicate what helped produce Augustine as well as to transmit a broad range of diagnostic tools for understanding what Augustine produced. Such are the general aims of literacy in the study of religion.

The key to such literacy, I am suggesting, is not arriving at some subject matter in common. The reality (and desirability) of blurred genres makes such a goal impossible. Rather, the key lies in possessing and transmitting common skills. This is what scholars of religion should be cultivating: not methodological orthodoxy, simplicity, essentialism, or definitional purity, but complex, sophisticated powers of analysis, interpretation, and explanation.[63] As Rorty remarks in his discussion of philosophy, the idea "is to *let* the institutional tail wag the pseudo-scientific dog. It is to admit that our geniuses invent problems and programs *de novo*, rather than being presented with them by the subject-matter itself, or by the 'current state of research.' "[64] Establishing a place for religion in the curricular structures of modern colleges and universities rests not on whether scholars in other departments are convinced that Religious Studies has proven itself as a human science, but on the extent to which those scholars are impressed by the intellectual perspicuity of the faculty and students in the Religious Studies department. If the study of religion rests its future on scholars whose methodological orthodoxy ensures that they canonize only Hume, Comte, Marx, Durkheim, Freud, Jung, and Turner, then it is in very deep trouble. *Better to resolve this academic case of conscience in terms of liberty rather than law.* Better first to attract the best and the brightest into the study of religion and let more flowers bloom.

Conclusion

The pursuit of purity in the study of religion, complete with the search for essentialist definitions and scientific objectivity, leads to an intellectual cul-de-sac. It fails on several counts, especially in its quest for simple ascriptions, which are then to be applied in a deductive manner to the "subject matter of religion." At the very least, the quest for purity appears to legitimize the interests of historians and social scientists with essentialist language,[65] often fueled by misperceptions about how the social sciences and the humanities are configured or are experiencing reconfiguration in colleges and universities today. It confuses confessional with apologetical discourse and equates non-naturalistic inquiry with theology, as if there were no alternative modes of inquiry. Moreover, it is wedded to a monocausal understanding of religion in relation to human motives, overlooking the dialectical interaction that can occur between religion and social movements. One would think that the classic works of Weber and Troeltsch had never been written.

For these reasons the quest for purity in the study of religion is a will-o'-the-wisp. We would do better to proceed inductively and hermeneutically, not abstractly and scientifically, seeking to produce a new generation of scholars who are intent on further genre bending. Then, and perhaps only then, will students of religion develop their interpretive perspicuity, their appreciation for the liberating winds of pluralism, and their sensitivities to moral and religious complexity.

CHAPTER NINE

Casuistry, Poetics, and Rhetoric

Particularity and Contingency

It is now time to take account of the elements that have shaped our inquiry into, and practice of, casuistry. Central to my concerns has been the importance of what Aristotle calls "the particulars" in moral reflection. This terminology refers to variable matters, the focus of practical inquiry, as opposed to invariable matters, the object of theoretical analysis. As I remarked in chapter 1, a basic requirement of casuistry is to attend carefully to complex details, the contingencies and vagaries of human experience. Casuistry demands that we examine the data and interpretations that surround a given case, that we work through appearances in order to find those that are most reliable. I sought to illustrate this point in subsequent chapters, each of which attempts to lay out empirical and other features of a case in the process of formulating a reasonable judgment. In chapter 8 I sharpened this concern for particulars by contrasting a "poetic" method with theoretical, abstract rationality: The former is inductive, interpretive, and empirical, focusing on particular practices or commitments; the latter is more general and mechanical, invoking an essentialist principle and applying it deductively.

In this chapter I want to develop more fully how "particularity" and variability bear upon practical reasoning, and how they ought to affect our expectations of what casuists produce (or ought to produce). Drawing from the work of Aristotle on ethical reasoning, perception, and public discourse, I will proceed along two related levels, the epistemological and methodological.

On the epistemological level, attention to particularity requires an understanding of practical reasoning as *poetic*. The fact that casuistry demands attention to particularity means that we must develop skills of interpretive perspicuity, the power to discern the importance of morally relevant details and to apprehend their interrelationships in human affairs. Understood in poetic terms, casuistry has an aesthetic dimension, focusing our attention on the configurations, nuances, and subtexts of moral particulars.

On the methodological level, attention to particularity invites us to envision casuistry as *rhetorical*. Understood in this way, practical deliberation is local, topical, and persuasive, producing sound judgments about substantive issues of the day rather than airtight demonstrations about what abstract, theoretical principles entail for human action. A rhetorical approach to practical reasoning bids us to draw upon presumptions and paradigms that have stood the test of time, and to develop them in light of immediate social concerns. Eschewing the need to construct abstract, impersonal principles and a deductive methodology, a "rhetorical casuistry" sidesteps the inclination in ethical theory to view the moral life from Olympian heights, detached from concrete existential needs, practices, and concerns.

I hope to sharpen these features of casuistry by contrasting them with two influential approaches in ethics today—applied ethics and narrative ethics. Casuistry is more inductive and dialectical than the former, and more inclined to deliberate and produce judgments than the latter. Of course, Aristotle was no casuist, and it would be a mistake to suggest that he articulates a theory of practical rationality that can be directly appropriated for casuistry today.[1] But his account of moral deliberation is sufficiently robust to suggest several ways of sharpening the distinctive aspects of casuistical reasoning. Let us explore these features of practical rationality, the poetic and the rhetorical, in turn.

Poetic Justice

At first glance the notion that casuistry has a poetic dimension seems wrongheaded. Owing to the work of Aristotle, *poetics* has acquired literary connotations, suggesting a mode of discourse attentive to plot, character, catharsis, and tragic reversal. For Aristotle, moreover, *poetics* also denotes artisanship, an excellence of making (*poiēsis*).[2] It does not typically suggest acts of virtue or vice. Given this Aristotelian legacy, the term *poetics* seems distant from practical deliberation and social criticism. Indeed, Aristotle goes to some length to distinguish between *poiēsis* and *phronēsis* (practical wisdom). His main point is that in *phronēsis* we are involved with ourselves—our character or

223

identity. In *poiēsis*, by contrast, the artist is involved in making something else. *Poiēsis* has an instrumental dimension, but practical reasoning is worthy in and of itself, not for what it produces outside the agent. Practical wisdom involves self-knowledge and self-deliberation, and we are not at our own disposal in the same way that an artisan's materials are available in the act of making something.[3] Aristotle thus distinguishes sharply between moral action and the productive arts, remarking, "Neither is acting making nor is making acting."[4]

This book is premised on the opposite idea, namely, that casuistry involves us in poetic activity, understood not in terms of craftsmanship or producing a work of art, but in terms of what it takes to *decipher* such a product: the powers of interpretive perspicuity. I call such powers "poetic," hoping to suggest that practical reasoning is not merely a passive endeavor in which the mind serves as a blank slate. Rather, the mind contributes something in the process of reasoning. It plays a creative, inventive role, requiring us to use our moral imagination. We "make" insofar as we must "make sense" of experience, confronted as we are with the variables of a situation. Making may not be acting, strictly speaking, but we would be ill-equipped to act rightly without first making sense of our contexts or cases.

The importance of deciphering and coordinating the details of experience cannot be overemphasized. But this means that a sharp distinction between *poiēsis* and *phronēsis* is overdrawn. As Aristotle himself recognizes, those who excel in practical reasoning must pay close attention to the variables of a situation. Persons of virtue are producers of meaning, engaged in sense-making activity as a first step toward determining the right thing to do from within a cluster of possibilities. Furthermore, his awareness in the *Nicomachean Ethics* that *eudaimonia* depends upon external goods suggests that contingencies can obstruct our path to happiness, and the *Poetics* provides an account of the tragic effect of contingencies on one's chances for the good life. When we ignore their place in human experience, relying on goodwill or earnestness alone, contingencies may produce unexpected and tragic reversals of fortune. *Phronēsis* and *poiēsis*, then, are not irrelevant to each other. Indeed, Aristotle suggests precisely the opposite point: We fail to make sense of contingencies at our peril, leaving ourselves vulnerable to bad luck.[5]

For these reasons ethics is not an exact science in the same sense as geometrical reasoning. The moral life is immersed in the realm of contingency, which resists crisp, logical formulations or algorithmic procedures. Aristotle thus writes: "Up to what point and to what extent a man must deviate before he becomes blameworthy is not easy to determine by reasoning, any more than anything else that is perceived by the senses; such things depend on particular facts, and the decision [*krisis,* also discernment, judgment] rests with perception."[6] Because such facts do not come prepackaged, deciphering their details requires us to acquire powers of imagination and interpretation, the ability to perceive the morally relevant features of our experience.

Aristotle thus insists not only that our powers of perception are valuable for the moral life, but that they are inexorably linked to virtue or vice. He writes:

> Now someone may say that all men desire the apparent good, but have no control over the appearance, but the end appears to each man in a form answering to his character. We reply that if each man is somehow responsible for his state of mind, he will also be himself somehow responsible for the appearance [of the end].[7]

We are responsible for the way in which *phainomena*—appearances—present themselves to us as we deliberate about how to act. Our optical powers, in other words, are never value-free. Rather, how we construe our problems is a function of the kinds of persons we happen to be. Descriptions, it is often said, are not morally neutral. As Nancy Sherman remarks about Aristotle's ethics,

> Much of the work of virtue will rest in knowing how to construe the case, how to describe and classify what is before one. An agent who fails to notice unequivocal features of a situation which for a given community standardly require considerations of liberality, apparently lacks that virtue. It is not that she has deliberated badly, but that there is no registered response about which to deliberate.[8]

Sherman rightly observes that book 6 of the *Nicomachean Ethics* develops this line of argument by drawing several parallels between *phronēsis* and perception. Aristotle states that *phronēsis* is like an "eye of the soul," a power of sight or insight.[9] Practical wisdom is "concerned with the ultimate particular fact, since the thing to be done is of this nature." But these particulars, Aristotle adds, are "the object not of scientific knowledge but of perception, not the perception of qualities peculiar to one sense but a perception akin to that by which we perceive that the particular figure before us is a triangle."[10] Moral discernment is not merely a matter of being able to identify pieces of information in a positivistic way, like an odor or a color, when we turn to experience. Rather, as Aquinas writes, our powers of discernment require "an interior sense," contrasted with the "external senses" by which we perceive empirical data.[11] Powers of discernment enable us to discriminate, as discrimination is understood in art, literary, film, or music criticism. Those who are "discriminating" are able to pick out the salient features of a work of art, those appearances that demand special attention. No less than in the arts, we must generate strong readings in the moral life. Thus understood, *phronēsis* does not entail "seeing," simply understood, but "seeing as."

Aristotle's emphasis on discernment and discrimination does not mean that he understands practical reasoning as lacking order or stability. The person of virtue is not someone who excels at clairvoyance, for *phronēsis* must draw on general rules. With the help of such rules the person of practical wisdom must be able to perceive the meaning of parts and wholes within the moral life. As I have remarked, the details of moral experience do not organize themselves for us. We need the power of vision to organize them and to identify their morally important features. For this reason Aquinas speaks of "virtues annexed to prudence" (or practical reasoning), referring to the optical skills necessary to render various aspects of the moral life intelligible.[12] Understood as a poetic activity, *phronēsis* asks us to make sense of parts, wholes, and their interrelationships in practical affairs. The person of practical wisdom, the *phronimos*, must be able to apprehend the practical import of concrete particulars. The *phronimos* articulates responses not to raw events, but to events that fall under an evaluative description.[13]

Without this form of moral insight it would be difficult to integrate our actions into a larger totality, the configuration of particulars within which we must situate our conduct. For Aristotle, acting according to virtue—selecting the mean between a pair of extremes— requires what David Wiggins calls "situational appreciation" of an agent's context. According to Wiggins, Aristotle provides a notion of *phronēsis* that "articulates the reciprocal relations of an agent's concerns and his perception of how things objectively are in the world."[14] In this way Aristotle blurs the distinction between aesthetics and morality. In Aristotle's ethics, there cannot be practical reasoning without interpretation, for action must be situated within a larger context in order to attain intelligibility and fittingness.

Emphasis on interpretation/perception means that our moral arguments are likely to be limited when we encounter others who disagree with our judgments. Whether we can convince others of our point of view will depend on our ability to show why cases or judgments should be seen in a certain way. The prospects for a common morality, in other words, will depend less on whether we can provide a knock-down logical demonstration than on whether interpretations and perceptions overlap to a sufficient degree to produce consensus. Arguments and counterarguments in casuistry typically surround the attempt to describe (or redescribe) a case; first and foremost we must ascertain the appropriate matrix for viewing the variables at hand.

For this reason, as Aristotle recognized, the powers of moral perception closely resemble the knowledge required by theoretical *nous,* since neither the universals of theoretical knowledge nor the particulars of practical reasoning allow for final, extra-linguistic justification. As Aristotle writes, *nous*

> is concerned with the ultimates in both directions; for both the first terms and the last are objects of intuitive reason and not of argument, and the intuitive reason which is presupposed by demonstrations grasps the unchangeable and first terms, while the intuitive reason involved in practical reasonings grasps the last and variable fact.[15]

As we approach the limits of theoretical knowledge (the grasp of universals) or practical reasoning (decision about particulars), we reach an end to what we can prove.[16] At that point our moral knowledge depends on intuition rather than on discursive argument. In this vein Aristotle remarks, "For these variable facts are the starting points for the apprehension of the end, since the universals are reached from the particulars; of these therefore we must have perception, and this perception is intuitive reason."[17]

In these respects, then, practical reasoning is poetic: Deliberation needs interpretation, a "seeing as," an ability to ascertain what is at stake in this or that situation. We must therefore speak of practical reasoning as an art rather than a science, for it is not easily formalized into a technique that admits of systematized training. Powers of discrimination and interpretation are unsystematic and, in part, idiosyncratic, depending on our individual talents of apprehension. But *art* does not denote "bad" or "imperfect" science.[18] Rather, practical reasoning is an art because its subject matter (the contingency of experience) does not admit of any fixed, unchanging formulations. The ideal of scientific demonstration or geometrical rationality is an inappropriate standard for moral reasoning: As ahistorical and universal, it is ill-suited as a method for reckoning with the variabilities of human life. Instead artistic, poetic skills are needed, for they enable us to discriminate within the particulars of experience, to ascertain what is demanded in the case, with its kaleidoscopic details.

By this Aristotelian account of interpretation, poetics, and practical reasoning we commit an injustice to the moral life by imposing the standard of geometrical demonstration on ethical inquiry. We fail to give concreteness and particularity their just due, bleaching them of their colorful details in our quest for abstract, timeless ethical principles. Thus it is instructive to recall Aristotle's adage about practical reasoning, which he contrasts with his view of scientific inquiry: "It is the mark of an educated man to look for precision in each class of things just so far as the nature of the subject matter admits."[19] Scientific reasoning—*epistēmē*—deals with immutable truths, and can arrive at unchanging certainty. But for Aristotle practical deliberation is different. It can only speak with "such premises to indicate the truth roughly and in outline," because its subject matter—human experience—is intractably particular, subject to variety or change.[20] Practical reasoning must address itself to human affairs, which are immersed in the realm of flux and diversity. Seeking to make sense of the particulars, to ascertain their moral salience, a poetic approach is more fitting—and more just—to the subject matter of the moral life itself.

Yet if it is true that without the skill of interpretation our practical deliberations would be deficient, the converse is also true: Without the exercise of deliberation, our powers of interpretation would suffer. For in the process of deliberating and arriving at moral judgments we shed light on the concrete meaning of our presumptions and paradigms. Our "seeing as" is broadened, enriched, and possibly revised in the ongoing exercise of forming practical judgments. For this reason Aristotle argues that the virtue of *phronēsis* is aided by experience or ongoing practice. "People of practical wisdom," he writes, are those to whom experience "has given . . . an eye [with which] they see aright."[21] This kind of vision is to be contrasted with knowledge that can be perfected in the abstract sciences:

> While young men become geometricians and mathematicians and wise in matters like these, it is thought that a young man of practical wisdom cannot be found. The cause is that such wisdom is concerned not only with universals but with particulars, which become familiar with experience, but a young man has no experience.[22]

Similarly, Aquinas characterizes the virtuous "interior sense" as that which is "seasoned by memory and experience, and so ready to meet the particular facts encountered."[23] Our powers of description in practical affairs are refined by the repeated exercise of forming judgments, by deliberating again and again about matters of flux and contingency.

In order for us to grow in practical wisdom, in other words, interpretation and deliberation must inform each other, dialectically. Casuistical inquiry must move back and forth between paradigms and presumptions on the one hand and experience on the other. A dialectical casuistry allows interpretation and social criticism, perception and judgment, to enrich each other in complex, nonformalized ways. Indeed, the idea that practical wisdom is aided by experience suggests that interpretation and social criticism, vision and judgment, are symbiotic.[24]

Rhetoric and Practical Reasoning

When Aristotle writes that "it is the mark of an educated man to look for precision in each class of things just so far as the nature of the subject matter admits," he is not simply saying that we can only speak "roughly and in outline" about practical affairs. He adds, "It is evidently equally foolish to accept probable reasoning from a mathematician and to demand from a rhetorician scientific proofs."[25] Here Aristotle is speaking methodologically, inviting us to consider how practical reasoning, along with its attention to particulars, might be understood in rhetorical terms.

Aristotle's account of rhetoric stands within his more general understanding of method, which he divides into two sorts: analytic and dialectic. An analytic method concerns matters of necessity, and is able to produce findings that are invariable. This method plays a vital role in the natural sciences, mathematics, and logic. In logic, Aristotle observes, the conclusions of the analytic method can never be novel; it operates within a closed system, and its results are tautological. The validity of a proposition in geometry, for example, rests on the meaning of and internal connections between the terms employed. In the natural sciences, the analytic method draws inferences from the unchanging essences of plants or animals. As used in logic or the sciences, the method is demonstrative, impersonal, and abstract.

Dialectical rationality, in contrast, draws upon generally accepted opinions—presumptive beliefs that have stood the test of time and experience.[26] It concerns things that are variable and contingent, matters "that could be otherwise." Further, it relies on and develops our common interpretations about how to live. As Martha Nussbaum remarks about Aristotle's practical philosophy, dialectical inquiry is "a method that is thoroughly committed to the data of human experience and accepts these as its limits."[27] Whereas analytic inquiry draws on abstract first principles, dialectic invokes our cultural vocabularies. When we reason from common interpretations and presumptions we can produce genuinely new insights, since we are dealing with substantive matters and not matters of necessity or formal validity. Moreover, because the dialectical method pertains to contingency, it includes the task of deliberation (we cannot deliberate about necessities).[28] This method is central to poetics, ethics, and politics, and its goal is to secure agreement about controversial issues in these domains. As Chaim Perelman observes, dialectical inquiry "seeks through argumentation the acceptance or rejection of a debatable thesis."[29] The results of dialectic are probable, not certain: They cannot be fixed and final; they can be true generally and for the most part.

An offshoot of dialectic, rhetoric shares all of these characteristics. However, it differs insofar as dialectic attempts to change minds, whereas rhetoric endeavors to move us to action. The practical counterpart to dialectic, rhetoric includes a motivational, agential dimension, seeking to induce new modes of *praxis*. *Rhetoric* refers to the art of persuasion, the skill of moving an audience to embrace a judgment about a matter of public importance.[30] Rhetoric bears upon our attitudes, feelings, and prejudices, and therefore has both cognitive and noncognitive dimensions. According to Aristotle's moral psychology, human beings cannot be motivated by appeals to reason alone; our desires and passions must be engaged as well. He understands rhetoric as that device by which individuals and communities can be inspired to act. Departing from Plato's deprecation of rhetoric as a form of sophistry and verbal artifice, Aristotle claims that it can have legitimate aims—moving individuals and communities toward praiseworthy ends—and thus merits philosophical inquiry.

In particular, rhetoric has three dimensions: As a deliberative exercise it recommends actions to be pursued or avoided; as a legal or forensic exercise it accuses and defends; and as an epidectic exercise it praises or blames past actions.[31] In all of these dimensions it concerns itself with producing reasonable judgments about matters of fairness and goodness, the basis for the good life.

Accordingly, rhetoric's subject matter is similar to that of ethics: Both focus on "ultimate particulars," the right and the good, and the variability of human affairs. Insofar as the moral life and rhetoric require judgments within a specific set of circumstances, both must attend to the particularities and appearances to which we must actively respond.[32] For this reason practical deliberation and rhetoric share several methodological features, which bear directly upon casuistical inquiry as I have sought to develop it in this book. Those features are seven in number.

First, as I have said, practical reasoning and rhetoric *share a certain kind of object*, namely, matters that are contingent or changeable: that which could be otherwise. "For it is about our actions that we deliberate and inquire," Aristotle writes, "and all our actions have a contingent character; hardly any of them are determined by necessity."[33] Rhetoric and *phronēsis* are both deliberative arts, concerned with this-worldly affairs and how we might improve our circumstances. In this respect they both seek to render judgments about issues of everyday life.

This connection between practical reasoning and rhetoric on the one hand and contingency on the other brings us to a second parallel: *Neither rhetoric nor moral deliberation can rest on absolute, unchanging ethical first principles.* Rather, they draw upon premises that hold generally and for the most part—generalizations that are trustworthy on the whole, but that might have to give way in exceptional or unique cases. For Aristotle, progress in rationality must begin from a particular point of view, enshrined in our commonplaces, which are refined (or revised) in public discourse and practical deliberation.

In rhetoric this more relaxed, provisional approach to argumentation is typified in its use of two principal devices: the enthymeme (or practical syllogism) and the example. Both play a role in arguments about contingencies: "the example being an induction, and the enthymeme a syllogism about such matters" [i.e., contingencies].[34] Moreover, both provide a shorthand for commonplaces and presumptions that have stood the test of time. The enthymeme—the practical syllogism used in rhetoric—does so by using premises that presume upon an audience's acceptance of often unstated assumptions. As James C. Raymond writes, the enthymeme "can express in a condensed and elliptical manner chains of logical connections that would be complex indeed if the assumptions themselves had to be demonstrated."[35] The example functions similarly by articulating a model or paradigm for action. Using examples, the rhetor invokes cultural vocabularies and conventions in order to engage an audience's current concerns—issues of the day—rather than timeless, theoretical matters. As products of experience, they hold generally but not infallibly, providing a gestalt for organizing our perceptions.

Casuistry has several affinities with this Aristotelian account of rhetoric. Indeed, the presumptions and common opinions that help shape the enthymeme are virtually identical to the presumptive claims that operate in casuistical reasoning. Presumptions are prima facie: They are generally binding unless they clash with another important virtue or obligation.[36] When conflicts occur, one set of concerns will have to yield, given the judgment that competing obligations are more pressing. The burden of proof is placed on those who wish to trump presumptions when they conflict with other moral duties. They allow for discretion, the ability to see how far they should be put aside or bent given the circumstances of a case.[37] Presumptions in rhetoric and casuistry thus resemble precedents in legal reasoning: They point us in the direction of what is generally advisable, but what is finally imperative may differ, depending on a fuller account of the situation.[38]

In this respect presumptions in rhetoric and casuistry express prejudices or anticipatory judgments. As I remarked in chapters 1 and 2, prejudices can provide substantive starting points for knowledge. Our common opinions are not, and need not be, value-neutral. But neither are they crippling or wholly determinative of our final point of view. They function as a moral compass, orienting us in a certain direction. Prejudices articulate general, uncontroversial beliefs or shared assumptions. They allow us to "foreground" important ideas in the process of forming arguments or seeking consensus in public discourse and debate.

Consider as well the similarities between the example in rhetoric and the paradigm in casuistry: Both provide a model or exemplar for reasoning about cases. As Raymond observes, *example* in Aristotle's *Rhetoric* does not mean *instance*, but *pattern*. Examples are paradigmatic, similar to a matrix in learning a language. "Type cases" enable us to infer analogically how, for example, to conjugate a verb in a foreign language. By providing a gestalt, an organized way of seeing, paradigms in rhetoric and casuistry enable us to coordinate a particular set of data into an intelligible pattern. Moreover, they are more or less unambiguous, requiring no elaborate explanation. As a result, we can use them to reason about more complicated matters, proceeding from "typical" cases to those that are novel, ambiguous, or more elaborate.[39]

Third, the fact that rhetoric and practical reasoning work within the realm of the variable means that we must have *modest expectations about their results.* Not only do they begin with truths that hold generally and for the most part, they also generate probable (but not certain) conclusions. Aristotle writes: "Conclusions that state what is merely usual or possible must be drawn from premises that do the same, just as 'necessary' conclusions must be drawn from 'necessary' premises."[40] In other words, because enthymemes and examples draw from commonplaces that have stood the test of experience, they cannot produce fixed and final results. To hope for precision and certainty in the realm of experience would be to impose expectations of necessity upon variable matters. We would thereby overlook what Aristotle considers the distinguishing mark of experience, namely, that it could have been otherwise. Instead we must be sure to look for precision only insofar as the nature of the subject matter admits, and contingency does not admit of invariable conclusions.

Accordingly, we ought to expect from rhetoric and casuistry not airtight demonstrations, but "quasi-logical arguments."[41] As Jonsen and Toulmin write, such arguments "establish their particular conclusions presumptively or probably, not 'necessarily.'"[42] *Probable reasoning* refers to the fact that moral verdicts must weigh different sides of an issue, producing a solution that favors one alternative over another. (Such a view is not, strictly speaking, probabilism, as that is technically understood in casuistry.)[43] The general idea is that moral reflection must assess pros and cons on the way toward resolving a contested issue. Verdicts about such issues are arguable, given the fact that some arguments count against them. They are fallible and revisable, lacking the expectations of certitude that surround analytic inquiry.

The fact that rhetoric and practical reasoning develop in response to variable matters brings us to a fourth resemblance: They produce *local rather than universal knowledge.*[44] Both speak to issues of the moment, problems that bear upon a group of people in a specific space and time. What is variable is a function of experience, and experience is always situated in the ongoing life of a people. For Aristotle, there is no such thing as "variability" or "experience" in the abstract.

Accordingly, both rhetoric and practical reasoning are topical, tied to the issues of the day for a particular public. Knowledge is "local" in both spatial and temporal terms: Its audience comprises a specific group of people, bound together at a particular time by a common set of needs, commitments, or problems. The goal of rhetoric and practical deliberation is not to produce conclusions that are removed from practical, everyday affairs, but to insert human inquiry into the turbulence of experience. Conceived in this way, Toulmin writes, rhetoric and practical reasoning are "timely not timeless, concrete not abstract, particular not universal, local not general."[45]

A fifth resemblance turns on the fact that *rhetoric and practical reasoning are not disinterested.* To the contrary: Rhetoricians aim to persuade an audience to embrace a certain point of view by appealing to our passions, interests, memories, and cultural vocabularies. The rhetor is driven by particular interests, not the least of which is the desire to persuade. Similarly, in casuistry the aim is to render judgments that are reasonable and fair, to move us to accept the conclusions of practical deliberation.

But the partisan character of rhetoric and *phronēsis* cuts deeper than the fact that neither aims at value-neutral conclusions. Both rely on commonplaces and shared interpretations, which bear the effects of history and culture. As I noted earlier in this book, in casuistry it is important to consider how cultural forces shape our habits of perception, our anticipatory judgments, our presumptions and paradigms.[46] A genuinely self-reflexive ethics and rhetoric must investigate the ways in which history affects our descriptions and judgments. History and culture are the bearers of interests, requiring not only interpretive perspicuity, but also a hermeneutics of suspicion. Rhetoric and practical reasoning must include a self-critical component, given their reliance on historical precedents and conventions. Once again, rhetoric and practical reasoning are fallible, vulnerable to the effects of social, cultural, and ideological forces. As products of history, they bear the marks of human finitude.

Sixth, and related to this last parallel, rhetoric and practical reasoning have an important *noncognitive dimension.* For Aristotle, rhet-

233

oric and practical reasoning both draw upon information provided by feeling and affect. Virtue for Aristotle involves doing virtuous actions and taking pleasure in them.[47] Our deliberative processes are not impersonal and cerebral, but engage our entire selves, holistically.

Children provide an instructive example. They often "read" situations affectively, relying on their emotions to interpret a situation as threatening, playful, serious, or silly. Childrearing includes, among other things, training the emotions, enabling children to trust their affections as interpretively reliable. Children learn that anger and resentment can be trustworthy in interpreting betrayal, or that the experience of magnanimity can include the feeling of authentic joy. They also learn that some emotions—laughing throughout the movie *Schindler's List,* for example—are inappropriate, premised on a distorted perception of the moral features of a film depicting the Holocaust. Such emotions are premised on an inadequate set of affective interpretations about horror and genocide. Training is necessary not because the emotions are irrational or deceptive—quite the contrary. Rather, training is needed because feelings carry with them responses and judgments, and without a reliable set of feelings, judgments can go awry.[48] For this reason Aristotle joins Plato in insisting that "we ought to have been brought up in a particular way from our very youth . . . so as both to delight in and to be pained by the things that we ought."[49]

The point holds, with modifications, for adults as well. We have feelings about situations insofar as we consciously or unconsciously describe them in a certain way. When those interpretations are revised, our feelings typically change. For example, when friends sense that my emotions are out of line with a situation, they offer an alternative description of the event. When the situation is more adequately redescribed, my feelings are transformed. As a result of such conversations, I can conclude, for example, "Yes, given the alternatives, my physical at the doctor's office wasn't so traumatic, and I ought to appreciate his diagnosis and counsel." Conversely, when our feelings about a situation change, they carry with them a transformed set of interpretations, a new perspective for assessing what really matters in the case at hand. So I might remark, "I felt disoriented and remorseful after my father died, but I am restored after the cathartic ritual of his funeral. I can now look back upon his life, his relationship with me, and his place in society with gratitude and esteem." In such instances, our interpretations and affections are symbiotically related. Moral evaluations rely on the exercise of an imaginative and affective "feel" for an experience, and without such feelings our overall assessments would be incomplete and perhaps misleading.

234   Aristotle considered these points about the affections and moral

reasoning to be obvious. In the *Rhetoric* he argues that orators ought to engage the passions of an audience because persuasion cannot occur unless the whole self is moved by an argument. As I noted earlier, rhetoric has an agential dimension, which for Aristotle includes affect and imagination. He thus encourages rhetors to draw upon a variety of oratorical tools to tap the memories, symbolic associations, logical capacities, and emotive range of their audiences.

A similar point shapes Aristotle's ethics. Although he adopts the Platonic distinction between the rational and nonrational parts of the soul early in the *Nicomachean Ethics,* he soon qualifies that distinction to emphasize the fluid boundary between reason and emotion. The virtues of reason ought to generate the intellectual virtues, such as *phronēsis,* while the nonrational element of the soul ought to generate the virtues of character, such as temperance and liberality.[50] But to separate these virtues would be a mistake. We cannot be moved to act except by a force that combines the cognitive and the noncognitive elements of our nature, reason and desire. "Choice," Aristotle writes, "is either desiderative reason or rationative desire."[51] Our motivational wellsprings include what appears attractive to us. To reason as if such forces were somehow alien to our nature would be inhuman.

As Sherman observes, for Aristotle the emotions "are not blind feelings, like itches or throbs, but intentional states directed at articulated features of an agent's environment."[52] They provide an important interpretive touchstone in the moral life insofar as they register the responses of the self in its depth and complexity. If I betray a friend, by Aristotle's account, my (virtuous) self-interpretation should include not only rational censure, but also the feeling of shame.[53] Without such feelings my self-interpretation would be deficient, having failed to elicit the full features of my personality. Thus Aristotle writes that "in general pleasure and pain may be felt both too much and too little, and in both cases not well; but to feel them at the right times, with reference to the right objects, towards the right people, with the right motive, and in the right way, is what is both intermediate and best, and this is characteristic of virtue."[54] Accordingly, as L. A. Kosman remarks, virtue in the Aristotelian account includes "being properly affected."[55]

It would be a mistake, then, to develop casuistry with an impersonal, arid ideal of human rationality. Instead, Aristotle suggests that practical reasoning ought to engage various dimensions of moral argument, including our prejudices and passions about a moral issue, in order to determine which are the most trustworthy. Accordingly, in casuistry it is often necessary to include an account of the opinions and interpretations that surround a case. Those opinions often shape a culture's reading of a social issue, leading us to feel a certain way.

Presumptions are often shaped affectively by how prior commentators have interpreted and evaluated our moral concerns. Casuistry must enter into dialogue with cultural perceptions that accompany a case, seeking to ascertain which (if any) offer a trustworthy account.

Finally, and seventh, rhetoricians are free to address *heterogeneous topics*. Nothing is "off limits" to the orator engaged in public speaking. Indeed, for Aristotle rhetoric has no particular subject matter: "It is not concerned with any special or definite class of objects."[56] It can range freely, tied to no "appropriate" issue of the day. Rhetoric is defined in terms not of its content, but of its aim: persuasion.

The effect of this point is to blur the distinction between "high" and "low" issues in rhetoric. Rhetors are not "better" if they focus primarily on issues of high culture—intellectual, artistic, or political debates, for example. Rather, rhetors are good or bad depending on their arts of persuasion, regardless of the subject matter at hand.

Earlier in this book I suggested that casuists might take some cues from this insight.[57] Aristotle's notion that nothing is off limits for rhetoric can be applied to practical reasoning as well. Practical deliberation is not, or ought not be, concerned with any special or definite class of objects—other than the obvious concern (relevant to rhetoric as well) to determine right and good action. What is important for casuists, like rhetoricians, is the extent to which they can engage our powers of social criticism about issues of the day. Unfortunately, however, academic ethics is generally averse to most issues in mass culture. Such issues are widely perceived as "lowbrow"—to be contrasted to "high art" in the scholarly guild: deontology, utilitarianism, eudaimonism, social and political theory, professional and applied ethics, etc. As a result, contemporary ethics is remarkably conservative, paying little attention to the cultural forces that actually affect a vast majority of people. Aristotle's view of rhetoric suggests that much of the attention that goes into the standard account of religious and philosophical ethics might be redirected toward some uncharted terrain.

Via Media

The idea that casuistry has a poetical dimension and a rhetorical methodology paves a middle way between two influential approaches in contemporary moral theory: applied ethics and narrative ethics. Casuists share with applied ethicists a desire to produce judgments about human conduct and institutions, yet they also echo the narrativists' emphasis on envisioning human conduct within its context or circumstances. Owing to the importance that casuists place on judgment and vision, they can seek the best of both worlds.

Applied ethics, as I have noted, is modeled on a geometrical, deductive account of practical reasoning. The general approach is to take an abstract principle and apply it to a problem in a "top down" fashion, or to pick out features of a situation and ascertain whether they abide by a more general rule. Cases are resolved by subsuming them under principles that are crafted antecedent to experience.[58]

Consider, for example, Alan Donagan's *The Theory of Morality*. As the title suggests, Donagan's book is a theoretical project, developing a single, incorrigible principle of morality, prior to and independent of any specific cases. Echoing Kant, Donagan's principle is accessible to all rational persons and needs no theistic sanction. This principle states, "It is impermissible not to respect every human being, oneself or any other, as a rational creature."[59] Donagan calls this the "fundamental principle of morality" because, he argues, it articulates the core of traditional Western morality, as that has been developed in Hebrew and Christian ethics. It more or less coheres with biblical and Talmudic teachings, Thomist moral philosophy, and (most notably) Kantian ethics.[60]

One obvious question is how to specify the meaning of this principle so that it can pertain directly to everyday experience. If we are able to determine more precisely what respecting persons involves, then we can amplify the content of morality. Injunctions that specify the fundamental principle, Donagan argues, will always fit one of three schemas:

(1) It is always permissible to do an action of the kind K, as such;
(2) It is never permissible to do an action of the kind K;
(3) It is never morally permissible not to do an action of the kind K, if an occasion occurs [in] which one can be done.[61]

The first schema articulates what we may do; the second what we may never do; the third what we are obliged to do, when possible.

Obviously these schemas are entirely formal. But when they are combined with the fundamental principle of morality, they begin to produce more practicable concepts. The first schema, when joined with the fundamental principle, produces the (derivative) schema, "No action of the kind K, as such, fails to respect any human being as a rational creature." Likewise, when the second and third schemas are combined with the fundamental principle, they respectively state, "All actions of the kind K fail to respect some human being as a rational creature," and "If an occasion occurs on which an action of the kind K can be done, not to do it will fail to respect some human being as a rational creature."[62]

In addition, more specific premises exist, which must satisfy one of the three derivative schemas. Such "specificatory premises" aim to

"identify a species of action as falling or not falling under the fundamental generic concept of action in which every human being is respected as a rational creature."[63] Although Donagan does not apply
his theory to actual, concrete cases, his overall plan is to provide a
conceptual model for bringing various kinds of activity under the
supreme principle of respecting human beings as rational creatures.
As we descend from the fundamental principle to specificatory premises, we proceed from general moral directives to specific rules.

The practical question facing this approach is how we can discover
specificatory premises satisfying the three schemas. How, in short,
are we to deal with cases in light of specific rules? Moral judgments
themselves cannot be guided by more rules, for that would introduce
a set of rules for applying rules, which themselves would require further rules. The obvious danger of generating an infinite regress of
rules would arise. Seeking to forestall this problem, Donagan writes,

> The moral system that may be derived from the fundamental principle
> ... may ... be described as a "simple deductive" system according to
> Robert Nozick's classification, or as an informal analytical one. The
> structure consisting of fundamental principle, derived precepts, and
> specificatory premises is strictly deductive; for every derived precept is
> strictly deduced, by way of some specificatory premise, either from the
> fundamental principle or from some precept already derived. But that
> structure is not the whole of the system. For virtually all the philo-
> sophical difficulties that are encountered in deriving that structure
> have to do with establishing the specificatory premises; and that is
> done by unformalized analytical reasoning in which some concept
> either in the fundamental principle or in a derived precept is applied
> to some new species of case.[64]

In Donagan's view, this unformalized reasoning has important parallels with common-law jurisprudence, as described by Edward H. Levi.
In its attempt to deal with concrete problems, this reasoning occurs
in three stages. First, a legal concept is established by comparing and
analyzing cases; second, the concept is applied to new cases; third,
reasoning by example with new cases goes so far that the concept
breaks down and must be replaced by another.[65]

But Donagan quickly modifies this parallel, especially the possibility that the legal (or moral) concept in question might eventually fail
in the ongoing process of application. Rather, the fundamental principle of morality is fixed and secure, which means that we must be
"confident that the concepts in terms of which it is formulated are
not liable to break down when applied to new and unforeseen cases."
Accordingly, those who accept traditional morality "must hold that a

point has been reached beyond which only reasoning of the kind found at the second of Levi's stages is called for."[66]

Yet if only the second of Levi's stages is allowed, then it is unclear whether Donagan can accept the common-law analogy. His views lie closer to the model of civil-law reasoning, involving a quite different methodology. In common law, as he rightly notes, we reason from precedent cases to similar ones, and extract more general principles along the way. The process is lateral and incremental, beginning from established verdicts that are embedded in cases and then branching out to analogous ones. A civil-law approach, on the other hand, begins with principles that are established in advance of cases, and applies them by determining which principles subsume which cases.[67] The process in this latter model is vertical, proceeding from the general principles to specific precepts in a "top down" fashion. The fundamental moral principle, and its derivatives, are to be understood independently of the cases to which they apply. The task of practical reasoning is to pick out features of an act that cohere, or fail to cohere, with an already established precept.

As I have said, Donagan's approach shares with casuistry the goal of producing judgments. Both the moral geometer and the casuist engage in problem-solving activities, seeking to provide answers to tangible, practical questions. Neither shies away from making moral decisions or from talking openly about moral quandaries. But it should be apparent that casuistry as I have tried to present it in these pages differs from Donagan's model of practical reasoning in at least two ways: in its dialectical approach to experience in general and in its analogical approach to novel experience in particular. In both instances casuistry is more open than applied ethics to revision, new interpretations, and the corrigibility of its presumptions and paradigms.

Casuistry enjoys a dialectical, symbiotic relation with experience, in contrast to Donagan's unilateral, deductive approach. Elegant as his model might be as a philosophical theory, it lacks resources for drawing from the lived realities and existential complexities of the moral life. It remains closed to the contributions that practical reasoning might make to our interpretive capacities. Casuists, in contrast, assume that experience can contribute to the refinement of presumptions and paradigms, that we grow in moral wisdom through the ongoing exercise of practical deliberation and the habits it produces. Experience, then, does not simply produce a set of instances that typify one or another principle. Rather, casuistry allows for a more inductive, interpretive method, in which moral meanings are produced, clarified, revised, or strengthened in the very process of forming judgments. Put simply, in applied ethics experience is "out

239

there," to be subsumed under a more general principle. In casuistry, one's experiences and habits contribute to the formation of presumptions and paradigms, which in turn are brought to bear upon the variabilities of the moral life.

Also, casuists and moral geometers deliberate about new cases differently. In both approaches, analogical reasoning is needed when dealing with novelty. But the geometer reasons analogically from a case that typifies the fundamental principle to another case. The precedent case is normative insofar as it "instances" the more general rule, providing that rule with material content.[68] New cases are evaluated in terms of their consistency with the explicit or implicit terms of the precedent case. Throughout this process, moreover, the fundamental principle itself is incorrigible to revision; its meaning is mediated by the precedent case. Casuists deliberate similarly to the extent that they seek convergences and divergences between precedents and novel cases. For casuists, however, the process presupposes a greater measure of corrigibility and possibility for revision. Novel cases produce fresh occasions for interpreting presumptions and paradigms. In the process, it is possible for casuists to generate new meanings for our moral understandings, given the richness and polyvalence of the materials on which they rely.

For casuists, cases are noteworthy not simply (or primarily) because they embody a principle. They provide what Jonsen and Toulmin aptly call a locus of certitude, a foundation from which similar cases can be considered on substantive terms.[69] Case-based reasoning is not held together by a chain of propositions, internally linked by their formal relations. Rather, cases are integrated into a complex network, requiring us not only to recognize substantive analogies between them, but also to coordinate them with a concern for circumstances, presumptions, and authoritative opinions toward the end of persuading an audience. In this way casuistical argument resembles rhetorical discourse: Both accumulate many kinds of reasons in the hope of presenting the favored position in a good light. As Jonsen and Toulmin remark, in case-based reasoning the force of argument comes from "the accumulation of reasons rather than from the logical validity of the arguments or the internal coherence of a single 'proof.'"[70] The resolution of our moral questions relies less on the grasp of abstract connections and moral algorithms than on the practical understanding of concrete cases.

The importance of experience and interpretation in the moral life has been amplified by the other influential strand of ethics I mentioned, narrative ethics. Developed by Alasdair MacIntyre against the idea that morality is a series of episodic decisions, disconnected from one's character and social context, narrative ethics has sought to emphasize the importance of personal identity, the excellences of character (the virtues), and the individual and collective stories in which those excellences find intelligibility.[71] Within this approach, narratives enable us to coordinate discrete moral decisions into a comprehensive, integrated account. Emphasis shifts from doing to being, from deeds and rules to character and life's journeys. Rather than ask whether features of an action are consistent with an incorrigible principle, narrative ethicists focus on skills that enable us to achieve moral goods, understood within a particular life story or set of interlocking stories.

Like casuistry, this approach is unsatisfied with the invocation of invariable principles and their deductive application as a recipe for the moral life. To the casuist and the narrativist, applied ethics seems prosaic, removed from the passions that touch us in our everyday experience. Moreover, both casuists and narrativists often insist that we attend to the richness and complexity of experience. Narratives, like cases, ask that we become, in the words of Nussbaum, "finely aware and richly responsible" concerning the context, feelings, relationships, and duties of day-to-day life.[72] Accordingly, narrativists and casuists emphasize poetic virtues: interpretive perspicuity, sensemaking, and the ability to provide "strong readings" of experience. But on two important issues casuists and narrativists have reasons to diverge. The first concerns the self that is involved in practical reasoning; the second concerns the appropriate devices for carrying out such reasoning.

First, recall two occasions of casuistry, doubt and perplexity.[73] In doubtful cases, we are unsure about the meaning or applicability of a presumption or paradigm. We are met by an ambiguity about the range of a rule's application, for example. One goal of practical reasoning is to ascertain how to apply a vague or general piece of moral knowledge. To this end, as I observed in chapter 1, casuists typically attempt to *specify* the meaning of our duties, to develop *paradigms* and *taxonomies* to classify actions, to reason *analogically* from familiar paradigms to new cases, and to attend in various ways to the *circumstances* that surround the case in question. In all of these endeavors casuists aspire to clarity and precision, providing a form of moral therapy for the doubting conscience.

A second, quite different occasion results from the experience of moral conflict. Here the conscience is not met with a dubious obligation in need of specification; rather, the conscience is bound by two clear and specific rules, one of which requires us to sacrifice the other. The conscience is not doubtful about whether a duty applies; it is rather perplexed about *which* duty ought to prevail when at least two are relevant. 241

Both "doubt" and "perplexity" suggest some measure of alienation or self-division. In one way or another I am separated, if only momentarily, from the obligations that should guide my action. Yet casuistry's acknowledgment of alienation or division is difficult to reconcile with narrative ethics, which views narrative as the antidote to doubt and perplexity. Casuists are engaged with quandaries of conscience, with cases that ask, How should one act? Narrative ethicists, in contrast, view the attention to quandaries and decisions as one of the great pitfalls of modernity.[74]

Consider, for example, what MacIntyre says about narrative as a central feature of selfhood and virtue. MacIntyre writes of the "concept of selfhood, a concept of self whose unity resides in the unity of a narrative which links birth to life to death as narrative beginning to middle to end."[75] For MacIntyre, narratives provide intelligibility for our actions, enabling us to contextualize our conduct, to make sense of our intentions in light of the circumstances that surround this or that activity.[76] In order to render an action intelligible, MacIntyre writes,

> we identify a particular action only by invoking two kinds of context, implicitly if not explicitly. We place the agent's intentions . . . in causal and temporal order with reference to their role in his or her history; and we also place them with reference to their role in the history of the setting or settings to which they belong. In doing this, in determining what causal efficacy the agent's intentions had in one or more directions, and how his short-term intentions succeeded or failed to be constitutive of long-term intentions, we ourselves write a further part of these histories. Narrative history of a certain kind turns out to be the basic and essential genre for the characterisation of human actions.[77]

Narratives provide order and unity to human life, coordinating our intentions into an overarching, teleological account. The self that emerges, then, is a kind of integral agent, *one whose purposes are tied together over time.*

The need for decisions and judgments, MacIntyre argues, is a function of modernity's great confusion about the nature of the good life and the virtues that such a life requires. We quarrel over cases because we possess only fragments of morality, disconnected from their classical roots. Indeed, our disagreements are a function of a widespread cultural emotivism, in which we are able only to express our feelings; we cannot reason or deliberate together. In the modern age, MacIntyre avers, our culture is crippled by widespread disagreement and a corresponding inability to articulate a shared set of convictions or standards of moral rationality.

MacIntyre contrasts our modern predicament with a vision of the unified self, situated in a common, coherent tradition or story. The goal of this self is not to deliberate about particulars, but to develop a virtuous life within a narrative quest. Indeed, MacIntyre's account of narrative ethics appears to leave little room for doubts, conflicts, and practical reasoning in a life of virtue. He rather depicts such conflicts as symptoms of social and cultural fragmentation. Narrative quests provide order to the moral life so that a person's life "can be conceived and evaluated as a whole."[78] Emphasis falls not on deliberating about particulars, but on personal identity, the formation of character. And personal identity, he adds, "is just that identity presupposed by the unity of the character which the unity of a narrative requires. Without such unity there would not be subjects of whom stories could be told."[79] Narrative provides a genre in the service of an undivided, unconflicted character, one that is not anxious about practical decisions or conflicts of duties. Doubts and conflicts presuppose a self that is at least temporarily alienated from itself or its familiar moral codes. Indeed, by MacIntyre's account the fact of division bespeaks a weakness of character.

In contrast, casuistry presupposes the value, indeed the richness, of what Aristotle called *phronēsis,* or practical wisdom in the face of particulars, with their many duties and obligations. As I have argued earlier, casuistry seeks to deliver us from those occasions in which rules are unclear, when conflicting rules pull us in opposite directions, or when we must ascertain degrees of moral culpability.[80] Such occasions are typically a function of competing duties, loyalties, and roles. Casuistry thus teaches that negotiating the demands of the moral life requires more than a simple appeal to strength of character. Rather, our character must be put to practical use, and casuists seek to show how we are to put morality into action. Accordingly, in casuistry we need not be threatened by quandaries, conflicts, and complex situations. Self-division and the concomitant need to deliberate practically arise not from a weak character, but from a thoughtful and multifaceted one. Casuistry develops in the service of a reflective clientele, those who appreciate moral complexity and the arduousness of deliberation about particulars.[81] It is thus better suited to an account of the moral self as pluralistic and elaborately involved in diverse affairs, a self that is held together less by a unified narrative than by a variety of roles in public and private life.

Casuists and narrativists also differ on the proper device for moral reflection: Should it be presumptions and paradigms, on the one hand, or stories, on the other?

Consider, once again, presumptions and paradigms. As I indicated earlier, both condense a chain of arguments or assumptions about the moral life. The presumption distills a commonplace of ethical belief in the form of prima facie duties or obligations, which provide starting points for practical deliberation and judgment. Similarly, paradigms offer a way of seeing, a gestalt for viewing a moral case. In this sense they are "exemplary," providing models on which to base practical reasoning. Moreover, paradigms constitute a taxonomy, a system of classifying moral action. Casuists often proceed by first providing a clear, brief definition of an action—intervention, abortion, lying, theft—before moving through an analysis of a particular case or policy.

To this view of casuistry, narrative ethics presents one important difference: Narratives are not clear and uncontroversial, but murky. It is usually difficult to see through them until the end, and even then the interpretation of the narrative is often up for grabs. Given that a narrative typically includes a plot, a subplot, character development, connections (and shifts) between episodes, reversals of fortune, setting (and setting changes), monologue, dialogue, narrative voice, and denouement, narrative conventions would seem to make practical reasoning interminable. Indeed, it remains unclear on the narrativists' account what kinds of judgments their approach would produce. Presumptions and paradigms, in contrast, enable casuists to proceed more efficiently toward specific judgments about cases. Presumptions and paradigms are more or less self-evident. They furnish an ethical shorthand in the process of practical reasoning, a clear point of departure for the practice of social criticism.

Casuistry and Heterogeneity

The fact that casuistry must attend to the variabilities of human experience suggests that casuists must draw on a variety of diagnostic instruments for analysis. If, as Aristotle knew, moral experience resists simple descriptions and incorrigible principles, then we need a wide range of tools to unearth what is at stake in the experiences we assess. Indeed, in the *Rhetoric* Aristotle reminds us that, when rendering judgments, rhetors must combine a variety of oratorical devices: story, peroration, argument, maxim, refutation, and joke (to name a few). When we engage in public speech about variable matters, no single set of discourses will do.[82]

Throughout this book I have sought to take a general cue from the Aristotelian embrace of heterogeneity in public discourse. We have seen the pertinence of casuistry for understanding the (overlapping) work of social critics, philosophers, strong poets, religious critics, medical ethicists, cultural commentators, and scholars of religion. Although the cases we have examined hardly exhaust the problems we face today, I have used them to illustrate some of the diverse discourses that ought to shape moral inquiry and contribute to public philosophy: philosophy of science, legal reasoning, comparative religion, literary theory, ideological criticism, theology, hermeneutics, and moral philosophy. Moreover, I have sought to draw upon paradigms, presumptions, and latent meanings in the course of casuistical analysis. My aim has been to enrich our view of casuistry by using resources from scientific, legal, humanistic, and social scientific inquiry. True, these are not identical to Aristotle's rhetorical devices, literally understood. But the more general point for Aristotle is that practical reasoning takes us into an array of complex experiences, and no single set of diagnostic tools can generate a sufficiently rich description of our cases.

How these discourses are brought to bear will vary, of course, according to the case and the casuist in question. But our lack of a clear recipe for their use should not set up obstacles to practical deliberation. Quite the contrary: We must view casuistry as an eclectic, interdisciplinary inquiry. Casuistry invites genre bending, for which there is no simple, algorithmic formula or procedural menu. Eclecticism and heterogeneity are not a bane for casuistry—not when it is understood in its full promise, as a poetics of practical reasoning.

Notes to Introduction

1. Blaise Pascal, *The Provincial Letters,* trans. and with an introduction by A. J. Krailsheimer (New York: Penguin Books, 1967).

2. Jeremy Taylor, *Dissuasive from Popery,* in *The Whole Works* (London, 1849), vol. 6, p. 274, cited in Margaret Sampson, "Laxity and Liberty in Seventeenth-Century English Political Thought," in *Conscience and Casuistry in Early Modern Europe,* ed. Edmund Leites (Cambridge: Cambridge University Press, 1988), 72. It is important to note, however, that Taylor himself produced a huge tome of casuistry. See Jeremy Taylor, *Ductor Dubitantium, or The Rule of Conscience* (London: Angel in Ivy-Lane, 1660).

3. For an instructive historical discussion of the polemical successes of Pascal and the Jansenists, see Sampson, "Laxity and Liberty in Seventeenth-Century English Political Thought," 72–96.

4. For a discussion of presumptions, see J. Philip Wogaman, *A Christian Method of Moral Judgment* (Philadelphia: Westminster Press, 1976), chap. 2 and passim. Wogaman's frequent use of the idea of "exceptions" to presumptions may suggest that he sees the alternatives to presumptions only in terms of liberty from prescribed laws. But a careful reading shows that for Wogaman exceptions may include honoring competing duties or goods in situations of moral conflict. See ibid., 51–52. I will clarify the difference between situations of liberty against law and situations of moral conflict, in which two duties or goods compete for allegiance, in chapter 1. Wogaman's language of presumptions is expansive and includes reference to the structure of theological truth claims, which I eschew in this book.

5. This description closely follows that provided by Albert R. Jonsen and Stephen Toulmin, *The Abuse of Casuistry: A History of Moral Reasoning* (Berkeley: University of California Press, 1988), 257.

6. See, e.g., Nancy Sherman, *The Fabric of Character: Aristotle's Theory of Virtue* (Oxford: Clarendon Press, 1989), 28–44.

7. Indeed, by this account we should not sharply distinguish between legal reasoning and the creative dimensions of practical judgment. For a discussion, see Hans-Georg Gadamer, *Truth and Method,* 2d rev. ed., trans. Joel Weinsheimer and Donald G. Marshall (New York: Crossroad, 1991), 324–41. I will take up these issues more fully in chapter 9.

8. See n. 5. For theological and historical discussions of casuistry, see Nigel Biggar, "The Case for Casuistry in the Church," *Modern Theology* 6

(October 1989): 29–51; James F. Keenan and Thomas A. Shannon, eds., *The Context of Casuistry* (Washington, D.C.: Georgetown University Press, 1995).

9. Jonsen and Toulmin, *The Abuse of Casuistry,* chap 15. See also Stephen Toulmin, "The Tyranny of Principles," *Hastings Center Report* 11 (December 1981): 31–39.

10. Aristotle reserves the ideal of contemplating timeless truths for the few of the leisured classes. Those involved in practical affairs, on the other hand, have more complex circumstances to confront, and to them Aristotle offers up his account of practical deliberation. See Aristotle, *The Nicomachean Ethics,* trans. W. D. Ross, in *The Basic Works of Aristotle,* ed. and with an introduction by Richard McKeon (New York: Random House, 1941), bk. 10, chaps. 6–9.

11. Stephen Toulmin, "How Medicine Saved the Life of Ethics," *Perspectives in Biology and Medicine* 25 (1982): 742.

12. Aristotle, *Nicomachean Ethics,* 1142a23, 1142b27–28. Interpreters of the virtue tradition often distinguish sharply between character on the one hand and ethical deliberation about specific problems on the other. According to this enormously popular interpretation, *character* is a term designating virtue or vice *tout court.* Ethical inquiry seeking to provide answers to specific problems is connected with "quandary ethics," the solving of moral dilemmas. This book is premised on the claim that such a distinction is the source of a misplaced debate if not a colossal mistake. See, e.g., Edmund Pincoffs, "Quandary Ethics," in *Revisions: Changing Perspectives in Moral Philosophy,* ed. Stanley Hauerwas and Alasdair MacIntyre (Notre Dame, Ind.: University of Notre Dame Press, 1983), 92–112.

13. In chapter 9 I will discuss how this optical dimension is pertinent to Aristotle's practical philosophy as well.

14. For an argument on behalf of legal reasoning as public philosophy in a democratic culture, see Mary Ann Glendon, *Rights Talk: The Impoverishment of Political Discourse* (New York: Free Press, 1991).

15. John D. Arras, "Getting Down to Cases: The Revival of Casuistry in Bioethics," *Journal of Medicine and Philosophy* 16 (1991): 30. Arras remarks that casuistry today should "(1) use real cases, (2) make them long, richly detailed, and comprehensive, (3) present complex sequences of cases, (4) stress the problem of 'moral diagnosis,' and (5) be ever mindful of the limits of casuistical analysis" (29). I have written this book with all five of Arras's concerns in mind.

16. Ibid., 45.

17. The danger of extrinsicism has been the subject of Charles Curran's many writings about the Catholic manualist tradition. See, e.g., Charles E. Curran, *Themes in Fundamental Moral Theology* (Notre Dame, Ind.: University of Notre Dame Press, 1977), chap. 2 and passim. Extrinsicism is similar to deductivism, which I address in chapter 2, insofar as both proceed in a "top down" fashion. But extrinsicism is different insofar as it imposes a principle, or set of principles, without consulting the kind of experience that is to be assessed. In ethics, extrinsicism often goes by the name *legalism.*

18. Thomas S. Kuhn, *The Structure of Scientific Revolutions,* 2d ed. (Chicago: University of Chicago Press, 1970), chap. 3.

Notes to Chapter One

1. Shakespeare, *King Richard III* 5.3.195–96.

2. One caveat in this regard concerns the question, Who is, or was, a casuist? This is a difficult issue, for two reasons. First, casuistry did not emerge as a systematic examination of cases until after 1000 C.E., when a professional class of canon lawyers and confessors emerged in Western Europe. And casuistry did not materialize as a widely recognized genre until the sixteenth and seventeenth centuries, when Catholics, Puritans, and Anglicans began producing tomes devoted to case studies. Yet elements of casuistry were laid down much earlier, in the sacred and legal writings of Judaism, Greek and Stoic philosophy, and early Christian literature.

Second, some authors were "casuists," but not exclusively. Jeremy Taylor, for example, produced an enormous work of casuistry, but he wrote several treatises on other subjects. Labeling him a "casuist" fails to describe the full range of his authorship.

To avoid these problems, I will use the term *casuist* to speak broadly about those who have contributed in one way or another through the centuries to casuistical inquiry, either in piecemeal or systematic ways. The point here is not to carry out a history of casuistry, but to examine the questions, tools, and habits of mind that enable us to think casuistically. For useful historical surveys, see Kenneth E. Kirk, *Conscience and Its Problems: An Introduction to Casuistry*, 4th ed. (London: Longmans, Green and Co., 1948); Jonsen and Toulmin, *The Abuse of Casuistry*.

3. Kirk, *Conscience and Its Problems*, 321.

4. Aristotle, *Nicomachean Ethics* 1137b10–31.

5. It should be noted that *probable* in ethics means "provable" or "arguable," as opposed to the ordinary sense of *probable*, which, as a modal term, qualifies the certainty of one's expression. Ordinarily, to say that something is probably the case is to say that the odds are in its favor, that it is more likely than not to be true. A probable statement, then, is reliable even if it is not certain. For a discussion of probable reasoning, see Stephen Toulmin, *The Uses of Argument* (Cambridge: Cambridge University Press, 1958), chap. 2. For useful discussions of probabilism in casuistry, see Jonsen and Toulmin, *The Abuse of Casuistry*, 167–70; John Mahoney, *The Making of Moral Theology: A Study of the Roman Catholic Tradition* (Oxford: Clarendon Press, 1987), 135–43; *The Westminster Dictionary of Christian Ethics*, 2d ed., s. v. "Casuistry" by Thomas Wood.

6. In this respect, casuistry is not unlike ordinary language. At the very least, casuistry's relationship to theory resembles Wittgenstein's understanding of the relationship between ordinary language and philosophy. Accordingly, elaborate theories of interpretation emerge in ethics, Wittgenstein might say, when casuistry "goes on a holiday."

7. Kirk, *Conscience and Its Problems*, 159.

8. For a discussion of specification in light of some recent ethical theories, see Henry S. Richardson, "Specifying Norms as a Way to Resolve Concrete Ethical Problems," *Philosophy and Public Affairs* 19 (Fall 1990): 279–310.

My discussion of rules and presumptions in casuistry is meant to underscore the fact that casuistry does not eschew principles in the exercise of moral reasoning. But this should not obscure the fact that casuistry differs from superficially similar appeals to principles in ethics, owing to the emphasis that casuists place on interpretation. To date, there is nothing like a poetics of principlism that resembles the kind of casuistical poetics I am developing here. This important difference is overlooked in Tom Beauchamp's instructive discussion of principles and casuistry in recent ethics. See Tom L. Beauchamp, "Principles and Other Emerging Paradigms in Bioethics," *Indiana Law Journal* 69 (Fall 1994): 955–71.

9. Aquinas, *Summa Theologiae*, II-II, Q. 66, A. 5.

10. Ibid., A. 7.

11. Ibid., ad. 2.

12. Kuhn, *The Structure of Scientific Revolutions*, chap. 3.

13. Ibid., 10–15.

14. Ibid., 45.

15. Ibid., 189.

16. Jonsen and Toulmin, *The Abuse of Casuistry*, 35.

17. Henry Davis, *Moral and Pastoral Theology*, vol. 2 (New York: Sheed and Ward, 1938), 171–86.

18. Joseph Fletcher, *Situation Ethics: The New Morality* (Philadelphia: Westminster Press, 1966).

19. Aristotle, *Nicomachean Ethics* 1160a2–8.

20. Richard A. McCormick, *How Brave a New World? Dilemmas in Bioethics* (Garden City, N.Y.: Doubleday and Co., 1981), 69.

21. Daniel C. Maguire, *A Case for Affirmative Action* (Dubuque, Ia.: Shepherd, 1992).

22. David Novak, *Law and Theology in Judaism* (New York: Ktav Publishing, 1974), 121.

23. My language of presumptions and paradigms follows Aristotle's distinction between enthymemes and examples in *Rhetoric* 1357a14. By *enthymeme* Aristotle has in mind a form of argumentation that draws on commonly held assumptions; by *example* (*paradeigma*) he has in mind not merely an illustration, but a model from which we can reason analogically.

I presuppose this distinction when I discuss presumptions, paradigms, and moral discourse about war in chapter 2. I will rely on that discussion, in turn, when I set out to solve a case in medical ethics in chapter 6. The more general methodological features of casuistry understood in these terms will emerge when I attempt to connect features of practical reasoning with Aristotle's view of rhetoric in chapter 9.

24. Aquinas, *Summa Theologiae*, I-II, Q. 97, A. 3.

25. For an important discussion, see Charles Taylor, *Philosophical Arguments* (Cambridge: Harvard University Press, 1995), chap. 9.

26. Aristotle, *Nicomachean Ethics* 1143b14.

27. For a discussion of custom and common law, see Benjamin N. Cardozo, *The Nature of the Judicial Process* (New Haven: Yale University Press, 1921), 58–66.

28. I do not wish to distinguish sharply between ambiguity and conflict as occasions of casuistry. Conflicts of general values—e.g., between liberty and equality in the political realm, or between respecting patient autonomy

and providing patient benefit in the medical realm—may generate the need to rank values and to specify more clearly each value's range of application. But that need arises from their generality, not their specificity, returning us to the hermeneutical concerns of the previous section.

29. For an account of presumptions in rhetoric, see Chaim Perelman and L. Olbrechts-Tyteca, *The New Rhetoric: A Treatise on Argumentation,* trans. John Wilkinson and Purcell Weaver (Notre Dame, Ind.: University of Notre Dame Press, 1969), 70–74.

30. Nicholas Rescher, *Dialectics: A Controversy-Oriented Approach to the Theory of Knowledge* (Albany: State University of New York Press, 1977), 30.

31. Richard A. Epstein,. "Pleadings and Presumptions," *University of Chicago Law Review* 40 (1972–73), 558–59, cited in Rescher, *Dialectics,* 32.

32. Rescher, *Dialectics,* 36.

33. Cardozo, *The Nature of the Judicial Process,* 20.

34. Ibid., 35.

35. See Kirk, *Conscience and Its Problems,* 270, 321, 327, 388–94.

36. For a discussion, see Thomas L. Shaffer, *On Being a Christian and a Lawyer: Law for the Innocent* (Provo, Ut.: Brigham Young University Press, 1981), chaps. 6–9. Yet Shaffer is drawn more toward narrative ethics, overlooking the resources that casuistry might provide for his discussions of legal ethics. Shaffer wants to call attention to the dilemmas that arise within a lawyer's work, yet he fails to note the tensions between his discussion of legal dilemmas and the main lines of narrative ethics.

37. See, e.g., Aquinas, *Summa Theologiae,* II-II, Q. 26.

38. Cicero, *On Duties,* ed. M. T. Griffin and E. M. Atkins (Cambridge: Cambridge University Press, 1991), 107.

39. Ibid., 121. Cicero's logic has parallels with rule utilitarianism, as described in William Frankena, *Ethics,* 2d ed. (Englewood Cliffs, N.J.: Prentice-Hall, 1973), 39–43.

40. Cicero, *On Duties,* 108.

41. Michael Walzer, *Just and Unjust Wars: A Moral Argument with Historical Illustrations,* 2d ed. (New York: Basic Books, 1992), chaps. 3, 8. These are not Walzer's only concerns; sovereignty plays a prominent role as well. See ibid., 51–63.

42. Ibid., 54.

43. Ibid., 251.

44. Ibid., 260.

45. Augustine, *On Lying,* in *The Nicene and Post-Nicene Fathers,* ed. Philip Schaff (Grand Rapids, Mich.: Eerdmans, 1956), 475.

46. For a general discussion, see Mahoney, *The Making of Moral Theology,* 48–58.

47. Augustine, *On Lying,* 477.

48. Aristotle, *Nicomachean Ethics* 1101a1–3.

49. Ibid., 1109a33–35.

50. The phrases are taken from Reinhold Niebuhr, *The Nature and Destiny of Man,* vol. 1, *Human Nature* (New York: Charles Scribner's Sons, 1941), 219–27.

51. I am aware that this case presupposes the judgment that elective abor-

tions are evil. For a nurse who is materially implicated in conduct judged as such, the act is excused if competing considerations prevail.

52. The distinction is put forward with characteristic clarity by Aquinas, *Summa Theologiae,* I-II, Q. 64, A. 7, where he articulates his influential view of the ethics of homicide in self-defense.

53. For an important discussion of the relative superiority of this distinction over the rule of double effect, see Philippa Foot, *Virtues and Vices* (Berkeley: University of California Press, 1978), chap. 2.

54. For a discussion, see Johann P. Sommerville, "The 'New Art of Lying': Equivocation, Mental Reservation, and Casuistry," in *Conscience and Casuistry,* ed. Leites, 175.

55. Augustine, *On Lying,* 469.

56. Gerald Kelly, *Medico-Moral Problems* (St. Louis: Catholic Hospital Association, 1958), 128–41; James J. McCartney, "The Development of the Doctrine of Ordinary and Extraordinary Means of Preserving Life in Catholic Moral Theology before the Karen Quinlan Case," *Linacre Quarterly* 47 (August 1980): 215–24. The literature on this distinction is immense, and is reviewed by Richard C. Sparks, *To Treat or Not to Treat? Bioethics and the Handicapped Newborn* (Mahwah, N.J.: Paulist Press, 1988). The distinction is central to many living wills today.

57. To be sure, whether all natural treatments may be withheld or withdrawn from terminally ill patients is a torturous issue. For a discussion, see James J. Walter and Thomas A. Shannon, "The PVS Patient and the Forgoing/Withdrawing of Medical Nutrition and Hydration," in Walter and Shannon, eds., *Quality of Life: The New Medical Dilemma* (Mahwah, N.J.: Paulist Press, 1990), 203–23.

58. Augustine, "On the Good of Marriage," in *Treatises on Marriage and Other Subjects,* trans. Charles T. Wilcox, et al., ed. Roy J. Deferrari (Washington, D.C.: Catholic University of America Press, 1969), 30.

59. See, e.g., Aquinas, *Summa Theologiae,* I-II, Qq. 72, A. 5; 74, A. 10; II-II, Q. 59, A. 4.

60. See, e.g., John Calvin, *Institutes of the Christian Religion,* bk. 2, chap. 8, par. 58.

61. In contemporary Roman Catholic moral theology, attempts have been made to reinterpret mortal sin in terms of Karl Rahner's notion of a "fundamental option." The point of the reinterpretation is to shift attention from individual deeds to the overall orientation of the self in its basic freedom—either toward or away from God's gift of self-communication. See Karl Rahner, *Theological Investigations,* vol. 6, trans. Karl-H. and Boniface Kruger (New York: Seabury, 1974), 178–96.

62. I am grateful to Professor Ted Koontz, Director of Peace Studies at Associated Mennonite Biblical Seminaries, for helping me see this point. I have sought to refine this idea in "Casuistry, Pacifism, and the Just-War Tradition in the Post–Cold War Era," in *Peacemaking: Moral and Policy Challenges for a New World,* ed. Gerald F. Powers, Drew Christiansen, and Robert T. Hennemeyer (Washington, D.C.: U.S. Catholic Conference, 1994), 199–213.

63. Ambrose, *De Officiis Ministrorum,* III, iv.

64. See Aquinas, *Summa Theologiae*, I-II, Q. 108, A. 4.

65. A considerable amount of work in recent Catholic ethics has sought to develop the perfectionist dimensions of Christian life, following the statement from the Second Vatican Council that "all the faithful are invited and obliged to holiness and the perfection of their own state of life." See *Lumen gentium*, in *Vatican Council II: The Conciliar and Post-Conciliar Documents*, ed. Austin Flannery (Northport, N.Y.: Costello Publishing, 1975), par. 42. On this issue the council documents follow Aquinas, *Summa Theologiae*, II-II, Q. 184, A. 3.

66. Augustine, "On the Good of Marriage," 20, 45, 46.

67. *Encyclopedia of Bioethics*, 1st ed., s. v. "Obligation and Supererogation" by Thomas J. Bole III and Millard Schumacker.

68. Augustine, *On Lying*, 475.

69. For a discussion, see John C. Ford and Gerald Kelly, *Contemporary Moral Theology*, vol. 1 (Westminster, Md.: Newman Press, 1958), chap. 9.

70. See ibid., 157.

Notes to Chapter Two

1. See Kenneth R. Timmerman, *The Death Lobby: How the West Armed Iraq* (Boston: Houghton Mifflin, 1991), 374. Timmerman provides an extensive account of Hussein's pursuit of military prowess, data from which I will draw on below.

2. For a rigorous discussion, see Martin L. Cook and Phillip A. Hamann, "The Road to Basra: A Case Study in Military Ethics," *Annual*, Society of Christian Ethics (1994): 207–28.

3. This account is compiled from information provided by Micah L. Sifry and Christopher Cerf, eds., *The Gulf War Reader: History, Documents, Opinions* (New York: Random House, 1991); Andrew Rosenthal, "U.S. and Allies Open Air War on Iraq," *New York Times*, 17 January 1991, 1; Joel Brinkley, "Allies Intensify Bombing of Iraqi Troops," *New York Times*, 20 January 1991, 1; R. W. Apple, Jr., "80 of Iraq's Planes Now in Iran," *New York Times*, 29 January 1991, 1; R. W. Apple, Jr., "Iraq Navy Threat Ended, Allies Say," *New York Times*, 3 February 1991, 1; R. W. Apple, Jr., "Air War Is Pressed," *New York Times*, 23 February 1991, 1; R. W. Apple, Jr., "Allied Units Surge through Kuwait," *New York Times*, 27 February 1991, 1; R. W. Apple, Jr., "Chaos Reported in Basra, Iraq," *New York Times*, 3 March 1991, 1; Patrick E. Tyler, "'Clean Win' in the War with Iraq Drifts into Bloody Aftermath," *New York Times*, 31 March 1991, 1(E); Russell Watson, et al., "Iraq's Power Play," *Newsweek*, 13 August 1990, 17–21; Russell Watson, et al., "Saddam's Last Stand," *Newsweek*, 4 March 1991, 18–37; Andrew Whitley, "Kuwait: The Last Forty-Eight Hours," *New York Review of Books*, 30 May 1991, 17–18; Theodore Draper, "The Gulf War Reconsidered," *New York Review of Books*, 16 January 1992, 38–45; Theodore Draper, "The True History of the Gulf War," *New York Review of Books*, 23 January 1992, 46–53.

4. James F. Childress, "Just-War Criteria," in *War or Peace? The Search for New Answers*, ed. Thomas A. Shannon (Maryknoll, N.Y.: Orbis, 1980), 40; U.S. Catholic Bishops, *The Challenge of Peace: God's Promise and Our*

Response (Washington, D.C.: United States Catholic Conference, 1983), par. 121.

5. By my account, then, pacifists have a limited basis for drawing on just-war criteria as a framework for social criticism. I do *not* wish to suggest that pacifists are able to use the just-war tradition to arrive at the conclusion that any particular war can be justified, for that would require them both to affirm and to deny the justification of war. At the very least, pacifists must reject the condition of just cause, and ought to find the assumptions of right intention to be unacceptable. One example of a pacifist drawing upon just-war criteria is Stanley Hauerwas (with Richard John Neuhaus), "Pacifism, Just War, and the Gulf," *First Things* 13 (May 1991): 40.

6. Yet many pacifists do not adopt pacifism on the basis of this mandate, as Hauerwas argues. See ibid., 39 and passim.

7. I wish to thank Bill Meyer and Gabriel Palmer-Fernandez for requesting clarification on this point, although they may not agree with how I have developed it here.

8. See, e.g., LeRoy Walters, "Five Classic Just-War Theories: A Study in the Thought of Thomas Aquinas, Vitoria, Suarez, Gentili, and Grotius" (Ph.D. diss., Yale University, 1971); Frederick H. Russell, *The Just War in the Middle Ages* (Cambridge: Cambridge University Press, 1975); James Turner Johnson, *Just War Tradition and the Restraint of War: A Moral and Historical Inquiry* (Princeton, N.J.: Princeton University Press, 1981); Lisa Sowle Cahill, "Nonresistance, Defense, Violence, and the Kingdom in Christian Tradition," *Interpretation* 38 (October 1984): 380–97.

9. See John Howard Yoder, *When War Is Unjust: Being Honest in Just War Thinking*, with an introduction by Charles P. Lutz (Minneapolis: Augsburg, 1984); John Howard Yoder, "Just War Tradition: Is It Credible?" *Christian Century*, 31 March 1991, 295–98.

10. See, e.g., Michael Walzer, "Perplexed," *New Republic*, 28 January 1991, 14; Alan Geyer, "Just War and the Burdens of History," *Christian Century*, 6–13 February 1991, 135; J. Bryan Hehir, "The Moral Calculus of War," *Commonweal*, 22 February 1991, 125–26; John Langan, "An Imperfectly Just War," *Commonweal*, 1 June 1991, 361–65.

11. Patrick Jordan, "A No-Hands-Tied War: Neither Just or Right," *Commonweal*, 8 March 1991, 148–49.

12. See, e.g., Richard John Neuhaus, "Just War and This War," *Wall Street Journal*, 29 January 1991, sec. 1, 16(A); James Turner Johnson, "Just War Tradition and the War in the Gulf," *Christian Century*, 6–13 February 1991, 134–35; James Turner Johnson and George Weigel, *Just War and the Gulf War* (Washington, D.C.: Ethics and Public Policy Center, 1991).

13. See, e.g., Johnson, *Just War Tradition and the Restraint of War*, chaps. 6, 7; William V. O'Brien, *The Conduct of Just and Limited War* (New York: Praeger, 1981), 55–70.

14. Jeffrey Stout, "Reflections on Virtue and War," unpublished paper delivered at the annual meeting of the American Academy of Religion, November 1985, for which I served as respondent. I thank Stout for permission to quote his analogy in full.

Stout introduced the analogy to refute the validity of presumptive duties in just-war criteria. As will become clearer below, in my judgment the analogy actually works to support the logic of presumptive duties in the ethics of surgery, harm, or war. Stout developed his views in light of the ethics of Thomas Aquinas on war. My own views on Aquinas's ethics, and the pertinence of the language of presumptive duties for his treatment of homicide in self-defense, are developed in Richard B. Miller, *Interpretations of Conflict: Ethics, Pacifism, and the Just-War Tradition* (Chicago: University of Chicago Press, 1991), chaps. 1, 2.

15. *The Westminster Dictionary of Christian Ethics*, 2d ed., s. v., "Conflict of Duties," by A. C. Ewing.

16. See Childress, "Just-War Criteria," 40–42.

17. See Gadamer, *Truth and Method*, 271–79, 299.

18. I am combining the discussions of "presumptions" and "presentation" in Chaim Perelman, *The Realm of Rhetoric*, trans. William Kluback, with an introduction by Carroll C. Arnold (Notre Dame, Ind.: University of Notre Dame Press, 1982), 24–26, 35–40.

19. For an alternative interpretation of the logic of just-war tenets, see Paul Ramsey, *Speak Up for Just War or Pacifism: A Critique of the United Methodist Bishops' Pastoral Letter, "In Defense of Creation,"* with an epilogue by Stanley Hauerwas (State Park: Pennsylvania State University Press, 1988), 109–10.

20. For a discussion of ordinary and extraordinary means in medicine, see chapter 1.

21. As with virtually all analogies in casuistry, this one has its limits. In this case, there are four.

First, in surgery there is no adequate analogy for the foreseen, unintended death of individuals in battle. The analogy breaks down, in other words, once we compare the relationship of parts to wholes in medicine and in war, respectively. The surgeon is permitted to attack part of the organism (a diseased element) for the sake of the whole. But surgeons are not allowed to attack the entire person. Or doctors may battle a disease that can infect a group of individuals, as in the fight against the plague, or polio, or AIDS. But at least in the United States, doctors are not permitted intentionally to kill any person or group when carrying out medical duties. The image of the individual as a scene of battle is limited, because it can all too easily obscure the damage to and the deaths of persons that occur in the battles of war. In war, individuals—not just diseased elements of individuals—may be killed intentionally. Killing in war assumes a magnitude that has no exact parallels with battles waged in an operating room.

Second, the analogy between war and medicine is dangerous, for it might suggest that there are factions in the world who are diseased and who should be removed to create social or international health. The analogy suggests that in war one side is like a doctor curing the human race of its infirm elements. This is an ominous idea, if for no other reason than that it can be connected too easily to racial and religious prejudices. The Germans, for example, used such notions to justify removing the "contaminating" presence of Jews and other minorities from Europe in their quest to "purify" the Aryan race. In the era after the Holocaust, the notion of war as a means of removing disease cannot but be associated with Nazi eugenics and other atrocities.

Third, different kinds of obligations surround the duty to intervene medically and militarily, as I shall make clearer below. Suffice it to say here that in the ethics of war there is no duty to intervene in all cases in order to save others from unjust aggression; in cases of third-party intervention political factors may be relevant, and appropriate duties to the self may proscribe taking risks on behalf of others. During the 1970s and 1980s, for example, virtually no just-war theorist argued that the United States was morally obligated to send soldiers to fight on behalf of Afghanistan against the Soviet Union. But for doctors the case is different: Political factors are irrelevant; doctors are morally obligated to treat others regardless of nation, race, or creed. And, although doctors may weigh duties to themselves in difficult instances, appeals to such duties are significantly more controversial in the case of medical nontreatment than they are in the case of military nonintervention.

Fourth, perhaps the most obvious limit to the analogy between war and surgery is that war sends people to operating rooms and emergency wards for medical care. Medical care aims to help people to leave the medical ward, not to send them there.

22. There are other forms of intervention, e.g., in a secession, in a civil war, or to carry out a humanitarian intervention, which I shall not consider here. For a discussion of these types of intervention, see Walzer, *Just and Unjust Wars,* chap. 6; J. Bryan Hehir, "Intervention and International Affairs," in *The American Search for Peace: Moral Reasoning, Religious Hope, and National Security,* ed. George Weigel and John Langan (Washington, D.C.: Georgetown University Press, 1991), 137–61; Kenneth R. Himes, "Just War, Pacifism, and Humanitarian Intervention," *America* 169 (August 14, 1993): 10–15, 28–31; and Kenneth R. Himes, "The Morality of Humanitarian Intervention," *Theological Studies* 55 (March 1994): 82–105.

23. My views about the difference between self-defense and intervention draw loosely from Walzer's discussion of self-defense, protection, and intervention in *Just and Unjust Wars,* chaps. 4 and 6. It should be noted that I am using intervention here in a broader sense. Walzer confines his notion of intervention to circumstances in which an outside party enters the affairs of another in the cases of secession, civil strife, or internal oppression. Such acts can be justified, in the right circumstances, as exceptions to what he calls the "legalist paradigm," namely, the standard warrant for justifying the use of force. The legalist paradigm justifies war in the cases of self-defense and third-party protection. But viewing third-party protection as Walzer does may obscure the ways in which it differs from the case of self-defense, especially in an action by an international coalition. Such differences will be developed below.

24. That the United Nations coalition is a third party acting on behalf of one sovereignty invaded by another distinguishes the case in the Persian Gulf from cases in which human rights are systematically violated *within* one nation by its own military or police forces, e.g., South Africa, or China during the events of Tiananmen Square. This is only to say that third-party interven-

tion is easier to justify than second-party intervention: In the former case boundaries have already been crossed by an aggressor; in the latter case the intervening party would be invading a sovereign nation, which requires additional justification.

This difference seems to be overlooked by those who suggest that U.S. actions on behalf of Kuwait are incongruous with the failure of U.S. leaders to intervene in China or South Africa, thereby establishing a double standard for intervention. See, e.g., Maureen Dowd, "Bush's Holy War: The Crusader's Cloak Can Grow Heavy on the Shoulders," *New York Times*, 3 February 1991, sec. 4, 1–2(E); David O'Brien, "Daunting Questions," *Commonweal*, 8 February 1991, 85; "Statement by Jim Wallis," in *Just War and the Gulf War*, ed. Weigel and Johnson, 149.

25. See the U.S. Catholic Bishops, *The Challenge of Peace*, par. 101.

26. Such holism may also be appropriate in cases of second-party intervention, e.g., humanitarian intervention to rescue victims from their own regime. Again, judgments deriving from proportionality and reasonable hope for success would be relevant.

27. See G. E. M. Anscombe, "The Justice of the Present War Examined," in *War in the Twentieth Century: Sources in Theological Ethics*, ed. Richard B. Miller (Louisville: Westminster/John Knox Press, 1992), 129. So, too, with the medical analogy: The illness is the cause, but the restoration of health must be the intention. Cause and intention, in other words, are not synonymous.

28. H. Richard Niebuhr, "The Grace of Doing Nothing," *Christian Century*, 23 March 1932, 380.

29. Timmerman, *The Death Lobby.*

30. Ibid., 41, 157.

31. Ibid., xxviii–xix, 18, 22, 32, 34, 59.

32. Ibid., 106.

33. Ibid., 112, 189, 293, 304.

34. Ibid., 153.

35. Ibid., 116–18.

36. Ibid., 262.

37. Ibid., 394.

38. Ibid., 278.

39. Ibid., 167–68.

40. Ibid., 42–43, 59.

41. Ibid., 248.

42. Ibid., 185, 422. See also the appendix to Timmerman's study, which provides extensive data about arms sales from Western nations to Iraq from 1975 to 1990.

43. Ibid., 203. Consider this example: In July 1990, only one month before the invasion of Kuwait, a firm in New Jersey was about to ship high-temperature furnaces to manufacture nuclear weapons in Iraq when the U.S. government was alerted by a former official from the Defense Department. The transfer was quickly blocked. The firm had notified the Commerce Department twice that its furnaces had nuclear applications, but it was repeatedly encouraged by the government to pursue the business. See Kenneth R.

Timmerman, "Surprise! We Gave Hussein the Bomb," *New York Times*, 25 October 1991, 15(A); Draper, "The Gulf War Reconsidered," 46–53, at 51.

44. Cited in Draper, "The Gulf War Reconsidered," 52.

45. Ibid.

46. See Thomas L. Friedman, "Envoy to Iraq, Faulted in Crisis, Says She Warned Hussein Sternly," *New York Times*, 21 March 1991, 1.

47. Draper, "The Gulf War Reconsidered," 53.

48. See Patrick E. Tyler, "Iraq: A Clear and Continuing Danger," *New York Times*, 1 December 1991, 1(E).

49. I do not mean to suggest that collective action is new. I only wish to point out that an international authorization of collective action raises questions about the ethics of allocating burdens among those who ally themselves in war.

50. See Gary C. Hufbauer and Kimberly A. Elliott, "Sanctions Will Bite—and Soon," *New York Times*, 14 January 1991, 15(A).

51. "Letter to President Bush: The Persian Gulf Crisis," *Origins* 20 (November 20, 1990): 397–400. The position of the U.S. Catholic bishops is echoed in the editorial, "Patience and Resolve," *Commonweal*, 11 January 1991, 3.

52. For an account of positions taken by other religious organizations in the United States, see Peter Steinfels, "Beliefs," *New York Times*, 5 January 1991, sec. 1, 9.

53. Walzer, *Just and Unjust Wars*, 2d ed., xiv.

54. Thomas C. Schelling, *Arms and Influence* (New Haven: Yale University Press, 1966), 79–80.

55. I wish to thank John Lovell for helping me see this point, although he may not agree with how I have developed it here.

56. Tom L. Beauchamp and James F. Childress, *Principles of Biomedical Ethics*, 3d ed. (New York: Oxford University Press, 1989), 147–50; Fred M. Frohock, *Special Care: Medical Decisions at the Beginning of Life* (Chicago: University of Chicago Press, 1986), 64–65. I should add that Beauchamp and Childress reject the distinction that I am arguing for here.

57. As McMahan shows, this distinction is relevant to more than medical cases. Although he eschews discussion of ordinary and extraordinary means, his comment would seem to hold in either kind of case.

McMahan goes on to point out that there are important distinctions to be drawn within the category of withdrawing aid, that some forms of withdrawal are killing whereas other forms only let an individual die. By his account, removing forces from Kuwait before repelling Iraq from Kuwaiti borders would be analogous to a medical physician who removes operative aid that has been provided but needs continuation to be effective. This kind of case, McMahan argues, should be classified in terms of allowing to die, not killing. See Jeff McMahan, "Killing, Letting Die, and Withdrawing Aid," *Ethics* 103 (January 1993): 250–79, at 272.

58. Francisco de Vitoria, *De Indiis et de Iure Belli Relectiones*, in *War and Christian Ethics*, ed. Arthur F. Holmes (Grand Rapids, Mich.: Baker Book House, 1975), 135. The case Vitoria has in mind concerns relations between Native Americans and invading Spaniards. The Spaniards, Vitoria argues, are

obligated to honor the dominion of, and carry out peaceful dealings with, the indigenous population. Yet Vitoria also recognizes that Native Americans, understandably fearing for their welfare, might unite in an effort to drive out Spaniards from their territory. According to Vitoria, the Spaniards may act to defend themselves within the limits of permissible self-protection. Vitoria's point is that in such a case we may speak of justice on both sides, "seeing that on one side there is right and on the other side there is invincible ignorance."

59. This is one way in which *ad bellum* criteria affect the way in which *in bello* restraints should be interpreted and rigorously applied.

60. Miller, *Interpretations of Conflict,* chap. 8.

61. Johnson and Weigel, *Just War and the Gulf War,* 66–67.

62. Indeed, it is noteworthy that Weigel fails to mention the condition of relative justice among the criteria of the just-war tradition.

63. Johnson and Weigel, *Just War and the Gulf War,* 66–70.

64. A similar point is made by James F. Childress, following Joel Feinberg on the distinction between acts that are just and those that are justified: The same act need not be both just and justified. In the context of just-war reasoning, this means that a war may be justified even if it is not entirely just. Yet if this is true, then Childress may press a point too far when he states, "Only when a war is both just and justified does a state have a *jus ad bellum.*" By my argument, relative justice allows a state to use force even if it has not perfectly satisfied all conditions of the *jus ad bellum.* A war that is "imperfectly just," in other words, is one that is justified but not entirely just, given the multiplicity of duties imposed by just-war tenets. See James F. Childress, *Moral Responsibility in Conflicts: Essays in Nonviolence, War, and Conscience* (Baton Rouge: Louisiana State University Press, 1982), 83–84.

Relative justice, as I have described it, ought to function self-reflexively in just-war theory, requiring us to assess the merits of our judgments and to be cognizant of competing and conflicting claims that may be generated by the variety of just-war conditions.

65. See Reinhold Niebuhr, *Christianity and Power Politics* (New York: Charles Scribner's Sons, 1940), chap. 1.

66. "Human Life in Our Day," in *Renewing the Earth: Catholic Documents on Peace, Justice and Liberation,* ed. David J. O'Brien and Thomas A. Shannon (Garden City, N.Y.: Doubleday, 1977), pars. 135–45.

67. An account of the overall battle plan is provided in R. W. Apple, Jr., "Done. A Short, Persuasive Lesson in Warfare," *New York Times,* 3 March 1991, sec. 4, 1(E), 3(E).

68. For those who apply *ad bellum* criteria in holistically to Operation Desert Storm, this judgment about proportionality necessarily weakens the argument of those (e.g., the U.S. Catholic bishops) who sought to support a strategy of compellence as an alternative to war. If, as I am suggesting, the foreseeable risks were not as grave as others have suggested, then invoking proportionality to support the imperative of sanctions becomes more difficult.

69. For a discussion of material and formal acts, see chapter 1.

70. It is wrong to say that the rule of double effect applies *in bello* criteria by attending exclusively to matters of intention and ignoring the importance

of consequences. This error helps shape Alan Geyer and Barbara G. Green's assertion that the rule of double effect is "casuistic" (understood pejoratively) in *Lines in the Sand: Justice and the Gulf War,* with a Foreword by Kermit D. Johnson (Louisville, Ky.: Westminster/John Knox Press, 1992), 24.

71. Thus it is difficult to say whether the bombing of the Amariya air-raid shelter in Baghdad on February 13, 1991, was immoral. See Caryle Murphy, "Amariya: Where One Raid Killed 300 Iraqis," *Washington Post,* 23 June 1991, 17(A).

72. Dilip Ganguly, "Baghdadis More and More Demoralized by Raids," *New York Times,* 22 February 1991, 6(A).

73. Barton Gellman, "Allied Air War Struck Broadly in Iraq," *Washington Post,* 23 June 1991, 1(A), 16(A).

74. *New York Times,* 23 March 1991, cited in Draper, "The True History of the Gulf War," 40.

75. Gellman, "Allied Air War Struck Broadly in Iraq," 16(A); see also George Lopez, "Not So Clean," *Bulletin of the Atomic Scientists* 47 (September 1991): 30–35.

76. Reuven Kimelman, "Judaism and the Ethics of War," *Proceedings of the Rabbinical Assembly* (1987), 14–15.

77. For this inference from Aquinas's treatment of homicide and war, see Miller, *Interpretations of Conflict,* 24–27.

78. John C. Ford, S. J., "The Morality of Obliteration Bombing," in *War in the Twentieth Century,* ed. Miller, 138–77.

79. Ibid., 157.

80. I assess the merits of Ramsey's argument in light of an account of prima facie duties in *Interpretations of Conflict,* chap. 6.

81. I do not mean to suggest that Ramsey would have drawn these implications from his discussions of deterrence to assess the Gulf War.

82. Gellman, "Allied Air War Struck Broadly in Iraq," 16(A). See Alberto Ascherio, et al., "Effect of the Gulf War on Infant and Child Mortality in Iraq," *New England Journal of Medicine* 327 (September 24, 1992): 931–33, which concludes that the Gulf War and trade sanctions produced a threefold increase in mortality among Iraqi children under five years of age.

83. For several discussions, see Sifry and Cerf, eds., *The Gulf War Reader,* 355–91; Caryle Murphy, "Iraqi Death Toll Remains Clouded," *Washington Post,* 23 June 1991, 1(A), 17(A).

84. Kirk, *Conscience and Its Problems,* 308.

Notes to Chapter Three

1. For a discussion of permissions and duties in casuistry, see chapter 1.

2. See, e.g., John Rawls, *A Theory of Justice* (Cambridge: Harvard University Press, 1971); John Rawls, *Political Liberalism* (New York: Columbia University Press, 1993); Bruce A. Ackerman, *Social Justice in the Liberal State* (New Haven: Yale University Press, 1980); Ronald Dworkin, "Liberalism," in *Private and Public Morality,* ed. Stuart Hampshire (Cambridge: Cambridge University Press, 1978), 113–43; Amy Gutmann, *Liberal Equality* (Cambridge: Cambridge University Press, 1980).

3. Michael J. Sandel, "Morality and the Liberal Ideal," *New Republic*, 7 May 1984, 17.

4. These views are developed with varying emphasis in Stanley Hauerwas, *The Peaceable Kingdom: A Primer in Christian Ethics* (Notre Dame, Ind.: University of Notre Dame Press, 1983); Glendon, *Rights Talk;* William F. May, *The Physician's Covenant: Images of the Healer in Medical Ethics* (Philadelphia: Westminster, 1983), 116–30; Michael Sandel, *Liberalism and the Limits of Justice* (Cambridge: Cambridge University Press, 1982); Charles Taylor, *Philosophical Papers*, vol. 2, *Philosophy and the Human Sciences* (Cambridge: Cambridge University Press, 1985), chap. 7; Charles Taylor, *Sources of the Self: The Making of Modern Identity* (Cambridge: Harvard University Press, 1989); Alasdair MacIntyre, *After Virtue: A Study in Moral Theory* (Notre Dame, Ind.: University of Notre Dame Press, 1981); Michael J. Sandel, "The Procedural Republic and the Unencumbered Self," *Political Theory* 12 (February 1984): 81–96; Nancy L. Rosenblum, *Another Liberalism: Romanticism and the Reconstruction of Liberal Thought* (Cambridge: Harvard University Press, 1987).

5. It might seem that the distinction between realists and idealists roughly parallels the distinction between duties to the self and duties to others. But this parallel is wrong, or at least very misleading. It is by no means the case that realists or liberals have no basis for endorsing duties to others, or that those who endorse duties to others cannot be liberals or realists. It is rather the case that realists/liberals suggest that a philosophic ethic that ranks duties to the self below duties to others will have a difficult time finding widespread adherence.

6. Rawls, *A Theory of Justice*, 573.

7. Ibid., 178.

8. Ibid.

9. Sandel, *Liberalism and the Limits of Justice*, 33.

10. See, e.g., Allen E. Buchanan, "Assessing the Communitarian Critique of Liberalism," *Ethics* 99 (July 1989): 853; Will Kymlicka, "Liberalism and Communitarianism," *Canadian Journal of Philosophy* 18 (June 1988): 181; Charles Larmore, "Political Liberalism," *Political Theory* 18 (August 1990): 339–41; Nancy L. Rosenblum, "Pluralism and Self-Defense," in *Liberalism and the Moral Life*, ed. Rosenblum (Cambridge: Harvard University Press, 1989), 215; Judith Shklar, "The Liberalism of Fear," 22, and Susan Moller Okin, "Humanist Liberalism," 39, in *Liberalism and the Moral Life*, ed. Rosenblum. The term *political morality* is preferred to *political theory*, since liberalism seeks, among other things, to establish moral limits to the power of the state.

11. Rawls, *A Theory of Justice*, 7; *Political Liberalism*, 11–12, 257–88; cf. John Rawls, "The Basic Structure as Subject," *American Philosophical Quarterly* 14 (April 1977): 159–65.

12. John Rawls, "Justice as Fairness: Political Not Metaphysical," *Philosophy and Public Affairs* 14 (Summer 1985): 245; Rawls, *Political Liberalism*, 13, 58–59.

13. See, e.g., Rosenblum, "Pluralism and Self-Defense," 212; Stephen Holmes, "The Permanent Structure of Antiliberal Thought," in *Liberalism and the Moral Life*, ed. Rosenblum, 227–53 passim; Amy Gutmann, "Com-

munitarian Critics of Liberalism," *Philosophy and Public Affairs* 14 (Summer 1985): 318; Michael Walzer, "The Communitarian Critique of Liberalism," *Political Theory* 18 (February 1990): 6–23.

For one attempt to show how communitarian views might make a difference in public policy, see Stanley Hauerwas, *A Community of Character: Toward a Constructive Christian Social Ethic* (Notre Dame: University of Notre Dame Press, 1981), chap. 12. Hauerwas joins his concerns in religious ethics to the debate between liberals and communitarians by associating liberalism with Ernst Troeltsch's category of "church." For Hauerwas, liberalism and "church" designate the attempt to accommodate one's ethical or religious message to the terms and assumptions of the wider culture. Accommodation is the price paid, Hauerwas argues, by the attempt to render one's views "public." He is critical of this accommodation, since it means that one must compromise one's distinctive identity, that one must play by rules set by alien terms, forces, or interests. Yet he is reluctant to construe his communitarian views along the lines of Troeltsch's alternative category, namely, sect.

14. Charles Taylor, "Cross-Purposes: The Liberal-Communitarian Debate," in *Liberalism and the Moral Life*, ed. Rosenblum, 161.

15. Ibid., 160–63.

16. See, e.g., Richard Rorty, "The Priority of Democracy to Philosophy," in *Objectivity, Relativism, and Truth*, vol. 1, *Philosophical Papers* (Cambridge: Cambridge University Press, 1991), 175–96; Jeffrey Stout, *Ethics after Babel: The Languages of Morals and Their Discontents* (Boston: Beacon Press, 1988), 227–28.

17. Rawls, *A Theory of Justice*, 4–6, 219–21, 453–62.

18. The issues surrounding moral motivation become hidden from view by liberals who restrict themselves to questions of political morality or philosophical methodology, because such questions eschew reference to the self and its loyalties. See, e.g., the essays in R. Bruce Douglass, Gerald M. Mara, and Henry S. Richardson, eds., *Liberalism and the Good* (New York: Routledge, 1990), all of which examine the goods implied in or presupposed by liberal philosophy, yet none of which broaches the issue of liberalism's feasibility. Rawls himself acknowledges this lacuna in political philosophy, noting that it provides the fundamental issue for his sequel to *Theory*. See Rawls, *Political Liberalism*, xv–xxx, 140–44.

19. See Rawls, *Theory of Justice*, 60–63; for a fuller discussion, see 298–310.

20. Ibid., 531.

21. Ibid., 138 (emphasis mine).

22. Ibid., 399 (emphasis mine).

23. I realize that these six lines differ from those Rawls explicitly enumerates, which I believe are incomplete. See *A Theory of Justice*, 513, for Rawls's own reasons for stability in his argument.

24. Ibid., 14.

25. Ibid., 101.

26. Utilitarian theorists might retort that such a request is hardly asking a "sacrifice," but I will not pursue that issue here.

27. Rawls, *A Theory of Justice*, 103.

28. Ibid.

29. Ibid., 102, 494.

30. Ibid., 494.

31. Ibid., 105.

32. Ibid., 570–71. Yet Rawls concedes that this temptation toward cheating cannot be altogether mitigated. Thus the need for state coercion to ensure that justice is served. See ibid., 267–68.

33. Ibid., 177–78.

34. Ibid., 500.

35. Ibid., 501.

36. Rawls seems to identify benevolence, self-sacrificial acts, and self-abnegation with each other when he discusses utilitarianism. Throughout his argument, the first two categories refer to ethical dispositions or acts, while the latter refers to individual psychology. The general point seems to be that utilitarianism is unstable insofar as it requires altruism, and altruism breeds self-abnegation. Whatever else might be said about these terms, surely Rawls's suggestion that self-sacrifice cannot spring from persons of robust self-esteem, or that altruism is somehow deflating, is not obvious.

37. Rawls, *A Theory of Justice*, 181.

38. Ibid., 536–37.

39. Ibid., 528.

40. Ibid., 575.

41. Ibid., 529.

42. Ibid., 448. Compare Durkheim: "As richly endowed as we may be, we always lack something, and the best of us realize our own insufficiency. That is why we seek in our friends the qualities that we lack, since in joining with them, we participate in some measure in their nature and thus feel less incomplete." Emile Durkheim, *The Division of Labor in Society,* trans. George Simpson (New York: Free Press, 1933), cited in Samuel H. Beer, "Liberty and Union," *Political Theory* 12 (August 1984): 366.

I must leave aside the question of whether Rawls's discussion of pluralism and complementarity coheres with his Kantian aversion to contingency. At the very least, his sixth reason for affirming the good of liberal culture in *Theory* suggests that liberal citizens will find themselves vulnerable to the contingencies of others' individual initiatives and pursuits of perfection. Indeed, Rawls commends the notion of dependence over and against the idea of self-sufficiency (529). Yet this notion of dependence seems incompatible with the fifth reason I have cited among Rawls's affirmations of liberal culture, namely, the idea that the nature of the self as invulnerable to contingency is revealed when justice is ranked above the good. The ontologies of the fifth and sixth reasons, in short, pull in opposite directions.

43. See, e.g., Milton Fisk, "History and Reason in Rawls' Moral Theory," in *Reading Rawls: Critical Studies on Rawls' "A Theory of Justice,"* ed. Norman Daniels (Stanford, Calif.: Stanford University Press, 1989), 53–80.

44. I say "in this respect" because even as Rawls adjusts his theory he is reluctant to abandon the idea that his views are universal in the sense that they may extend "appropriately to specify a reasonable conception of justice among all nations." For a discussion, see John Rawls, "The Domain of the

Political and Overlapping Consensus," *New York University Law Review* 64 (May 1989): 251, n. 46.

45. John Rawls, "Kantian Constructivism in Moral Theory," *Journal of Philosophy* 77 (September 1980): 518.

46. Ibid., 519, 564; Rawls, "Justice as Fairness," 228–30; Rawls, *Political Liberalism*, xx–xxx, 48–66.

47. Rawls, "Kantian Constructivism," 540; Rawls, *Political Liberalism*, 9–10.

48. Rawls, "Justice as Fairness," 225; Rawls, *Political Liberalism*, 13.

49. Rawls, "Justice as Fairness," 225; Rawls, *Political Liberalism*, 13–14.

50. John Rawls, "The Idea of an Overlapping Consensus," *Oxford Journal of Legal Studies* 7 (1987): 6; cf. Rawls, *Political Liberalism*, 192.

51. Rawls, "Justice as Fairness," 228; Rawls, *Political Liberalism*, 8.

52. Rawls, *Political Liberalism*, 14.

53. Rawls, "Justice as Fairness," 230.

54. Rawls, *Political Liberalism*, 15.

55. Rawls, "Justice as Fairness," 247; cf. Rawls, *Political Liberalism*, 12.

56. Rawls, "Social Unity and Primary Goods," 184; Rawls, *Political Liberalism*, 38.

57. Rawls, "The Idea of an Overlapping Consensus," 20; cf. Rawls, *Political Liberalism*, 151–52.

58. Rawls, "The Idea of an Overlapping Consensus," 20–21; cf. Rawls, *Political Liberalism*, 213–54.

59. Rawls, "The Idea of an Overlapping Consensus," 20–21.

60. Rawls, "Social Unity and Primary Goods," 184.

61. Rawls, "The Priority of Right and Ideas of the Good," *Philosophy and Public Affairs* 17 (Fall 1988): 262; Rawls, *Political Liberalism*, 193.

62. Rawls, "The Priority of Right," 267; Rawls, *Political Liberalism*, 199.

63. See chapter 1.

64. Rawls, "Kantian Constructivism," 534–35; Rawls, "Justice as Fairness," 232, n. 15; Rawls, *Political Liberalism*, 11–15, 29–35.

65. This qualification is overlooked by those who suggest that Rawls's adjustments require him to reverse the *philosophical* relationship between the right and the good. True, Rawls's refinements clearly implicate his theory in democratic polity, requiring him to presuppose a society occupied by individuals and groups each pursuing various conceptions of the good. But this only means that the good is prior to the right, chronologically as it were, not philosophically. Those who read Rawls as committing himself to a revised understanding of the relationship of the right and the good ignore the fact that justice as fairness can be excavated from a pluralistic democracy without committing itself to a substantive view of the good of human beings, and that his notion of the moral person is linked to his view of the citizen. See, e.g., William Galston, "Moral Personality and Liberal Theory," *Political Theory* 10 (November 1982): 506; Chantal Mouffe, "Rawls: Political Philosophy without Politics," in *Universalism vs. Communitarianism*, ed. David Rasmussen (Cambridge: MIT Press, 1990), 223; L. Gregory Jones, "Should Christians Affirm Rawls' Justice as Fairness? A Response to Professor Beckley," *Journal of Religious Ethics* 16 (Fall 1988): 252–55.

66. Rawls, "The Priority of Right," 270.

67. Rawls, "Kantian Constructivism," 525; Rawls, "Social Unity and Primary Goods," 164–65; Rawls, *Political Liberalism*, 19–20.

68. Rawls, "Justice as Fairness," 241; Rawls, *Political Liberalism*, 30.

69. Rawls, "Kantian Constructivism," 544–45; Rawls, *Political Liberalism*, 144–46, 154–58.

70. Rawls, "The Priority of Right," 270; Rawls, *Political Liberalism*, 203.

71. Rawls, "The Priority of Right," 270; Rawls, *Political Liberalism*, 203.

72. Rawls, "The Priority of Right," 270; Rawls, *Political Liberalism*, 203.

73. Rawls, *A Theory of Justice*, 399.

74. Rawls, "The Priority of Right," 270; Rawls, *Political Liberalism*, 203.

75. Robert Bellah, et al., *Habits of the Heart: Individualism and Commitment in American Life* (Berkeley: University of California Press, 1985).

76. Pluralism provides one occasion of casuistry, as I argued in chapter 1: Our competing duties—obligations that accrue to our various roles and activities—need to be sorted out. Liberalism and casuistry can thus contribute to each other in subtle and important ways.

77. The phrase *partial memberships* is borrowed from Michael Walzer, *Obligations: Essays on Disobedience, War, and Citizenship* (Cambridge: Harvard University Press, 1970), 7.

78. John Stuart Mill, *On Liberty*, ed. and with an introduction by Currin V. Shields (Indianapolis: Bobbs-Merrill, 1956 [1859]), 64.

79. Ibid., 53.

80. Ibid., 43.

81. Ibid., 49.

82. Rosenblum, "Pluralism and Self-Defense," 225.

83. See, e.g., Richard Rorty, *Contingency, Irony, and Solidarity* (Cambridge: Cambridge University Press, 1989).

84. For a discussion, see Rosenblum, *Another Liberalism*, 143–47.

85. See, e.g., H. Richard Niebuhr, *Radical Monotheism and Western Culture, with Supplementary Essays* (New York: Harper and Row, 1943).

86. These ideas of the sovereignty of God and natural law morality roughly parallel the categories of divine voluntarism and divine essentialism, as these ideas are developed in the fine study by Edmund Santurri, *Perplexity in the Moral Life: Philosophical and Theological Considerations* (Charlottesville: University of Virginia Press, 1987), 78–79 and passim.

87. "Declaration on Religious Liberty," in *Vatican Council II: The Conciliar and Post-Conciliar Documents*, par. 2.

88. Ibid.

89. Ibid., par. 3.

90. Ibid., par. 1.

91. Ibid., par. 3.

92. I realize that I am invoking the idea of an overlapping consensus differently from Rawls. Rawls intends the idea to show that different visions of the good abide by moral principles that coincide with the basic terms of his theory of justice. Liberalism is stable because nonliberal theories can converge with the working premises of contract doctrine. But because Rawls's views are circular and doubtfully neutral we must take another tack, one

provided by the goods of partial memberships. The experience of partial memberships, and their liberating effects, is a good secured and protected by contract doctrine. It provides a source of stability for liberalism because it is possible to embrace the goods of partial memberships and still abide by a nonliberal vision of the good.

93. It is doubtless true, as David H. Smith has reminded me, that adherents of religions who find themselves at home in a liberal culture may very well be "liberal" in the eyes of their more conservative religious compatriots. For example, Christians or Muslims who tolerate religious diversity would appear to have absorbed certain basic tenets of liberalism as a philosophical doctrine, at least when their attitudes are contrasted with those of Christian or Islamic fundamentalists. The different attitudes between moderate and conservative religious groups toward religious liberty would suggest that liberalism is not as neutral as it purports to be. Is it not the case that Islamic or Christian fundamentalists would have more difficulty tolerating other points of view than would moderate Muslims or Christians in a liberal society? If so, does this not suggest that living in a liberal society requires an embrace of liberalism *as a comprehensive doctrine?*

To these questions liberals can simply reply that liberalism demands no more of fundamentalists than it requires of an intolerant group. Liberalism's boundaries, as it were, are fixed not by philosophy but by the requirements of justice, *derived from liberalism as a political morality.* Fundamentalists who have little tolerance for diversity can thus be treated like other intolerant groups, and liberalism must reckon with the problem (in Rawls's words) of "tolerating the intolerant." Not all intolerant groups are to be tolerated, Rawls rightly argues, and the basis for deciding when to draw the line is determined largely by the requirements of civic order. The presence of intolerant groups may very well provide cases in which liberalism experiences severe strains. For a discussion of tolerating the intolerant, see Rawls, *A Theory of Justice,* 216–21.

94. It may very well be true, as Walzer observes, that liberalism needs "periodic communitarian correction." Yet when viewing communitarianism as the return of the repressed we ought to remember, as Rosenblum observes, that "repression serves a crucial need," that "what is unconscious is repressed because it is dark, dirty, or dangerous." See Walzer, "The Communitarian Critique of Liberalism," 6–23, at 15; Rosenblum, "Pluralism and Self-Defense," 217.

Notes to Chapter Four

1. Rawls, *Theory of Justice,* 12. In subsequent works, Rawls has clarified the details of this idea, viewing the original position as a "device of representation" in which parties are to be seen as representing "free and equal citizens who are to reach an agreement under conditions that are fair." See Rawls, "Justice as Fairness," 237.

2. For a discussion of the bewildering range of meanings, see Lilian Furst, *Romanticism in Perspective: A Comparative Study of Aspects of the Romantic Movements in England, France, and Germany,* 2d ed. (London: Macmillan, 1979), 17–26; 50–52. On romanticism as a sensibility, see Rosenblum,

Another Liberalism, 1–2; George W. Stocking, Jr., ed., *Romantic Motives: Essays on Anthropological Sensibility* (Madison: University of Wisconsin Press, 1989), 5–7.

3. For a discussion, see Alasdair MacIntyre, *Three Rival Moral Versions of Moral Enquiry: Encyclopaedia, Genealogy, and Tradition* (Notre Dame, Ind.: University of Notre Dame Press, 1990), chap. 1.

4. Furst, *Romanticism in Perspective*, 84.

5. For an illuminating discussion, see Ashton Nichols, *The Poetics of Epiphany: Nineteenth Century Origins of the Modern Literary Movement* (Tuscaloosa: University of Alabama Press, 1987), chap. 1.

6. See Furst, *Romanticism in Perspective*, 117–36.

7. Nichols, *Poetics of Epiphany*, 21.

8. Chaim Perelman, *The New Rhetoric and the Humanities: Essays on Rhetoric and Its Applications* (Boston: D. Reidel, 1979), 166.

9. Taylor, *Sources of the Self*, 379.

10. Ibid., 419.

11. Earl Wasserman, *The Subtler Language* (Baltimore: Johns Hopkins University Press, 1968), 10–11.

12. George W. Stocking, Jr., "Romantic Motives and the History of Anthropology," in *Romantic Motives*, ed. Stocking, 3–9.

13. See, e.g., Roberto Mangaberia Unger, *Knowledge and Politics* (New York: Free Press, 1975), 72–76, and *The Critical Legal Studies Movement* (Cambridge: Harvard University Press, 1986), chap. 1.

14. For a discussion, see Rosenblum, *Another Liberalism*, chap. 7.

15. For an illuminating discussion, see H.-D. Kittsteiner, "Kant and Casuistry," in *Conscience and Casuistry*, ed. Leites, 185–90.

16. Michael Walzer, *Spheres of Justice: A Defense of Pluralism and Equality* (New York: Basic Books, 1983).

17. Walzer, *Just and Unjust Wars*, xvi. Walzer puts cases to good use in this book as well. Here I shall focus chiefly on his account of justice within communities rather than between them.

18. Walzer, *Spheres of Justice*, xiv.

19. Ibid.

20. Ibid., xv.

21. Ibid., 100–103.

22. Ibid., 26.

23. Ibid., xiv.

24. See Michael Walzer, *Interpretation and Social Criticism* (Cambridge: Harvard University Press, 1987), 20.

25. Walzer, *Spheres of Justice*, xiv.

26. Walzer, *Interpretation and Social Criticism*, 21. Elsewhere Walzer tropes the distinction between realism and utopianism in Jewish terms, contrasting the "Exodus politics" of this-worldly liberation with the "messianic politics" of revolution and a return to Edenic conditions. See Michael Walzer, *Exodus and Revolution* (New York: Basic Books, 1985), chap. 5 and passim. The role of Jewish refrains in Walzer's thought will be taken up shortly.

27. Walzer, *Spheres of Justice*, 5.

28. For a discussion, see Furst, *Romanticism in Perspective*, 57–77.

29. Throughout this chapter I will use these terms heuristically. I do not mean to suggest that ancient Israelites saw prophets and priests, or covenantal and levitical tendencies, as mutually exclusive.

30. Walzer, *Spheres of Justice*, 318. See also Michael Walzer, "Liberalism and the Art of Separation," *Political Theory* 12 (August 1984): 315–30.

31. Walzer, *Spheres of Justice*, 28.

32. Ibid., 20.

33. Ibid., 7.

34. Ibid., 86–91.

35. Ibid., 6

36. Ibid., 9.

37. Ibid., 10.

38. Ibid., chap. 4. In principle, monopoly and dominance possess the seeds of injustice, but because eliminating monopoly would be impossible without a strong state apparatus, Walzer attends primarily to the problems posed by dominance. See ibid., 14–17.

39. Ibid., xv.

40. Michael Walzer, *Thick and Thin: Moral Argument at Home and Abroad* (Notre Dame, Ind.: University of Notre Dame Press, 1994), chap. 1. It remains unclear how Walzer's notion of minimal morality in *Thick and Thin* can do the kind of work that the morality of human rights accomplishes in his treatment of international conflict in *Just and Unjust Wars*.

41. Walzer, *Spheres of Justice*, 313.

42. Ibid., 26.

43. Ibid., 320 (emphasis mine).

44. Ibid., xiv (emphasis mine).

45. Ibid., 15.

46. Ibid., xiv–xv.

47. Ibid., 320.

48. Walzer, *Just and Unjust Wars*, 19.

49. Walzer, *Spheres of Justice*, 9.

50. Ibid., 83.

51. Ibid., 313.

52. Walzer, *Just and Unjust Wars*, 251–55 and passim. For a brief discussion, see chapter 1 herein.

53. Walzer, *Spheres of Justice*, 29.

54. For a trenchant critique of antiliberals' appeals to community, see Stephen Holmes, "The Permanent Structure of Antiliberal Thought," in *Liberalism and the Moral Life*, ed. Rosenblum, 230–31.

55. Walzer, *Spheres of Justice*, 31–32. This identification between a community and the state marks a departure from Walzer's earlier position, in which he drew a clear distinction between the state and what he called "secondary associations with claims to primacy." See Walzer, *Obligations: Essays on Disobedience, War, and Citizenship*, chap. 1.

56. Walzer, *Spheres of Justice*, 82–83.

57. Ibid., 62 (emphasis in original).

58. Ibid., 63–64.

59. Ibid., 321.

60. Ibid., 7–8; chap. 2 passim.

61. Ibid., 9; cf. Walzer, *Interpretation and Social Criticism*, 43; *Just and Unjust Wars*, xv.

62. See the account of Mercy College in Dobbs Ferry, New York, in Joseph Berger, "A College Links Raises for Teachers to Recruiting of Students," *New York Times*, 10 June 1995, 31. Mercy College's plan also included reducing faculty salaries by 7 percent should enrollment remain unchanged.

63. Mary Douglas, *Purity and Danger: An Analysis of the Concepts of Pollution and Taboo* (Boston: Ark Paperbacks, 1984), 53. For a theological discussion, see Jon D. Levenson, *Creation and the Persistence of Evil: The Jewish Drama of Omnipotence* (San Francisco: Harper and Row, 1988).

64. Douglas, *Purity and Danger*, 53.

65. Ibid.

66. See, e.g., Ronald Dworkin, "To Each His Own," *New York Review of Books*, 14 April 1983, 4–5; Brian Barry, "Social Criticism and Political Philosophy," *Philosophy and Public Affairs* 19 (Fall 1990): 360–73.

67. For an instructive typology of evil, see Paul Ricoeur, *The Symbolism of Evil*, trans. Emerson Buchanan (Boston: Beacon Press, 1967).

68. On strong poetry, see Harold Bloom, *The Anxiety of Influence* (New York: Oxford University Press, 1973).

69. The problem of representation to which I am obliquely referring has assumed crisis proportions in anthropology. See James Clifford, *The Predicament of Culture: Twentieth Century Ethnography, Literature, and Art* (Cambridge: Harvard University Press, 1988), chap. 1; George E. Marcus and Michael M. J. Fischer, *Anthropology as Cultural Critique: An Experimental Moment in the Human Sciences* (Chicago: University of Chicago Press, 1986), chaps. 1–3; Clifford Geertz, *Works and Lives: The Anthropologist as Author* (Stanford, Calif.: Stanford University Press, 1988); John Van Maanen, *Tales of the Field: On Writing Ethnography* (Chicago: University of Chicago Press, 1988).

70. The phrase, Smith notes, was coined by Alfred Korzybski. See Jonathan Z. Smith, *Map Is Not Territory: Studies in the History of Religions* (Leiden: E. J. Brill, 1978), 309.

71. Jonathan Z. Smith, *Imagining Religion: From Babylon to Jonestown* (Chicago: University of Chicago Press, 1982), xi.

72. I want to thank David Boeyink for helping me see this point.

73. In the abortion case the sphere in question would be security and welfare, which is distributed according to the principle of need.

74. Walzer, *Spheres of Justice*, 313.

75. Ibid., 15. Whether this use of political power accords with our shared understandings of its proper role is a problem for Walzer that I will not pursue here.

76. Walzer, *Just and Unjust Wars*, 19.

77. Donald Davidson, "On the Very Idea of a Conceptual Scheme," *Proceedings of the American Philosophical Association* 47 (1973–74): 5–20.

78. Walzer, *Spheres of Justice*, 82–83.

79. Walzer, "Liberalism and the Art of Separation," 320.

80. Walzer, *Spheres of Justice*, 243–44.

81. Walzer subsequently ruminates about this problem; see Michael Walzer, *What It Means to Be an American* (New York: Marsilio Press, 1992), chap. 4.

82. For the correspondence between Curran and the Sacred Congregation for the Doctrine of the Faith, see Charles E. Curran, *Faithful Dissent* (Kansas City, Mo.: Sheed and Ward, 1986), sec. 2; for Curran's account of the proceedings at CUA, see Charles E. Curran, *Catholic Higher Education, Theology, and Academic Freedom* (Notre Dame, Ind.: University of Notre Dame Press, 1990), 210–39.

83. Walzer, "The Art of Separation," 316.

84. For a discussion of these difficulties in the Catholic context, see Richard A. McCormick, *The Critical Calling: Reflections on Moral Dilemmas since Vatican II* (Washington, D.C.: Georgetown University Press, 1989), chaps. 4 and 6 and passim.

85. Walzer, *Spheres of Justice*, 198.

86. Ibid., 203.

87. Ibid., 206.

88. Ibid., 10.

89. Ibid., 232.

90. For a discussion of Walzer's theory from a feminist perspective, see Susan Moller Okin, *Justice, Gender, and the Family* (New York: Basic Books, 1989).

91. Walzer, *Spheres of Justice*, 240.

92. More recently Walzer has remarked that insofar as groups like the family resemble the sphere of political power, they should be subject to democratic rules. But this recommendation, while intuitively attractive, would nonetheless compromise Walzer's emphasis on the spheres (and their relative independence) that make up our social world. See Walzer, *Thick and Thin*, 58.

93. M. H. Abrams, *Natural Supernaturalism: Tradition and Revolution in Romantic Literature* (New York: Norton, 1971).

94. Consider, for example, the eleven essays in David Miller and Michael Walzer, eds., *Pluralism, Justice, and Equality* (New York: Oxford University Press, 1995). Each essay provides independent commentary on *Spheres of Justice;* none broaches the issue of religion in relation to Walzer's views.

Notes to Chapter Five

1. Terry Eagleton, *Literary Theory: An Introduction* (Minneapolis: University of Minnesota Press, 1983), 178 (emphasis in original).

2. For a lucid and engaging discussion of these and other currents in literary criticism, see ibid., passim.

3. As Peter Steinfels reports, eight out of ten Catholics in a 1992 poll disagreed with the statement, "Using artificial means of birth control is wrong," and nine out of ten told a *New York Times* poll in 1987 that "someone who uses artificial birth control can still be a good Catholic." See Peter Steinfels, "Papal Birth-Control Letter Retains Its Grip," *New York Times,* 1 August 1993, 1. Moreover, Gustav Niebuhr writes that in a Gallup poll of Catholics taken in 1992, 87 percent agreed with the statement that "the church should permit couples to make their own decisions" about birth con-

trol. See Gustav Niebuhr, "Sex, Catholics and Papal Words: 25 Years Later, Encyclical on Birth Control Is Divisive," *Washington Post*, 25 July 1993, 1. A *New York Times*/CBS poll in 1994 reported the following level of agreement with the statement, "Someone can be a good Catholic if she or he practices artificial birth control": eighteen to twenty-nine years of age, 98 percent; thirty to forty-four years, 91 percent; forty-five to sixty-four years, 85 percent; sixty-five and older, 72 percent. See Peter Steinfels, "Future of Faith Worries Catholic Leaders," *New York Times*, 1 June 1994, 1(A), 12(A). Discussions of the scholarly commentary on *Humanae vitae* are numerous. For a reliable digest, see Mahoney, *The Making of Moral Theology*, chap. 7.

4. The most prominent contributions are anthologized in Charles E. Curran and Richard A. McCormick, eds., *Readings in Moral Theology No. 3: The Magisterium and Morality* (Mahwah, N.J.: Paulist Press, 1982).

5. Catholic Theological Society of America, *Report of the Catholic Theological Society of America, Committee on the Profession of Faith and the Oath of Fidelity* (n.p.: Catholic Theological Society of America, 1990), 123.

6. For a discussion, see *Commonweal*, 8 September 1989, 455–56. Among Catholic conservatives, anniversaries of *Humanae vitae* continue to inspire international conferences and religious gatherings, e.g., the International Congress of Moral Theology (Rome, 1988), the "Trust the Truth" symposium (Princeton, 1988), the Twelfth Human Life International World Conference (Houston, 1993), the International *Humanae Vitae* Conference (Omaha, 1993), and the Institute on Religious Life (Mundelein, Illinois, 1993).

7. This terminology is to be distinguished from notions of intrinsic and extrinsic probability, which I define in chapter 1.

8. Another natural method is total abstinence, which I will not examine here.

9. We have seen a similar attempt to join the right and the good in chapter 3, where I discussed Rawls's effort to form a nonutopian political philosophy. Both Rawls and Paul VI attempt to provide an answer to the question of moral motivation. In Paul VI's case, the question takes the following form: Why ought we to accept his casuistry about procreation apart from its appeal to the natural law? *Humanae vitae* replies by arguing that, however strange or rigorous this ethic might first appear, couples will have a better relationship if they practice natural forms of birth control than if they use artificial forms.

10. See, e.g., Ralph McInerny, "Whither the Roman Catholic Theologian?" *Fidelity* 1 (August 1982): 18–24; Charles R. Pulver, "Dissenting Theologians Have Lost Their Faith," *Wanderer*, 30 April 1992, 4.

11. I recognize here that I am using *paradigm* to designate an approach to morality rather than an exemplary case. Catholic sexual ethicists tend to handle cases like nonprocreative sexuality with competing gestalts about how properly to understand the laws of "natural" activity. As I will make clearer below, those two gestalts are understood as "physicalist" and "personalist."

Readers familiar with the literature on Catholic sexual morality know that the case of contraception functions paradigmatically insofar as various cases in sexuality and medicine are reasoned about in analogous terms. Conservative and liberal treatments of, say, homosexual relations or artificial insemination in Catholic morality draw from arguments that shape conservative or liberal treatments of contraception.

Accordingly, different verdicts about the ethics of contraception provide the prism for reflecting about the meaning of the natural in other domains of sexual or medical ethics. For this reason it is unwise to draw a sharp distinction between the paradigm of natural law morality and the paradigm case of contraception. In much of the literature in Catholic ethics, the two paradigms have dialectically informed each other in overt or covert ways.

In many respects this polyvalence surrounding *paradigm* as pertaining to (1) gestalts of the natural law and (2) exemplary cases echoes Kuhn's different uses of the term. For a discussion of "normal science" and paradigms, see Kuhn, *The Structure of Scientific Revolutions*, 2d ed., chap. 3 and epilogue.

12. For a discussion, see Richard A. McCormick, *Notes on Moral Theology, 1965–1980* (Lanham, Md.: University Press of America, 1981), 218–19.

13. For a discussion of formal and material acts, see chapter 1.

14. Bernard Häring, "The Inseparability of the Unitive-Procreative Functions of the Marital Act," in *Contraception: Authority and Dissent*, ed. Charles E. Curran (New York: Herder and Herder, 1969), 176.

15. Augustine, "On the Good of Marriage," 24.

16. Häring, "The Inseparability of the Unitive-Procreative Functions," 177.

17. See John T. Noonan, "An Almost Absolute Value in History," in *The Morality of Abortion: Legal and Historical Perspectives*, ed. Noonan (Cambridge: Harvard University Press, 1970), 38; and *Contraception: A History of Its Treatment by the Catholic Theologians and Canonists* (Cambridge: Harvard University Press, 1965), 438; James V. Ricci, *One Hundred Years of Gynaecology, 1800–1900* (Philadelphia: Blakiston Co., 1945), chap. 1.

18. In many respects these developments in the Catholic casuistry of contraception illustrate a situation in which new facts challenge standard ways of seeing, causing a wholesale overhaul of a paradigm. Jonsen and Toulmin cite such instances as an occasion of casuistry. I see them as less an occasion than a problem for casuistry, which I call the problem of novelty. I take up this problem in the next chapter. For a discussion, see Jonsen and Toulmin, *The Abuse of Casuistry*, 326.

19. For a discussion, see Noonan, *Contraception*, 438–40.

20. Häring, "The Inseparability of the Unitive-Procreative Functions," 179, citing *Humanae Vitae*, par. 13.

21. Augustine by no means expected intercourse among the virtuous to be devoid of pleasure, at least in this life. Procreative sexuality without sensual pleasure—the ideal of the Stoics and of Clement of Alexandria—was conceivable for Augustine only in the state of sinlessness, in paradise or for the saints in heaven. See Augustine, *The City of God*, trans. Henry Bettenson, with an introduction by David Knowles (New York: Penguin Books, 1972), bk. 14, par. 23.

22. For a discussion of negative and positive duties, see chapter 1.

23. For a discussion, see Curran, *Themes in Fundamental Moral Theology*, chap. 1.

24. McCormick, *Notes on Moral Theology*, 219.

25. Attempts to introduce personalist language into official Catholic teaching after *Humanae vitae* nonetheless find the physicalist paradigm irresistible. Consider the pastoral letter by the U.S. Catholic bishops, *To Live in Christ Jesus*. The bishops translate the "unitive" and "procreative" aspects of intercourse into the "love-giving" and "life-giving" meanings of intercourse, respectively, and refer to these as "real human values and aspects of human personhood." The bishops' language lends the impression that they have embraced the physicalist critique and now understand intercourse in moral and intersubjective rather than in physicalist terms. But that impression is wrong. According to the bishops, "The love-giving and life-giving meanings of marital intercourse are real human values and aspects of human personhood. Because they are, it is wrong to act deliberately against either. In contraceptive intercourse the procreative or life-giving meaning of intercourse is deliberately separated from its love-giving meaning and rejected; the wrongness of such an act lies in the rejection of this value." The same would be true of natural forms of birth control, unless of course physicalism undergirds the bishops' understanding. Such an assumption would allow them to distinguish artificial from natural forms of birth control and say that natural methods are love-giving *and* life-giving. But to consider intercourse during infertile periods as "life-giving" is, of course, absurd. Couples who plan to have intercourse only during infertile periods are no less deliberate in their attempt to separate the love-giving from the life-giving aspects of intercourse than are those using artificial contraception. See U.S. Catholic bishops, *To Live in Christ Jesus: A Pastoral Reflection on the Moral Life* (Washington, D.C.: United States Catholic Conference, 1976), par. 46.

26. McCormick, *Notes on Moral Theology*, 220.

27. See also Häring, "The Inseparability of the Unitive-Procreative Functions," 187–89.

28. Those who abide by the official Catholic teaching, of course, are not required to procreate prolifically. This fact is often overlooked by those who infer that *Humanae vitae* establishes a mandate for couples to produce offspring. The encyclical allows couples to limit their number of offspring, so long as they use so-called natural methods. My point here is that personalists are better equipped than those who abide by the encyclical's logic to question the wisdom of producing numerous offspring.

In the literature of the Catholic right, the idea of procreating prolifically is celebrated by James A. Weber, "Let's Hear It for Population Growth!" *Wanderer*, 15 May 1975, 1, 6. Weber's thesis is that more people *do* more, and that those who live in poverty today nonetheless have higher living standards than primitive societies of an earlier era. See also Mary Arnold, "A Primer for Radical Mothers," *Fidelity* 5 (August 1986): 20–24. Arnold laments the fact that many middle-class mothers limit their offspring to two, yet fails to recognize the links between this fact and larger global and environmental needs.

29. This line of thought is suggested in James M. Gustafson, *Ethics from a Theocentric Perspective*, 2 vols. (Chicago: University of Chicago Press, 1981, 1984), 2:227–46.

One attempt to redeem Paul VI's line of argument would be to distinguish between nonconceptive acts (abstaining from intercourse during fertile periods) and anticonceptive acts (using artificial contraception). The goal is to produce an alternative taxonomy that requires us to distinguish abstinence from contraceptive sexuality. See, e.g., William E. May, *Human Existence, Medicine, and Ethics: Reflections on Human Life* (Chicago: Franciscan Herald Press, 1977), 120–25; John Finnis, *Moral Absolutes: Tradition, Revision, Truth* (Washington, D.C.: Catholic University of America Press, 1991), 85–89.

Yet the problem with this taxonomy is that it detaches "not acting to procreate" (during fertile periods) from the *overall* purposes of "natural birth control." Such a redescription accomplishes little, morally speaking, since it obscures the nonprocreative intentions that shape the couple's overall actions. To be sure, "natural birth control" is not *contra*ceptive, since it does not seek to obstruct conception. Yet failing to describe such "natural methods" apart from the couple's more comprehensive commitments and intentions produces precisely the kind of sophistry for which casuists are, unfortunately, all too easily disparaged. To rest one's case on the distinction between "not acting to procreate" and "acting not to procreate" is intelligible only if we describe "natural birth control" absent reference to nonprocreative intentions. This distinction misdescribes the purposes to which the couple must, of necessity, commit themselves in natural family planning. But if we see *nonconceptive* plans and *contraceptive* actions as both *nonprocreative,* the distinction fails to produce a difference of any moral importance.

In other words, couples engaged in natural family planning who abstain from intercourse during fertile periods are not adequately classified as "not acting to procreate." If they carry out plans to have intercourse during infertile periods they are also "acting not to procreate."

30. In making this remark, I do not mean to suggest that widespread use of natural contraception would be or is successful. Yet it is fair to impute such a suggestion to *Humanae vitae,* given what Paul VI says about the desideratum of scientifically perfecting natural techniques, which I shall discuss below. Further, defenders of *Humanae vitae* hold that natural methods can be shown to be highly successful. See, e.g., Ben Luther, "Family Planning? Naturally!" *Wanderer,* 15 July 1976, 8–9.

31. André E. Hellegers, "A Scientist's Analysis," in *Contraception,* ed. Curran, 232.

32. Mark Kline Taylor, *Remembering Esperanza: A Cultural-Political Theology for North American Praxis* (Maryknoll, N.Y.: Orbis Books, 1990), 114.

33. For a discussion of nature and culture as troped by gender, see Sherry B. Ortner, "Is Female to Male as Nature Is to Culture?" in *Woman, Culture, and Society,* eds. Michelle Zimbalist Rosaldo and Louise Lamphere (Stanford, Calif.: Stanford University Press, 1974), 67–87.

34. The only other place in the document in which *vir* appears without being joined to *uxor* or *mulier* is par. 24, which refers to the "men of science" (*viros scientiarum*). But this reference occurs in an appeal to scientists to improve the methods of natural birth control. That is, it appears outside Paul VI's treatment of the morality of contraception.

35. Simone de Beauvoir, *The Second Sex,* trans. H. M. Parshley (New York: Vintage Books, 1974), 809.

36. Ricci, *One Hundred Years of Gynaecology,* 5.

37. Harvey Graham, *Eternal Eve: The History of Gynaecology and Obstetrics* (Garden City, N.Y.: Doubleday, 1951), 492–94.

38. Ibid., chap. 17.

39. Edwin M. Jameson, *Obstetrics and Gynecology* (Paul B. Hoeber, Inc., 1936), 61.

40. Ricci, *One Hundred Years of Gynaecology,* 23–24.

41. Michel Foucault, *The History of Sexuality,* Vol. 1: *An Introduction* (New York: Vintage Books, 1980), chap. 1.

42. See Ricci, *One Hundred Years of Gynaecology,* chap. 1; Graham, *Eternal Eve,* 442–44.

43. Cited in Ricci, *One Hundred Years of Gynaecology,* 37.

44. Hanna Klaus, "The Virgin Mary and the Human Body," *Fidelity* 3 (February 1984): 15.

45. Ibid.

46. Ibid.

47. Paul Marx, "Why Pro-Lifers Should Oppose Contraception," *Fidelity* 2 (July 1983): 28.

48. Ibid., 30.

49. Monica M. Migliorino, "Why Contraception Is Evil," *Homiletic and Pastoral Review* 87 (April 1987): 61–62 (emphases hers).

50. John Tracy, "*Humanae vitae* and the Ovutektor," *Month* (January 1982), 7.

51. Ibid. Donald envisages a more advanced microammeter which will register either a red or a green light.

52. Carol Jackson Robinson, "The Most Private Property," *Wanderer,* 31 May 1973, 4.

53. Marx, "Why Pro-Lifers Should Oppose Contraception," 30.

54. For a discussion, see chapter 1.

55. Carol Jackson Robinson, "Male Chauvinist Pigs, Marriage, and the New Catholic World," *Wanderer,* 7 August 1975, 4.

56. E. Michael Jones, "The Asymmetry of the Sexes," *Fidelity* 1 (March 1982): 13.

57. Ibid.

58. Ibid.

59. James G. Bruen, Jr., "Women at War with Themselves," *Fidelity* 9 (October 1990): 13; cf. Harold Voth, "The Women's Movement," *Fidelity* 2 (September 1983): 22; Thomas Droleskey, "Dressed to Kill," *Wanderer,* 13 May 1993.

60. Bruen, "Women at War," 13 (emphasis mine).

61. Ibid.

62. Sheldon Vanauken, "The Iron Law of Home," *Fidelity* 5 (August 1986): 19.

63. Ibid., 18 (second emphasis mine).

64. Ruth Price, "Can We Afford Two Career Families?" *Fidelity* 1 (September 1982): 21.

65. Ibid.

66. James G. Bruen, Jr., "Captain Hook in Drag," *Fidelity* 6 (September 1987): 21.

67. Hence the many conferences celebrating *Humanae vitae,* in which groups carry banners with quotations from the encyclical. For an account of a conference in Omaha (1993), attended by over 4,500 people, see Peggy Moen, "*Humanae Vitae* Conference Emphasizes Joy and Celebration," *Wanderer,* 5 August 1993, 1.

68. Paraphrasing Rorty, *Contingency, Irony, and Solidarity,* 17.

Notes to Chapter Six

1. Søren Kierkegaard, *Works of Love,* trans. Howard and Edna Hong, with a preface by R. Gregor Smith (New York: Harper and Row, 1962), 318.

2. Robert C. Cefalo and H. Tristam Englehart, "The Use of Fetal and Anencephalic Tissue for Transplantation," *Journal of Medicine and Philosophy* 14 (1989): 27.

3. Ignacio Madrazo, et al., "Transplantation of Fetal Substantia Nigra and Adrenal Medulla to the Caudate Nucleus in Two Patients with Parkinson's Disease" (letter), *Journal of the American Medical Association* 318 (January 1988): 51; "British Fetal Implants," *New York Times,* 19 April 1988 (no author), 9(C); Sandra Blakeslee, "Fetal Cell Transplants Show Early Promise in Parkinson Patients," *New York Times,* 12 November 1991, 3(C); "Doctors Implant Frozen Fetal Cells," *New York Times,* 13 December 1988 (no author), 8(C); Gina Kolata, "Evidence Is Found That Fetal Tissue Transplants Can Ease a Brain Disease," *New York Times,* 7 May 1992, 11(B); Curt R. Freed, et al., "Transplantation of Human Fetal Dopamine Cells for Parkinson's Disease," *Archives of Neurology* 47 (May 1990): 505–12.

4. Blakeslee, "Fetal Cell Transplants," 3(C).

5. Dorothy Vawter, Warren Kearney, Karen G. Gervais, Arthur L. Caplan, Daniel Garry, and Carol Tauer, *The Use of Human Fetal Tissue: Scientific, Ethical, and Policy Concerns* (Minneapolis: Center for Biomedical Ethics, University of Minnesota, 1990), 1.

6. Andrew M. Munster, et al., *Severe Burns: A Family Guide to Medical and Emotional Recovery* (Baltimore, Md.: Johns Hopkins University Press, 1993), 26.

7. Tamar Lewin, "Medical Use of Fetal Tissues Spurs New Abortion Debate," *New York Times,* 16 August 1987, 1.

8. Vawter, et al., *The Use of Human Fetal Tissue,* 4.

9. Warren E. Leary, "U.S. Panel Backs Research Use of Fetal Tissue from Abortions," *New York Times,* 17 September 1988, 1(A). NIH contracted with the Poynter Center at Indiana University, which prepared a position paper for a national panel charged with reviewing policy on the use of fetal tissue for transplantation. The following chapter grew out of research in connection with that grant. See David H. Smith, Judith A. Granbois, Richard B. Miller, Robin Levin Penslar, and Carol J. Weil, "Using Human Fetal Tissue for Transplantation and Research: Selected Issues," in *Report of the Human Fetal Tissue Transplantation Research Panel,* vol. 2 (Bethesda, Md.: Department of Health and Human Services, National Institutes of Health, 1988), F1–F43.

10. Robin Toner, "Clinton Orders Reversal of Abortion Restrictions Left

by Reagan and Bush," *New York Times*, 23 January 1993; Sharon Begley, et al., "Cures from the Womb," *Newsweek*, 22 February 1993, 49.

11. *Appendix: Research on the Fetus*, National Commission for the Protection of Human Subjects of Biomedical and Behavioral Research: 1975, DHEW Publication No.[OS], Washington, D.C., 76–128.

12. Kuhn, *The Structure of Scientific Revolutions*, chap. 3.

13. Ibid., 10–15.

14. Ibid., 189.

15. Jonsen and Toulmin, *The Abuse of Casuistry*, 252.

16. The just-war tradition is not a paradigm in the sense that a paradigm provides a taxonomy or classification system. It is more accurate to say that just-war criteria function paradigmatically: They specify in an exemplary way how we can provide a justification and limitation for certain acts that occur within institutional contexts. In this way the just-war tradition can operate as a model from which we can develop other forms of research, and according to which we can reason analogically.

17. Aristotle, *Nicomachean Ethics* 1141b15.

18. Toulmin, "How Medicine Saved the Life of Ethics," 742.

19. Immanuel Kant, *Foundations of the Metaphysics of Morals*, trans. Lewis White Beck (Indianapolis: Bobbs-Merrill, 1976 [1785]), 47.

20. James Walters and S. Ashwal, "Anencephalic Infants as Brain Donors and the Brain Death Standard," *Journal of Medicine and Philosophy* 14 (1989): 79–87.

21. Kierkegaard, *Works of Love*, 325 and chap. 9.

22. For a discussion of the connection between the duty not to harm and more general attitudes about suffering, see Miller, *Interpretations of Conflict*, 42–46.

23. Blakeslee, "Fetal Cell Transplants," 3(C).

24. In order to make this point about conflicting claims, a social theory of the self must be presumed. Without such a theory, the idea that some persons' needs place demands on others would be difficult to understand. Nevertheless, the presumptive weight of the duty not to instrumentalize favors the claims of the fetus.

25. Uniform Anatomical Gift Act, 1968, rev. 1987.

26. Albert R. Jonsen, "Transplantation of Fetal Tissue: An Ethicist's Viewpoint," *Clinical Research* 36 (April 1988): 218.

27. UAGA, section 1.

28. Questions about criteria of fetal death have become problematic given the prospect of harvesting anencephalic fetuses. The general argument on behalf of using different criteria for determining whether anencephalic children may be harvested is the claim that the whole-brain criterion for death is inadequate, since anencephalics do not develop a whole brain. Lacking a whole brain, anencephalics never cross the threshold from gestation to human life. And, because this threshold is never crossed, it makes no sense to talk about crossing the threshold from human life to death according to the paradigm provided by persons with a whole brain. An alternative criterion for anencephalic death is necessary, one that defines the anencephalic as

dead despite the functioning of the brain stem. This criterion would allow doctors to make anencephalic infants' organs available without the restrictions that would obtain in cases of those who had crossed the threshold from gestation to human life.

However, since the issue of this chapter concerns the use of human abortuses, I prescind from adjudicating the different views about criteria of anencephalic death. For discussions of brain death and anencephaly, see volume 14 of the *Journal of Medicine and Philosophy*, which is devoted entirely to the subject.

29. Mary B. Mahowald, "Introduction," *Clinical Ethics* (April 1988): 188.

30. Alan Fine, "The Ethics of Fetal Tissue Transplants," *Hastings Center Report* 18 (June/July 1988): 5–8.

31. Windom's memo was included in the materials to be studied by those drafting position papers (see n. 8).

32. James B. Nelson and J. Rohricht, *Human Medicine: Ethical Perspectives on Today's Medical Issues* (Minneapolis: Augsburg, 1984), 32–39.

33. LeRoy Walters, "Ethical Issues in Fetal Research: A Look Back and a Look Forward," *Clinical Research* 36 (April 1988): 209–14.

34. Mark Bowden, "Fetal Tissue: An Ethical Debate," *Philadelphia Inquirer*, 6 October 1987, 3(H).

35. Congregation of the Doctrine of the Faith, "Instruction on Respect for Human Life in Its Origin and on the Dignity of Procreation: Replies to Certain Questions of the Day," in *Bioethics*, 3d ed., ed. Thomas A. Shannon (New York: Paulist Press, 1987), 600.

36. LeRoy Walters, "Ethical Issues in Experimentation on the Human Fetus," *Journal of Religious Ethics* 2 (1974): 41; cf. Paul Ramsey, *The Ethics of Fetal Research* (New Haven: Yale University Press, 1975); McCormick, *How Brave a New World?*

37. James T. Burtchaell, "University Policy on Experimental Use of Aborted Fetal Tissue," *IRB: A Review of Human Research* 10 (July/August 1988): 9; see also Robert Barry and Darrel Kesler, "Pharaoh's Magicians: The Ethics and Efficacy of Human Fetal Tissue Transplants," *Thomist* 54 (October 1990): 597.

38. Edwin F. Healy, *Medical Ethics* (Chicago: Loyola University Press, 1956), 101.

39. Ibid., 103.

40. At least one ethicist who has thought about the relationship between the ethics of war and the ethics of medicine, Paul Ramsey, would question my reasoning here. As I argued against Ramsey in a discussion of war, it is possible to overdraw the distinction between intending and foreseeing a moral evil. Overdrawing such a distinction may wrongly exonerate us from the duty to reduce untoward consequences of our actions, even if those consequences are only foreseen but unintended. Are we not sometimes obligated to reduce the foreseen, deleterious effects of our good intentions when we can?

The specifics of my argument took the following form: In assessing Ramsey's ethics of war and deterrence, I argued that a "thin" account of intention surrounding the use of nuclear weapons allows him to endorse a theory of deterrence that relies on the prospect of unintended, foreseen collateral damage in the course of nuclear war. The commitment to a discriminate nuclear war ought to shape the intention of military policy, but the prospect of foreseen, unintended effects of such policies menaces the opponent, strengthening deterrence. Ramsey endorsed the prospect of disproportionate collateral damage as a means to a morally tenable deterrent. A "thicker," more robust notion of moral intention, on the other hand, would raise questions about such collateral damage, even in discriminate targeting. Just-war criteria with a thicker account of intention would not permit the prospect of disproportionate damage as a means to an end. A thicker account of intention, moreover, would require military planners to reduce (or intend to reduce) foreseen harms as part of a fully moral act. Military planners ought to limit as much as possible the foreseen, unintended collateral damage of discriminate targeting. Unfortunately for Ramsey, such efforts would attenuate those factors on which his theory of deterrence rests.

Ramsey's question in the present context could take the following form: Does my argument on war, deterrence, and intention "bite back"? Wouldn't a morally robust account of intention require researchers who condemn elective abortion to reduce those instances on which their procurement of tissue relies? Does an argument on behalf of procuring tissue as foreseen but unintended not rely on the same "thin" account of intention for which I criticize Ramsey in a discussion of war? Ramsey might observe the irony that my criticisms of his ethics of war ought to inform the medical issue under consideration here, leading to a more conservative treatment of cooperation than I have allowed.

To these observations I would argue that a consistent account of "thick" intention would indeed require persons who transplant fetal tissue to seek to reduce the occasion of procurement if they object to elective abortion. But this does not mean that fetal tissue from elective abortions may not be used. It means only that insofar as such tissue is available, those who transplant it are not implicated in a wider set of practices from which they may wish to dissociate themselves. The same dissociation seems more difficult in the military profession, where targeting and deterrence stand in a tighter causal nexus. Abortion and procurement are related differently than targeting and deterrence so long as the barriers mentioned in the second and third sections of this chapter are observed. These barriers would proscribe abortion as a premeditated means of procuring fetal tissue.

For a discussion of intention in the tactics of war, see chapter 2; for a discussion of Ramsey on war and deterrence, see my *Interpretations of Conflict*, chap. 6.

41. Burtchaell, "University Policy," 10; cf. Walters, "Ethical Issues in Experimentation," n. 10.

42. For a discussion of permitting and consenting to actions, see chapter 1.

Contemporary official Catholic teaching is vague about the moral problems surrounding cooperation. In their 1983 pastoral letter, the U.S. Catholic bishops devote a section to moral questions facing individuals employed in the defense industry. The relevant issue concerns cooperation, although the bishops fail to raise it. Despite the fact that "the defense industry is directly involved in the development and production of . . . weapons of mass destruction," those who may cooperate in the production of such weapons are not admonished to leave their work. Instead, "those who remain in these industries or earn a profit from the weapons industry should find in the Church guidance and support for the ongoing evaluation of their work."

It is unfortunate that the bishops did not address the question of formal and material cooperation, since employment in some defense industries stands within a causal nexus of military strategies that the bishops clearly condemn, for example, the use of strategic nuclear weapons for counter-population targeting. If recent Catholic teaching is reluctant to question actions that stand within such a causal nexus, it seems incongruous that it would raise questions about cooperation in the procurement of fetal tissue, where transplantation does not contribute causally to elective abortions. See U.S. Catholic Bishops, *The Challenge of Peace*, par. 319.

43. Mahowald, "Introduction," 187.

44. McCormick, *How Brave a New World?* 78.

45. McCormick would doubtless agree that policy about fetal experimentation ought not do the work of revising cultural attitudes about abortion. See ibid., 81.

46. Congregation of the Doctrine of the Faith, "Instruction on Respect for Human Life in Its Origin," 600.

47. Sissela Bok, "Fetal Research and the Value of Life," in *Appendix: Research on the Fetus*, 2–6, 2–7.

48. Burtchaell, "University Policy," 9.

49. Healy, *Medical Ethics*, 112.

50. Given what I have said about Nazi experimentation lacking initial justification, it would seem that Burtchaell's analogy concerns scandal rather than cooperation. Burtchaell could argue that, as a practice in which another's sin is foreseen but not wished, Nazi experimentation was an instance of illicit indirect scandal, since the experimentation lacked sufficient reason.

Yet even if this is correct, the Nazi analogy fails to show that comparable evils surround the use of fetal tissue. In the case of transplanting fetal tissue, the possibility of indirect scandal is justified by the act's having sufficient reason as medical therapy. Unlike the case of Nazi experimentation, transplanting fetal tissue can satisfy the criteria for overriding the prima facie duty not to use others merely as means to ends. Other safeguards, mentioned below, are designed to prevent scandal from increasing.

51. Ramsey, *The Ethics of Fetal Research*, 93–98; McCormick, *How Brave a New World?* 72–80; Burtchaell, "University Policy," 8; Barry and Kesler, "Pharaoh's Magicians," 597.

52. For an account of women who decide to abort, see Linda B. Franke, *The Ambivalence of Abortion* (New York: Random House, 1978).

53. I recognize that many people already justify these abortions as therapeutic.

54. For a discussion of the problem of the tyranny of principles in casuistry, see Jonsen and Toulmin, *The Abuse of Casuistry*, 1–20, 264–65.

Notes to Chapter Seven

1. Augustine, *City of God*, bk. 12, chap. 7.

2. Clifford Geertz, *The Interpretation of Cultures* (New York: Basic Books, 1973), 100.

3. Robert Pear, "Panel Calls on Citizens to Wage National Assault on Pornography," *New York Times*, 10 July 1986, 1 and 10.

4. One exception is the work of Ronald Dworkin in moral and legal philosophy. See Ronald Dworkin, *A Matter of Principle* (Cambridge: Harvard University Press, 1985), 335–72; "Liberty and Pornography," *New York Review of Books*, 15 August 1991, 12–15; "The Coming Battle over Free Speech," *New York Review of Books*, 11 June 1992, 55–64; "Women and Pornography," *New York Review of Books*, 21 October 1993, 36–42.

5. I also surveyed violent homosexual pornography in order to sharpen some of the distinctive features of the heterosexual materials that I will discuss in this chapter. Magazines like *Sandmutopia Guardian* cater to heterosexual and homosexual readers and thus intersperse photographs of straight couples with photographs of bound men, often with erections. Like the more explicitly homosexual magazine *DungeonMaster*, this magazine includes information about clothing (mostly leather goods), personal ads, phone sex, mail-order items, clubs, whips, genital tormentor clips, fashionwear, reading materials, instructions for building one's own torture chamber or dungeon, ads for other magazines, porn movie reviews, and tools to accentuate pain and arousal, such as the elastroator (pliers designed to place rubber rings on the nipples). Often, as in the magazine *Bound and Gagged*, narratives are autobiographical, with little reference to the themes of sexual compensation or vigilantism. The narratives, in other words, make more of an attempt to adopt realistic conventions, purporting to provide documentaries. This approach accords with what might be called the more positivistic or scientific orientation of gay pornography. Along these lines, *Bound and Gagged* regularly includes the feature "Bond Aid," in which readers write in with medical questions. The answers provided by the column are written by David Stein and Richard Sommers, M.D.

6. Carol J. Clover, "Her Body, Herself: Gender in the Slasher Film," *Representations* 20 (Fall 1987): 196.

7. It seems anomalous to call pornography a speech-act because it lacks a recognizable verbal component. Thus, pornography seems to lack what is called locutionary and illocutionary force; pornography is neither a verbal proposition or inscribable utterance (locution) nor a verbal utterance that includes a performative element (illocution, e.g., "I promise," or "I apologize"). Seen as a form of bidding that effects various responses from the viewer, however, pornography best approximates what has been labeled a "perlocutionary" speech-act. According to Paul Ricoeur, perlocutionary discourse "is the discourse as stimulus. It acts, not by my interlocutor's recognition of my intention, but sort of energetically, by direct influence upon the emotions and the affective dispositions." See Paul Ricoeur, *Hermeneutics and the Human Sciences*, trans., ed., and with an introduction by John B. Thompson (Cambridge: Cambridge University Press, 1981), 200.

8. I do not wish to suggest that aesthetics and hermeneutics are entirely separate domains of inquiry. Certainly literary works are enjoyed as works of art. The distinction lies in the fact that aesthetics commonly analyzes sensory percepts whereas hermeneutics commonly deciphers meanings. See the *Encyclopedia of Philosophy*, s. v. "Aesthetics, Problems of," by John Hospers.

9. Richard Stivers, *Evil in Modern Myth and Ritual* (Athens: University of Georgia Press, 1982), 11–13.

10. Compare Clover's analysis of the horror/slasher film, "Her Body, Herself," 190.

11. George Steiner, "Night Words: High Pornography and Human Privacy," in *The Pornography Controversy: Changing Moral Standards in American Life*, ed. Ray C. Rist (New Brunswick, N.J.: Transaction Books, 1975), 204–5.

12. Joseph Slade, "Pornographic Theaters off Times Square," in *The Pornography Controversy*, ed. Rist, 119–39.

13. Ibid., 136–39.

14. Ibid., 135.

15. Ibid., 139.

16. See, e.g., Edward Donnerstein, "Pornography: Its Effect on Violence against Women," in *Pornography and Sexual Aggression*, ed. Donnerstein and Neil M. Malamuth (Orlando, Fla.: Academic Press, 1984), 53–81; James Weaver, "The Social Science and Psychological Research Evidence: Perceptual and Behavioral Consequences of Exposure to Pornography," and Diana E. H. Russell, "Pornography and Rape: A Causal Model," both in *Pornography: Women, Violence and Civil Liberties*, ed. Catherine Itzin (New York: Oxford University Press, 1992), 284–309; 310–49.

17. Donnerstein himself equivocates about drawing causal conclusions from his research. Cf. Donnerstein, "Pornography," 78, 80.

18. Harold J. Gardiner, S. J., "Moral Principles toward a Definition of the Obscene," in *The Pornography Controversy*, ed. Rist, 164. I have tried to rehearse, in chapter 5, how this line of thought would bear upon matters of sexuality and nonprocreative intercourse.

19. I am assuming for this criticism that when Gardiner fashioned his argument the audience of pornography was predominantly male. The trend toward a mixed audience is only very recent. For a discussion of this latter trend, see Linda Williams, *Hard Core: Power, Pleasure, and the "Frenzy of the Visible"* (Berkeley: University of California Press, 1989), chap. 8.

20. Eva Feder Kittay, "Pornography and the Erotics of Domination," in *Beyond Domination: New Perspectives on Women and Philosophy*, ed. Carol Gould (Totowa, N.J.: Rowman and Allanheld, 1984), 150.

21. Ibid., 161.

22. Ibid., 145–46, 171.

23. For a survey, see Karl F. Morrison, *The Mimetic Tradition of Reform in the West* (Princeton: Princeton University Press, 1982); for a constructive appropriation of *mimēsis* in Gadamer, Kierkegaard, and Ricoeur, see William Schweiker, *Mimetic Reflections: A Study in Hermeneutics, Theology, and Ethics* (New York: Fordham University Press, 1990).

24. Aristotle, *Poetics*, 1448b4–24, 1450a15–20.

25. Ricoeur, *Hermeneutics and the Human Sciences,* 291–93.

26. Ibid., 292; see also 179–80.

27. It might be objected that Dionysian rituals were nihilistic insofar as they often included sacrifice, including human sacrifice. However, the Dionysian sacrifice and the subsequent eating of raw flesh and drinking of blood were sacramental, a ritual quest for unity with the deity that was part of a larger quest for immortality. Moreover, these rituals were linked to vegetation worship and nature worship; they were thus tied to the cycle of the life process. Death was located within the larger cycle of death and rebirth; fatality, thus construed, was not an end in itself. Indeed, the presence of death did not serve to annihilate distinctions between life and death, but to reaffirm them. For discussions of the Dionysia and Dionysian rituals, see W. K. C. Guthrie, *The Greeks and Their Gods* (London: Methuen and Co., 1950), 178–82; Lewis Farnell, *The Cults of the Greek States,* vol. 5 (Oxford: Clarendon, 1909), 180–85.

28. Rosemarie Tong, "Feminism, Pornography and Censorship," *Social Theory and Practice* 8 (1982): 1–17.

29. Ibid., 4.

30. Elaine Scarry, *The Body in Pain: The Making and Unmaking of the World* (New York: Oxford University Press, 1985), 44–45.

31. Ibid., 50.

32. Ibid., 45.

33. René Girard, *Violence and the Sacred,* trans. Patrick Gardiner (Baltimore: Johns Hopkins University Press, 1977).

34. Ibid., 271.

35. Ibid., chaps. 2, 4 passim.

36. Ibid., 27, 33.

37. The argument is implied in Irene Diamond, "Pornography and Repression: A Reconsideration," in *Women: Sex and Sexuality,* ed. Catharine R. Stimpson and Ethel Spector Person (Chicago: University of Chicago Press, 1980), 142.

Notes to Chapter Eight

1. For a discussion of the role of doubt and ambiguity as an occasion of casuistry, see chapter 1.

2. Melford E. Spiro, "Religion: Problems of Definition and Explanation," in *Anthropological Approaches to the Study of Religion,* ed. Michael Banton (London: Tavistock, 1963), 97.

3. I am using "comprehensive vision" here in a way that echoes Rawls's view of a "comprehensive moral doctrine." For a discussion, see chapter 3.

4. Ray L. Hart, "Religious and Theological Studies in American Higher Education: A Pilot Study," *Journal of the American Academy of Religion* 59 (Winter 1991): 715–827 (hereafter "Hart report").

5. J. Samuel Preus, *Explaining Religion: Criticism and Theory from Bodin to Freud* (New Haven: Yale University Press, 1987), xix.

6. This formulation suggests that the differences between theology and the study of religion are not always dramatic. About the study of religion and theology at the turn of the century, for example, Eric J. Sharpe remarks:

Certainly there was a time when scholarship sought to free itself from the deductive and hence ultimately authoritarian methods of religious confessionalism, siding with historical science over against what was felt to be the dead hand of religious orthodoxy. *But this was precisely what liberal religion was doing during the same period.* . . . Liberalism is a many-headed beast, and is especially hard to grasp in those cases (and there are many of them) in which liberals themselves find difficulty in stating their own case with clarity. But if we identify two of its distinguishing features as an insistent moralism and a quest for human universals, coupled with a belief in the infinite educability of the human race, then perhaps we can begin to see how the line of Religion and the line of Religious Studies are (when viewed from a particular angle) not two lines, but one.

Sharpe's comments provide a different reading of the relation between theology and Religious Studies than Preus's. Seeking to display a revolutionary difference between theology and Religious Studies, Preus eschews any discussion of theological thought in his account of the rise of the naturalistic paradigm for the study of religion. (The point will be discussed below.) See Eric J. Sharpe, "Religious Studies, the Humanities, and the History of Ideas," *Soundings* 71 (Summer/Fall 1988): 251 (emphasis in original).

Preus's views depend on a Kuhnian view of conceptual change as *revolutionary,* which may not be necessary to sustain his thesis about the rise of a nontheological paradigm for studying religion. For an important critique of Kuhn's theories of revolutionary paradigm shifts, see Stephen Toulmin, *Human Understanding: The Collective Use and Evolution of Concepts* (Princeton, N.J.: Princeton University Press, 1972), 70–106.

7. Toulmin, *Human Understanding,* 379.

8. Ibid., 380.

9. Ibid., 380–81.

10. Hans H. Penner and Edward A. Yonan, "Is a Science of Religion Possible?" *Journal of Religion* 52 (1972): 133.

11. Hans H. Penner, "Criticism and the Development of a Science of Religion," *Studies in Religion* 15 (1986): 164–75, at 174–75.

12. Penner and Yonan, "Science of Religion," 115. Those conditions are:

(1) The definiens (the defining term) must articulate the conventional connotation of the definiendum (the term that is being defined).

(2) The definiens should not be wider or narrower than the definiendum.

(3) The definiens should not include any expression that occurs in the definiendum; it should avoid circularity.

(4) Ambiguous, figurative, or obscure language should not be used.

(5) The definiens should not be stated negatively unless the definiendum is also negative.

13. Ibid., 131. In a later work, Penner defines religion as "a verbal and nonverbal structure of interaction with superhuman being(s)." See Hans H. Penner, *Impasse and Resolution: A Critique of the Study of Religion* (New York: Peter Lang, 1989), 7.

14. Frederick Ferré, "The Definition of Religion," *Journal of the American Academy of Religion* 38 (March 1970): 3.

15. Ibid., 14.

16. Ibid., 6. Ferré's definition of religion is developed on pp. 8–11.

17. Ludwig Wittgenstein, *Philosophical Investigations,* 3d ed., trans. G. E. M. Anscombe (New York: Macmillan, 1968), pars. 38–47.

18. Ibid., par. 67.

19. Ibid., par. 66 (emphases in original).

20. I do not wish to be understood as embracing an antitheoretical position here. The data of religion do not simply explain themselves, and we need theoretical constructs to facilitate understanding. So it may very well be that definitions of religion are not fruitless. All I am arguing is that they are unnecessary as a first step toward defining *Religious Studies.*

21. Donald Wiebe, "Postulations for Safeguarding Preconceptions: The Case of the Scientific Religionist," *Religion* 18 (January 1988): 17.

22. Ibid.

23. Preus, *Explaining Religion,* xx (emphasis in original).

24. Ibid., ix.

25. Ibid., xvi.

26. Ibid., 209.

27. Ibid., xxi.

28. See, e.g., George A. Lindbeck, *The Nature of Doctrine: Religion and Theology in a Postliberal Age* (Philadelphia: Westminster Press, 1984); John Milbank, *Theology and the Social Sciences: Beyond Secular Reason* (Cambridge, Mass.: Basil Blackwell, 1991); William Placher, *Unapologetic Theology: A Christian Voice in a Pluralistic Conversation* (Louisville, Ky.: Westminster/ John Knox Press, 1989); John Howard Yoder, *The Priestly Kingdom: Social Ethics as Gospel* (Notre Dame, Ind.: University of Notre Dame Press, 1984). At most, these authors might embrace an "ad hoc apologetics," described as making "a case for the reasonableness of Christian belief not by referring to some putatively neutral datum of experience to which the Christian religion conforms but, rather, through the skillful demonstration of how our common and everyday world in its variety really conforms to the biblical world." For a discussion, see William Werpehowski, "Ad Hoc Apologetics," *Journal of Religion* 66 (July 1986): 282–301, at 284.

In a study of Karl Barth's writings on religion, Garrett Green seeks to show the relevance of Barth's critique of religion for religious studies. Green has in mind the antitheological stance of many secular theorists in the study of religion today, and seeks to show how and where they might learn from Barth. He argues that nontheological approaches to the study of religion themselves include faith presuppositions and agendas, and that Barth's critique of religion shares various lines with Durkheim and Freud. For these reasons, Green concludes, Barth ought to belong within the canon of authors taught in religious studies programs.

The problem with Green's argument is that having presuppositions does not put a secular approach to religion on the same plane as a theological approach, especially when that theology is developed along Barthian lines, with strong christological claims. Stated differently, the distinctiveness of secular approaches vis-à-vis theological orientations is not undermined by the fact that the former are not methodologically neutral. Discovering that positivism is an ideal honored in the breach hardly opens the door to christocentric approaches to the study of religion.

We ought not overlook the question put to the academy by Preus. That question is not whether some approaches are methodologically neutral, but whether nontheological approaches can provide a reasonable explanation of the origin and continuation of religious belief and practice. Green fails to indicate whether Barth would accept the terms of such a question, given the strictures of Barth's dogmatic method. And, even if Barth could find some way to address that question, it remains unclear why non-Barthians should find much of interest in what he says, except to count the number of methodological hoops through which he jumps in his dogmatics in order to arrive at an assessment of religion similar to that provided straightforwardly by Enlightenment accounts. See Garrett Green, "Challenging the Religious Studies Canon: Karl Barth's Theory of Religion," *Journal of Religion* 75 (October 1995): 473–86.

29. Wiebe, "Postulations," 13 (emphasis mine); compare Preus, *Explaining Religion,* xix.

30. Ibid. See also Penner, *Impasse and Resolution,* chap. 1.

31. For an instructive account of the *epoché* in phenomenology, see James G. Hart, *The Person and the Common Life: Studies in Husserlian Social Ethics* (Dordrecht: Kluwer Academic Publishers, 1992), 5–10.

32. See chapter 3.

33. Max Weber, *The Protestant Ethic and the Spirit of Capitalism,* trans. Talcott Parsons, with an introduction by Anthony Giddens (New York: Charles Scribner's Sons, 1958), 183; Ernst Troeltsch, *The Social Teaching of the Christian Churches,* trans. Olive Wyon, with an introduction by H. Richard Niebuhr (Chicago: University of Chicago Press, 1976), 23–37; 1002–4.

34. Wiebe, "Postulations," 14. The idea that explanatory theory is on the frontier of the study of religion is similarly endorsed by Robert S. Michaelsen, "Cutting Edges," *Journal of the American Academy of Religion* 59 (Spring 1991): 137–48.

35. Clifford Geertz, *Local Knowledge: Further Essays in Interpretive Anthropology* (New York: Basic Books, 1983), 24.

36. I am aware that Clifford and Geertz represent different models of ethnographic inquiry. The latter's notion of "thick description" operates in the hermeneutical camp, while the former invokes the ideas of heteroglossia and dialogical inquiry as understood by Bahktin. See Geertz, *The Interpretation of Cultures;* Clifford, *The Predicament of Culture,* chap. 1.

37. Geertz, *Local Knowledge,* 10.

38. Ibid., 19.

39. This view was made famous by Max Müller, and is reported anecdotally in Ari L. Goldman, *The Search for God at Harvard* (New York: Random House, 1991), 33. For a discussion of Müller's views, see Eric J. Sharpe, *Comparative Religion: A History* (New York: Charles Scribner's Sons, 1975), chap. 2.

40. Stephen D. Crites, scribe, "The Religion Major: A Report" (Atlanta, Ga.: Scholars Press, 1990), 9; cf. Ivan Strenski, "Our Very Own 'Contras': A Response to the 'St. Louis Project' Report," *Journal of the American Academy of Religion* 54 (Summer 1986): 333. Strenski's argument—that allowing a place for theology in the study of religion constitutes a reactionary, counter-revolutionary program—masks the antiliberal undercurrent in recent attempts to purge the study of religion of theological discourse. After his attack on the "re-theologizing" of Religious Studies, Strenski brings us breathlessly to the conclusion that some versions of theology might be acceptable in the study of religion if they operate under the rubric of hermeneutics, especially hermeneutics that is informed by comparative religious inquiry. Strenski adds that "we have hardly begun" this reconfiguration of theology. But even a cursory glance would show that recent theology made the hermeneutical turn well over a decade before Strenski's jeremiad. And he asserts, rather then shows, that recent trends in hermeneutics eschew the contributions of work in comparative religion.

Strenski's argument is directed in part against a book award in the American Academy of Religion for work in a "Constructive-Reflective" category. One difficulty with this award, he alleges, is that it recognizes work done not *about* religion but *for* it, advancing the interests of religion. In addition, the award suggests that other works that are awarded, e.g., in the Historical or Descriptive-Analytic categories, are not constructive or reflective. But Strenski cannot have it both ways, arguing *against* the notion of constructive work as advancing religion and *for* the idea that more works ought to be considered constructive.

41. Even with the study of religion firmly in place in many American colleges and universities, it is by no means clear that all scholars or devotees welcome comparative and cultural inquiries. See, e.g., Howard Eilberg-Schwartz's discussion of Judaism in relation to comparative or anthropological inquiries in *The Savage in Judaism: An Anthropology of Israelite Religion and Ancient Judaism* (Bloomington: Indiana University Press, 1990), chap. 4 and passim; cf. the Hart report, 744: Comments from Jewish institutions indicate that "most [faculty] play little attention to scholars who work on other subject matters in the field of religion."

42. Clifford Geertz, *Islam Observed: Religious Development in Morocco and Indonesia* (Chicago: University of Chicago Press, 1971).

43. Hart report, 764.

44. Donald Wiebe, "The Failure of Nerve in the Academic Study of Religion," *Studies in Religion* 13 (Fall 1984): 411. It may be that naturalism would allow for ethical approaches that are apodictic and foundational, as Charles Taylor observes. See Taylor, "Explanation and Practical Reasoning," in *The Quality of Life*, ed. Martha C. Nussbaum and Amartya Sen (Oxford: Clarendon Press, 1991), 208–31.

45. Hart report, 768–70. The idea that ethics (or feminism) would receive such a ringing endorsement seems strange for other reasons as well. In religious ethics today the canons of objective, public rationality are under siege, especially in increasingly influential narrative ethics. The general complaint, put forward most notably by Hauerwas, is that appeals to commonly shared

canons of reasoning are overly abstract, disconnected from the moral fabric of our everyday practices and communal ties. In other words, the popular endorsement of ethics in Religious Studies fails to take note of the strong—indeed militant—confessional currents in religious ethics. Echoing the Romantic rejection of Enlightenment rationalism, narrative ethicists are suspicious of the quest for objectivity. If sectarianism, rather than normativity, is the reason that theology should be banished, then religionists should be wary of several strong currents within the subfield of ethics. (Indeed, a new form of scholasticism—narrative scholasticism, which parrots and levels the original insights of narrative ethics—awaits us in religious ethics. But this development raises an independent set of problems in the subfield of ethics, which I will not address here.)

46. Preus, *Explaining Religion*, xii.

47. Smith, *Map Is Not Territory*, 290.

48. And "less" is not impossible. Consider the possibility of a philosophy department with one member who teaches about artificial intelligence and another who teaches about Jewish philosophies of history after the Holocaust. These colleagues have less in common with each other than they do with colleagues in computer science and religious studies, respectively. But they are nonetheless housed under one roof. Are we thus to conclude that their membership in the same philosophy department is a function of the fact that their respective pursuits are both "philosophy"?

49. More recently Smith seems to have modified his views, coming closer to my emphasis on sharing common skills and recognizing the contingency of our present intellectual mapping in colleges and universities. See Jonathan Z. Smith, "'Religion' and 'Religious Studies': No Difference at All," *Soundings* 71 (Summer/Fall 1988): 231–44.

50. Richard Rorty, *Consequences of Pragmatism: Essays 1972–1980* (Minneapolis: University of Minnesota Press, 1982), chap. 12.

51. Ibid., 213.

52. Ibid., 215.

53. This does not mean that confessionalists' green cards should be revoked, but that tolerating their participation in the wider study of religion may parallel tolerating the intolerant in liberal political philosophy. See Rawls, *A Theory of Justice*, 216–21.

54. Van Harvey, "Reflections on the Teaching of Religion in America," *Journal of the American Academy of Religion* 38 (March 1970): 28. Harvey's essay ought to be required reading in the graduate study of religion today.

55. The relevant literature is immense. One would have to mention John B. Cobb and David Ray Griffin, *Process Theology: An Introductory Exposition* (Philadelphia: Westminster Press, 1982); Edward Farley, *Ecclesial Reflection: An Anatomy of Theological Method* (Philadelphia: Fortress Press, 1982); Gustafson, *Ethics from a Theocentric Perspective;* John Hick, *God Has Many Names* (Philadelphia: Westminster Press, 1982); Gordon D. Kaufman, *The Theological Imagination: Constructing the Concept of God* (Philadelphia: Westminster Press, 1981); Sallie McFague, *Models of God: Theology for an Ecological, Nuclear Age* (Philadelphia: Fortress Press, 1987); Schubert Ogden, *The Reality*

of God (San Francisco: Harper and Row, 1977); Francis Schüssler-Fiorenza, *Foundational Theology: Jesus and the Church* (New York: Crossroad, 1984); Mark C. Taylor, *Erring: A Postmodern A/theology* (Chicago: University of Chicago Press, 1984); and David Tracy, *The Analogical Imagination: Christian Theology and the Culture of Pluralism* (New York: Crossroad, 1981). Reflecting the "would-be" or diffuse status of theology as a discipline, all of these authors raise hermeneutical and methodological issues. Only Gustafson makes explicit reference to an ostensive religious community—and a rather general one at that—when he articulates his "preference for the Reformed tradition."

56. Wiebe, "Postulations," 15; Strenski, "Our Very Own 'Contras,'" 323–35 passim.

57. Harvey makes a similar point in "Reflections," 28, and much that has been written since 1970 corroborates his judgment.

58. See, e.g., James M. Robinson, "Religious Studies as Humanizing Studies," *Soundings* 71 (Summer/Fall 1988): 212; Robert R. Hann, "Commitment, Theology, and the Dilemma of Religious Studies at the State University," *Horizons* 19 (Fall 1992): 263–76.

59. Peter Brown, *Augustine of Hippo: A Biography* (Berkeley: University of California Press, 1967); John Rist, *Augustine: Ancient Thought Baptized* (Cambridge: Cambridge University Press, 1994).

60. For an account of Freud's thought and its ethical implications, see Ernest Wallwork, *Psychoanalysis and Ethics* (New Haven: Yale University Press, 1993).

61. For an instructive discussion of agency in these terms, see Sandel, *Liberalism and the Limits of Justice*, 19–23, 133–64 and passim.

62. See, e.g., J. Patout Burns, "Augustine on the Origin and Progress of Evil," and William S. Babcock, "Augustine on Sin and Moral Agency," in *The Ethics of St. Augustine*, ed. William S. Babcock (Atlanta, Ga.: Scholars Press, 1991); G. R. Evans, *Augustine on Evil* (Cambridge: Cambridge University Press, 1982).

63. I am not arguing against explanatory methods as necessary and instructive in Religious Studies, only against the idea that such methods are sufficient as a paradigm for the study of religion.

64. Rorty, *Consequences of Pragmatism*, 218 (emphasis in original).

65. Strenski seems to concede as much. See "Our Very Own 'Contras,'" 326, n. 1.

Notes to Chapter Nine

1. Nonetheless, Aristotle's discussion of *philia* explores the conflicts of duties that surround civic friendship in the *Nicomachean Ethics*, bks. 8–9. Not without reason, W. D. Ross's translation refers to this section of Aristotle's writing as a "casuistry of friendship." See Aristotle, *Nicomachean Ethics*, p. 953.

2. Aristotle, *Nicomachean Ethics* 1140a1–24.

3. Gadamer, *Truth and Method*, 312–24.

4. Aristotle, *Nicomachean Ethics* 1140a6.

5. The connections between Aristotle's ethics and his theory of tragedy

have been developed by Martha C. Nussbaum, *The Fragility of Goodness: Luck and Ethics in Greek Tragedy and Philosophy* (Cambridge: Cambridge University Press, 1986). As Nussbaum makes clear, the importance of attending to the particulars is not premised for Aristotle on the desire to escape contingency or vulnerability in the moral life.

6. Aristotle, *Nicomachean Ethics* 1109b22.

7. Ibid., 1114a31–1114b3.

8. Sherman, *The Fabric of Character*, 29.

9. Aristotle, *Nicomachean Ethics* 1144a30.

10. Ibid., 1142a22–28.

11. Aquinas, *Summa Theologiae*, II-II, Q. 47, A. 3, ad. 3.

12. Ibid., I-II, Q. 57, A. 6. See also Thomas Aquinas, *Commentary on the Nicomachean Ethics*, vol. 2, trans. C. I. Litzinger (Chicago: Henry Regnery, 1964), 581.

13. For a similar discussion, see Gustafson, *Ethics from a Theocentric Perspective*, 1:333.

14. David Wiggins, "Deliberation and Practical Reason," in *Essays on Aristotle's Ethics*, ed. Amélie Oksenberg Rorty (Berkeley: University of California Press, 1980), 237.

15. Aristotle, *Nicomachean Ethics* 1143a35–b3.

16. For an illuminating discussion, see T. H. Irwin, "First Principles in Aristotle's Ethics," *Midwest Studies in Philosophy* 3 (1978): 252–69.

17. Aristotle, *Nicomachean Ethics* 1143b4–6. It is true, as Troels Engberg-Pedersen argues, that this perception rests on prior habituation, on what might be called training in making evaluative descriptions. For this reason Engberg-Pedersen argues that Aristotle's notion of intuition is not "raw," untutored perception. The point that Aristotle makes in the passage I cite here is that this perception is "intuitive" in the sense that it is nondiscursive. See Troels Engberg-Pedersen, *Aristotle's Theory of Moral Insight* (Oxford: Clarendon Press, 1983), chap. 7.

18. I am grateful to William F. May for enabling me to see this point.

19. Aristotle, *Nicomachean Ethics* 1094b24–26.

20. Ibid., 1094b21.

21. Ibid., 1143b14.

22. Ibid., 1142a13–15.

23. Aquinas, *Summa Theologiae*, II-II, Q. 47, A. 3, ad. 3.

24. In my discussion of the Gulf War this dialectical approach was most explicit. I suggested that, when applying just-war criteria to the war against Iraq, we begin by drawing on the tools of the just-war tradition. My suggestion was premised on the notion that just-war criteria provide a set of terms for discerning the morally salient features of war. But I also urged that we be mindful of the factors that do not fall automatically under standard ethical terms or categories, that our terms for interpreting conflict must be filled in with a fine-grained analysis of the war in question (as well as the factors that led up to the war). One point was to suggest that the Gulf War had several unusual features that do not fit easily into our commonplace terms of interpretation, but that these features must nonetheless be incorporated into final judgments about the war's relative justice or injustice. With this point in

mind I called attention to important ways in which the particulars of history and human experience can inform our ethical judgments.

Yet it would be mistaken to see chapter 2 as standing alone in this book as an example of dialectical casuistry, because all of the chapters have been designed to proceed dialectically between general concerns and particular cases. All of the previous chapters address a specific case with a more general issue in view: application, moral expectations, ideology, novelty, evil, and extrinsicism. One goal has been to throw new light on some familiar cases by beginning with a more comprehensive category to shape our perception of a particular case at hand. But in the process it was also hoped that the category itself would gain some richness and complexity—that what it means to apply paradigms (chapter 2), or to consider questions of moral motivation (chapter 3), or to engage in ideological criticism (chapter 5), or to reason analogically (chapter 6) can be illuminated in light of the case in question. This is one way in which this book has sought to create a symbiotic, dialectical relationship between interpretation and social criticism.

25. Aristotle, *Nicomachean Ethics* 1094b24–29.

26. Aristotle, *Topics* 100a31; 100b20–24.

27. Nussbaum, *Fragility of Goodness,* 245.

28. Aristotle, *Nicomachean Ethics,* bk. 3, chap. 3; bk. 6, chap. 6; cf. Aristotle, *Rhetoric* 1357a5–7.

29. Perelman, *The Realm of Rhetoric,* 4.

30. Aristotle, *Rhetoric* 1355b26.

31. Ibid., bk. 1, chap. 3.

32. Aristotle, *Nicomachean Ethics* 1098b31–1099a6.

33. Aristotle, *Rhetoric* 1357a26.

34. Ibid., 1357a15.

35. For an instructive discussion, see James C. Raymond, "Enthymemes, Examples, and Rhetorical Method," in *Essays on Classical Rhetoric and Modern Discourse,* ed. Robert J. Conners, Lisa S. Ede, and Andrea A. Lunsford (Carbondale: Southern Illinois University Press, 1984), 144.

36. Here I do not wish to suggest that Aristotle literally held to a theory of prima facie duties, only that such a theory generally coheres with Aristotle's more relaxed understanding of moral principles and their application.

37. Aristotle, *Nicomachean Ethics* 1137b28–31.

38. For an example of casuistry that is informed by this account of presumptive duties, see chapter 2.

39. For an illustration of casuistry that is informed by this account of paradigms, see chapter 6.

40. Aristotle, *Rhetoric* 1357a28.

41. Perelman, *The Realm of Rhetoric,* chap. 7 and passim.

42. Jonsen and Toulmin, *The Abuse of Casuistry,* 73.

43. See chapter 1.

44. For examples drawn from political philosophy, see chapters 3 and 4.

45. Stephen Toulmin, "The Recovery of Practical Philosophy," *American Scholar* 57 (Summer 1988): 341.

46. For discussions, see chapters 1, 4, 5.

47. Aristotle, *Nicomachean Ethics* 1099a17–21, 1104a23–b16, 1105a1–16.

48. For an outstanding discussion of emotions, religion, and the moral life, see Paul Lauritzen, *Religious Belief and Emotional Transformation: A Light in the Heart* (Lewisburg, Pa.: Bucknell University Press, 1992).

49. Aristotle, *Nicomachean Ethics* 1104b12.

50. Ibid., 1103a3–25.

51. Ibid., 1139b4.

52. Sherman, *Fabric of Character*, 45.

53. For a more general discussion, see Aristotle, *Nicomachean Ethics* 1105a3–6, 1144b30–1145a7.

54. Ibid., 1106b19–24.

55. L. A. Kosman, "Being Properly Affected: Virtues and Feelings in Aristotle's Ethics," in *Essays on Aristotle's Ethics*, ed. Rorty, chap. 7.

56. Aristotle, *Rhetoric* 1355b35.

57. See chapters 5 and 7.

58. For useful discussions of this approach to medical ethics, see Barry Hoffmaster, "The Theory and Practice of Applied Ethics," *Dialogue* 30 (Summer 1991): 213–34, and "Can Ethnography Save the Life of Medical Ethics?" *Social Science and Medicine* 35 (December 1992): 1421–31.

59. Alan Donagan, *The Theory of Morality* (Chicago: University of Chicago Press, 1977), 67.

60. Ibid., 57–66.

61. Ibid., 67.

62. Ibid., 67–68.

63. Ibid.

64. Ibid., 71–72.

65. Ibid., 68, drawing from Edward H. Levi, *An Introduction to Legal Reasoning* (Chicago: University of Chicago Press, 1949), 8–9.

66. Donagan, *Theory of Morality*, 68.

67. For an instructive discussion, see Arras, "Getting Down to Cases," 32–33.

68. Presumably, precedent cases are what Donagan calls the "specificatory premises" of his system; his terminology is not always clear.

69. Jonsen and Toulmin, *The Abuse of Casuistry*, 16–20.

70. Ibid., 256.

71. MacIntyre, *After Virtue*, chaps. 14–16.

72. Martha Craven Nussbaum, *Love's Knowledge: Essays on Philosophy and Literature* (New York: Oxford University Press, 1990), 148–67, citing Henry James.

73. For a discussion, see chapter 1.

74. In addition to MacIntyre's *After Virtue*, chaps. 1–4, see Pincoffs, "Quandary Ethics." Stanley Hauerwas endorses casuistry within his framework of narrative ethics, but it remains unclear how or why narrativists would adopt the tools of casuistry, as I shall point out below. See Hauerwas, *The Peaceable Kingdom*, chap. 7.

75. MacIntyre, *After Virtue*, 191.

76. Ibid., 198–209.

77. Ibid., 194.

78. Ibid., 191.

79. Ibid., 203.

80. For a discussion, see chapter 1.

81. In a subsequent work MacIntyre seeks to correct the impression that he has overlooked Aristotle's understanding of practical reasoning about particulars. But he fails to reckon with the occasions of practical reasoning and the implications for the self that they pose. See Alasdair MacIntyre, *Whose Justice? Which Rationality?* (Notre Dame, Ind.: University of Notre Dame Press, 1988), chap. 8.

82. Jeffrey Stout puts forward a similar view of eclecticism and interdisciplinarity when he describes the work of the moral *bricoleur* in *Ethics after Babel*, 293.

Abrams, M. H. *Natural Supernaturalism: Tradition and Revolution in Romantic Literature*. New York: Norton, 1971.

Aristotle. *The Basic Works of Aristotle*. Edited and with an introduction by Richard McKeon. New York: Random House, 1941.

Arras, John D. "Getting Down to Cases: The Revival of Casuistry in Bioethics." *Journal of Medicine and Philosophy* 16 (1991): 29–51.

———. "Principles and Particularity: The Role of Cases in Bioethics." *Indiana Law Journal* 69 (Fall 1994): 983–1014.

Augustine. *Treatises on Marriage and Other Subjects*. Translated by Charles T. Wilcox, et al. Edited by Roy J. Deferrari. Washington, D.C.: Catholic University of America Press, 1969.

Barry, R., and D. Kesler. "Pharaoh's Magicians: The Ethics and Efficacy of Human Fetal Tissue Transplants." *Thomist* 54 (October 1990): 575–609.

Beauchamp, Tom L. "Principles and Other Emerging Paradigms in Bioethics." *Indiana Law Journal* 69 (Fall 1994): 955–71.

Bellah, Robert N., et al. *Habits of the Heart: Individualism and Commitment in American Life*. Berkeley: University of California Press, 1985.

Biggar, Nigel. "The Case for Casuistry in the Church." *Modern Theology* 6 (October 1989): 29–51.

Bloom, Harold. *The Anxiety of Influence*. New York: Oxford University Press, 1973.

Buchanan, Allen E. "Assessing the Communitarian Critique of Liberalism." *Ethics* 99 (July 1989): 852–82.

Burke, Kenneth. *A Rhetoric of Motives*. Berkeley: University of California Press, 1969.

Childress, James F. *Moral Responsibility in Conflicts: Essays in Nonviolence, War, and Conscience*. Baton Rouge: Louisiana State University Press, 1982.

———. "Dissociation from Evil: The Case of Human Fetal Tissue Transplantation Research." *Social Responsibility: Business, Journalism, Law, Medicine* 17 (1991): 32–49.

Cicero. *On Duties*. Edited by M. T. Griffin and E. M. Atkins. Cambridge: Cambridge University Press, 1991.

Clifford, James. *The Predicament of Culture: Twentieth Century Ethnography, Literature, and Art*. Cambridge: Harvard University Press, 1988.

Clifford, James, and George E. Marcus, eds. *Writing Culture: The Poetics and Politics of Ethnography* (Berkeley: University of California Press, 1986).

Clover, Carol J. "Her Body, Herself: Gender in the Slasher Film." *Representations* 20 (Fall 1987): 187–228.

Crites, Stephen (scribe). "The Religion Major: A Report." Atlanta: Scholars Press, 1990.

Curran, Charles E., ed. *Contraception: Authority and Dissent.* New York: Herder and Herder, 1969.

———. *Catholic Higher Education, Theology, and Academic Freedom.* Notre Dame, Ind.: University of Notre Dame Press, 1990.

Davidson, Donald. "On the Very Idea of a Conceptual Scheme." *Proceedings of the American Philosophical Association* 47 (1973–74): 5–20.

Davis, Henry. *Moral and Pastoral Theology.* 4 vols. New York: Sheed and Ward, 1938.

Donagan, Alan. *The Theory of Morality.* Chicago: University of Chicago Press, 1977.

Douglas, Mary. *Purity and Danger: An Analysis of the Concepts of Pollution and Taboo.* Boston: Ark Paperbacks, 1984.

Douglass, R. Bruce, Gerald M. Mara, and Henry S. Richardson, eds. *Liberalism and the Good.* New York: Routledge, 1990.

Draper, Theodore. "The Gulf War Reconsidered." *New York Review of Books,* 16 January 1992, pp. 38–45.

———. "The True History of the Gulf War." *New York Review of Books,* 23 January 1992, pp. 46–53.

Dworkin, Ronald. "Liberty and Pornography." *New York Review of Books,* 15 August 1991, pp. 12–15.

———. *A Matter of Principle.* Cambridge: Harvard University Press, 1985.

———. "Women and Pornography." *New York Review of Books,* 21 October 1993, pp. 36–42.

Eagleton, Terry. *Literary Theory: An Introduction.* Minneapolis: University of Minnesota Press, 1983.

Elshtain, Jean Bethke. *Democracy on Trial.* New York: Basic Books, 1995.

Engberg-Pedersen, Troels. *Aristotle's Theory of Moral Insight.* Oxford: Clarendon Press, 1983.

Ferré, Frederick. "The Definition of Religion." *Journal of the American Academy of Religion* 38 (March 1970): 3–16.

Flannery, Austin, ed. *Vatican Council II: The Conciliar and Post-Conciliar Documents.* Northport, N.Y.: Costello Publishing, 1975.

Foot, Philippa. *Virtues and Vices.* Berkeley: University of California Press, 1978.

Ford, John C., and Gerald Kelly. *Contemporary Moral Theology,* vol. 1. Westminster, Md.: Newman Press, 1958.

Foucault, Michel. *The History of Sexuality.* 4 vols. Translated by Robert Hurley. New York: Vintage Books, 1980.

Furst, Lilian. *Romanticism in Perspective: A Comparative Study of Aspects of the Romantic Movements in England, France, and Germany.* 2d edition. New York: Macmillan, 1979.

Gadamer, Hans-Georg. *Truth and Method.* 2d revised edition. Translated by Joel Weinsheimer and Donald G. Marshall. New York: Crossroad, 1991.

Galston, William A. "Moral Personality and Liberal Theory." *Political Theory* 10 (November 1982): 492–519.

Geertz, Clifford. *The Interpretation of Cultures.* New York: Basic Books, 1971.

———. *Islam Observed: Religious Development in Morocco and Indonesia.* Chicago: University of Chicago Press, 1971.

———. *Local Knowledge: Further Essays in Interpretive Anthropology.* New York: Basic Books, 1983.

———. *Works and Lives: The Anthropologist as Author.* Stanford, Calif.: Stanford University Press, 1988.

Geyer, Alan, and Barbara G. Green. *Lines in the Sand: Justice and the Gulf War.* Foreword by Kermit D. Johnson. Louisville: Westminster/John Knox Press, 1992.

Girard, René. *Violence and the Sacred.* Translated by Patrick Gardiner. Baltimore, Md.: Johns Hopkins University Press, 1977.

Glendon, Mary Ann. *Rights Talk: The Impoverishment of Political Discourse.* New York: Free Press, 1991.

Gustafson, James M. *Ethics from a Theocentric Perspective.* 2 vols. Chicago: University of Chicago Press, 1981, 1984.

Gutmann, Amy. "Communitarian Critics of Liberalism." *Philosophy and Public Affairs* 14 (Summer 1985): 308–22.

Hart, Ray L. "Religious and Theological Studies in American Higher Education: A Pilot Study." *Journal of the American Academy of Religion* 59 (Winter 1991): 715–827.

Hauerwas, Stanley. *The Peaceable Kingdom: A Primer in Christian Ethics.* Notre Dame, Ind.: University of Notre Dame Press, 1983.

Hauerwas, Stanley, and Richard John Neuhaus. "Pacifism, Just War, and the Gulf." *First Things* 13 (May 1991): 39–45.

Hehir, J. Bryan. "Intervention and International Affairs." In *The American Search for Peace: Moral Reasoning, Religious Hope, and National Security,* edited by George Weigel and John Langan. Washington, D.C.: Georgetown University Press, 1991.

Himes, Kenneth R. "Just War, Pacifism, and Humanitarian Intervention." *America* 169 (August 14, 1993): 10–15, 28–31.

———. "The Morality of Humanitarian Intervention." *Theological Studies* 55 (March 1994): 82–105.

Itzin, Catherine, ed. *Pornography: Women, Violence and Civil Liberties.* New York: Oxford University Press, 1992.

Johnson, James Turner. *Just War Tradition and the Restraint of War: A Moral and Historical Inquiry.* Princeton, N.J.: Princeton University Press, 1981.

———. "Just War Tradition and the War in the Gulf." *Christian Century* (February 6–13, 1991): 134–35.

Johnson, James Turner, and George Weigel. *Just War and the Gulf War.* Washington, D.C.: Ethics and Public Policy Center, 1991.

Jonsen, Albert R., and Stephen Toulmin. *The Abuse of Casuistry: A History of Moral Reasoning.* Berkeley: University of California Press, 1988.

Kant, Immanuel. *Foundations of the Metaphysics of Morals.* Translated by Lewis White Beck. Indianapolis: Bobbs-Merrill, 1976 [1785].

Keenan, James F., and Thomas A. Shannon, eds. *The Context of Casuistry.* Washington, D.C.: Georgetown University Press, 1995.

Kelly, Gerald. *Medico-Moral Problems.* St. Louis, Mo.: Catholic Hospital Association, 1958.

Kierkegaard, Søren. *Works of Love.* Translated by Howard and Edna Hong, with a preface by R. Gregor Smith. New York: Harper and Row, 1962.

Kimelman, Reuven. "Judaism and the Ethics of War." *Proceedings of the Rabbinical Assembly* (1987), 8–26.

Kirk, Kenneth E. *Conscience and Its Problems: An Introduction to Casuistry.* 4th edition. London: Longmans, Green and Co., 1948.

Kittay, Eva Feder. "Pornography and the Erotics of Domination." In *Beyond Domination: New Perspectives on Women and Philosophy.* Edited by Carol Gould. Totowa, N.J.: Rowman and Allanheld, 1984.

Kuhn, Thomas S. *The Structure of Scientific Revolutions.* 2d edition. Chicago: University of Chicago Press, 1970.

Kymlicka, Will. "Liberalism and Communitarianism." *Canadian Journal of Philosophy* 18 (June 1988): 181–204.

Langan, John. "An Imperfectly Just War." *Commonweal* (June 1, 1991), 361–65.

Larmore, Charles. *Patterns of Moral Complexity.* Cambridge: Cambridge University Press, 1987.

———. "Political Liberalism." *Political Theory* 18 (August 1990): 339–60.

Leites, Edmund, ed. *Conscience and Casuistry in Early Modern Europe.* Cambridge: Cambridge University Press, 1988.

Levi, Edward H. *An Introduction to Legal Reasoning.* Chicago: University of Chicago Press, 1949.

Mahoney, John. *The Making of Moral Theology: A Study of the Roman Catholic Tradition.* Oxford: Clarendon, 1987.

McCormick, Richard A. *How Brave a New World? Dilemmas in Bioethics.* Garden City, N.Y.: Doubleday, 1981.

———. *Notes on Moral Theology, 1965–1980.* Lanham, Md.: University Press of America, 1981.

———. *Notes on Moral Theology, 1981–1985.* Lanham, Md.: University Press of America, 1985.

MacIntyre, Alasdair. *After Virtue: A Study in Moral Theory.* Notre Dame, Ind.: University of Notre Dame Press, 1981.

———. *Three Rival Moral Versions of Moral Enquiry: Encyclopaedia, Genealogy, and Tradition.* Notre Dame, Ind.: University of Notre Dame Press, 1990.

———. *Whose Justice? Which Rationality?* Notre Dame, Ind.: University of Notre Dame Press, 1988.

McMahan, Jeff. "Killing, Letting Die, and Withdrawing Aid." *Ethics* 103 (January 1993): 250–79.

Malamuth, Neil M., and Edward Donnerstein, eds. *Pornography and Sexual Aggression.* Orlando, Fla.: Academic Press, 1984.

Mill, John Stuart. *On Liberty.* Edited and with an introduction by Currin V. Shields. Indianapolis: Bobbs-Merrill, 1956.

Miller, Richard B. *Interpretations of Conflict: Ethics, Pacifism, and the Just-War Tradition.* Chicago: University of Chicago Press, 1991.

————, ed. *War in the Twentieth Century: Sources in Theological Ethics.* Louisville, Ky.: Westminster/John Knox Press, 1992.

Neuhaus, Richard John. "Just War and This War." *Wall Street Journal,* January 29, 1991.

Nichols, Ashton. *The Poetics of Epiphany: Nineteenth Century Origins of the Modern Literary Movement.* Tuscaloosa: University of Alabama Press, 1987.

Niebuhr, H. Richard. *Radical Monotheism and Western Culture, with Supplementary Essays.* New York: Harper and Row, 1943.

Noonan, John T. *Contraception: A History of Its Treatment by the Catholic Theologians and Canonists.* Cambridge: Harvard University Press, 1965.

Novak, David. *Jewish Social Ethics.* New York: Oxford University Press, 1992.

Nussbaum, Martha Craven. *The Fragility of Goodness: Luck and Ethics in Greek Tragedy and Philosophy.* Cambridge: Cambridge University Press, 1986.

————. *Love's Knowledge: Essays on Philosophy and Literature.* New York: Oxford University Press, 1990.

Okin, Susan Moller. *Justice, Gender, and the Family.* New York: Basic Books, 1989.

Outka, Gene, and Paul Ramsey, eds. *Norm and Context in Christian Ethics.* New York: Charles Scribner's Sons, 1968.

Pascal, Blaise. *The Provincial Letters.* Translated and with an introduction by A. J. Krailsheimer. New York: Penguin, 1967.

Paul VI. *Humanae Vitae.* Boston: Daughters of St. Paul, 1968.

Penner, Hans H. "Criticism and the Development of a Science of Religion." *Studies in Religion* 15 (1986): 164–75.

Penner, Hans H., and Edward A. Yonan. "Is a Science of Religion Possible?" *Journal of Religion* 52 (1972): 107–33.

Perelman, Chaim. *The New Rhetoric and the Humanities: Essays on Rhetoric and Its Applications.* Boston: D. Reidel, 1979.

————. *The Realm of Rhetoric.* Translated by William Kluback, with an introduction by Carroll C. Arnold. Notre Dame, Ind.: University of Notre Dame Press, 1982.

Pilarcyzk, Daniel. "Letter to President Bush: The Persian Gulf Crisis." *Origins* 20 (November 29, 1990): 397–400.

Preus, J. Samuel. *Explaining Religion: Criticism and Theory from Bodin to Freud.* New Haven: Yale University Press, 1987.

Ramsey, Paul. *The Ethics of Fetal Research.* New Haven: Yale University Press, 1975.

Rawls, John. *A Theory of Justice.* Cambridge: Harvard University Press, 1971.

————. "The Basic Structure as Subject." *American Philosophical Quarterly* 14 (April 1977): 159–65.

————. "The Domain of the Political and Overlapping Consensus." *New York University Law Review* 64 (1989): 233–55.

————. "The Idea of an Overlapping Consensus." *Oxford Journal of Legal Studies* 7 (1987): 1–27.

———. "Justice as Fairness: Political Not Metaphysical." *Philosophy and Public Affairs* 14 (1985): 223–51.

———. "Kantian Constructivism in Moral Theory." *Journal of Philosophy* 77 (September 1980): 515–72.

———. *Political Liberalism.* New York: Columbia University Press, 1993.

———. "The Priority of Right and Ideas of the Good." *Philosophy and Public Affairs* 17 (Fall 1988): 251–76.

Rescher, Nicholas. *Dialectics: A Controversy-Oriented Approach to the Theory of Knowledge.* Albany: State University of New York Press, 1977.

Ricci, James V. *100 Years of Gynaecology, 1800–1900.* Philadelphia: Blakiston, 1945.

Ricoeur, Paul. *Hermeneutics and the Human Sciences.* Translated, edited, and with an introduction by John B. Thompson. Cambridge: Cambridge University Press, 1981.

Rist, Ray C., ed. *The Pornography Controversy: Changing Moral Standards in American Life,* New Brunswick, N.J.: Transaction Books, 1975.

Rorty, Amélie Oksenberg, ed. *Essays on Aristotle's Ethics.* Berkeley: University of California Press, 1980.

Rorty, Richard. *Consequences of Pragmatism.* Minneapolis: University of Minnesota Press, 1982.

———. *Contingency, Irony, and Solidarity.* Cambridge: Cambridge University Press, 1989.

———. *Objectivity, Relativism, and Truth,* vol. 1, *Philosophical Papers.* Cambridge: Cambridge University Press, 1991.

———. *Essays on Heidegger and Others,* vol. 2, *Philosophical Papers.* Cambridge: Cambridge University Press, 1991.

Rosaldo, Michelle Zimbalist, and Louise Lamphere, eds. *Woman, Culture, and Society.* Stanford, Calif.: Stanford University Press, 1974.

Rosenblum, Nancy L. *Another Liberalism: Romanticism and the Reconstruction of Liberal Thought.* Cambridge: Harvard University Press, 1987.

———, ed. *Liberalism and the Moral Life.* Cambridge: Harvard University Press, 1989.

Ross, Susan A. "The Bride of Christ and the Body Politic: Body and Gender in Pre-Vatican II Marriage Theology." *Journal of Religion* 71 (July 1991): 345–61.

Ross, W. D. *Foundations of Ethics.* Oxford: Clarendon, 1939.

Sandel, Michael. "Democrats and Community." *New Republic* (February 22, 1988), 20–23.

———. *Liberalism and the Limits of Justice.* Cambridge: Cambridge University Press, 1982.

———. "Moral Argument and Liberal Toleration: Abortion and Homosexuality." *California Law Review* 77 (1989): 521–38.

———. "Morality and the Liberal Ideal." *New Republic* (May 7, 1984), 15–17.

———. "The Procedural Republic and the Unencumbered Self." *Political Theory* 12 (February 1984): 81–96.

Scarry, Elaine. *The Body in Pain: The Making and Unmaking of the World.* New York: Oxford University Press, 1985.

Schaff, Philip, ed. *The Nicene and Post-Nicene Fathers.* Grand Rapids, Mich.: Eerdmans, 1956.

Schelling, Thomas C. *Arms and Influence.* New Haven: Yale University Press, 1966.

Sharpe, Eric J. *Comparative Religion: A History.* New York: Charles Scribner's Sons, 1975.

Sherman, Nancy. *The Fabric of Character: Aristotle's Theory of Virtue.* Oxford: Clarendon, 1989.

Sifry, Micah L., and Christopher Cerf, eds. *The Gulf War Reader: History, Documents, Opinions.* New York: Random House, 1991.

Smith, Jonathan Z. *Imagining Religion: From Babylon to Jonestown.* Chicago: University of Chicago Press, 1982.

———. *Map Is Not Territory: Studies in the History of Religions.* Leiden: E. J. Brill, 1978.

———. "'Religion' and 'Religious Studies': No Difference at All." *Soundings* 71 (1988): 231–44.

Sparks, Richard C. *To Treat or Not to Treat? Bioethics and the Handicapped Newborn.* Mahwah, N.J.: Paulist Press, 1988.

Stocking, George W., Jr., ed. *Romantic Motives: Essays on Anthroplogical Sensibility.* Madison: University of Wisconsin Press, 1989.

Stout, Jeffrey. *Ethics after Babel: The Languages of Morals and Their Discontents.* Boston: Beacon, 1988.

Strenski, Ivan. "Our Very Own 'Contras': A Response to the 'St. Louis Project' Report." *Journal of the American Academy of Religion* 54 (Summer 1986): 323–35.

Taylor, Charles. *Philosophical Papers,* 2 vols. Cambridge: Cambridge University Press, 1985.

———. *Sources of the Self: The Making of Modern Identity.* Cambridge: Harvard University Press, 1989.

Thomas Aquinas, Saint. *Summa Theologiae.* Blackfriars Edition. New York: McGraw-Hill, 1972.

Timmerman, Kenneth R. *The Death Lobby: How the West Armed Iraq.* New York: Houghton Mifflin, 1991.

Toulmin, Stephen. *Human Understanding: The Collective Use and Evolution of Concepts.* Princeton, N.J.: Princeton University Press, 1972.

———. "How Medicine Saved the Life of Ethics." *Perspectives in Biology and Medicine* 25 (Summer 1982): 736–50.

———. "The Recovery of Practical Philosophy." *American Scholar* 57 (Summer 1988): 337–52.

———. "The Tyranny of Principles." *Hastings Center Report* 11 (1981): 31–39.

———. *The Uses of Argument.* Cambridge: Cambridge University Press, 1958.

U.S. Catholic Bishops. *The Challenge of Peace: God's Promise and Our Response.* Washington, D.C.: United States Catholic Conference, 1983.

Vawter, Dorothy E., et al. *The Use of Human Fetal Tissue: Scientific, Ethical, and Policy Concerns.* Center for Biomedical Ethics, University of Minnesota, 1990.

Walters, LeRoy. "Ethical Issues in Experimentation on the Human Fetus." *Journal of Religious Ethics* 2 (1974): 33–75.

Walzer, Michael. "The Communitarian Critique of Liberalism." *Political Theory* 18 (February 1990): 6–23.

———. *Exodus and Revolution.* New York: Basic Books, 1985.

———. *Interpretation and Social Criticism.* Cambridge: Harvard University Press, 1987.

———. *Just and Unjust Wars: A Moral Argument with Historical Illustrations.* 2d edition. New York: Basic Books, 1992.

———. "Liberalism and the Art of Separation." *Political Theory* 12 (August 1984): 315–30.

———. *Obligations: Essays on Disobedience, War, and Citizenship.* Cambridge: Harvard University Press, 1970.

———. "Perplexed." *New Republic* (January 28, 1991), 13–14.

———. *Spheres of Justice: A Defense of Pluralism and Equality.* New York: Basic Books, 1983.

———. *Thick and Thin: Moral Argument at Home and Abroad.* Notre Dame, Ind.: University of Notre Dame Press, 1994.

———. *What It Means to Be an American: Essays on the American Experience.* New York: Marsilio Press, 1992.

Wiebe, Donald. "Postulations for Safeguarding Preconceptions: The Case of the Scientific Religionist." *Religion* 18 (1988): 11–19.

Williams, Linda. *Hard Core: Power, Pleasure, and the "Frenzy of the Visible."* University of California Press, 1989.

Wittgenstein, Ludwig. *Philosophical Investigations.* 3d edition. Translated by G. E. M. Anscombe. New York: Macmillan, 1968.

Yack, Bernard. "Community and Conflict in Aristotle's Political Philosophy." *Review of Politics* 45 (1985): 92–112.

Yoder, John Howard. "Just War Tradition: Is It Credible?" *Christian Century* (March 31, 1991), 295–98.